OTTOMANS, TURKS AND THE BALKANS

OTTOMANS, TURKS AND THE BALKANS

Empire Lost, Relations Altered

Ebru Boyar

Tauris Academic Studies
London • New York

Published in 2007 by Tauris Academic Studies, an imprint of I.B.Tauris & Co Ltd
6 Salem Road, London W2 4BU
175 Fifth Avenue, New York NY 10010
www.ibtauris.com

In the United States of America and Canada distributed by Palgrave Macmillan
a division of St. Martin's Press, 175 Fifth Avenue, New York NY 10010

Copyright © 2007 Ebru Boyar

The right of Ebru Boyar to be identified as the author of this work has been asserted by
the author in accordance with the Copyright, Designs and Patent Act 1988.

All rights reserved. Except for brief quotations in a review, this book, or any
part thereof, may not be reproduced, stored in or introduced into a retrieval system, or
transmitted, in any form or by any means, electronic, mechanical, photocopying,
recording or otherwise, without the prior written permission of the publisher.

Library of Ottoman Studies 12

ISBN: 978 1 84511 351 3

A full CIP record for this book is available from the British Library
A full CIP record is available from the Library of Congress

Library of Congress Catalog Card Number: available

Printed and bound in India by Replika Press Pvt. Ltd
From camera-ready copy edited and supplied by the author

To my parents, Mediha and Yunus Boyar

CONTENTS

Notes on Transliteration, Dates and Names ix

Acknowledgements xi

Introduction 1

1. History-Writing in the Late Ottoman/Early Republican Era 9

2. 'A Belt of Large Dumplings': The Definition of the Balkans 29

3. The Representation of the Balkans 42

4. The Balkan Peoples and the Balkan States 72

5. The Multi-Images of the Balkans 82

Conclusion 141

Notes 148

Bibliography 209

Index 237

NOTES ON TRANSLITERATION, DATES AND NAMES

All texts in Ottoman Turkish have been transliterated into modern Turkish orthography and no diacritical marks are used. Dates have been given in both *Hicri* (A.H.) or *Mali* and *Miladi* (A.D.). In cases where it is impossible to establish whether the Ottoman date is *Hicri* or *Mali*, the *Miladi* (A.D.) equivalent for both is given, that for *Mali* being in brackets.

Surnames have been given in brackets when the period referred to preceeds the surname law of 1934.

ACKNOWLEDGEMENTS

I would like first to express my deep gratitude to Dr. Kate Fleet, who supervised the Ph.D. thesis upon which this book is based. She not only taught me about how to do research but also showed me what a good academic should be. She never ceased to be interested in my work, was always there when I needed her and never lost patience with me.

I should like to thank Professor Palmira Brummett, Dr. George Dedes, Miss Julian Chrysostomides, Professor Salih Özbaran, Dr. Tuba Çavdar, Dr. Svetla Ianeva, Dr. Stefka Parveva and Dr. Svetlana Ivanova.

I am most grateful to the Skilliter Centre for Ottoman Studies which opened new horizons for me, not only because of its invaluable collection but also because of the stimulating environment which it provided. I should like to thank Newnham College very much both because it has the Skilliter Centre and also for its friendly and supportive environment. I am also most grateful to the library of the Türk Tarih Kurumu and for the efficiency and kindness of the personnel working there. In particular I should like to thank Mustafa Sönmez. The staff of both the Başbakanlık Osmanlı Arşivi in İstanbul and the Başbakanlık Cumhuriyet Arşivi in Ankara were unfailingly helpful. Even when the Başbakanlık Osmanlı Arşivi was at its busiest, the staff continued to be most efficient. This made my research times in the archives both enjoyable and productive. The staff at the Oriental Department of the National Library of St Cyril and St. Methodius in Sofia, too, were extremely helpful. I should also like to thank l'Istituto per l'Oriente in Rome, the library of the Faculty of Oriental Studies, Cambridge and the Cambridge University Library.

I am most grateful for the financial support throughout my Ph.D. from YÖK (The Turkish Higher Educational Council) and the Cambridge University Overseas Trust which gave me the Mehmet Fuat Köprülü Scholarship.

Finally I am deeply indebted to my family who have trusted and supported me throughout.

INTRODUCTION

> The land which my grandfather ploughed and into which he poured his soul
> Has gone and will never come back![1]

In 1913 the Ottoman empire lost its soul, or that at least was how many felt. The Balkans, symbolising far more than territory, was at the very heart of what made the empire. Its loss plunged the Ottoman intellectual elite into a search for what had gone, and drew the Ottomans into a complex of sensations, shame, grief, anger and a questioning about their own identity. Beaten by their own subjects, their great empire brought down by 'former shepherds and servants,'[2] the Ottomans felt an overwhelming sadness for the alienation of a land that had been theirs for centuries and regret for the blood which they had pointlessly shed for it.

The trauma of the loss of the Balkans was shattering for the Ottomans and its reverberations were felt in the early Republic and beyond. It coloured the mind-set of the new Turkish elite and shaped their way of thinking about their neighbours, about Europe and about themselves. However much political relations with their Balkan neighbours might be good, the edge of bitterness and anger remained, and surfaced whenever a conflict appeared.

> Balkan nationalism does not resemble the nationalism of other nations. Balkan nationalism has a special, bloody history full of raids, assassinations, bombs and banditry. Balkan nationalism is rapacious, barbarous. Balkan countries resemble zoos for wild animals, behind every frontier there is a bloodthirsty nationalism which consists of teeth and claws separated from each other by

iron bars. These nationalisms continuously stretch out their claws against each other between the bars of the frontiers and tear each other to pieces. However barbarous they were when they jointly attacked us, they were equally vicious, as we saw after the Balkan War, when they were at each other's throats.[3]

Although these words were written in 1920, these sentiments continued.

Angered over the loss of the Balkans, the Ottomans and later the Turks also suffered an acute sense of injustice, that the Balkan peoples, for whom they had done so much, should have turned on them in this way, and that the Europeans should have always taken their side, despising the Turks as barbarous and uncivilised. This the Europeans continued to do well into the Turkish Republic.

This book considers the development of the Ottoman/Turkish intellectual relationship with the Balkans and tries to understand in what ways the loss of the Balkans coloured Ottoman/Turkish self-perception and shaped the relations of the empire and later the Republic with the outside world.

Sources

In trying to understand the place of the Balkans in the Ottoman/Turkish mentality, one of the main primary sources is clearly the history-writings of the period. The standard histories such as Ahmed Cevdet Paşa's *Tarih-i Cevdet* (Cevdet's History) or Mustafa Nuri Paşa's *Netayic ül-Vukuat* (The Consequences of Events), were written by historians from within the establishment, Ahmed Cevdet Paşa, for example, being the official court historian (*vakanüvis*), and thus reflect the establishment view of history and of the Balkans. These histories are also important in that they became the standard reference works for later generations. Apart from these standard histories, there are the history text books written for schools, both those written by famous historians such as Mehmed Fuad (Köprülü), Ahmed Refik (Altınay) and Ali Reşad who were very important historians both of the late Ottoman and early Republican eras, and historians who were not well known such as Lütfiye Hanım. These texts responded very much to the needs of state education and were thus a reflection of what the state wanted to inculcate the population with, and were very important for the development of national identity. Some text books, such as *Resimli ve*

Haritalı Osmanlı Tarihi (The Illustrated Ottoman History with Maps) written by Ahmed Rasim, the well-known journalist and writer, or the Türk Tarihi Tetkik Cemiyeti (later, Türk Tarih Kurumu, the Turkish Historical Society) publications *Tarih III* (History III) and *Tarih IV* (History IV), then became standard works for later historians. Kemal Karpat for example made considerable use of *Tarih IV* in his book *Turkey's Politics: The Transition to a Multi-Party System* published in 1959.[4]

A further type of history used in this study consists of histories specifically related to the Balkans, such as Kamil Kapudan's book on Montenegro or Halil Yaver's books on Bulgaria, as well as books published by military publishing houses such as Askeri Matbaa and Askeri Deniz Matbaası and written by military officers, including the works of Halil Sedes on Ottoman military campaigns against the Serbs, in Montenegro, in Bosnia-Herzegovina and against the Bulgarians, and that of Mithat Işın on Crete. By combining these various types of histories, it is possible to gain a more in-depth understanding of how the Balkans was represented in the histories of the late Ottoman/early Republican period and of the relation of the Balkans to the creation of a national identity in the early Republican era.

The second kind of sources examined is literary works of fiction. Such works were written either with a didactic purpose, such as the stories of Ömer Seyfeddin, or were the outcome of the author's personal experience, as was the case, for example, of Halide Edib (Adıvar) or Yakup Kadri (Karaosmanoğlu). For these authors too, conveying a message was much more important than writing a literary piece. Used in conjunction with the histories, these sources further enable one to develop a more nuanced understanding of the intellectual environment in which the representation of the Balkans was shaped.

It is obvious that when dealing with memoirs, the third type of source considered in this study, caution is necessary since memoirs are subjective and are often written considerably later than the period which they are describing, and thus use language and concepts that belong to this later period. Şevket Süreyya Aydemir, for example, wrote his memoirs, *Suyu Arayan Adam* (The Man Seeking Water), in 1959, while Galip Kemali Söylemezoğlu wrote his memoirs of his time in the Ottoman embassy in Athens between 1913 and 1916, in 1946. Others, although more contemporary to events described, were written with the aim of justifying the author's conduct, such as the memoirs of Cemal

Paşa, published in 1922. Nevertheless, such sources are of considerable importance for an understanding of the perceptions of the period, even if coloured by the later experiences of the author who was inevitably influenced by the period in which he was writing.

In contrast to the first three types of sources used in this study, the histories, literary works and memoirs, the fourth group, official documents such as official correspondence, instructions issued by the government in İstanbul or Ankara, reports to İstanbul or Ankara, embassy correspondence and translations from the foreign press, were not designed to inculcate a particular understanding or put across any specific message, but were the working documents of the state. As such, they are essential for an understanding of government perception and indicate to what extent the picture given by the histories, the literary works and the memoirs were reflected in official state policy.

Historical Outline

The period of the late nineteenth century, from the last years of the Tanzimat, the period of reform and modernization initiated by sultan Abdülmecid in 1839 with the declaration of the *Gülhane Hatt-ı Hümayunu*, to the early years of the Turkish Republic, witnessed a series of transformations and convulsions which turned a 600-year-old empire with territories stretching from North Africa across the Middle East to Europe, into a new nation-state struggling for survival in the aftermath of the cataclysm of the First World War. It was in this climate that the Ottoman, and later the Turkish, intellectuals developed their perceptions of state and identity and sought for ways to survive within the changing political scene.

While this period, from around 1861 with the coming to the throne of Abdülaziz, to the end of the Second World War, is usually taken as being two distinct and discrete eras, the pre-and post-1923 periods, divided by the fault line formed by the creation of the Turkish Republic, from the point of view of intellectual history this period should be seen rather as one continuum in which ideas flowed from the Ottoman to the Turkish period and were modified in time but which did not undergo any sudden or abrupt transformation. There was thus no schism intellectually between the pre- and the post-1923 eras.

The later Tanzimat era saw the rise of intellectual opposition to the government with the establishment of the group which came to be known as the Young Ottomans (Genç Osmanlılar) and whose leading members included Namık Kemal, Ziya Paşa and Şinasi. Unhappy with the level of bureaucratic authority and with the direction which the Tanzimat reforms had taken, this group called for the promulgation of a constitution. After a period of political difficulty, Abdülhamid II (1876-1909) came to the throne promising to proclaim the constitution which he duly did in 1876. A sultan of great political ability, Abdülhamid however had no intention of allowing his authority to be restricted by the constitution and soon found a pretext to prorogue it. From now on, throughout his long reign, Abdülhamid sought to legitimise his rule, control opposition and ensure the survival of the state. Nevertheless, he was faced with mounting opposition from the Young Turk movement, which called for the re-establishment of the constitution and parliament, and was opposed to the autocratic rule of the sultan. Many of the Young Turks fled to Europe or, in the case of Mizancı Murad, to Cairo, from where they continued their vocal opposition, publishing journals and newspapers in which the Ottoman sultan was attacked. The Young Turks gradually gained support, significantly among the army officers who, in 1908, threatened to march on İstanbul from Thessaloniki and thus forced Abdülhamid to bring back the constitution and recall parliament. Abdülhamid's position, however, was now extremely weakened and in 1909 he was forced to abdicate in favour of his brother, Mehmed V (1909-1918).

While opposition to Abdülhamid built up among the intellectuals, he was also faced with the stark reality of European control which left him with very little room to manoeuvre either in order to prevent the shrinking of the territory of his empire, or to control his economy and to use what financial resources he had for the economic development of his state in the way he saw fit. Following the Russian advance which took Russian troops to the outskirts of İstanbul and which ended with the most unsatisfactory (from an Ottoman point of view) Treaty of San Stefano, the 1878 Congress of Berlin restructured the Ottoman empire. This Congress, run entirely by the European powers and at which neither the Ottomans nor those from the new Balkan entities had any effective say, produced an independent Serbia, Romania, Montenegro and an autonomous Bulgaria.

Economically too, the Ottoman empire was caught in the vice of European control. After a series of financial problems, the Ottoman state sank into bankruptcy and shortly afterwards, in 1881, into European hands with the setting up of the Public Debt Administration, a body run predominantly by the British and the French and into which Ottoman input was minimal.

After the abdication in 1909 of Abdülhamid, power was *de facto* in the hands of the İttihad ve Terakki (the Committee of Union and Progress), although this party did not establish itself in undisputed control until after the elections of 1912. The post-1908 period provided a new climate for intellectual expression. It was a period in which the intelligentsia tried to redefine Ottomanism, which had been the predominant ideology of the Young Ottomans and utilized in the Abdülhamidian era, to create an effective sense of identification with the state. This attempt gave way to a move to emphasise instead the Turkishness of the state.

The post-1908 period was also one of mounting dangers due to the clash between the Great Powers. The Balkan states united in 1912 to attack the Ottomans who were only rescued from complete disaster in the Balkan Wars by the failure of this Balkan alliance which fell apart when Bulgaria and Serbia went to war over the territories won in the first Balkan War. The Balkan Wars represented a massive psychological shock for the Ottoman intellectuals whose despair is evident in the writings of the period.

The outbreak in 1914 of the First World War, which in fact signalled the beginning of the end not only for the Ottoman empire but for the political order of the day, was seen by Ottoman politicians, in particular Enver Paşa, who, together with Cemal Paşa and Talat Paşa, controlled the government in the war years, as an opportunity for the Ottomans to escape the European stranglehold and gain territorial rewards. Instead, the empire ended, carved up by the victors.

In the immediate aftermath of the war, the Ottoman empire was in ruins. With the encouragement in particular of the British, the Greeks invaded Anatolia in 1919, initially with great success. The sultan in İstanbul, Vahideddin, who came to the throne as Mehmed VI in 1918, cooperated totally with the Allies and put up no opposition to the dismemberment of his empire and the granting of a small remnant as a rump Turkish state in north-west Anatolia.

Opposition to the stance of the sultan, and then to the Allied occupation of İstanbul which took place in 1920, grew and hardened around the leadership of Mustafa Kemal (Atatürk) who was to drive the Greeks out of Anatolia during the Kurtuluş Savaşı (National Liberation War) and to establish an alternative government in Ankara. It was with this government and not with the sultan in İstanbul that the Allies were forced ultimately to negotiate. The Treaty of Sèvres, which was concluded in 1920 with the Ottoman government in İstanbul and which divided up the territorial spoils among the victors, was replaced by the Treaty of Lausanne (1923) and the new Turkish Republic was declared. From now on until 1946 the Republic was governed by a one-party system under the Cumhuriyet Halk Fırkası/Partisi (Republican People's Party) led by Mustafa Kemal.

The new government was faced with two major tasks: to reconstruct the country which had been reduced to ruins and whose population had been devastated by wars, and to create a Turkish citizen. For this it was essential that the country remain at peace, and the government made great efforts to ensure that Turkey stayed out of any military conflict in the international arena. Turkey did not enter the Second World War, for example, until 1945. Much of the infrastructure of Anatolia had been destroyed and a major programme of railway construction, agricultural development and industrialisation was introduced. The population had been reduced and debilitated dramatically not just by war but also by diseases such as malaria, syphilis, tuberculosis, cholera and trachoma. The government undertook an extensive health programme aimed both at treating these diseases and educating the population about disease prevention. The government was concerned not merely with the physical condition of its people but also with their minds for it aimed to transform the population into modern, educated Turkish citizens by means of education and propaganda designed to instil a sense of national identity. All these changes and reforms initiated by the Republican government infiltrated into every aspect of the life of the population.

The intellectuals in this new nation-state had been involved in the post-1908 search for an effective identity in the rapidly changing environment of the Ottoman empire in the period immediately before the outbreak of the First World War. The same intellectuals, who now emerged from a decade of continuous warfare, were faced again with the need to create an identity, this time not for an empire but for a new nation, for although the Turkish nation-state now existed physically, it did not yet have what might be termed a mental existence. From 1923 onwards the intellectuals played a major role in ensuring the survival of this new state, which was by no means a foregone conclusion, by developing a sense of belonging both to the Turkish state and to the people within the nation-state.

1
HISTORY-WRITING IN THE LATE OTTOMAN/EARLY REPUBLICAN ERA

As E. H. Carr once wrote 'when we attempt to answer the question, What is History?, our answer, consciously or unconsciously, reflects our own position in time, and forms part of our answer to the broader question of what view we take of the society in which we live.'[1] The relation of the human being to history is present-oriented, since the questions that shape the perception of the past are prepared in the present. It could even be argued that the answers to such questions, moreover, are required more to meet the needs of the present than to shed light on the events of the distant past in its own right. In fact, as the well-known Turkish writer and literary historian of the early Republican era, Ahmet Hamdi Tanpınar, wrote in his *Beş Şehir* (Five Cities), since the past always exists, we have constantly to work through and come to terms with it in order to live as ourselves, that is with our true essential being and 'identity.'[2]

Language and history, as Akçuraoğlu Yusuf, the well-known historian, pioneer Turkist and head of the Türk Tarihi Tetkik Cemiyeti (T.T.T.C.), later the Türk Tarih Kurumu (The Turkish Historical Society), noted, 'are the most important factors in keeping and developing an identity of a nation.'[3] The importance of history in connection with national identity was repeated by A. Fuat Baymur in his 1945 book on teaching history:

> History has an important role in the awakening of national identity, in its nourishment and its taking root. They say rightly

that history brings the "feeling of being rooted." Indeed it is through this that a connection between us and our ancestors is established. We know about their style of life, thinking and feeling, and their struggles, we understand what we owe them, we have learned our duties towards the next generation. As Schopenhauer said, a nation can only attain [national] consciousness through history. Then, again as has been rightly said, if the past lives inside us, our nation will be able to have a future.[4]

Indeed, an essential factor in Turkish national identity creation in the early Repulican era was the use of history. In the 1930s' history-writing was very much under state direction and was perceived as a central part of the changes brought about by the new regime. Earlier, under Abdülhamid II too, history was considered both as a potential tool of and as a threat to the state, while under the İttihad ve Terakki, history was used to increase the loyalty of the population to the state and at the same time to denegrate the autocratic rule of Abdülhamid II. It was also seen as a means of creating an "Ottoman citizen." This functionality of history was the same for the Ottomans as it was for the Turks of the new Republic, for history-writing formed a continuum through the late Ottoman/early Republican period and was not fundamentally affected by the change from a multi-religious empire to a "homogenized" nation-state. The Ottoman components of history-writing, the understanding of history, the historians themselves and the histories they wrote were all carried on into the early Republican era.

One major development in the second half of the nineteenth century was that modern European history-writing started to influence Ottoman historiography, and Ottoman historians began to adopt historical methods from the European model. Müşir Süleyman Paşa, who was later considered a pioneer 'Turkist' in *Türk Yılı* (The Turkish Year), published by the Türk Ocakları (Turkish Hearths), was one of the first Ottomans to write about the method of history using European methodology in his book *Mebani-i İnşa* (The Foundations of Composition), published as a school history text for military school students in 1871.[5] Several years before, in 1863, Ahmed Vefik Paşa, well-known for his dictionary *Lehçe-i Osmani* (The Ottoman Dictionary), based his approach to the methodology of history in his *Hikmet-i Tarih* (The Wisdom of History) on an attempt to bring together the European and Islamic methods of history-writing. His well-known history text book, *Fezleke-i Tarih-i Osmani* (An Outline of Ottoman History), which was for a long time used as a school textbook, was organized according to European style, dividing the history into sections according to century, and giving chapters for each reigning sultan. Similarly, Gelenbevizade Ahmed Tevfik Bey, the secretary (*katip*) of Abdülhamid II, published *Hamidet ül-Usul* (In Praise of Methodology) in 1878, in which he discussed the methodology of history by synthesising Arabic sources, such as Ibn Khaldun, and French sources.[6]

Like his contemporaries, Namık Kemal, the most well-known member of the Young Ottomans, too, was very well aware of European publications on the Ottoman empire, Islam and the European style of history-writing. However, he did not entirely adopt European methodology in his historical works. Although he saw history as something different from a story, this did not necessarily result in his acceptance of European methodology for the 'fen-i tarih' (science of history), since European historiography, far from being superior to Islamic historiography, was, in his view, inferior.[7] Although therefore conscious of European methodology and of the difference between history and story-telling, Namık Kemal did not see any necessity to adopt this methodology in order to write history. Later, early Republican writers such as Mükrimin Halil Yinanç, a product of the late Ottoman education system, and Mehmed Kaplan, who was shaped by Republican education, criticised Namık Kemal's historical works for not being "scientific" since they did not differentiate between myth and reality and their arguments were based not on documents but on intuition.[8]

While, with the growing awareness of European methodology, how history was to be written was thus changing through the second half of the nineteenth and early twentieth centuries, why it was written did not. The idea that history should have a mission, an aim, led to the development of an understanding of the functionality of history in the late Ottoman and early Republican eras. Although the conviction that history should serve an aim remained the same throughout this period, what this aim should be changed according to contemporary needs. Instead of replacing the old aims with new ones, the old aims were modified and new ones were added. In this historical continuum, the state, however, always remained central in the definition of the aims of history.

Such centrality is clear from very early on. Ahmed Vefik Paşa in his *Fezleke* praised the Ottoman dynasty and sought to bolster the legitimacy of the state and dynasty by demonising any kind of attempt to undermine the power of the centre and the sultan in the eyes of the sultan's subjects.[9] Ahmed Cevdet Paşa, the most well-known history-writer of the nineteenth century, saw history very much from a central state point of view. A Tanzimat bureaucrat and court historiographer, *vakanüvis*, he recorded the events in the Ottoman empire in the years between 1188/1774-1241/1825 in his well-known chronicle *Tarih-i Cevdet* (Cevdet's History), which was published while he was alive and became an important source for the era it covered. Even in the early Republican era, Ahmed Cevdet's chronicle was a major reference work for the new history-writing project of the 1930s' which aimed to produce a new history for the new nation-state, and Akçuraoğlu Yusuf used it for the book which he wrote as part of the project for rewriting Turkish history, *Türk Tarihinin Ana Hatları* (Main Lines of Turkish History).[10]

Although Ahmed Cevdet Paşa aimed, especially in *Tarih-i Cevdet*, to contribute to the Ottoman 'science of history' (ilm-i tarih), his understanding of science did not come from an embedded positivism, but rather his historical approach was shaped by a traditional understanding of *ilim*.[11] Ahmed Cevdet Paşa perceived the aim of writing history as being that of providing lessons by showing the mistakes of the past.[12] This was also very much the approach of Mustafa Nuri Paşa (1824-1889) who held various high administrative posts during his life time and wrote *Netayic ül-Vukuat*, a major Ottoman history and much used as a source by later historians. Here, too, history was seen as having the didactic message of teaching the lessons of the past so that future generations might avoid such mistakes. Perceiving history as a means of providing lessons was prevalent in the Ottoman-Republican historical continuum.

Not only such *paşa* historians, who can be considered as the direct representatives of the existing government, but also the "oppositional" element within the Ottoman intellectuals perceived history as a very important political and social tool. Namık Kemal saw history as something usable by the state, since history, by illustrating past glories and past mistakes, would provide the necessary knowledge for the successful survival and progress of the state.[13] In the introduction of his *Osmanlı Tarihi* (Ottoman History), published in 1887, Namık Kemal discussed the benefits for the state and the Ottoman nation (*millet*)[14] of learning history and he asked 'if a *millet*'s history is not known, from where can the reasons, known or unknown, for progress and perpetual [survival] be learned?'[15]

It was not merely a matter of the history which the *millet* should know, but also of what it should not. Under Abdülhamid II, history became increasingly a tool of the state and one which the sultan sought both to control and to manipulate. Censorship under Abdülhamid is often taken as a major impediment to history-writing, although this censorship in fact developed gradually during his reign and was not the hard and fast feature which it has sometimes been portrayed as.[16] According to Adnan Adıvar, Ziya Paşa's and Namık Kemal's books, for example, were freely read until 1889.[17] Later, however, some of the history books in circulation, such as Müşir Süleyman Paşa's school text book on world history and Namık Kemal's *Osmanlı Tarihi*, were banned in 1303/1887.[18] But this did not automatically lead to the abolition of history courses in schools, as was argued in the post-Abdülhamidian period,[19] for, as part of the control of the information flow in this period, Abdülhamid II wanted to manipulate history-writing according to the needs of the regime in its fight for the survival of both the sultanate and the state.[20] The texts in this period avoided relating the losses of the Ottoman empire, and were also inclined to ignore recent political history. While not all writing specifically for the sultan, the historians in this period, like their predecessors, prayed for the health and success of the current sultan and treated with great care any sensitive issues which might be seen as giving justification for discontent among Ottoman subjects of the state.[21] For instance, the representation of the French Revolution in the Tanzimat histories as an illegitimate act of the people which led to disorder continued to be reproduced during the Abdülhamidian era in works such as Abdurrahman Şeref's *Tarih-i Devlet-i Osmaniye* (The History of the Ottoman State), which was produced as a school text book in 1318/1900, and Ali Cevad's *Mükemmel Osmanlı Tarihi* (Complete Ottoman History).[22] The subject was later completely removed from the curriculum[23] and books about the French Revolution were classed as 'detrimental.'[24]

In this period, histories had to be checked by and obtain permission from the Ministry of Education before being published. This mechanism ensured that such publications were in accordance with the political requirements of the day. The regime was not able to control what was written, but was able to control, through censorship, what was published in Ottoman-controlled lands. Histories were either not given permission for publication, or were banned and collected after publication, while those published outside Ottoman control, in, for example, Cairo, which were deemed detrimental, were forbidden entry.

In 1887, Namık Kemal's *Osmanlı Tarihi,* Vol. I, *Medhal* (Introduction) was published with the permission of the Ministry of Education. Namık Kemal submitted his work to Abdülhamid II together with a letter dated 28 Teşrin-i evvel 1303 (9 November 1887).[25] Although Abdülhamid II apparently held the book in high esteem, he banned it immediately after its publication, ordering that existing copies be destroyed on the grounds that certain words and phrases in the book might be open to misuse.[26] While censorship resulted in the banning of Namık Kemal's books, this ban served merely to increase interest for, as Abdülhamid's Minister of Internal Affairs, Mehmed Memduh Paşa pointed out, banning material resulted in an increased interest in such 'forbidden' texts.[27] Namık Kemal's books in general, and his history in particular, became very popular in those censored years. In his memoirs, Namık Kemal's son Ali Ekrem Bolayır wrote that even the draft of his father's history was a source of curiosity for people and a source of fear for the family even after the death of his father, since this interest in the history could have attracted the attention of the palace and jeopardized the family's security.[28]

Censorship under Abdülhamid contributed to the shape of history-writing in the pre-1908 period by strengthening state control of history and thus ensuring what kind of history was published and what history was taught in schools. Under Abdülhamid, as had been the case before, the concept of the mission of history was prevalent, regardless of the political stance of the historians. History was didactic, its purpose to show the lessons of the past for the betterment of the future. Despite the political differences between the intellectuals of this era, their aim remained the same: to bolster the power of the Ottoman state. This was to be done either through an increase in the power of the central authority brought about by re-establishing the traditional order in the provinces, or through increasing the power of the state by renewing the loyalty of the Ottoman subjects to it based on the idea of union (*ittihad*). While the 'conservative'[29] Ahmed Cevdet, who wrote a semi-historical autobiography, *Maruzat* (Matters (submitted to a superior)), for Abdülhamid II during whose reign the second edition of his *Tarih-i Cevdet* was published, advocated the former approach, the 'nationalist'[30] Namık Kemal supported the latter. History was thus seen as a means not only of legitimizing the existing dynasty or the state, but also of halting its decline. Abdülhamid II was very aware of the potential of history both as a threat to the legitimacy of his power and the image of the state, and as a means of manipulating the minds of his subjects. If there is any shift in the writing of history from the Tanzimat period to the era of Abdülhamid, it is in Abdülhamid's keen grasp of the power of history as a tool for state control.

The post-1908 era witnessed a boom in the number of publications in general, and publications in history in particular, due to the decline of Abdülhamidian censorship. However, the objectives behind history-writing increased rather than altered, and new objectives were added to those of increasing the loyalty of Ottoman subjects to the state and of bolstering the power of central authority. Now the Abdülhamidian regime was to be de-legitimised, although care was taken not to undermine the legitimacy of the dynasty, and an Ottoman "citizen" was to be created by adopting the methods of European nationalism. However, this did not mean following a "nationalist" design for a nation, but involved rather the locating the new citizen in an Ottoman context, that is not in an homogenous centralized state, but, paradoxically, within a multi-religious, non-homogenous empire.

In this environment, an attempt to institutionalise history-writing was made with the establishment of the Tarih-i Osmani Encümeni (Ottoman Historical Commission), whose first president, Abdurrahman Şeref, had a position in the new constitutional government. From 1910 onwards, this Commission began to publish a journal, *Tarih-i Osmani Encümeni Mecmuası* (The Journal of the Ottoman Historical Commission), which changed its name in 1924 to *Türk Tarih Encümeni Mecmuası* (The Journal of the Turkish Historical Commission).[31] The ideological stance of the Commission was entirely dependent on the political climate of the country. The Commission, which started as Ottomanist (that is within an imperial outlook), became Turkist, emphasizing the Turkishness of the state, in the later period of the İttihad ve Terakki era. In 1335/1917, the Commission published

Osmanlı Tarihi (Ottoman History) written by Necib Asım (Yazıksız), who was then a professor of Turkish history and language in the Darülfünun (the first Ottoman university established in 1863), and Mehmed Arif, then a professor of Ottoman history in the Darülfünun. The book gave substantial space to the pre-Ottoman era as well as a seperate section on the Turks from the period before the creation of the Ottoman empire. The introduction written by the Tarih-i Osmani Encümeni drew attention to the necessity of learning history, for history was a 'classroom of example' (dershane-i ibret).[32]

For Köprülüzade Mehmed Fuad, one of the most important historians of the early Republican era as well as an important politician, writing Ottoman history required more than a belief in the necessity of history. Although he apparently appreciated the *Osmanlı Tarihi* of Necib Asım and Mehmed Arif, he argued that because of the lack of European-style methology or developed use of source material, a proper 'national history' of the Ottoman empire could not be written.[33] To obtain maximum benefit from history-writing, it was essential that it be presented according to the European model, that is that it be 'scientific.' A year later, in the same journal in an article 'Tarihde Usul' (Methodology in history), Emin Ali wrote about Euro-centric historiography, referred to in his time as the modern understanding of history, which developed in the nineteenth century. In this article he emphasized the absolutely essential relationship between documents and history, stating that without documents there was no history.[34] While he underlined the necessity of cataloguing documents, he also discussed professional history-writing, focusing on the vital importance of education in *ilm-i tarih*, the science of history, in what he called an apprenticeship period.

However, as Emin Ali pointed out, before everything, before any discussion of methodology, it was first necessary to understand what history was. For Emin Ali, history had a role as a court of judgment in which tyrants were sentenced. History inspired morality (*ahlak*), conscience (*vicdan*) and virtue (*fazilet*), and, in particular, patriotism (*vatanperverlik*). For Köprülüzade Mehmed Fuad, too, history was at the service of the state and the nation. Writing in 1913, he argued that an Ottoman/Turkish literary history would be an important means to prove the existence of Turkish/Ottoman civilization. 'Such a work, which will bring to life, clearly and completely for centuries to come not only the poems of the Turks but also the manifestations of Turkish thought and civilization, will be not only a national but also, at the same time, a human and scientific monument.'[35] In order to accomplish this goal of creating a substantial and comprehensive account of Ottoman/Turkish literature, Köprülüzade Mehmed Fuad argued for the importance of methodology and against a strict positivism that would lead the historian to simplistic conclusions. He underlined that 'a good historian should strive not to take the narrow rules of the natural sciences but the scientific soul which prevails in research in these sciences.'[36] In this highly significant article, he reviewed contemporary European historiography and scrutinized works on Turkish/Ottoman literature. However, 20 years later, in the first Turkish History Congress in 1932, he ended his speech 'Türk Edebiyatına Umumî Bir Bakış' (A general survey of Turkish literature), with a quotation from his 1913 article, not about methodology but about the mission of this 'scientific' enterprise:[37]

> For this great national and scientific monument which still lacks building materials, every Turkish youth who is an enthusiast of the history of literature should strive to bring at least one stone which accords with the methodology which has been explained, because the magnificent monument which will be brought into existence by demonstrating the uniqueness of the Turkish national genius of the great and distinguished Turkish nation which has shown itself throughout the centuries in various phases, will drive future generations to the same aim of being unique. How can a more noble and divine aim than this for an historian of Turkish literature be imagined?[38]

The great benefits expected from history-writing, as seen by Köprülüzade Mehmed Fuad and Emin Ali, were carried over into the Republican era. In a 1928 article, 'Tarih İlimdir' (History is a science), Ahmed Refik, the well-known and prolific historian of the late Ottoman and early Republican era, elevated history to a supra-human level, attributing to it a non-scientific, metaphysical characteristic which separated it from the other sciences. History, rather than being a mental construction of human beings to record events according to time, was that which implemented the orders of God and was therefore a natural part of the human condition.[39]

While the perception of history as an essential component in the construction of the state and in strengthening national unity continued in the Republican era, the historians of this era argued not over the purpose of history but over the place of Ottoman history in the history-writing of the new Republic. In 1924, after one and half years' teaching in Baku University, Muhittin (Birgen), the chief editor of the newspaper *Tanin* during the First World War and a member of the İttihad ve Terakki, advocated a new history-writing based on the character of the new state, rather than the continued use of Ottoman history texts even if such texts were modified. Using a materialist understanding of history and following his conviction about the relation between sociology and history, he argued that the new Turkish nation was not a continuation of the Ottoman empire, for the empire had been a repressive, non-Turkish power which had tyrannized the Turks for over 700 years.[40] Unlike, for example, Köprülüzade Mehmed Fuad and Ahmed Refik, who continued to attempt to unify Ottoman history and Turkish history by Turkifying Ottoman history, Muhittin called for a new history written on the basis of the total rejection of the Ottoman past as a part of Turkish history. According to him, 'the solution to the problem of Ottoman and Turkish history cannot be procured by sticking the word "Turk" onto the tail of the word "Ottoman".'[41] Muhittin's rejection of Ottoman history was not, however, accepted. In the second congress on Turkish history, Afet (İnan), an important figure of the Turkish History Thesis (which sought to stress the importance of Turkish history and Turkish achievements and to give the new Republic a national history), and foster daughter of Mustafa Kemal, integrated Ottoman history into the Turkish History Thesis thus giving it an official recognition. The history of the 'nation' was differentiated from the history of the 'dynasty,' and the Turkish nation became the main "owner" of the Ottoman empire, which was defined according to the needs of the Turkish Republic.[42]

A further problem was, for some, the way Ottoman history had been written. This was not so much a problem of the place of Ottoman history, but the style. In 1934, Necip Ali, the editor of *Ülkü Halkevleri Mecmuası*, a popular monthly journal published by the Halkevleri (the People's Houses),[43] argued that the 'Ottoman History Thesis,' a term used in this period for Ottoman history-writing, was no more than a collection of stories of the warrior-like conquests of a 600-year-old nomad tribe. Such history, by failing to present this 'nomad tribe' as the legitimate occupier of Anatolia, gave a pretext to anyone wishing to invade, and nourished the common European perception of the Turk, whom, he argued, 'other nations wanted to perceive ... as a foreign and enemy nation, belonging to the yellow race, settled in Asia Minor and Europe.'[44]

With the introduction of the Turkish History Thesis in the 1930s, the functionality of history as a state intellectual tool became more formalized and the aims of history-writing became clear.[45] In the first congress on Turkish history, Akçuraoğlu Yusuf gave the outlines of what history should be and how it should be used for the creation of a national identity. According to him, every nation legitimately wrote history from its own perspective. Therefore the Turkish historians, too, should write history according to their national interests rather than adopting or merely copying the histories written from the perspectives of other nations. He chose *Umumi Tarihi* (Universal History)[46] of Ali Reşad, an important historian of the late Ottoman and early Republican era, to demonstrate the threat posed to the national interests by a history based on translation of European sources which were already biased against the Ottoman empire.[47] This point made by Akçuraoğlu Yusuf in the first Turkish History Congress was repeated by Falih Rıfkı (Atay) in his article on the second Turkish History Congress (1937) in which he said: 'The image of the colourful and barbarian Turk reached even into Turkish schools due to lack of Ottoman awareness and through translations.'[48] History-writing was thus to be important also in bolstering national self-confidence, an essential element in a viable and rooted national identity.

History was not merely important, at a national level, in the creation of a national identity within the country, but, written in accordance with certain methodological rules taken from western historiography, was also important for the integration of the Turkish nation into the western world and for gaining the respect and recognition of the West. A. Zeki Velidi Togan, who wrote a well-known book on methodology in history published in 1950 and based predominantly on his lecture notes from 1929-1932 and 1939 onwards,[49] considered history as a tool that would lead to the destruction of the eastern inferiority complex in relation to the West. This could, he felt, be achieved through integrating the eastern, that is Arabic, Persian, Indian and Central Asian, understanding of history and history books with those from the West. This would lead to a universal understanding of history which was neither western nor eastern.⁵⁰ Peyami Safa, a well-known writer and journalist, summarised the aim behind this attempt to write a new 'Turkish history':

> To break up the inferiority complex which gnaws at the roots of the national consciousness of the Ottoman child who thinks of himself as a dried, crooked and shrunken branch of an underdeveloped Asian race, a consciousness which was half awakened after the disasters of Bosnia-Herzegovina, Tripoli, the Balkans and Sèvres, after proving to him in one instance that he can enter the European civilized world and making him believe in the possibility of a transition from the single and imposing mass of his history as old as man to a great living organism, to place the stamp of the huge and eternal truth of Turkey on his soul. Well, this is one of the most fundamental bases of Atatürk's nationalist and civilizational revolution.⁵¹

For Mustafa Kemal Atatürk, history was the means to change the western perception of Turkey and to erase the European conception of the Turk as 'incapable of any form of civilization,' as lazy in time of peace and destructive and barbarous in war.⁵² According to Yakup Kadri Karaosmanoğlu in his book about Atatürk written shortly after Mustafa Kemal's death,

> neither the victory of Dumlupınar nor the Lausanne peace, nor the many political, social, cultural and economic revolutionary changes which followed them had yet shaken off the world's hostile perception and negative view of the Turkish nation. This man who had at one stroke uprooted all the centuries-old superstitions embedded in his country had been totally unable to wipe this black stain of ignorance from the mind of the western world, which was considered the essential source of objective knowledge, justice and truth.⁵³

The only way to fight against this western mind-set was to write a new national history of the Turks.

Either Ottoman or Turkish, either conservative or radical, all Ottoman/Turkish⁵⁴ historians in the late Ottoman/early Republican period perceived history as a useful means to reach a political or social aim of the state regardless of whether they used modern historical techniques or not. The reason for this centrality of the state in the historians' approach lies in the relation between the state and the intellectuals of whom the historian was a part. The Ottoman/Turkish historian, as a member of the intelligentsia, existed in a direct relation with the state rather than with any class. This dimension of the Ottoman/Turkish historian differs from Gramsci's understanding of the intellectuals as 'the dominant group's "deputies" exercising the subaltern functions of social hegemony and political government.'[55] In the late Ottoman and early Republican era, the intellectuals functioned as the 'deputies' of a state, whose power was not merely physically coercive. In this Ottoman/Turkish continuum, what was created was a "state" hegemony, not a specific "class" hegemony.

The nature of this link between the state and the historian in the late Ottoman and early Republican era lies in the fact that most of the historians in this period were either directly employed or indirectly supported by the state, or educated in the schools which were shaped by the state according to its priorities. For example, in the late nineteenth century, the historians were administrative or military bureaucrats, such as Ahmed Vefik Paşa and Mustafa Nuri Paşa, or state chroniclers who worked as the official historians of the state, such as Lütfi Efendi, or writers of text books for the state schools, which were shaped according to the needs of the political authority, such as Lütfiye Hanım and Ali Cevad, who was also an officer and teacher.[56]

On occasion an historian could be both bureaucrat, state chronicler and writer of school text books. Ahmed Cevdet Paşa was both a high state official, *vakanüvis*, and one of the authors of a text book on Ottoman grammar for schools, as well as being an important legal figure.[57] Abdurrahman Şeref wrote history text books and taught history in state schools, including the Mekteb-i Sultani, today Galatasaray Lisesi, which was established to give a European style of education, and the Mülkiye Mektebi, established to train bureaucrats for the state. He was also headmaster of both these schools. After the re-introduction of the constitutional government, he became the last *vakanüvis* and a minister in the cabinet. Coming from the Abdülhamidian establishment, Abdurrahman Şeref continued to be an important intellectual figure in the post-1908 period, and became the first president of the Tarih-i Osmani Encümeni. Despite his age, he became an MP in the first Turkish Parliament in Ankara.[58]

Even those historians who were at one point in opposition to the government, such as Murad Bey, a leading figure among the Young Turks, were still very much part of the state apparatus and did not have any "extra-state" perception. Known either as Mizancı after *Mizan*, a newspaper he continued to publish in exile, or Tarihçi (historian), Murad Bey, who wrote *Tarih-i Umumi* (Universal History) and later, after 1908, *Tarih-i Ebulfaruk* (History of Ebulfaruk), is an interesting example of the symbiotic relation between political power and the intellectual within the Ottoman context. He was born in Dagistan and immigrated to the Ottoman empire when he was a student in the İstavropol (Stavropol in the North Caucasus) High School. He was married to Hasibe Hanım, the daughter of Hilmi Molla from one of the well-established families of İstanbul[59] and worked as a highly paid history teacher in the Mülkiye Mektebi.[60] From there he moved to a well-paid position in the Public Debt Administration. While with the Public Debt Administration, he submitted a memorandum (*layiha*) to the sultan on changes he perceived as necessary in the running of the state.[61] His suggestions were not, however, accepted by Abdülhamid, and, angered by this rejection, Murad Bey left for Cairo, moving from there to Paris and Geneva. He was later convinced to return to İstanbul by the sultan's agent, Ahmed Celaleddin Paşa, and subsequently, on his return in 1887, lost credibility among the Young Turks.[62] Namık Kemal, too, later considered an important figure of Turkish patriotism, had spent much of his life as a state official, and, as a letter he wrote to his son-in-law Rıfat Bey shows, he was very ready to negotiate with the palace about the content of his *Osmanlı Tarihi* in order to obtain permission for its publication.[63]

This tight bond between historian and state comes out clearly in Abdülhamid's memoirs, written in 1333/1917, in which he explained how he perceived the link between the state and intellectual:

> If I had been an enemy of literature, I would not have given a salary to [Namık] Kemal Bey until his death from my own pocket, nor would I have taken his son into my service. If I had been an enemy of literature, I would not have taken so much reproach and spoilt behaviour from [Recaizade Mahmud] Ekrem Bey and Ebüzziya [Tevfik] Bey. If I had been an enemy of literature, I would not have found myself performing acts of benevolence such as paying Abdülhak Hamit Bey's debts as well as providing

him with a high salary. If I had been an enemy of literature and the science of history, I would not have consented to [Mizancı] Murad Bey's remaining in government service on an ample salary until the last moment of my sultanate, putting up with all his unreasonableness, Murad Bey who wanted at one point to work against my throne and crown. No, I say again, I was a true and compassionate friend of writers. If I had been their enemy, I had the men to strike authors and writers down in the middle of the street.[64]

In the post-1908 period, the relation between the state and historian took a different shape. But, although such direct state control may have been lifted, the inherent bond between historian and state remained. Although Enver Ziya Karal argued in 1946 that there was no state intervention in history-writing in the post-Abdülhamidian period, thus allowing for the dissemination of unfounded European views of Turkish history with little or no critical analysis,[65] the official abolition of censorship and the decline of state control in fact merely lessened direct state intervention. Historians continued to be part of the state establishment, either working for it or having close links with, for example, the İttihad ve Terakki, or producing text books for the state schools in accordance with the programme prepared by the Ministry of Education. Political pressure continued to be exerted. In his memoirs Cavid Bey, the Finance Minister of the İttihad ve Terakki government, wrote that the Minister of Interior in the post-İttihad ve Terakki government, Mehmed Ali Bey, advised Süleyman Kâni (İrtem), Abdullah Zühtü and Ahmed Refik (Altınay) to write books against the İttihad ve Terakki. Ahmed Refik's *İki Komite İki Kıtal* (Two Committees Two Massacres) and *Kafkas Yollarında* (On the Road to the Caucasus) thus portrayed the İttihad ve Terakki unfavourably.[66]

In the early Republic the closeness between historian and state, with the historian very much part of the state apparatus, was criticized in a debate on the role of the historian. As early as 1924, the organic relation between state and intellectual within the Ottoman context was underlined by Muhittin (Birgen). Taking the 'kapıkulu[67] cemiyeti' as a social class[68] made up of the privileged subjects of the empire who controlled 'the sword and the book,' the army and the *ulema*, and were defined according to their allegiance to the sultan regardless of their nationality, Muhittin described the contemporary historians as '*kapıkulu* historians' (kapıkulu müverrihi), unable to adapt themselves to the nation-state. In 1934, Reşit Galip, the Minister of Education, claimed that the Republic inherited a history based on the writings of those who were the officials of the palace, or who relied on such works, and were engaged in writing the history of the sultan and the dynasty. This understanding of history, which Reşit Galip referred to as the 'Ottoman History Thesis' (Osmanlı Tarih Tezi), focused only on bolstering the allegiance of the subjects to the caliphate and the sultanate. In this history, the nation was inconsequential, this history was thus not the history of the nation, but of something alien.[69]

The Darülfünun was seen as an institution which reproduced this type of Ottoman history-writing, and was attacked by Muhittin who regarded it as responsible for this inability of historians to transform themselves from empire historians to historians of the nation-state. This line of thinking continued among the "leftist" element of the new Republican regime. These intellectuals had a socialist outlook and had relations with the Soviet Union, many having been educated there. In August 1932, Burhan Asaf, an important writer of the 'national leftist' journal *Kadro*,[70] accused the Darülfünun professors present at the first Historical Congress of failing to grasp the Congress's message: 'to reach independence too in the understanding of national history' (millî tarihi görüşte de istiklâle varmak).[71] This attack in *Kadro* was part of the journal's search for new intellectuals for the new Turkey to replace the old Darülfünun intellectuals, a search expressed by Şevket Süreyya (Aydemir), an important writer for this journal: 'We are looking for a new idea, a new man for a new life. Our yearning and inclination are only for the new.'[72] Such attacks were part of a campaign against the "dinosaur" Darülfünun and its failure to produce history suitable for the needs of the new state. As a result of such attacks, reforms began in 1933. The Darülfünun was closed and replaced by İstanbul University.[73] Many professors did not find work in the new university because of their failure to meet the criteria set by the needs of the political and social reforms, including the new movement in history-writing, as defined by the state,[74] which was now to be national history written according to the dictates of the state. Turkish history was the history of the nation, that is the state, for now 'nation is the state.'[75] The position of the historian thus very much resembled that of his predecessor in the Ottoman period. The historian became a servant of the state which gave him a duty. The existence of intellectuals, in particular of the historian, was now very much tied to the survival of the state. The historian now had a more institutionalized role within the state machinery than he had had before.

From the late Ottoman era to the Republican era, the "location" of the historian within the state did not change, although the state transformed itself from a multi-religious empire to a nation-state. The new republic sought to raise its own state historians in order to cultivate the idea of history defined according to the needs of the state. The Turkish History Thesis of the 1930s' was an attempt to speed up the production of this new history and disseminate it to the people, the *halk*.

One important part of dissemination was the writing of popular history. This move towards a more popular history-writing had in fact developed earlier and it could even be argued dates back to Namık Kemal's popular historical works, such as *Devr-i İstila* (The Period of Conquest) which consisted of short biographies of the sultans down to the reign of Süleyman the Magnificient.[76] However, the differentiation between academic and popular history books actually began to develop in the post-1908 era as the result of the increase in literacy and schooling during Abdülhamid's reign, an increase in the number of publications, and the social-engineering policies adopted by the new regime in order to create an Ottoman "citizen" by adopting the methods used by the European nation-states. Similar to popular religious books, which simplified religious dogmas and gave clear-cut distinctions between good and evil, heaven and hell, and sometimes included illustrations of, for example, hell and *sırat köprüsü* (the bridge leading to Paradise), popular historical texts, such as Ahmed Refik's three-volume *Kadınlar Saltanatı* (The Sultanate of the Women) published in 1332/1914 (1916) and 1923, were produced in a style similar to that of popular folk stories.[77]

Popular history, however, was not limited to history books. Similar themes, for example the glorification of the Ottoman past which carried a religious overtone, were integrated into literary works such as poems and short stories, especially those published in journals and newspapers. Mehmed Akif (Ersoy), Ziya Gökalp, Yahya Kemal (Beyatlı) and Mehmed Emin (Yurdakul) used these themes in their poems, as did Ömer Seyfeddin in his popular short stories.

This differentiation between academic and popular history books further developed during the Republican era. In a letter written in 1942 to the Cumhuriyet Halk Partisi (Republican People's Party) in response to a request from the party for an evaluation of a book, *Bulgaristan Tarihi* (Bulgarian History), written by a teacher Osman Nuri Peremeci who had requested financial assistance from the party as he was himself unable to meet the cost of printing, Şemseddin Günaltay, the president of the Türk Tarih Kurumu (Turkish Historical Society), gave his judgment that the book was not academic, but that, after some minor changes, it could make a useful 'book for the public' (halk kitabı).[78] Later that same year the book was published under the title *Tuna Boyu Tarihi* (The History of the Bank of the Danube) incorporating the changes Şemseddin Günaltay had asked for.[79] The Cumhuriyet Halk Partisi was very involved in the advancement of popular history, providing popular books for the libraries of the Halkevleri (The People's Houses).[80] Authors approached the party requesting that their books be purchased for the Halkevleri libraries. Yaşar Nabi Nayır, an important writer and publisher of the early Republican period, for example, requested that the Cumhuriyet Halk Partisi buy his book, *Balkanlar ve Türklük* (The Balkans and the Turkishness), for the Halkevleri libraries, claiming that the book would serve to increase patriotic and national 'training' (terbiye) of the Turkish youth. Upon his request 150 copies of his book were bought for the Halkevleri libraries.[81]

History was not merely for the people but also for the pupils. While the primary school history texts which were written in simpler language than those for secondary schools and aimed to convey a simple and direct message to the pupils, resembled popular history books, most of the history text books written for high schools and universities, such as Ali Reşad's *Tarih-i Osmani* (Ottoman History) of 1329/1911 for Mülkiye Mektebi and *Asr-ı Hazır Tarihi* (Contemporary History) of 1926 for high schools, may be considered as academic texts which had little or no popular features. The high school or university texts of the late Ottoman and early Republican era, in fact, were mostly based on the lecture notes of the professors, which were either compiled by the professors themselves or from notes taken by their students.

School text books played an important part in the shaping of identity by inculcating the school children with patriotic feelings and loyalty to the fatherland, and training them to be good citizens. In 1327/1911, Ahmed Refik ended his history for the second year of the middle school (*rüşdiye*) with advice for children:

When the name of the Ottomans is called to mind, keep before your eyes the things which you have read, the former condition of our *millet*, the former glory of Ottomanism and the former honour of our soldiers. Work with all your mind to preserve this honour. You can only prove your love of the *millet* and loyalty to the fatherland in this way. Only history can teach you these lessons. That is why you must, lovingly and thoughtfully, read Ottoman history which teaches you the conditions of your fatherland and the greatness of your *millet*.[82]

İhsan Şeref, a history teacher and a school text book writer, in his 1926-school text, drew a link between history and national feelings:

We too have a history. And a very glorious one. Its name is the history of the Anatolian Turks. Everyone must absolutely know the history of their own nation. If we do not know our history, we can have no national feeling. Such people who have no feeling for nation, no feeling of nationalism are no use to you, me or anybody else.[83]

Not only were children inculcated with feelings of patriotism, but also with a sense of the need for history. *Türk Çocuklarına Tarih Notları* (History Notes for Turkish Children), published in 1929, considered history not only as illuminating and a guide for contemporaries but also a 'useful teacher' for the next generations.[84] This same understanding of history as a useful teacher was repeated, almost word for word, in a history text prepared for high schools as part of the project of re-writing history.[85] This was the first of a four-volume history which was written under the personal supervision of Mustafa Kemal Atatürk,[86] according to whom, history 'was the truest guide to what a nation was capable of and what it could achieve.'[87] This idea of history as a useful means for understanding the present was echoed by Afet İnan in a conference paper she gave in 1944 when she talked about the importance of history for everybody and for every occupation, since history enabled an examining and understanding of the reasons for contemporary events.[88] In his 1928 poem, Fazıl Ahmet (Aykaç) imagined how history, as an old teacher, would narrate the National Liberation War and the reforms. He used this imagined history-writing as a projector to the future of the Republic in order to narrate the contemporary successes, especially of Mustafa Kemal as leader of the nation.[89]

2

'A BELT OF LARGE DUMPLINGS': THE DEFINITION OF THE BALKANS

> The idea prevalent in some quarters that the line of the Balkans is a strong one is a mistake. The Balkans are nothing more than a belt of large dumplings, so to speak, which permit infantry to wind around them in all directions, making roads as they go for artillery and transport trains. [...] The southern slopes are steep, while the northern are easy of access in hundreds of places. [...] The continuous line being impossible, it is an error to suppose that the Balkans will ever interpose a serious barrier to an intelligent and determined attack from the Bulgarian side of the mountains.[1]

The journey of the term "the Balkans" from being 'a belt of large dumplings' to one of the world's most "infamous" regional designations in the twentieth century was a fast one. According Mark Mazower, the term came in at the end of the nineteenth century to replace the designation 'Turkey in Europe' which no longer corresponded to the geographical area for which it had until then been used.[2] Maria Todorova's approach to the term, "the Balkans" is more theoretical than Mark Mazower's. Looking very much from within the region, her concern is to find out why the term came to have such pejorative connotations. Neither of these two authors, however, considers the Ottoman/Turkish aspect of the question. While Todorova does mention the term in Turkish, her understanding of it is flawed, for she describes 'Balkanlar' as being in Turkish 'a personal noun in the plural [used] to designate the states of the Balkan Peninsula.' As in

English, however, the word can mean both the states and the region in general. It does not mean the Balkan states alone. While Todorova assigns to it a neutral and non-pejorative meaning, again, as in English, the term may or may not carry a pejorative connotation.[3]

The word *balkan* has various meanings within the late nineteenth- and early twentieth-century Ottoman context. In the dictionaries of the period, the term *balkan* means mountain or chain of mountains or mountainous, thus not necessarily being a regional geographical definition. Ahmed Vefik Paşa, in his dictionary *Lehçe-i Osmani*, defines *balkan* as a mountain and *balkan dağı* as the chain of mountains in Rumeli.[4] Şemseddin Sami defines *balkan* as 'a steep or forest-covered chain of mountains, a chain of mountains.'[5] He also defines the same word in his *Dictionnaire Turc-Français* as 'Chaîne de montagnes couvertes de forêts; le mont Hemus; le Balkan.'[6] Şemseddin Sami, in his encyclopaedic dictionary of the world, also refers to the *Balkan* mountain to the east of the Caspian, which was located, he says, in a gulf, also called *balkan*.[7]

The dictionary definition of the term *balkan* also appears in the texts of the period. In 1294/1877 Kamil Kapudan in his book on Montenegro used *balkan* to mean mountainous, referring not only to Rumeli but also to Anatolia.[8] While Murad I crossed the 'büyük Balkan' from the East in Namık Kemal's account of the early development of the Ottoman state,[9] storms and downpours crossed the Balkans, that is the mountains, sweeping westward from Europe to İstanbul in Ahmed Lütfi Efendi's narration of daily events.[10] The Balkan mountains were also important strategic geographical locations. In his account of the defense of Plevne (Pleven) written in 1316/1898 (1900), Ahmed Cemal, who as Cemal Paşa was later to become one of the three main figures of the İttihad ve Terakki and Navy Minister, takes the Balkan mountains as a main definition point together with the Danube to locate Plevne.[11] For Kazım Karabekir, later a major figure of the First World War and of the National Liberation War, the Balkans, the mountains, were a hot bed of bandits who threatened the power and security of the state.[12]

The term *balkan* could also be used in the phrase *Balkan Şeb-i Ceziresi*, the Balkan Peninsula, here referring to a specific geographical location and not merely the Balkan mountain range. In Ali Cevad's dictionary *balkan* is used both for the mountain range and for the peninsula: 'Balkan is the name of a chain of mountains running East to West from Eastern Rumeli to Bulgaria in the Ottoman Europe which gives its name to the peninsula on which it is found.'[13] Şemseddin Sami describes the *Balkan Şeb-i Ceziresi* as the most eastern of the three big peninsulas in Europe which was

> bounded to the north by Austria and Hungary, to the north-east by Russia, to the east by the Black Sea and the Bosphorus, to the south by the Sea of Marmara and the Dardanelles, the Aegean and the Mediterranean, and to the west by the Greek and Adriatic sea and by Dalmatia, and it lies between ´30 ° 36 and ´30 ° 47 latitude north and ´20 °15 and ´40 °29 longitude east.'[14]

According to Şemseddin Sami, this area, which had been Ottoman territory since the end of the Middle Ages, consisted of the territories of the European section of the state and was known as Ottoman Europe or Rumeli (Turquie d'Europe) which were for Şemseddin Sami the same. However, Şemseddin Sami notes that 'recently,' with the gaining of independence of various parts of this territory, this name, Ottoman Europe or Rumeli (Turquie d'Europe), no longer covered the whole area which began to be called instead the Balkan Peninsula.[15]

It is thus clear that in the late nineteenth century Rumeli did not mean the same thing as the Balkan Peninsula. In a geography textbook of 1318/1900 (1902), Rumeli was equated only with the Ottoman empire in Europe: 'Avrupa-i Osmaniye = Rumeli-i Şahane.'[16] In the Republican era, Rumeli was increasingly used interchangeably with the Balkans. In a 1934 city guide of İstanbul prepared by the İstanbul municipality, Rumeli was defined, in the section devoted to the history of the city, as the Balkan Peninsula: 'The reason for the Greeks and Orthodox still being called (Rum) and the Balkan Peninsula (Rumeli) in Turkish, and for Anatolia earlier being called (Diyari Rum) by the Arabs and Muslims stems from the fact that these places were the lands of Ancient Romans and the people there were their subjects.'[17] In *Tarih III*, Rumeli and the Balkans were used as interchangeable geographical designations:

> The emperor thought that in the event of the Ottoman Turks crossing to Rumeli and marching against the Bulgarians and the Serbs, İstanbul would for a period be out of danger. [...] Gelibolu became the naval base for military actions and for the series of conquests which the Ottomans made in the Balkans. [...] As was

said before, before the Ottoman Turks crossed into the Balkans, the Balkan Peninsula became the setting for invasions and migrations of the Thracians in the period before Christ, and the Huns, the Avars, the Bulgars after.[18]

However, this interchangeability of the two terms was not universally accepted and Rumeli did not equate with the Balkans in everyone's imagination. Nahid Sırrı, the author of a travel account on Edirne written in 1941, for example, clearly did not think of Rumeli and the Balkans as being one and the same, for he described his feeling while waiting in Sirkeci, the departure point in İstanbul for travelling into the Balkans and from where he was to go to Edirne, as one of breathing 'the air of Thrace, or even the more distant air of old Rumeli.'[19]

Such interchangeability and confusion can be seen in Halil İnalcık's 1943 book, *Tanzimat ve Bulgar Meselesi* (The Tanzimat and the Bulgarian Question), in which he differentiates 'Rumeli Eyaleti' from Rumeli,[20] and where the Balkans and Rumeli as non-specified regional designations seemed to be used interchangeably,[21] although the Balkans sometimes also appear to be referring to a greater region than Rumeli.[22] In 1995 İnalcık "fixes" the interchangeability of the terms and defines Rumeli as 'the geographical name given to the Balkan peninsula by the Ottomans, also the name of the Ottoman province which included this region.'[23]

Interestingly, for many late twentieth-century Ottoman historians the terms Rumeli and the Balkan Peninsula continued to be interchangeable, the entry for Rumeli in the index of Donald Quataert's book *The Ottoman Empire 1700-1922*, for example, reading 'Rumeli, *see* Balkan Peninsula.'[24] Recently, a hybrid term, 'the Ottoman Balkans' has been introduced to define the Ottoman territories in Europe,[25] but this term, too, fails to convey the meaning which both the terms Rumeli and the Balkans contain.

In fact the term Rumeli can be seen as an Ottoman-centric term whereas the Balkan Peninsula is very much a Euro-centric term. Even though the terms may on occasion overlap in the geographical area they cover, they reflect different political outlooks. Şemseddin Sami's definition of Rumeli as the European part of the Ottoman empire seems more applicable to the nineteenth-century Ottoman conception of the region.[26] In Şemseddin Sami's definition, Rumeli was defined according to the Ottoman empire and was not a fixed term, for the region it defined shrank in the nineteenth and early twentieth century. Although officially, with the introduction of the provincial system in the Ottoman empire in 1867, there was an attempt to fix locations and Rumeli became the name of one of the provinces, this did not prevent the utilization of the term *Rumeli* with its subjective Ottoman-centric meaning, Rumeli, for example, being used to designate the Ottoman territory in Europe as distinct from the separate, new Balkan states of Bulgaria, Serbia, Romania, Greece and Bosnia in Ahmed Nazmi's map of Rumeli from 1329/1911.[27] In his 1946 dictionary, Mehmet Zeki Pakalın gives both meanings of Rumeli:

> Rumeli: is the name given to the part of the Ottoman empire in the European continent.
> The Province of Rumeli: is the name given to one of the large provinces of the Ottoman empire on the European continent. The province included the following places: Thessaloniki, Skolpje, Okhrida, Velbužd, Delvinon, Valona, Elbasan, Prizren, Dukagin, Kruševac, Vilčetrin, Ioannina, Smederovo, Janevo.[28]

In contrast to Rumeli, the terms Balkan Peninsula and the Balkans, however, are Euro-centric and politically loaded terms replacing the European term 'Turkey in Europe.' Marriott, writing on the Eastern Question in 1917, referred to 'the lands which the geographers of the last generation described as *Turkey in Europe*, but for which political changes compelled us to seek a new name. The name generally given to that segment is *The Balkan Peninsula*, or simply *The Balkans*.'[29] This clearly demonstrates the political content of this term which did not reflect geographical reality. While in 1917 'Turkey in Europe' as an area was considerably smaller than it had been in the late nineteenth century, it still existed. In the same way as the Ottoman term Rumeli, which Şemseddin Sami equates with Turquie d'Europe, remained in use despite the shrinking of the area to which it was applied, so too could the European term have continued to be used.

In fact, the term "the Balkans" as a regional designation began to be used around the late 1870s' and its introduction seems directly related to European belief in the imminent end of the Ottoman empire in the post-Berlin Congress period. A former eastern correspondent of *The Times* in his article, 'Diplomacy in the Balkans' dated October 27,

1885, discusses the success of diplomacy in delaying 'an explosion in the Balkans' and refers to the 'little Balkan governments.'[30]

This term cannot be considered a pure and fixed topographical designation, and the borders of this region fluctuated even in the European understanding. For example, while according to an Ottoman translation of a newspaper item based on an interview with the German Chancellor Prince Bismarck in 1298/1881, the Balkan Peninsula includes Greece, Serbia, Bulgaria and Eastern Rumeli,[31] in the 1903 map that was published in *The Times*, the Balkan Peninsula embraces 'Albania, Montenegro, Bosnia, Servia, Rumania, Bulgaria, Macedonia and Eastern Rumelia.'[32] Although the meaning of the term fluctuates and the territories included shift, the term essentially means in the European understanding of the period, both ex-Ottoman territories and those territories still under the Ottoman empire.

The Balkans were depicted as including the Ottoman European territories of Eastern Rumeli, Macedonia, Kosova, autonomous Bulgaria and Bosnia-Herzegovinia, which was *de facto* under the occupation of Austria-Hungary, together with the independent states of the region: Greece, Romania, Serbia and Montenegro. Thus, the Ottoman territories were alienated from the Ottoman empire itself and, at least at the level of discourse, gained a distinct identity through becoming a part of a non-Ottoman whole, that is the Balkans.

Ottoman awareness of this newly introduced word seems to exist from its first introduction with this new meaning, but this term appears to be more of a "pseudo-Ottoman" term rather than an "authentic" Ottoman phrase, in that it was used to translate the European term 'Balkan Peninsula,' as it was for example in the 1298/1881 interview with Bismarck in which the Balkan Peninsula was translated as 'Balkan Şeb-i Ceziresi.'[33] Ottoman archival documents including translations from the European press and consular reports from the Ottoman embassies in Europe include this term without translating it into any equivalent Ottoman word. However, despite this awareness, this new term, at least until the early twentieth century, was not internalized or used by the Ottoman historian in his designation of the region of which the term 'the Balkans' was supposed to be a definition. In neither late nineteenth-century history texts such as *Osmanlı Tarihi* of Ali Cevad, who interestingly defines the Balkans in his dictionary but does not use the term himself, nor early twentieth-century texts such as Abdurrahman Şeref's *Tarih-i Devlet-i Osmaniye*, does this term appear with this newly acquired European-originated meaning. In 1323/1907, Tüccarzade İbrahim Hilmi takes the Balkan Peninsula as a fixed geographical location and defines the Ottoman territories in Europe within the Balkan peninsula: "Ottoman Europe stands in the middle of the Balkan peninsula and covers more than half of its surface.'[34] But in another geography text book published in the same period, a 1325/1907 Ottoman geography text book, *Memalik-i Mahrusa-i Şahaneye Mahsus Mükemmel Mufassal Atlas* (The Complete Detailed Atlas of [the Lands of] the Protected Domains), the word *balkan* only appears as the name of the mountains between Bulgaria and Eastern Rumeli.[35] Despite the occasional use of the term in some history or geography books, *balkan* in its Euro-centric meaning was thus not internalized until the post-Abdülhamidian era.

Various possible explanations can be put forward for this lack of Ottoman internalisation of this term. It could be related to, for example, the effect of censorship under Abdülhamid II or could be a form of Ottoman intellectual response to the imposition of a European conceptualization. Although often referred to, censorship under Abdülhamid II is in fact not a well-defined phenomenon. While there are some documents giving general outlines of censorship based on previous experiences, the necessity of the day, and the personal perceptions of those who wrote the reports on censorship,[36] there is apparently no government-issued list of the words that were censored in this era. Even those lists which we do have did not include the word 'Balkan' in its newly-acquired meaning, while they did include words such as Armenia, Macedonia, and Crete.[37]

In his 1327 book on Abdülhamid II, Osman Nuri (Ergin), referred to an order of Tahsin Paşa one of the clauses of which stated, according to Osman Nuri, that 'the mentioning of names such as Armenia related to history and geography is forbidden.'[38] The validity of this statement was accepted without question and was repeated by Süleyman Kâni İrtem, who held various administrative posts between 1896-1924 and wrote history articles for the newspaper *Akşam* between 1925-1945. In one of his articles, he stated that 'the mentioning of names such as Armenia related to history and geography was forbidden.'[39] However this directive by Tahsin Paşa was in fact taken by Osman Nuri from Paul Fesch's book, *Constantinople aux derniers jours d'Abdul-Hamid* which was published in 1907,[40] while the actual existence of such as an order is disputed among historians.[41]

One might therefore have expected the word 'Balkans,' as a geographical location, to have been banned during the period of censorship. The fact that it was not, at least for part of the period, is clear from Tüccarzade İbrahim Hilmi's 1323/1907 geography text book, issued with the permission of the Ministry of Education, which used the phrase the Balkan Peninsula as a geographical designation.[42] The reliability of these kinds of lists for total clarification of Abdülhamidian censorship is questionable. They reflect only the particular period in which these journalists or newspaper owners functioned, and are therefore not representative of the whole Abdülhamidian era. Moreover, the main character of Abdülhamidian censorship was that it functioned according to the *ad hoc* decisions taken by the censor officials, based on their perceptions of what was "detrimental" or on the orders of the sultan or high officials who perceived a word as being "detrimental" at that particular moment. This flexibility of censorship does not, therefore, permit any clear-cut conclusions to be made over what was or was not banned throughout the period.[43]

In the school history text books of the post-1909 period much emphasis was placed on Abdülhamidian censorship, which was used to demonise his regime. According to these texts, words such as *vatan* (fatherland) and *millet*[44] were banned by Abdülhamid, motivated by his enmity towards any terms which would incite patriotic feelings for the fatherland as opposed to the sultan.[45] While such words may indeed have been censored in the daily press by the censor officials acting according to their perceptions of what was, at that moment, "detrimental," they did appear in the school history text books of the Abdülhamidian era, such as those written by Ahmed Vefik and Lütfiye Hanım.[46] According to the memorandum (*layiha*) submitted by Mizancı Murad to Abdülhamid in 1311/1895, the words 'vatan' and 'millet' were banned,[47] but Ali Cevad's school history text book published in 1316/1900-1 (1902) with the permission of the Ministry of Education, included both terms.[48]

It is thus clear that Abdülhamid's policy of censorship cannot be taken as the reason behind the lack of utilization of the term the Balkans, the amorphous character of such a censorship policy, based as it was on shifting perceptions of what was "detrimental" and thus in need of banning, making any definitive conclusions impossible.

The lack of internalisation of this idea can perhaps rather be interpreted as Ottoman intellectual resistance to the imposition of the European concept of the Balkans, although this is a difficult argument to develop largely due to the scarcity of material available from which to gage the level of such Ottoman intellectual resistance. Ottoman intellectual rejection of this European term was also a rejection of all that was implied behind it, for the term attempted to impose on the Ottoman empire borders which were obviously not identical to her late nineteenth-and early twentieth-century political and legal boundaries, and formed part of what might be described as a general "cognitive trimming" of the empire by Europe. The Ottoman provinces of Albania and Armenia, as well as Bulgaria and Eastern Rumeli, were represented in *The Times*, a newspaper often referred to, and taken seriously, by the Ottomans themselves, as independent of Turkey, while Kurdistan, another Ottoman province, was considered within Turkey.[49] This also underlines how much the representation of the Balkans, like Armenia, was accentuated by religious underpinning. What was of great significance in the European vision of the region was the religious denomination of the population of the area and European perception tended to be framed in religious terms. Europe thus interested itself in Armenia for example, while Kurdistan was apparently seen as lying outside any central European concern in what might be linked to a general perception of the Ottoman empire as an Islamic empire while the heavily Christian populated provinces within the empire were seen as something separate, almost as something not naturally part of the Ottoman world. In fact, European states had traditionally used Christianity as a pretext for interference in the internal affairs of the Ottoman state, the French supporting the Catholics, the British the Protestants and the Russians the Orthodox population. This European emphasis on religion, that is on Christianity, may possibly have been a factor in any Ottoman intellectual rejection of the Euro-centric term 'the Balkans,' for this term might have been perceived as also being religiously loaded. This argument, however, must remain speculative. Indeed, any argument of conscious rejection of the use of this Euro-centric term in general is not easy to prove due to lack of any documentary evidence, and is further undermined by the increase in the usage of the Balkans in its Euro-centric meaning in the post-1908 period.

While therefore neither censorship nor intellectual resistance can be taken as reasons for the lack of internalisation of the term 'the Balkans', the explanation may lie in the fact that the Ottomans did not need such a term, since they did not, unlike the Europeans, perceive the region any differently now from how they had before. For instance, in his biography of his father, Midhat Paşa, published in 1903 in English, Ali Haydar Midhat, who was a member of the Young Turks in exile, uses the term the Balkans and differentiates it from Adrianople (Edirne): 'He [Kıbrıslı Mehmed Paşa] now charged Midhat with the difficult and delicate mission of pacifying the disturbed provinces of Adrianople and the Balkans, and clearing them of the brigandage that infested them.'[50] In the French version of the book, published in 1908, the term "Balkans" was used with the same meaning: 'Mehmed Pacha confia à Midhat la difficile et délicate mission de pacifier les provines d'Adrinople et des Balkans et de les purger des bandes de brigands qui les infestaient.'[51] The Ottoman version of the book was first published in Cairo in 1322/1904, and, after the re-declaration of the constitution, the book was at last published in İstanbul. In both the Cairo and İstanbul editions, Midhat Paşa's appointment was narrated without any reference to "the Balkans" as a regional designation, *balkan* referring only to the Balkan mountains. Instead Ali Haydar Midhat referred to Rumeli:

> At the time when banditry increased on the right and middle wings of Rumeli and in particular on all sides of the Balkan mountains, when the incident of murder became very important both within the empire and internationally, then, as it was necessary to appoint someone with power, reputation and perseverance, the afore-mentioned [Kıbrıslı Mehmed Paşa] requested from the Babıali [the Ottoman government], without anyone knowing, that Midhat Efendi be appointed to this position and be given extraordinary powers in order to carry out his office.[52]

However, the term *balkan* did begin to be used by the Ottoman elite, not as a regional designation but as a political term to group together the states which were established in the Ottoman territories in Europe, as early as the 1890s'. Mehmed Arif, in his book published posthumously by his sons in Cairo in 1321/1903 and in İstanbul in

1328/1910, used the concept 'Balkan hükümetleri' (the Balkan governments) to define the states established on Ottoman territory: 'It is again history which, using the name Balkan governments, gives new life to the Romanians, Serbians, Montenegrins and Bulgarians, each in the form of independent government.'[53]

The texts following the 1908 Revolution increasingly use the term *balkan* as a geographical designation as well as the common name of the governments established on Ottoman European lands. However, although the term itself appeared more and more in the texts of the era, the meaning(s) attributed to the term was not always clear or consistent. In 1324/1908, in his *Musavver Bulgaristan* (Bulgaria Depicted), Captain Ragıb Rıfkı, uses the word *Balkan Şeb-i Ceziresi* to designate the Balkan Peninsula geographically. In the section devoted to the history of Bulgaria, Ragıb Rıfkı talks of the settlement of the Bulgarians in the Balkan Peninsula covering Thrace and Moesia.[54] He also uses the synonym of *Balkan Şeb-i Ceziresi*, 'Balkan Yarım Adası' (the Balkan Peninsula), the phrase used in modern Turkish.[55] The term was not only used as the name of the peninsula, but was also used to refer to a group of states in the ex-Ottoman territories in Europe. As early as 1327/1911, Ahmed Refik uses this word in his school text book prepared for the *rüştiye*. This text however, fails to give a clear idea about what 'the Balkans' is, and Ahmed Refik only uses it in the phrase 'Balkan hükümetleri,' which in itself is not clearly defined.[56]

This increasing use of the term the Balkans can in part be explained by an increase in the number of translations from European languages in which the Balkans was increasingly used with its newly-acquired meaning. Journalist-writer Ahmed Rasim, in the fourth volume of his massive work on Ottoman history, *Resimli ve Haritalı Osmanlı Tarihi* (Illustrated Ottoman History with Maps) published in 1330-1328/1912 and prepared as a school text book, used *balkan* with its Euro-centric meaning.[57] For his account of nineteenth-century Ottoman history, he made extensive use of Engelhardt's *La Turquie et le Tanzimat* relying on the translation by Ali Reşad published in 1328/1910.[58] The European term *balkan* was taken directly into the Ottoman by Ali Reşad who in effect did not translate it but simply used the European term, as was the case too with the Ottoman documents including translations from the European press and consular reports based on the information received through the European press. In an interesting twist, Ahmed Rasim then uses Engelhardt's terminology and argument to support the argument in an Ottoman source, the *Mirat-ı Hakikat* (The Mirror of Realities) of Mahmud Celaleddin Paşa, on the reasons for the Bulgarian uprising, one of which was general disturbance over excessive taxes.[59]

With the Balkan War, the term in its Euro-centric meaning apparently became a part of Ottoman vocabulary, and the war between the Ottoman empire and the alliance of Bulgaria, Greece, Montenegro, and Serbia was called 'the Balkan War' (Balkan Harbi) in Ottoman histories. The term 'Balkan' appeared in several forms in two publications from 1912 and 1913, *Bulgar Vahşetleri* (Bulgarian Barbarity) and *Rumeli Mezalimi ve Bulgar Vahşetleri* (Atrocities in Rumeli and Bulgarian Barbarity) where the terms such as 'Balkanlar' (the Balkans), 'Balkan mezalimi' (the Balkan Atrocities), 'Balkanlılar' (the Balkan peoples), 'Balkan Hükümetleri' (the Balkan governments) are used.[60] In a small pamphlet from 1330/1914, Hüseyin Kazım curses the Albanians as they were the real reason for the 'Balkan ittifakı' (the Balkan alliance).[61] Ahmed Salah Aldin, who taught in the Law School and the Darülfünun, used *balkan* in its various forms as the mountains, the peninsula, as a geographical and political designation, and an alliance in his 1331/1915 book, *Makedonya Meselesi ve Balkan Harbi Ahiri* (The Macedonian Question and the Last Balkan War), which was based heavily on European sources.[62] The use of the term *balkan* in poems and stories also ensured that it formed part of the literary vocabulary and imagination.[63]

However, despite this increasing usage of the term with its Euro-centric meaning, made necessary for the Ottoman elite by the Balkan Wars, there were still atlases and dictionaries which did not use the term. Mehmed Eşref did not use the Balkans as a geographical designation in his 1330/1912-13 (1914-15) history atlas of world and the Ottoman empire.[64] Diran Kelekyan, in the *Dictionnaire Turc-Français* dated 1911, defined *balkan* in the same way as Şemseddin Sami had in his 1899 French-Ottoman dictionary, as: 'chaine de montagnes couvertes de forêts; le mont Haemus; le Balkan.'[65] In the 1330/1912-13 (1914-15) dictionary of Ali Seydi, *balkan* was defined as a chain of mountains covered by forests and the Balkan mountains as the mountains which stretched from West to East in Rumeli.[66] Only in the 1929 edition of his dictionary did Ali Seydi add 'because of this [i.e. because the mountains were called Balkan] that section is called the Balkan Peninsula' to the definition of *balkan* of 1330.[67] Although not clearly defined in the Ottoman intellectual mind, the term Balkans with its Euro-centric meaning had become part of the political vocabulary of the Ottoman elite by the last decade of the empire's existence.

The new Turkish Republic inherited both the concept of the Balkans and its fluidity from the late Ottoman era. Although the term was used in the histories of the early period, such as Ali Reşad's *Asr-ı Hazır Tarihi*,[68] there was no clear-cut geographical or even political definition of the term. Faik Sabri (Duran), well-known for his atlases and maps in the Republican era, did not use the Balkans as a regional geographical designation in his 1927 atlas prepared for primary schools, which included Turkey and her neighbours as well as the other parts of the world in the map entitled 'Türkiye ve Etrafındaki Komşu Hükümetler Haritası' (Turkey and the surrounding neighbour governments), and the Balkans was only used as the name of the chain of mountains in Bulgaria.[69] In 1931, however, in the atlas prepared as part of the project of re-writing history, *Türk Tarihinin Ana Hatları Atlası* (The Atlas of the Main Lines of Turkish History), there is a map of the region called '1878-1915 Arasında Balkan Memleketleri' (The Balkan countries between 1878-1915). According to this map, the Balkans as a region is defined according to the Balkan states, the Balkans thus being a political designation rather than a geographical one.[70]

The political significance of the term is very clear in the discussions preceding the conclusion of the Balkan Pact. As Albania was not to be involved in the agreement, Turkey did not wish to use the term Balkan. The only major difference between the draft proposals prepared by the Greek Foreign Ministry and those drawn up by the Turkish Foreign Ministry and the Greek ambassador in Turkey concerned the use of the term 'Balkanique.' While the text prepared by Athens referred to 'les Hautes Parties Contractantes, désireuses d'assurer le maintien de l'ordre territorial existant actuellement dans la péninsule Balkanique,' that prepared by Ankara referred to 'les Hautes Parties Contactantes [sic.], désireuses d'assurer la paix et le maintien de l'ordre établi entre les cinq pays.' Similarly the Athens text used the term 'leurs frontières Balkaniques,' the Ankara version 'leurs frontières communes.'[71]

In the 1930s', the term "the Balkans" was an integral part of Turkish geographical and political vocabulary. However, like the European usage, the Ottoman-Turkish usage of the term was political more than geographical. The borders of the region were defined not according to fixed latitudes and longitudes, but according to changing political borders and alliances.

3

THE REPRESENTATION OF THE BALKANS

The late nineteenth-century Ottoman historian was the eyewitness of most of the events leading up to the establishment of the nation-states in the Ottoman European territories. In some cases, as with Ahmed Cevdet Paşa, Ahmed Vefik Paşa, and Mustafa Nuri Paşa, the historians themselves became actors in the events, due to their administrative and military positions in the Ottoman state, and thus actors in the history which they were writing. Even if the historians were not always directly involved in the events, their lives were effected by the developments in the empire. With the new century, the Ottoman historian now had to cope with the already existing *de jure* or *de facto* nation-states while witnessing their consolidation of power at the expense of the Ottoman empire. Although Greece became independent in 1830, her expansion continued during the nineteenth and early twentieth centuries due to her claims over Macedonia, Crete and the Aegean islands. Modern Greece, thus, is the product of almost a hundred years of confrontation with the Ottoman empire. Bulgaria too expanded at Ottoman expense. After the Congress of Berlin (1878), autonomous Bulgaria invaded Eastern Rumeli and had claims over Macedonia. Serbia and Montenegro made territorial gains, a united Romania was created and continued its enlargement in the twentieth century. Therefore, although, with the exception of Albania and Bosnia-Herzegovina, which was invaded and later, in 1908, annexed by Austria-Hungary, all the Balkan states were products of the nineteenth century, their modern shape was the production of the twentieth.

While the Republican historian could be considered different from his predecessors in that he was not writing under the empire but was an historian of one of the new nation-states which emerged out of the empire, he, in fact, essentially narrated the uprisings and conflicts in Ottoman European territory, the reasons behind them and their results in the same way as did his predecessors.

The Words of Narration

In order to understand the Ottoman-Turkish perception of the troubles in the Balkans and the rise of the nation-states, the vocabulary used to define the 'Balkan' uprisings or, as they were later called, the 'national movements,' in Ottoman and Republican historiography must first be considered since such terms shed light on the mentality that lay behind them. Certain words are commonly used by the late nineteenth-century Ottoman historians to narrate and interpret the events in the European territories of the Ottoman state in the nineteenth century. These words continued to be used by the twentieth-century Ottoman historians to describe the same events and, further more, these were carried into the Republican era and used by the historians of the nation-state.

The most-used word in the texts to define the Balkan movements, regardless of the events or size of the uprising, is *ihtilal*. Both the Greek uprising of 1821, which resulted in the establishment of the Greek nation-state, and a small uprising in Nevesin (Nevesije, a town in Herzegovina) in 1292/1875 are called 'ihtilal.'[1] *İhtilal* is used for uprisings against state authority or for local disorder in provinces or parts of the empire, such as in Mecca,[2] or in the capital, İstanbul. The protests of the *medrese* students over the arrests and punishments of those responsible for the *Kuleli Vakası* in 1276/1859,[3] the social unrest in the capital due to the decline of the value of *kaime*, paper money,[4] and the upheavals in the Balkans were thus all described as *ihtilal*.

However, the meaning attributed to the term *ihtilal* might stem from the attitude of a certain historian to a particular event. Ahmed Cevdet Paşa's representation of the French Revolution (Fransız İhtilali) reflected his discontent with the change of the existing order brought about by the common people. He commented that it was strange that although the aim of the French in bringing about a revolution was to acquire independence, liberty, equality and freedom, what they ended up with was an absolutist government of a base people in which the rules were those such as murdering the innocent.[5] For Kemalettin

Şükrü, writing in 1931, however, the 'Great French Revolution' (Büyük Fransız İhtilali) was 'a national uprising which won the right to be called a great revolution' and it further 'demonstrates a lesson in awakening by showing how a nation which had for a long time groaned under the tyranny of the palace and the oppression of the aristocracy, and which had been left hungry and had been dragged down into poverty, finally uniting, freed itself from all those yokes.'[6]

In 1331/1913-14, the year instability in the Ottoman political scene was at its peak, Hancızade Mehmed Remzi discussed *ihtilal* as a central concept of the Ottoman post-1908 political scene, dominated by a series of governmental changes which created constant instability in the country. He thought of *ihtilal* in conjunction with 'hatred, envy, and slander.'[7] He perceived of 'his-i ihtilal,' a feeling or desire for overturning order, as stemming from greed for individual power and the rejection of morality.[8] This trend, according to the author, was the result of a shift in the traditional understanding of state and society:

> Once the Ottoman state was founded on virtues which brought prosperity and victory. The youth were moved by a great feeling of security and trust, a deep feeling of being followers and of submission. For this reason a government could keep its position for a long time. It was possible to preserve order, to assure social harmony and to manage well the political balances. But today the morality which had become for us a pious tradition, has disappeared. The young man, confronting the elders, felt in himself the confidence of a grown man. In fact, a chain of events which brought about this result was the events of fate. But it was not possible to contain this result, which was natural and justifiable to a certain degree, at the point which was necessary. Nobody knows their limits, nobody is contented with his rights, everyone wants easily and quickly to be granted the happiness of reaching the highest positions.[9]

This change in the traditional structure of society led to the establishment of unstable and weak governments. The disaster of the Balkan Wars, according to Hancızade Mehmed Remzi, proved this decline on the political scene.[10]

In the years of the Turkish National Liberation War, naming the war was an important issue for the legitimization process. Ağaoğlu Ahmed, a pioneer Turkist, in a series of articles in 1922 in the official newspaper of the Ankara government, *Hakimiyet-i Milliye*, attempted to prove that the Ankara government was the legitimate representative of the people and therefore disobedience to the sultan was legitimate.[11] According to the author, 'if rebellion is defined as movement against the direction which society has taken,' the real rebels were the sultan and the İstanbul government since they were the ones who opposed the agreed order of Ankara.[12] After negating the legitimacy of the sultan and the İstanbul government, Ağaoğlu Ahmed tried to give a name to the action of the Ankara government. According to him, this was not *ihtilal*, for '*ihtilal*, with the meaning uprising or revolt, is an event which is always temporary, definitive and limited. Revolts are sudden and either they succeed in reaching their limited goals, or not, but they always die down again suddenly.'[13] Nor was it *inkılap*, for '*inkılap*, with the meaning of revolution, signifies a rising up which a defined society, although it has developed and progressed both spiritually and materially, has carried out in order to remove obstacles which prevent a change of the regime to which it is subjected, and of the political and social institutions.'[14] This was a 'a national movement' (hareketi milliye) which included both *ihtilal* and *inkılap*, but went deeper than both. It was a movement started as a result of a spontaneous feeling among the 'unconscious' (gayri-şuurî) villagers for self-defence against the actions of the enemy. This first initial reaction was not based on any pre-planning, and later the leadership was taken over by intellectuals who, for Ağaoğlu Ahmed, gave the direction and order necessary for the success of a national movement. Therefore the national movement became a movement of both segments of the society which together created the nation.[15]

Ağaoğlu Ahmed's representation of the Turkish National Liberation War as a national struggle or liberation movement, and his differentiating it from *ihtilal* found its reflection in the early Republican history texts. The Turkish National Liberation War was thus defined as a national movement.[16] If the term rebellion was used within the context of this war, it was only in the sense of a "legitimate" rebellion against the sultan and had no impact on the general representation of the war as a national movement.[17]

Another word often used by Ottoman and Turkish historians to define these movements, which also denotes disobedience and rebellion, was *isyan*. Ahmed Cevdet describes the Serbian uprising of

1804 as *isyan*.[18] Sometimes *isyan* and *ihtilal* were used interchangeably in the same text, as in Cevdet Paşa's narration of the Hungarian revolt against Austrian authority in 1848.[19] In the 1920 school history text, Köprülüzade Mehmed Fuad used *isyan* and *ihtilal* with the same meaning.[20] In *Tarih III*, *ihtilal*, *isyan* and another word *kıyam* (revolt) were used interchangeably to define the Greek and Serbian uprisings.[21] The uprisings in the Balkans which ended with the establishment of the nation-states, although sometimes categorized as 'national' and sometimes as 'national movements,' continued to be called *ihtilal* and *isyan*. In a 1929 dictionary, *ihtilal* was defined as 'creation of disorder, mischief, intrigue. Creation of disorder by opposing the laws of the state; turning sour; turmoil,' and the French as 'altération, trouble, insurrection.'[22] *İsyan*, however, was defined as 'to be rebellious, rebelliousness, disobedience, sin,' and in French as 'révolution, révolte.'[23] Despite the similarity in meaning between these two terms, they were sometimes used to denote different events. Samih Nafiz Tansu attempted to differentiate *ihtilal* and *isyan*, *ihtilal* meaning actions directed against central authority while *isyan*, used together with 'milli' in the phrase 'national uprisings' (milli isyanlar), was the name given to the uprisings of the Balkan nations for their independence and freedom in the first half of the nineteenth century.[24] However, Tansu's narration of the Greek and Serbian 'national uprisings' was similar to the representations of the previous historians who had not called these uprisings 'national.'[25]

Other terms to denote uprising used by the historians of, in particular, the late nineteenth century, were *şuriş* (sedition), *iğtişaş* (riot, disturbance, insurrection, uproar) or *iğtişaşat* and *şekavet* (brigandage, villainy). *Fetret* was also used. Although the dictionary definition of this term is 'an interregnum between one reign and the succeeding one,'[26] the term was used by the historians with the meaning of rebellion or revolt. The late nineteenth-century historians such as Ahmed Cevdet, Ahmet Vefik and Ali Cevad used this term to refer to the Greek uprising.[27] This word is also used by Ahmed Vefik, and hence also by Ali Cevad, to define the governmental vacuum during the French Revolution.[28] In the later period, *fetret* was used more and more to denote the Greek uprising which was called 'Rum fetreti.'[29] This phrase became a cliché to denote the Greek uprising and was also used in some Republican texts.[30]

In both Ottoman and Republican histories, rebellion or uprising was often associated with fire, something which spread fast and could cause much damage if not controlled. Ahmed Cevdet Paşa wrote of the flaring up of the fire of revolution when discussing the accelaration of the French Revolution.[31] Ahmed Rasim compared the spreading of the uprising which began in Nevesin (Nevesije) in 1875, to other parts of the region with a spread of a fire.[32] This analogy continued in the Republican histories, the Morean uprising being described in *Tarih III* for example as 'a fire of revolt' (isyan ateşi) which could not easily be extinguished.[33]

Those involved in these uprisings in Rumeli, Ottoman Europe, are referred to as *eşkiya* (bandit), the word that was most popularly used, *asi* or, in the plural form, *usat* (rebel) or *şaki* (brigand, robber), or more generally, 'erbab-ı fesad' (people of sedition). Although Lütfi Efendi is considered very dull as a court historiographer, especially in comparison with Ahmed Cevdet Paşa, he used a variety of vivid, descriptive words in his narration of the Balkan uprisings. The rebels in Crete were 'usat' while the Greek soldiers coming to support them were 'nefer-i fesede' (soldiers of disorder, incitement) and their actions were 'the violent actions of harmful people' (hâşarâtīn harekât-ī vahşiyâneleri).[34] Moreover, Lütfi Efendi accused the Montenegrins of *serkeşlik* (disobedience especially used for the children who oppose their parents),[35] and used *tuğyan*, (insubordination or disobedience to the orders of God) to describe the rebellion in Bulgaria and Greece.[36] Such colourful depictions started to fade away in the twentieth-century Ottoman and Republican texts. Although some of these words were popularly used by later historians in similar contexts, the late nineteenth-century Ottoman narrative style was generally rejected in favour of a new simple and more direct style, mainly advocated by the young Ottoman intellectuals who sought to create a language which would be understandable by the ordinary people.[37] The words *eşkiya*, *asi*, and new words such as *isyancı* (rebel) and *ihtilalci* (rebel) were also used in these texts to denote those who were involved in uprisings.

Other words used repeatedly in the texts in relation to these uprisings and revolts demonstrate an understanding of the state as a kind of educator, as well as a father figure. The word *şımarmak*, for example, which means to be spoilt by indulgence, implies that such indulgence led these local people to rebel. This verb is used mainly when there is a lack of state authority, due to some concession granted under the guarantee of the Great Powers or to some delay in the state's forceful response to a situation.[38] The natural response to such "spoilt subjects" of the empire was the imposition of *terbiye* (education or training). Thus, the oppression of such uprisings was called *terbiye*.[39] Such vocabulary makes clear that society was not conceived of as something able to have its own thoughts independent of the state. Even if these Ottoman subjects were considered as in some way independent of the state, this was considered inappropriate and, further, was not taken seriously. Mustafa Nuri Paşa defines the Serbians who attempted to revolt in 1102/1691 as having fallen 'under the spell of obtaining independence,' exhibiting a belittling attitude to Serbian rebels.[40] All the terminology chosen to define and explain the nineteenth-century uprisings in the Ottoman European territories by the nineteenth-century Ottoman historians reflects this general understanding of state-society relations in the nineteenth-century Ottoman empire, stressing the central role of the state as a father figure in the lives of its people.

This understanding of the state was carried into the twentieth-century Ottoman and Republican historiography as a reflection of the centrality of the state in the mind-set of the Ottoman/Turkish historian. Not only did the Ottoman/Turkish historians follow their predecessors in their selecting of vocabulary to narrate the uprisings of the Ottoman subjects in the Balkans, but the Ottoman elite too used similar terminology to represent the independent Balkan states: Cemal Paşa, for instance, describes the Serbs after the Balkan Wars as being from the most spoilt Balkan state.[41]

The responses proposed to remedy this problem of revolt in the Ottoman European territories further provide important clues for an understanding of the mentality of the Ottoman/Turkish historian. The use of force is represented using a terminology which reflects the central position of the Ottoman state not only within Ottoman but also Republican history-writing. The two frequently used words to denote the Ottoman government's response to the uprisings in Ottoman histories and documents were *tenkil* and *tedib*. While, according to Şemseddin Sami's definition, both have meanings which are directly related to dealings with bandits and outlaws, *tenkil* meaning 'removal, banishment'[42] and *tedib* 'the application of the necessary rules to those who act against the law,'[43] the other meanings of both words are closely linked to other phrases which are used in the history texts in relation to the Ottoman government's handling of the uprisings in the Balkans.

Thus, *tenkil* also means 'the giving of a punishment which will be a warning to the others' and *tedib* means 'teaching good manners and behaviour, reprimanding.'[44] Phrases such as 'to be a lesson and an example' (ders ve ibret olmak) and 'to subdue' (taht-ı itaata almak) were used to represent Ottoman government actions against the subjects of the state who rebelled against its authority.

The Nationalist Movements or Spoilt Behaviour?

The uprisings, that are later called 'national movements' by twentieth-century historians, were neither "national" nor "movement" for the Ottoman historian in the nineteenth century. If the term 'movement' is taken to mean 'a course or series of actions and endeavours on the part of a body of persons, moving or tending more or less continuously towards some special end,'[45] for the Ottoman historian of the century the uprisings were not movements. These uprisings were not planned and consistent campaigns of rebellious people who, driven by a conscious and developing idea of nationhood, aimed at achieving independence from the Ottoman yoke and at establishing their own nation-states. Within a framework that perceives the people of this region as unable to govern themselves or act independently without outside intervention, it would hardly be possible to conceive of a vision of nationalism as a driving force.

Nationalism as a concept was a developing one even in nineteenth-century European intellectual thought. It is possible to see the reflection of this cognitive development on the Ottoman elite of the period. However, being aware of the development of a new concept in Europe did not result in an understanding of the concept similar to that in Europe. The Ottoman elite developed its own interpretation of the understanding of nationalism which was quite different from that accepted today. This understanding was very much affected by the empire paradigm valid within the state, the established status of people and groups, and the balance of power politics. According to that elite view, nationalism was not perceived as something which developed naturally within the society. Rather it was a different method of foreign intervention in Ottoman territory.

The words which are later seen as components of nationalism within modern Turkish vocabulary, such as *vatan, millet, kavim* and *cinsiyet* were used with different meanings, whose sense depends on context. İhsan Sungu in his frequently referred to work on the Young Ottomans tries to give fixed meanings to certain words that are used in the works of Namık Kemal. According to this study, *millet* is used for those who belong to the same religion, *ümmet* for those under the same state administration and *kavim* for people coming from the same race.[46] This approach, however, seems flawed. Attaching fixed meanings to words without regard to the specific context in which they are used and without acknowledging fluctuations of meaning not merely from author to author but from text to text of the same author in the highly dynamic environment of the Ottoman nineteenth century is unlikely to lead to any accurate understanding of the concepts of the time. In this context it should be remembered that the authors' priority was not that of developing concrete political theories, but of describing events.

Even the translation of the foreign word 'nationalism' into Ottoman points to the conceptual immaturity. At the end of the nineteenth century, Ahmed Cevdet Paşa translates the French 'nationalité' as 'kavmiyyet meselesi.' 'Cinsiyet' defined as a synonym of 'kavm,'[47] was used by Şemseddin Sami with a more limited meaning than 'nation.' He talks of two main 'cinsiyet' of Greece: the Greek and the Albanian. For Şemseddin Sami, 'Greek' (Yunani) is 'belonging to the country of Greece or being from the people of that country' and 'Greek' (Yunanlı) is 'a man of the Greek people.'[48] Mehmed Salahi, while travelling from Crete, encountered a young Greek man who described himself as Greek, although Mehmed Salahi then realized that he was in fact an Albanian from Ergiri (Argyro-Kastro). Mehmed Salahi commented in his account that 'the dissemination and spread of Greekness was being worked with a great deal of zeal and endeavour, and the zeal and endeavour for this cause had such serious results that they even made a person renounce and despise his own 'milliyyet' and people (cinsiyet) and be proud of joining another 'milliyyet'.'[49] This "unnatural" assumption of another 'milliyyet' led him to call this man a 'young corrupted Albanian Greek' (Arnavud bozması genc yunanlı [*sic.*]) and he disregarded him: 'I listened sometimes laughing sometimes objecting to the extravagant explanations of this silly young man, who had been disoriented by the disease of Greekness.'[50]

There is a further set of words used to define the identifications of local people in the region: those which denote religious categorization. The most commonly used word to refer to a religious community was 'millet' which meant 'a community sharing the same religion and sect.'[51] Not only in the texts of Ahmed Cevdet Paşa and Lütfi Efendi, but also in the texts of Namık Kemal, *din* (religion) and *mezhep* (sect) are the main common signifiers. Namık Kemal stresses the importance of Islam in transcending the differences of *cinsiyet* (race) and *lisan* (language), something which gives him a confidence in the future of the Ottoman empire.[52] Ahmed Cevdet Paşa discusses İşkodra (Škodra) almost entirely on the basis of confessional differences.[53] Lütfi Efendi, in *Tarih-i Lütfi*, discusses Crete in the context of a Christian-Muslim dichotomy. Lütfi Efendi's distress over the Christian betrayal of Muslims in Crete and on the Montenegrin borders is evident in the text.[54]

Such emphasis on religion does not necessarily lead to ignorance of other kinds of allegiances in society, especially in the century when the Great Powers used every asset at their disposal to tighten their allegiances with the different groups in the empire. *Kavim/kavm* and *cins/cinsiyet* are the words used to mean tribal and racial relations. Ahmed Cevdet Paşa also uses Ibn Khaldun's term, *asabiyya*,[55] spirit of kinship in the family or tribe, together with *kavm*.[56] However, while common language and common education were other references used to show different allegiances, in the final analysis religion overwhelms all these differences,[57] and continues to be pivotal in the historians' identifications.

A third set of terms used in the texts but not directly related to the Balkans demonstrates that Ottoman historians were aware of the existence of terms such as "nationalism" and "fatherland." However, the meanings which they attributed to these words are different from the twentieth-century understandings of these concepts, and the meanings reflect their general world vision. As mentioned before, Ahmed Cevdet Paşa translates *nationalité* as *kavmiyyet meselesi*, literally the question of race or tribe. He explains this as a new rule (*kaide*) which Napoleon III introduced during the Franco-Austrian war over Italian unification, whereby if a *kavm/kavim* did not want to accept the sovereignty of the state, than the state should acquiesce, although the exact implications of this are left unexplained.[58] The understanding of "nationalism" was political, and its application was bound to the consent of the parties; but these parties were not the local people who wanted "independence" or "unification" with another state. They were the states which governed them or states which had interests or contractual relationships such as international treaties that would give them a say in the application of this new rule. Hence, what led to the unification of Italy was not a "nationalism" which prepared a common base among the people of different Italian states and encouraged them to unite, but "nationalism" as a new rule in the balance of power game. In the Ottoman context, the application of this new rule existed because the Great Powers wanted it in order to manipulate and weaken the Ottoman empire. Ahmed Cevdet Paşa perceived this new approach as very harmful to the state's interests, as in the case of Montenegro.[59] Lütfi Efendi also approached the unification of Italy, as well as Germany, along these lines.[60]

While in the Republican histories nationalism is usually seen not merely as a political innovation injected by outside powers, but also as something springing from the people themselves, giving a sense of belonging to members of the society and uniting them, the concept of nationalism as a "foreign force" introduced for political reasons by an outside power still appears when dealing with the nineteenth century. Akçuraoğlu Yusuf, an important figure of Turkish nationalism, argues that Napoleon III's emphasis on nationalism was one of the important impetuses for Italian unification.[61] United Italy and Germany supported a 'racial policy' (Akvam ve ırk politikası), and in accordance with this policy, supported, according to Ahmed Rasim, the unification of Crete with Greece. Moreover, France too favoured this policy due to its ambitions over Belgium.[62]

For the symbolic father of Turkish nationalism, Namık Kemal, what was important about Italian or German unification was not the reason but the result: *ittihad,* union as a broad concept meaning union of all Ottoman subjects to increase the power of the state through centralization, through the decrease of the influence of European states in Ottoman territories, and through progress. Hence, for Namık Kemal, as for Ahmed Cevdet Paşa, the *Islahat Fermanı* of 1272/1856 was an 'İmtiyaz Fermanı,' Ferman of Concessions, since it caused the decline of the power of the state.[63] While, Namık Kemal praises the *Tanzimat Fermanı,* for, according to him, it had paved the way to deal effectively with the upheavals in the Balkans, Egypt and Syria,[64] he becomes very critical of the *Islahat Fermanı* and of those responsible for it, Ali and Fuad Paşas.

For the late nineteenth-century Ottoman elite what needed consideration was not any amorphous concept such as nationalism but what they saw as the concrete reasons for revolt. Therefore, nationalism, later regarded as the most important impetus for state building in the twentieth century, was not the power behind the rise of nation-states on the ex-Ottoman territories, the reasons for which were rather the weakness of the Ottoman state and the strength of the other states who were rivals of the Ottomans, such as Russia or Austria. Nationalism was not used as a term to define the Balkan uprisings, since it was not considered an appropriate tool to define these events, the nineteenth-century Ottoman historians preferring traditional identifications such as religion and explaining these uprisings as being due to concrete causes such as foreign intervention, corruption, and the inability of the state to display sufficient power.

The history texts from the early twentieth century started to focus on more idea-related explanations for the Balkan uprisings, although nationalism still did not appear as the all encompassing factor behind them. One such explanation was the concept of *intibah* or *uyandırma* (awakening). According to Şemseddin Sami, 'intibah,' which meant 'awakening, wakefulness,' also meant 'opposite of unawareness, shrewdness, vigilance.'[65] In the history texts, both 'uyanma' and 'intibah' were used to refer to the awakening of consciousness among Ottoman subjects or to their becoming aware of something which they had not been aware of before, Celaleddin Paşa, for instance, referring to the Serbs of Austria whose 'hearts and minds were awakened by Panslavism.'[66] Kamil Paşa, although he did not use the term 'awakening,' attempted to demonstrate the importance of the change in perception among Ottoman subjects of the reasons for their revolt and it was this process which was symbolized by the term 'awakening.' He drew attention to the activities of the Greeks who had been involved in sea trade during the troubled years of the Napoloenic era and were influenced by the liberal ideas (usul-u serbestiyesi) of Europe. These Greeks, according to Kamil Paşa, 'exerted themselves dropping revolutionary thoughts into the minds of those from the same religion (*mezhep*)' through schools which they set up.[67]

In the earlier years of the post-1908 period, the term 'awakening' was also used to refer to the functions of 'patriots' in the Abdülhamidian era who worked for the Ottoman *millet* (nation).[68] In this period, *millet* was considered a political community within the demarcated borders of a state which gave its allegiance to that particular state. The state, therefore, creates the *millet*. In 1327/1911, Ziya Gökalp, later one of the most important theoreticians of Turkish nationalism, defined *millet* not as a religious community but as a political one and differentiated it from *kavm*:

According to us a nation is a community which has political influence, that is "state power." Therefore "Osmanlılık" is certainly a nation. But the groups belonging to the Ottoman social structure, the component parts such as the Turk, the Greek, the Kurd, the Albanian, the Bulgarian, the Armenian, are not each a nation but consist only of a "tribe."[69]

This idea that a political community within a state equated to a nation was also reflected in histories narrating the establishment of the nation-states in the Ottoman European territories. For Ahmed Refik, 'the governments in the Balkans, because they were tired of Janissary oppression, rose one by one in revolt. Among them the Serbs rose several times.'[70]

Only 12 years later, Ziya Gökalp rejected his own, earlier, definition of *millet* as a political community within a state and confessed that this interpretation had been a mistake: 'Thirdly, a nation is not a sum of those living a shared political life within an empire. For example, it is a mistake to give the name Ottoman nation to all the subjects of the old Ottoman empire, because there were various nations within this mixture.'[71] Now he described the *millet* as a society whose members were connected by a bond which consisted of a shared moral education, *hars*, feelings.[72] In 1920, this idea of *millet*, emphasising a common bond stemming from a joint 'hars' (special forms which a civilization takes in every nation)[73] had already been used in *Ahd-ı Milli Beyannamesi* or *Misak-ı Milli* (The National Pact) and it was on the basis of this concept that the last Ottoman Parliament fixed the borders of the Ottoman lands. Due to its vagueness and generality, this definition of Ottoman territory allowed for the possibility of a wide application. Ottoman lands were those which were 'inhabited by the Ottoman Muslim majority united in religion, origin and aspiration, filled with mutual respect and feelings of loyalty to each other, and whose social and original (*ırkiye*) law is entirely in accord with the conditions of their surroundings.'[74]

By 1931, the definition of *millet* had become 'a political and social group which is made up of citizens united by language, culture and ideals.'[75] According to the second edition of *Tarih III*, national movements were 'the struggles of some of the human mass who are united by language or ideas and feelings and are called a nation to ensure their freedom and unity, and the vital conditions necessary for their development.'[76]

This new conceptualisation of nation led the Republican historians to approach the Balkan uprisings differently from the way in which their predecessors had. Although they used the term 'awakening,' as earlier historians had, they perceived this awakening as being the gaining of national consciousness. Köprülüzade Mehmed Fuad, for instance, stressed, as Kamil Paşa had done a decade before him, the importance for the uprisings of schools and churches in the dissemination of ideas, but, although he too approached the uprising from the perspective of the Ottoman state, he also underlined the importance of the existence of a common "national" bond among these people:

> The Moreans, who had a connection with the European nations through seamanship, learned, thanks to the church and the school, that they were slaves and that in order to free themselves from this [slavery] it was necessary to revolt. Their schools and churches taught them that they were Greek. The Morean young men who studied in Russia and other places in Europe strove for the liberation of their fellow nationals. The Russians, who wanted first to weaken and then to carve up the Ottoman state, gave a formidable amount of help to them. The Greek liberation society called 'Etniki Eterya' thus came into being and the Greek Patriarchate in İstanbul gave great support to it.[77]

For some Republican historians these two institutions, the church and the school, served to keep alive an old consciousness of identity such as 'the soul of old Byzantineness' (eski Bizanslılık ruhu) which, according Akçuraoğlu Yusuf, was important in the Greek uprising.[78] Churches played a major role in national 'awakening': 'Likewise in some places Serbian monasteries existed which had preserved their institutions by relying on old *fermans*. They transmitted national aspirations and traditions to the new generations, and in this way they prepared a suitable ground for a movement of national awakening.'[79]

In the Republican narration of nationalism and national movements, the French Revolution was accepted as the source of nationalism and national movements in Europe. The French Revolution was then linked to the uprisings in the Ottoman European territories in such a way that these uprisings became "national" due to this created organic link with the French Revolution and merely referring to the French Revolution implied "national ideas": 'The national movement which began in Europe with the French Revolution showed its effect soon afterwards among the Greeks of the Morea who had close ties with Europe on account of shipping and trade.'[80]

This narrative cliché later became a formal part of Turkish national history-writing, being integrated into *Tarih III*, and became an established "fact" that had to be integrated within the context of nationalism and national movements:

> Ideals of liberty and equality, nationalism and independence, which were thrown out by the French Revolution, came to the ears of the Christian subjects, who lived in the towns and had commercial contacts with Europe. These were slowly disseminated by them to other Christian *reaya*. At the time when the Ottoman Muslims had formed no clear idea of the French Revolution, the Greeks of Galata, Fener, Bucharest and the Aegean who had contacts with Europe, on the other hand, had more or less grasped the true nature of the event.[81]

However, the introduction in the Republican era of new explanations narrated using terminology which was derived from western ideas of nationalism, state-building and sovereignty did not mean a general shift in the essence of representation of the establishment of the Balkan states from the nineteenth-century Ottoman histories to those of the twentieth century. The significance of these terms lies more in the change in the self-identification and self-representation of the Ottoman historian than in a change of attitude towards these uprisings which rested largely on the idea of the centrality of the state.

The Centre-Periphery Paradigm

The character of the representation of the Balkans by the late Ottoman and early Republican historians was very much related to the general political developments within the state and Europe. As discussed earlier, the Ottoman world view in general and the Ottoman perception of the Balkans in particular was carried from the empire to the nation-state via the texts and the intellectuals themselves. Despite some revolutionary breaks with certain imperial ideas, such as the essentiality of the caliphate for the survival of the state, the idea of history was modified and transformed according to contemporary needs but not rejected by the Republican elite. The pivotal frame of reference, carried from the empire to the nation-state in relation to the representation of the establishment of nation-states in Ottoman lands, was the elite perception of the centre-periphery relationship within the Ottoman context. According to this perception, the elite of the centre perceived itself as a part of central government and its interests overlapped with the interests of the state. This attitude automatically led the elite to think and write taking the state as the centre of its narratives. This perception, thus, dictated the way the historians represented the establishment of the nation-states in Ottoman European territories and formed the paradigm within which they perceived these developments.

The late Ottoman historian in the centre identified himself neither with the sultan nor with the subject. The historian, now, became not the historian of the sultan or the Ottoman dynasty but the historian of the state of which the sultan was the integral figure-head. This understanding of the state is clear from the words of the Tanzimat *vezir* Fuad Paşa who described the four pillars of the Ottoman state to the British ambassador Stratford Canning as being 'the *millet* of Islam, the state of Turkey, the Ottoman monarchy and the capital city of İstanbul.'[82] This new understanding gave new responsibilities to the Ottoman historian: now, the historian would not only be responsible for writing a history of the Ottoman dynasty but also a history of the Ottoman empire of which the Ottoman dynasty was a part. The Ottoman historian who embraced the state-centric history writing as being the historian of the state perceived the uprisings and the establishments of the nation-states in the European territories of the Ottoman empire as a violation of the established center-periphery relation by the periphery and moreover saw the reasons for these uprisings not as stemming from the inner dynamics of the periphery but as being incited from "outside" the periphery.

This general understanding of the establishment of the Balkan nation-states remained the same in Republican historiography. Despite the transformation of the state apparatus from the multi-lingual, multi-religious and multi-ethnic empire to a "homogenous" nation-state, the elite of the new Republic was the elite of the centre in the empire. Although the nation-state managed to produce its own national elite in the 1930s', it was the elite of the Ottoman empire which created the main institutions of the new state. Even the so called "history revolution" did not change the attitude of the elite to the Ottoman past in general and the nineteenth-century history in particular. Although the Republic emphasised the pre-Ottoman history of the Turks as the dominant *ethnie* of the new nation-state and de-legitimised the İttihad ve Terakki governments and the late Ottoman dynasty, since the Republican political elite perceived them as immediate threats to the legitimacy of the new state as well as a challenge to their power, this centre-periphery paradigm, in which the uprisings and establishment of the nation-states in the European territories of the Ottoman empire were represented, essentially did not change.

According to the centre-periphery paradigm, the province as periphery was a dependent unit on the central government in İstanbul. The periphery could not have an existence or identity independent of the centre. This understanding naturally led to a perception of the supremacy of the centre over the periphery, with the periphery being a dependent, subservient being. The central government both imposed political power on the provinces, and, through its agents, controlled the local power bases, acted as intermediary in local conflicts and, especially in the nineteenth century, began to spread its influence into traditional communities through education, quarantine, military service, censorship and censuses. In return for this control, the centre promised the periphery "order" and "security." Any failure of control on the part of the central government was perceived as decline in the respectability and honour of the Ottoman state.[83]

During the nineteenth century, the Ottoman central government came more and more to intervene in the lives of its subjects and to play a more obtrusive role than it had before. While the centre thus redefined its role, there was no consciousness of any need to redefine periphery. Since the centre did not recognize the possibility of change in the role of the periphery, it considered any challenge to its power coming from the periphery as a challenge not from the periphery itself but from other outside centres of power. The centre could be outside the empire and was thus not limited to İstanbul alone. For Montenegro, for example, Russia was perceived as a centre while Montenegro itself was denied any independent significance. Kamil Kapudan, in his book on Montenegrin economics, politics, customs, geography and history, underlines the central position of Russia in Montenegro to which it supplied money, weapons, and even education for the youth who later revolted against the Ottoman empire. In the text there is a clear shift of centre from the Ottoman empire to Russia which was able to control the periphery, that is Montenegro.[84] A similar attitude is revealed in Mehmed Salahi's account of Crete. Mehmed Salahi, who was sent to the island as a government inspector to investigate the disorder there, locates Greece in the central role, attributing to it the role of what one might call a pirate centre.[85] Malicious ideas as well as weapons and teachers for the Christian schools came from Greece.[86] In 1326/1910, the link between Sofia and the Bulgarian comitadjis in Macedonia and the difficulty the Ottoman government experienced in repressing their activities is made clear in an article in *Genç Kalemler* in which the author wrote: 'So long as the strings of the revolutionary committee (*komita*) puppets are pulled in Sofia, it does not seem possible that the plans for future action can be improved.'[87] The perceived need of a centre for a periphery and the inability of any periphery to function independently of a centre is evident in Halil İnalcık's 1943 publication in which he explained that one of the reasons for the lack of a Bulgarian uprising for independence in the first half of the nineteenth century was that 'the Bulgarians, like the other Balkan nations, did not have an independent, more civilized (*medeni*) state nearby which could come to their aid.'[88]

The definition of "outside intervention" was not limited to the intervention of other states but included other Ottoman provinces or principalities, for in some cases this foreign intervention could simply refer to areas outside the particular location of the uprising or disorder. This relativity in the understanding of 'outside intervention' was, in fact, an extension of a lack of concept of the Balkans as a designation of any geographical and political whole, an identity which did not exist in Ottoman understanding.

This "outside intervention" was especially evident in cases of bandits or irregular troops, who could move from one area to another and find protection among the local people of that particular area due to the religious and ethnic mix of the Balkans. The Serbs could thus infiltrate easily from autonomous Serbia into Bosnia or Montenegro, Montenegrin bandits could function in Ottoman İşkodra (Škodra) and autonomous Bulgaria could support another autonomous province of the empire, Eastern Rumeli.

The Ottoman government's awareness of alternative centres of power for the periphery is reflected in the texts from the last quarter of the nineteenth century and was a reflection of the Ottoman historians' recognition of the weakness of the state in this period. Not only physical aid, such as weapons or soldiers, or schools and hospitals, but also the influence of ideas from outside on Ottoman subjects was considered a threat to the Ottoman state. In particular, the banning of books and newspapers and the strict entry controls imposed on books produced outside Ottoman territories, or even those from within the autonomous provinces, make clear the understanding of threat for the Ottoman state.

The physical presence of outside powers was something which the Ottomans of the later nineteenth century were forced more and more to come to terms with. While the appearance of a French consul in Travnik was viewed with suspicion by one of the characters in Ivo Andrić's *Bosnian Chronicle*, who commented 'We've lived for hundreds of years without consuls, and that's how we'll go on,' it was clear to others that this was a development which was here to stay: 'Never mind how you lived in the past, now you are going to have to live with a consul. That's how things are. And the consul will find things to do. He'll sit beside the Vizier giving orders, watching how the beys and agas behave and what the Christians are up to, and keeping Bunaparta informed about it all.'[89] Indeed, both the Ottoman periphery and centre had to learn to live with the consuls. While for the Ottoman government, which sought to decrease the influence of the foreign powers in its periphery while trying not to upset any Great Powers, such foreign presence was unattractive, for the periphery it was the reverse. The periphery now tried to play off all the "centres" which it had available to it.

The dealings of the Ottoman representatives in the periphery with the consuls of the Great Powers were careful and the demands and the interests of the local people were important reference points that were used against Great Power interests. In a letter written to the Italian consul in Ruse in response to the petition of the priest Alfonso Mulinari, the Ottoman authorities stipulated that 'since both the aforementioned priest Alfonso and the other subjects of the friendly states may travel and even choose to settle in every part of the Ottoman domains, the aforesaid priest too shall not be prevented from going to the place to which he wants to go.' However, two thirds of the villagers of the village of Belene (the modern town of Belene in the district of Pleven) to which the priest wished to go, did not want him as their priest. If, in spite of this, he persisted in going there and attempted to interfere in the 'spiritual affairs' (umur-u ruhaniyesi) of the villagers, problems, the authorities noted, could arise. In that case, the Ottoman government would take no responsibility, which would instead be the priest's.[90]

Putting the demands of the local people first was an important tactic of Ottoman policy of the late nineteenth century, as Abdülhamid's attempt to prevent the annexation of Ülgün (Dulcigno) by Montenegro shows. In a last ditch attempt to prevent this annexation, which was demanded by the Great Powers, Germany, Russia, Britain, Italy, France and Austria-Hungary, Abdülhamid II sent a telegraph to the German emperor, Wilhelm I, asking him to help the Ottoman government over this issue. The draft version of this telegraph included the phrase 'the wretched Muslim people should not be unjustly treated in any way,' but the word Muslim was dropped from the final version.[91] In the end, however, the Ottoman government was forced to agree to this annexation despite considerable Albanian opposition. In the Republican era, İrtem perceives Albanian resistance to the annexation of Ülgün as one of the fundamental events of the nineteenth century in Albanian national memory, in which it was seen as a reflection of the 'akide' (creed) 'God created nations before he created religions' (Allah milletleri dinlerden evvel vücude getirmiştir).[92] The Albanians, thus, now represented themselves as having been opposed to and separate from the Ottomans in relation to this annexation.

The loss of Ülgün in fact represented a blow to Albanian faith in the Ottoman state. The Muslims of Crete, too, were loosing their faith in the empire. On 20 June 1896, the Muslim members of the Meclis-i Umumi-i Vilayet (The General Provincial Assembly) of Crete published a pamphlet in Paris in French, the title of which was translated as *24 Mayıs Sene 1896'da Girid Vukuatı* (The incident of Crete on 24 May in the year 1896). This pamphlet was distributed all over the world (alemin her tarafında) with the aim of correcting the misinformation about the 1896 uprising circulating in Europe and naming those responsible for the revolt.[93] Following the publication of this pamphlet in Paris on 27 Haziran 1312 (1896), the Muslim members submitted a memorandum (*takrir*) to the consuls of the Great Powers whose 'display of love of humanity was evident' (mazahirat-ı insaniyet-i perveraneleri meşhud), and reminded them of the minority rights of the Muslims, while underlining that the aims of the Muslims of Crete were to live on the island peacefully with their 'compatriots' (vatandaş) and to work for the development of Crete.[94] These initiatives undertaken by the Muslims of Crete to create direct links with the European representatives on the island, and even with the European public, demonstrated that the Muslim subjects of the Ottoman empire too felt the need to appeal directly to the European powers, rather than relying entirely on the Ottoman central government to protect their interests.

The concerns of Ottoman subjects were not limited to issues of security or survival, but also involved everyday matters such as taxation and ways of avoiding payment. Obtaining foreign citizenship was helpful in this regard, Ahmed Cevdet Paşa for example referring to a certain Niko, who had been living in Ülgün (Dulcigno) for 60 years but had not being paying taxes since he held Austrian citizenship.[95]

Ottoman subjects could also slip from central control in other ways, and the line between the ordinary people and bandits was very blurred. In their histories, both Ahmed Lütfi Efendi and Ahmed Cevdet Paşa on occasion make no differentiation between bandit (*eşkiya*) and the local people who rebelled. In their writings, the local people could be oppressed and deceived by bandits and in turn become bandits opposing the authority of the state.[96] This thin line between *reaya* and bandit was an important reference point for the Ottoman subjects in the periphery with which to threaten the Ottoman government. In 1298/1881 a petition submitted to Abdülhamid II by the representatives of the Vlachs of Manastır (Bitolj), Tırhala (Trikala) and Yanya (Ioannina) is an example of such a warning: if the Ottoman government did not respond to their demands that Thessaly not be handed over to Greece, since this would mean their loosing their vital pastoral lands, the Vlachs, as well as Albanians of the region, would turn to banditry:

> Because the aforementioned Vlachs and the Albanians, made up of 20,000 families, cannot go as shepherds together with their flocks of sheep to Thessaly, and because they have no possibility of following another profession which will induce them to give up shepherding, they may oppose the handing over of Thessaly to Greece. In fact, they will unite and come together and if they are not successful, they will turn to banditry. In that case, while there

might be perfect security in the East, the condition of the aforementioned people will cause much difficulty and harm. Whatever happens, neither the Muslim nor the Christian Albanians can in any way rejoice at the destruction of the Vlachs, because they will think that the harm which befell the Vlachs will in the future also happen to them. For this reason, it can be inferred that they, taking up arms together with the Vlachs, will oppose the handing over of Thessaly to Greece.[97]

The awareness of this thin line was reproduced in the history texts of the post-Abdülhamidian period.[98] Loss of control over the subjects of the periphery was considered a symbol of the weakness of the Abdülhamidian government and was used as another tool to delegitimize his regime. Abdülhamid was much criticised in the post 1908 period for his perceived mishandling of Eastern Rumeli, which was regarded as an example of the weakness and incompetence of his government. Just after the Bulgarian declaration of the annexation of Eastern Rumeli in 1885, the Serbian government declared war against Bulgaria, thus creating an opportunity for the Ottoman government to restore its power there. The Ottoman government declared that the Bulgarian Principality was under the sovereignity of the Ottoman empire and therefore the Serbian declaration of war would be read as an attack against the Ottoman empire. The Ottoman government did not, however, extend any material support to the Bulgarian army and guaranteed not to intervene militarily over the issue, preferring to search for a diplomatic solution to restore the status quo in Eastern Rumeli.[99] Ragıb Rıfkı, in his book published in 1324/1908, highlighted the contradiction in Abdülhamid's policy:

> Here there is a strange issue: we extended our friendly assistance to them with no comprehensible reason, why? Because the Bulgarians were our subjects and an attack against them from outside meant an offence against Ottoman rights. This is a true thing; but was it not our rightful and legitimate duty to reprimand a presumptuous entity which directly attacked our rights and cleansed our trampled soil from its dark body?[100]

Another officer, Kazım Karabekir, who later became an important figure of the National Liberation War and early Republic, was more explicit than Ragıb Rıfkı in his condemnation of the Abdülhamidian government over its failure to protect Ottoman interests during the annexation of Eastern Rumeli by Bulgaria. In the talk he gave to the Edirne Military Council in 1328/1912 in Edirne he said:

> Towards the end of October [Teşrin-i evvel] a note came from İstanbul to Sofia: 'the Serbian attack on Bulgaria would be considered as an attack on the Ottoman empire. A note had been given to this effect to the Serbian government, too!' A misdirected threat! Having made no sound about the Bulgarians who were invading one of our large provinces, we then proceeded to declare war on those who had said something. Just as if we were preventing the independence of Bulgaria with this kind of action. The Bulgarians did not fail to express their thanks in practice for this unimaginable generosity: taking this note as security for Eastern Rumeli, they began to move their armies westward against Serbia.[101]

Not only was Abdülhamid clearly castigated for his handling of this issue, but the "periphery," here the Balkans, was also stigmatized as being merely a periphery, either of the Ottoman empire or of any other state regardless of its position as an independent state or not. Although in the Republican era, the idea of İstanbul, or here Ankara, being a centre vis-à-vis the Balkan states was not a reality, the concept of centre-periphery remained embedded in historical representation from the late empire through to that of the early Republic. The representation of the Balkans continued to be essentially framed within the centre-periphery paradigm even in the texts of the 1930s' and 40s'.

Late Ottoman/early Republican representation of the creation of the Greek nation-state is thus presented within this paradigmatic framework. The establishment of the Greek state as the first "independent" nation-state on Ottoman European lands occupies an important space in late Ottoman history-writing. Although the Danubian Principalities (contemporary Romania) obtained autonomy from the Ottoman empire initially under the Treaty of Küçük Kaynarca (1774), although this meant Russian patronage, and the Serbians gained their autonomy from the Ottoman state in 1816, later extended by the agreement of Bucharest and confirmed by an imperial order in 1830, the Ottoman historian perceived Serbia and the Principalities as a part of the Ottoman empire until the recognition of their legal independence by the Berlin Agreement in 1878. The Greek case was, therefore, the first example of Ottoman loss of territory to the creation of a nation-state. In fact, Greece, unlike the Serbian, Bulgarian or Romanian experiences, was the first nation-state in the nineteenth-century Ottoman landscape which gained its independence *de jure* within the Ottoman empire without having a long experience of autonomy.[102] For the Ottoman historian Greece was important both as a new nation-state created on Ottoman soil and also as a problematic "neighbour" and continuous threat to Ottoman territorial integrity and identity, due to Greek expansionist ambitions and the existence of a Greek population within the Ottoman empire.

The Ottoman historian perceived and evaluated the Greek case internally vis-à-vis the centre, and thus as an internal problem of the state, but also one very much influenced by outside intervention. Hence the Greek case, for the Ottoman historian, was not something that could be perceived as part of the universal idea that was European nationalism, and Ottoman histories, unlike modern literature on Greek independence, did not represent it as a case of nationalism. The establishment of the Philiki Etairia,[103] the first uprising of 1814 and the process unfolding towards the establishment of a nation-state - the Morean uprising, Great Power intervention which culminated in the burning of the Ottoman and Egyptian fleets at Navarino (1827) and the declaration of Greek independence - were all considered within this centre-periphery paradigm. This Ottoman representation of the Greek Independence War and the establishment of the Greek nation-state stayed essentially the same throughout the period from the last quarter of the nineteenth century to the early twentieth century.

There are three main themes which can be detected in Ottoman history-writing on the Greek case: the Morean uprising, the intervention of the Great Powers, and Tepedelenli Ali Paşa. The Morean uprising was called 'ihtilal,' 'isyan,' 'şuriş' or 'fetret,' an act against the authority of the Ottoman state and the creation of disorder. This uprising, called a 'national revolution' or 'national movement' by modern Balkan historians,[104] was not for the Ottomans an independent action, nor was it undertaken by a "nationally" or even "politically" conscious Greek people. In *Fezleke*, Ahmed Vefik Paşa, who actually ignored the establishment of the Greek state, described the Morean uprising in terms of Russian provocation and provocation by

Tepedelenli Ali Paşa.[105] Lütfiye Hanım, in her *Mirat-ı Tarih-i Osmani* which was heavily influenced by *Fezleke*, perceived the Greek case as the result of Russian provocation and incitement by Tepedelenli. This uprising gave a further opportunity to Russia to prey on a weakened Ottoman state which found itself in a difficult position, and to declare war with the aim of obtaining concessions for Greece, the Principalities and Serbia.[106] Therefore, for Lütfiye Hanım, too, the Greek uprising was dependent on the outside and she perceived the Morean uprising within the context of Ottoman relations with the Great Powers, in particular with Russia. Ali Cevad's *Mükemmel Osmanlı Tarihi* of 1316/1900-01 (1902), reproduces almost exactly the same perception of the Greek case, even using the same vocabulary.[107] These three texts were all used as school text books and were thus aimed at what Kashani-Sabet has described in her work on the development of Iranian nationalism as 'a captive and impressionable audience in students.'[108]

Other, non-school texts written and published in the last quarter of the nineteenth century such as *Tarih-i Cevdet* and *Netayic ül-Vukuat* were more sophisticated and voluminous. But, can we argue that they brought a different representation of the establishment of the Greek state? The reading of these and similar texts from the same period shows that it is difficult to give an affirmative answer to this question. Although, both *Tarih-i Cevdet* and *Netayic ül-Vukuat* are regarded as the most important historical texts of the period and even today are still used as important sources by historians of the Ottoman empire, their approach to the establishment of the Greek state was similar to that in Ahmed Vefik, Lütfiye Hanım and Ali Cevad. While Ahmed Cevdet Paşa was more sophisticated in his approach, his understanding was essentially the same. For him, the Greek uprising was the end result of the changing power structures in Rumeli where local power holders lost their respect for the representatives of the state in the periphery after the wars with Russia in 1182/1768 and 1200/1786, and sought to influence the policies of the centre through bribing the officials in İstanbul. Therefore, as the bribes increased, the burden on the *reaya* who were under the control of the local power holders increased. This created an enormous resentment and paved the way for uprisings, one of which was the Greek uprising.[109] This was not, however, something independent of outside intervention.

Mustafa Nuri Paşa, too, saw the root of the Greek uprising in the 1182/1768 Russian war, and, according to him, it was from that point on that the Russians envisaged the establishment of a Greek state.[110] However, contrary to Ahmed Cevdet Paşa's line of thinking, Mustafa Nuri Paşa considered the existence of Tepedelenli Ali Paşa in positive terms. Although Tepedelenli, a representative of local notables in the periphery, i.e. Rumeli, was able to challenge central authority, his dominance prevented the rising of both the Moreans, who were 'prepared for sedition,'[111] and their main supporter, Russia.[112] In both cases, as well as in the accounts of Ahmed Vefik, Lütfiye Hanım and Ali Cevad, the Morean uprising was not a nationalist movement but a periphery revolt against the Ottoman centre, provoked from outside.

In 1327/1911, Ahmed Refik, underlining as Mustafa Nuri Paşa had done, the rebellious character of the Morean who tended to revolt 'without any reason,' pointed out that when Tepedelenli was governor the Moreans were unable to do anything. Ignoring Tepedelenli's role in inciting the rebellion, Ahmed Refik concluded that the Moreans, who 'were always revolting and occupying the state's time unnecessarily' (daima isyan ederler, devleti yokdan yere meşgul ederlerdi), rebelled only after his death, and only when supported by the Russians and Europeans did they rebel totally.[113] This inherent inclination of the Moreans for rebellion became an important part of the narration of the Greek uprising in the Ottoman/Turkish history texts. In another school text for the second year of the *rüşdiye* which was also published in 1327/1911, Ali Reşad and Ali Seydi, for whom too the Greek uprising was the result of Russian provocation and European 'spoiling' (yüz verme),[114] highlighted this historical "inclination for rebellion" among the Moreans: 'Modern Greece was a province of the Ottoman state called the province of Morea (Mora eyaleti). Because they were excessively disobedient and spoilt, its people, on finding the opportunity revolted from time to time, but they could be taught a lesson by sending soldiers.'[115]

This inherent capacity for revolt continued to be a cliché in the definition of the Moreans during the Greek uprising in Republican history-writing. The Moreans who lived in the mountainous areas of the region were not 'submissive' to the Ottoman government and existed partially on 'banditry' (haydutluk).[116] This generalization spread from the Moreans and could be applied to 'Greeks' (Rumlar) in general, who were 'fundamentally inclined to revolt' (esasen isyana müstait olan Rumlar).[117]

There are three approaches within Ottoman historiography and that of the early Republic to Tepedelenli's influence on the Greek uprising and the state's reaction to him. According to the first approach, Tepedelenli Ali Paşa himself incited this rebellion against the Ottoman state in order to prevent the centre's attempt to crush him. The state response was therefore justified and Tepedelenli deserved his fate.[118] There was no questioning of whether the centre strategically underestimated the importance of Tepedelenli in keeping the Greeks of the area under control, or, in other words, whether the centre failed to use Tepedelenli, who was perceived as a threat to central authority, against the Greek rebels who wanted secession from the empire.

The second approach questioned the crushing of Tepedelenli, and argued that he was the only counter-power to the Greek rebels who would not have dared to revolt if he had kept his power base.[119] This was therefore a strategic mistake. There was, however, no question of apportioning blame to the sultan Mahmud II, since the person of the sultan was perceived as untouchable, and blame was instead laid at the door of Halet Efendi. This attitude to the person of the sultan was not always applied in texts published after 1909 where Abdülaziz and Abdülhamid II could be openly criticized.[120] According to this second interpretation of the events of the Greek uprising, Halet Efendi considered the amount of the annual present which he received from Tepedelenli insufficient and decided to organize a plot against him. In some texts, Halet Efendi was also accused of diverting the attention of the state from the Greek revolt to Tepedelenli Ali Paşa, since he was indebted to the Phanariots for whom he worked for a while.[121] He misinformed Mahmud II and incited the sultan to send troops to crush Ali Paşa.[122] Here the event was personalized: "wicked" Halet Efendi, for his own personal benefit, plotted against Tepedelenli, the only force which in fact could have prevented the secession of the Morea from the Ottoman empire. This narrative might be read as an example of the sacrificing of state/public interest to personal interest, here that of Halet Efendi.[123] For those who subscribed to the second interpretation, Ali Paşa's establishment of a power base against the central authority was preferable to the creation of a Greek state. According to Ahmed Müfid, the MP for Yanya (Ioannina), 'the Greek revolt was thought to be merely the result of incitement by Ali Paşa and the importance of the event was not understood in time. The damage done to the Ottoman state as a result of this was without doubt much greater than the harm caused by Tepedelenli Ali Paşa.'[124]

The third approach attempts to separate Tepedelenli Ali Paşa from the Morean uprising. It does not consider Ali Paşa's incitement of the uprising, and attributes it to Alexander Ypsilantis's exploitation of the opportunity created by the Ottoman army's preoccupation with Tepedelenli Ali Paşa's rebellion. Although Ypsilantis was unsuccesful, escaping to Austria where he died in prison, 'thrust' there by the Austrian government (Avusturya Hükûmeti tarafından tıkıldığı), the uprising did begin in the Morea.[125]

The tangible existence of foreign intervention on behalf of the Greeks was made blatantly clear for the Ottoman historians by the burning of the Ottoman-Egyptian fleet by the Great Powers at Navarino. After this incident, İbrahim Paşa left the Morea with his army and returned to Egypt, and the Ottoman empire found herself in a war with Russia which ended with Ottoman acceptance of Greek autonomy and later independence. The Ottoman historians offer various explanations for foreign intervention in the Greek case. The first is a very simplistic understanding based on the perception of states' actions as similar to human actions and hence motivated by pure jealousy,[126] justice and injustice, betrayal, like and dislike, friendship. Lütfiye Hanım explained the Russian war of 1243/1827 as being due to jealousy: 'In 1243 the enemy could not endure the good order of the state and before the difficulties of the Greek incident were over, Russia took on itself the Greek claim to independence and somehow or another even drew the states of England and France into an alliance.'[127] The second explanation is more sophisticated and more impersonal than the first. This explanation is based on the evaluation of the interests and interference of the European states in the Greek case as part of the Eastern Question and part of the general inter-state rivalry of the European powers in the East. Historians adopting this interpretation of the Greek case used the balance of power discussion to explain British and French intervention in the Morean uprising to counter Russian influence in the region.[128]

Although the first unsophisticated explanation was used mainly in the nineteenth-century texts, while the late nineteenth-and twentieth-century texts tended to use more sophisticated and more systematic interpretations, the more simplistic explanations still appear in these later writings due to the simple and didactic character of the texts. This simplistic interpretation continued to be used in the school text books of the later period. For Ahmed Refik, Russia, France and Britain unjustly sent a navy against 'us' to burn the Ottoman fleet at Navarino.[129] Ali Seydi and Ali Reşad wrote of this 'Navarino incident which will never be forgotten by the Ottomans' in their school history text book published in the same year and for the same year of the *rüşdiye*.[130] This burning of the Ottoman fleet at Navarino was regarded by Ahmed Hasır and Mustafa Muhsin as a 'trampling on international law and one of the stains which could not be wiped off the history of civilization.'[131]

In the Republican texts, although the development of a national consciousness among the Greeks, fostered by the dissemination of national ideas through churches and schools, was put forward as an important factor in the Morean uprising, the establishment of a Greek state without the intervention of the Great Powers was inconceivable.[132] Nationalism seemed secondary for the establishment of the Greek nation-state. Even so-called "national ideas" were imported from these Great Powers through education and trade. Köprülüzade Mehmed Fuad made clear the link between European intervention and the establishment of the Greek state in a section of his book called 'Balkanlar da Milliyet Fikirleri' (National Ideas in the Balkans): 'The idea of 'nationalism' which appeared at the beginning of the last century, the theory that 'every nation must be an independent state,' gave rise, in a very short time, to the birth of 'Greece,' with the help only of the European states.'[133] The dependent character of the uprising was thus made even clearer by assigning the 'national ideas' not to indigenous sources but, yet again, to outside powers, thus undermining the legitimacy of the uprising, represented by Greece itself as a national movement.[134]

The late nineteenth-century Ottoman historian thus represented the Balkans very much within the centre-periphery paradigm, assigning no concept of "sentient being" to the areas of the periphery whose very existence depended not on their own aspirations and actions but on a centre, be it İstanbul or elsewhere. Uprisings in the European territory of the Ottoman empire were not nationalist movements but simply the revolts of a periphery against the centre, motivated not by nationalism but due to outside provocation, a naturally rebellious character, or simply the bad behaviour of an over-pampered people. Although nationalism came to be used more and more in the interpretations of the later Ottoman historians and, especially, of those of the early Republic, essentially the late nineteenth-century understanding continued through into the Republic and the interpretation of the uprisings remained framed within the centre-periphery paradigm and explained largely using the arguments of the Ottoman historians of the nineteenth century.

4

THE BALKAN PEOPLES AND THE BALKAN STATES

In the meantime, the Ottoman army had already set out, and truths and untruths were spawned. But there was something that unsettled the people of the peninsula even more than the approaching army: the word "Balkan". Before the Turks even set foot on the peninsula, they baptized it and its people with this name, and this name stuck to them, like new scales on the body of an aged reptile. The people were at their wits' end. They twisted in their sleep as if they were trying to shake off this name, but the result was the opposite - the name clung to them all the more forcefully, as if it wanted to become one with their skin. They now realized that, divided as they had always been, they had never given their peninsula a name. Some had called it "Illyricum", some "New Byzantium", others had opted for "Alpania" because of the peninsula's alps, or "Great Slovenia" because of the Slav, and so on. Now it was too late to do anything, and so, without a common name, but with a name bestowed upon them by the enemy, they marched to battle and defeat. [1]

For Ismail Kadare, the peoples of the Balkans were 'baptized' by the Turk, the enemy, the other, the Turk who was also a curse on the region: 'The eleven peoples of the peninsula had to stumble along within a communal shell named "Balkan", and it seemed that nobody gave them a second thought, unless to anathematize them: "You cursed wretches!"'[2]

This picture presented by Kadare of the Balkan peoples welded into union by Ottoman imposition is far more related to a twentieth-century necessity than historical reality for not only did the Ottomans not give the name to the region but they did not have the concept of the Balkans as one region and of its peoples as one whole. In Ottoman histories, there was no concept of a "Balkan" attack, or an uprising by "the Balkan people," but rather regional insurrection by, for example, Montenegrins. The Balkans as a region and the Balkan people did not appear as a totality in these late nineteenth-century texts.

Ottoman definition of the peoples in the European territories of the empire was not based on nation-states or a well-demarcated region. The main identifier for the Ottoman elite was religion: Christian (Latin, Orthodox, Armenian), Muslim and Jewish. However, there was neither a clear juxtaposition of Christian *reaya* versus Muslim *reaya* nor an equality among Christians, nor even among Orthodox Christians. Just as the territorial borders could fluctuate, so could religious boundaries, due to variables other than religious ones, such as material benefit, customs, or simply the need to survive. This fluidity of borders was not merely something which existed in practice among the people but was recognized by the nineteenth-century Ottoman historians themselves. These historians approached this fluidity of boundaries among religious groups judgmentally. However, this judgmental approach does not necessarily imply a negative or positive attitude. The criterion, which the authors used in order to decide what was good or bad, was state-centric and based on the need for the maintenance of effective state control in the periphery. While for Mehmed Salahi, both Muslims and Christians were to be equally condemned in the uprisings in Crete, for Kamil Kapudan the Latin population of İşkodra (Škodra), together with the Muslim population, deserved praise, while the Orthodox population did not. Such judgments were thus not based on any religious criteria but purely on benefit to the central state.[3]

The self-identification of the Ottoman historian with the centre further drove him to perceive the people of the periphery as inferior. This is clear from the stereotypic and repetitive attributions made to different groups of people in the Ottoman European territories. According to Mehmed Salahi, the concessions given to the Cretans, regardless of their religion, were premature since they were not sufficiently advanced to handle them.[4] In the Republican texts, these "less developed" Cretans were 'rebellious' (ihtilalci)[5] and 'ill-tempered' (hırçın).⁶ A similar attitude is evident in Kamil Kapudan's approach to Montenegro. He represented Montenegrins as primitive in every aspect of life. Their houses were mere huts built of stone and dry tree branches with no modern furniture, such as sofas or armchairs. All existing signs of modernity in Montenegro, such as new weapons and a hospital, were provided by the Russian government. The Montenegrins were not even, for Kamil Kapudan, proper Christians and he called them 'half Christian' (nim Hristiyan) due to their religious customs, which were not in conformity with Orthodoxy.⁷ Although Ahmed Cevdet Paşa described the Montenegrin practice of cutting off the noses and ears of Muslims as barbarous ('âmelât-ı vahşiyâne'), he objected fiercely to European justification of Montenegrin behaviour which was based on the view that 'the Montenegrins are a barbarous people.'⁸ Thus, although Ahmed Cevdet Paşa regarded these actions as barbarous, he did not accept the European approach that what the Montenegrins did had to be accepted because they were barbarous and therefore not to be judged by the rules of civilized society. Ahmed Rasim too perceived this Montenegrin practice as barbarity: 'The barbarity which the Montenegrins deemed appropriate for Ottoman prisoners of war fostered hatred. They cut off their noses and ears and shooed the prisoners away.'⁹ This labelling of the Montenegrins as a people who were primitive and barbarous (vahşi) continued in the Republican era, and in 1933, Akçuraoğlu Yusuf described Montenegrins as 'half barbarous' (nim vahşi).¹⁰ Three years later, Halil Sedes, a retired army general, wrote of the Montenegrins' interest in war: 'For this people who lived deprived of prosperity, welfare and happiness, in short, the pleasures of life, in conditions of half savagery, war was perceived in fact as an agreeable occupation.' Montenegrins, whom 'the requirement of the natural formations of their county made powerful and strong,' and who 'because of their life style, shepherded and wandered, generally with guns on their shoulders,' living on hunting and even banditry won military esteem.¹¹

This belittling and reducing the rebelling Ottoman subjects to a level of primitive barbarity, evident in Ottoman representations of the Montenegrins, can also be seen in the use of the imagery related to pigs and pig herding. This seems to have appeared in the period of the Balkan Wars. In the poem, 'Balkanlar Destanı' (The Epic of the Balkans), first published in 1912, Ziya Gökalp refers to pig herders: 'God said that where the crescent appeared/ that place was Turan, so take it back,/ pig herders cannot be kings/ in the country of God, in Turan.'[12] This theme was picked up by Halil Sedes in his 1934 history of the Ottoman-Serbian campaign, when he described the profession of Kara Yorgi (Karadjordje Petrović), 'the grandfather of the royal house of modern-day Yugoslavia,' as that of a pig herder.[13]

Akçuraoğlu Yusuf also attributed this profession to Kara Yorgi and was dismissive of the Serbian rebels. At the head of the Serbian rebels

> there was a pig herder called Kara Yorgi, who had learned a little soldiering as an insignificant officer in Austria. The band gathered around him consisted only of pig herders who drove pigs in the mountains and forests, and who, because of their work, were always armed and accustomed to having no constraints, and highway robbers and village raiders who were shown and applauded in Serbian songs as if they were national heroes.[14]

In the school text books written by Ahmed Hasır and Mustafa Muhsin, the Serbs were merely peasants who herded pigs and cultivated corn. Miloš Obrenović, who was 'the long-time opponent and rival of Kara Yorgi' and who became 'the başknez (reis) of the Serbs,' was, in this account, a pig trader.[15]

In the same way as the Ottoman historians did not conceive any unity of Balkan peoples, so too did they fail to see any unity of Balkan states. Although, with the Berlin Treaty (1878), the Ottoman empire lost her suzerainty over Serbia, the Danubian Principalities and Montenegro, and was forced to accept the autonomy of Bulgaria, this crucial change in the map of the region did not find an immediate reflection in the Ottoman historiography of the area. The history texts which appeared after the Congress of Berlin followed the mind set of the pre-Congress period, despite the fact that the authors of these texts were well aware of the new shape of the region and what repercussions this new order might bring.

Indeed the Ottoman statesmen of the period were very well informed about the developments in Europe, a constant deluge of reports and telegrams arriving constantly in İstanbul from the Ottoman embassies in Europe, together with a mass of translations from various European newspapers. The Ottoman government was highly aware of the centrality of European politics for the survival of the empire. This did not however lead to any conception of a viable Balkan unit, for, although concerned over potential alliances between various Balkan states, the Ottoman government was convinced that no such unity would emerge without Great Power instigation, and no such Great Power support would, they felt, ever be forthcoming.

The Ottoman approach is made evident by the government's actions over the 'quadruple alliance,' rumours of which were reported to İstanbul in 1883. Alarmed, the Ottoman government asked its embassies in Europe to investigate whether this news was true or not.[16] The main reason for this agitation seems to have been the visit of the Bulgarian Prince Alexander to the Greek King George in Athens and his acceptance by the Greek government as a representative of an equal state in the region, as made clear by the Greek reception of him. Moreover, the private talk between the Prince and the King also attracted the attention of the Ottoman government and increased concerns over the possibility of an alliance, at least between Greece and Bulgaria.[17] The Bulgarian Prince's visit in the same month to Cetinje (Cetina), the capital of Montenegro, where he was received with great enthusiasm by both the Montenegrin government and by the people, further agitated the Ottoman authorities.[18]

Ottoman diplomats from Vienna and Rome telegraphed the government reporting that, on the basis of their correspondence with Austrian and Italian statesmen, there was no such quadruple alliance.[19] Further, the Ottoman ambassador in Berlin wrote that the German Emperor guaranteed the status-quo in the Balkan peninsula.[20] Although the Ottomans were concerned over any political alliance in the region and especially over Bulgarian intentions concerning Eastern Rumeli and the Balkan mountains,[21] the Ottoman government did not perceive the 'Balkan' states as a political, social or cultural whole which defined its identity thus. Any doubt the Ottoman government might have had over a possible alliance was erased by the assurance given by various Great Power representatives that the political incompatibilities of the Balkan entities made any such alliance impossible. This further strengthened Ottoman lack of any conception of a Balkan identity because no such indigenous structure was perceived and if any such structure were to emerge it would only be as a result of European intervention or support.

The action of the Serbian Prince, Milan Obrenović, in 1886 served to demonstrate further that in fact no such anti-Ottoman Balkan unity did exist. After acknowledging the lack of Ottoman trust in Serbia due to the events of the recent past, and the Serbian seizure of 'her natural right of independence,'[22] the Prince, urging the ambassador to 'let bygones be by-gones,' went on to propose an anti-Russian alliance against the increasing Russian influence in the Balkan Peninsula and even a possible Russian invasion of Bulgaria which would threaten the peace and order of the whole peninsula. The Ottoman empire was, for the Prince, the only state that could stand against Russian ambitions in the East. This proposal was repeated in a more cautious manner by the Serbian Minister of Foreign Affairs. After presenting the proposals, the Ottoman ambassador in Belgrade expressed his doubts that either the King or the Minister would have had the courage to propose this kind of an alliance against Russia without the knowledge and permission of Austria, who had considerable concerns over Russian influence in the region in which it, Austria, had a great interest. For the ambassador, therefore, this was in effect an Austrian plan against Russia which did not involve putting Austria herself at risk.[23] The Ottoman ambassador's view of behind-the-scenes Austrian involvement was in line with the Ottoman perception of the Balkan states as being in a peripheral position vis-à-vis the Ottoman empire and any other Great Power outside the region. This denial of any existence other than as a periphery for the Balkan region might also explain why any statement by the representatives of the Great Powers carried more weight than those of even the kings of the Balkan nation-states on issues directly related to the region, for such states could only function in relation to a centre be it Ottoman or one of the Great Powers. This idea that the Balkan entities needed centre(s) to exist blocked any conception of the region as an independent unit and its people as a whole even in the later Ottoman and early Republican era.

Apart from being denied an existence as a single entity, the Balkan states, rather in the way the peoples too were denigrated or belittled, were seen as being small states. The European description of the Balkan states as 'little Balkan governments,'[24] in contrast to the big states i.e. the Great Powers, was embraced by the Ottoman intellectuals as a reflection of the central position attributed to the Ottoman state. Bulgaria was referred to as 'little Bulgaria' by Mehmed Bey, a 'Young Turk' whom, the 'British archaeological traveller,'[25] William Ramsay met shortly after the 1908 Revolution while traveling to İstanbul by train. Mehmed Bey heavily criticised British intervention in Ottoman politics and protested that 'not even Russia had ever so openly and rudely dictated its desires to little Bulgaria, as England did in that case to Turkey.'[26] Greece too was represented as 'little' in a poem written during the Greco-Ottoman War in 1897, in which Vahyi Efendi, lieutenant commander from Crete, asked: 'Oh Greek, you took this kingdom but yesterday, can a puppy stand against a lion, I wonder?'[27] This belittling of the Greek state emerged again in the period of the unification of Crete with Greece, when the poet Akil Koyuncu referred to the Greek crown being a gift from the Ottomans.[28]

A few years later Ahmed Rasim wrote disparagingly of Greece, commenting that since Greece owed its existence to the Great Powers, it would inevitably be forced to capitulate to the pressure of the Allied powers and enter the war on their side, a fact which thus reduced Greece's so-called independence to nothing. 'Well,' as Ahmed Rasim said, 'these are the results of being raised under that sort of wing. The time always comes when the hand of the protector turns to torture.'[29]

For Cemal Paşa, the 'little' Balkan states were an irritation, due to their constantly raising an outcry over minority problems, problems which he agreed existed but which were not of major consequence and which could be sorted out without all this unnecessary fuss. For him, in fact, the problem was not the minorities but the noise created by the 'little Balkan governments.'[30] This categorization of the Balkan states as 'little Balkan states' continued in the Republican era. According to a 1945 school history text book, the Balkan alliance during the Balkan Wars was made between 'the little Balkan states' (Balkanlı küçük devletler).[31] Sometimes this categorization was used to refer to the nineteenth-century context. Halil İnalcık, for instance, refers in 1943 to 'the little Balkan states' (küçük Balkan devletleri), Romania, Greece and Serbia, which had left Ottoman sovereignty with Russian help.[32]

This vision of little Balkan states resulted in great frustration among the Ottoman elite, whose humiliation brought about by the defeat in the Balkan War was increased because these little states about whom they had spoken so disparagingly, were victorious over the Ottoman empire. Defeat at the hands of 'the little Balkan states' was seen as much more humiliating than defeat by the Great Powers. Akçuraoğlu Yusuf wrote in *Türk Yurdu* just after the Balkan Wars of the Ottoman shame and frustration created by being beaten by those who had been 'our subjects for five centuries.'[33] This feeling was echoed in another account written in the same period:

After ruling with total power over the three great continents of the world for 600 years, we were finally expelled from Rumeli. We were driven even out by our former shepherds and servants. We must not remove from our hearts until the Day of Judgment the pain of this insulting blow which we have received.[34]

This Ottoman despair at the end of the Balkan War was discussed much later by Yusuf Hikmet Bayur who explained Ottoman anger at the Balkan states' attempt to interfere, alongside the Great Powers, in the internal affairs of the Ottoman empire. The Balkan states aspired to be part of the Great Power club, to 'be a member of the court together with Great Powers, to give orders to the Ottomans and to pronounce sentence.'[35]

For the Ottoman historian of the nineteenth century, the Balkans as a unit did not exist. When, partly as a result of necessity, the Ottoman historian did begin to conceive of Balkan states, such states were 'little,' and their independence was a fiction for they were creatures of the Great Powers. This attitude coloured the 1930s' Turkish political scene and was influential in Turkey's dealings with her Balkan neighbours. For the Turkish ambassador in Athens who wrote a report on the proposed 'Balkan Union' (Balkan Birliği) for the Ministry of Foreign Affairs in 1932, what was important was not the individual Balkan states, such as Albania and Bulgaria, but the positions of the Great Powers, particularly Italy and France. The Great Powers, who all had their own, divergent interests in the region, were not likely to look with favour on the creation of a Balkan Union.[36] In fact, any such unity was threatened not merely by Great Power interest, but also, to an extent, by the regional players themselves. According to Professor Ormanjiyev, the head of the Executive Committee of the Society of Thrace (Trakya Cemiyeti İcra Komitesi Reisi) which aimed at the annexation of Eastern Thrace to Bulgaria, the Balkan Pact was a reflection of 'the injustices perpetrated against the Bulgarian nation which was beginning to rise yet again from the ashes like a phoenix.' Turkey was the main culprit of such injustice since it was the Ottoman empire which had expelled the Bulgarians in 1913. Greece too was guilty of expelling Bulgarians from its soil. Since the Balkan Pact was based on such injustice, it was, in the opinion of Ormanjiyev, doomed to failure.[37]

In the Republican era, the Balkans as a regional designation was very much political rather than geographical. For Ali Reşad in 1926 a Balkan state was one which had land in the Balkan Peninsula. Thus Austria-Hungary became a Balkan state by invading Bosnia and Herzegovina.[38] With the signing of the Balkan Pact, Turkey too, for the first time, became a Balkan state. For Yusuf Hikmet Bayur in 1935, the Balkans consisted of Albania, Bulgaria, Greece, Romania, Yugoslavia and Turkey.[39]

With the Balkan Wars, and more especially with the creation of the Repulic, the texts began to use the word 'Balkanlılar.'[40] But what exactly does this term signify? Literally it means the ones from the Balkans, but as used in late Ottoman and Republican contexts, these 'ones' were the nation states in the Balkans. The term did not mean Balkan peoples, a people united by a common social and cultural bond. Any such commonality existed only in the realm of discourse, and was used, for example, by Mustafa Kemal Atatürk in a speech given at the last session of the Second Balkan Conference in the Turkish Parliament in Ankara in 1931:

> Whatever social and political face the Balkan nations present, it is necessary not to forget that they have common ancestors from the same blood and from related tribes who came from Central Asia. The mass of people who for thousands of years came one after another along the northern and the southern routes of the Black Sea like waves of the sea and who settled in the Balkans, even though they carried different names, are in reality nothing other than [people] from sibling tribes who emerged from the same, single cradle with the same blood circulating in their veins.[41]

This idea of a Balkan commonality continued at the level of discourse after Atatürk's death. In a paper, published in 1946, in which he explained the reasons behind the creation of the Turkish History Thesis, Enver Ziya Karal quoted from Atatürk's speech which he used to demonstrate Atatürk's belief in 'the concord between nationality and humanity.'[42]

Such commonality was not, however, something reflected in the reality on the ground. Any Turkish desire to create common reference points was viewed in the Balkans with irritation, suspicion, or ridicule. In 1933 a translation into French from an article in a Bulgarian newspaper, *Zaria*, was sent from the Turkish embassy in Sofia to the Ministry of Foreign Affairs, and from there to the Prime Minister's Office. The letter, which noted that the article ridiculed the Turkish History Congress, drew attention to various sentences which referred to Turkey's desire, despite being merely a tiny state, to have itself recognized as a major power. The French translation of the article, entitled 'Les fantaisies des historiens turcs,' read as follows:

> Il y a quelque temps, à Ankara s'est tenu un grand congrès des historiens turcs. Il a été décidé que les plus célèbres historiens de Turquie écritvent [*sic.*] une vaste et juste histoire de la Turquie. Au congrès un historien turc a déclaré que les turcs étaient le plus vieux peuple de la terre. Il a fourni ses preuves à l'appui. Un autre historien est allé encore plus loin en affirmant devant le congrès que les premiers êtres humains, Adam et Eve, seraient également turcs... Comme preuve, il a montré que les noms de Adam et Eve répondent entièrement aux mots turcs d'homme et femme. Une autre preuve les paradis serait quelque part en Asie-Mineure, d'où plus tard les peuple turc envahit trimphalement [*sic.*] l'Europe. De tout temps les turcs ont souffert de la manie de turquiser tout, bien que jadis comme à présent ils n'aient été qu'un petit peuple. Au grande nation avec ses 13 millions d'habitants, n'a en vérité que cinq millions et demi de purs turcs. Rien d'étonnant que les historiens turcs veuillent maintenant turquiser Adam et Eve aussi.[43]

'Les fantaisies des historiens turcs,' existed also perhaps in the lack of an Ottoman conceptualization of a Balkan unity, either of peoples or states, and, coupled with this, a tendency to belittle the individuals and the individual states of the region. The later discourse construction of a common bond, evidenced in Mustafa Kemal's speech, was without any foundation in the new political scene in which there existed an array of Balkan states one of which was, for specific, pragmatic and not necessarily enduring reasons, the new Republic of Turkey.

5

THE MULTI-IMAGES OF THE BALKANS

Recurrent images of the Balkans appear in the history-writing from the late Ottoman to the early Republican period. The region was one of violence and barbarism, it was associated with migration and the spread of dangerous ideas, as well as sometimes offering a more positive example of the way forward to the historians both of the late Ottoman era and of the new Republic. It carried for both the Ottomans and the Turks a strong feeling of a fatherland in which the Danube played a significant role. Its image was also very closely bound up with two outside powers, Europe and Russia. What image applied depended in part on the author's own particular choice, which could be based on his own relation to the region, such as for example being an emigrant from the area, or related to the changing domestic or international political scene. Further, although the images were constant, the recipients were not. Thus the image of violence was applied to the Bulgarians by Mahmud Celaleddin Paşa in *Mirat-ı Hakikat*, but to the Greeks by Ahmed Rasim. Again in school history text books published after the National Liberation War, it was Greek violence against civilians which was used to portray "the Balkans" as a violent and immoral aggressor.

On occassion, government policy determined what image was applied to which state. By the 1930s' much was being written against Bulgaria and published by private publishing houses, while anti-Greek publications, so common in the 1920s, were rare. Turkey had problems over the territorial claims of both Greece and Bulgaria, expressed in their state anthems. The desire to conquer İstanbul, expressed very clearly in the Bulgarian national anthem, 'Shumi Maritza,' was well-known through Turkish publications of the period.¹ In contrast, the same desire on the part of the Greeks who sang 'With our king at our head, we will go and take İstanbul and Hagia Sophia' (Başımızda Kralımız olduğu halde, gidip İstanbulu ve Ayasofyayı alacağız) in 'the anthem of the Greek King,' remained unpublished in Turkish sources and such information was filed away in the Republican archives for the information of the government only.² Politically, Turkey was at this point cementing good relations with Greece and thus was prepared to ignore any such inconvenient expressions of national ambition. Relations with Bulgaria, were, however, not good. In 1933 Prime Minister İsmet İnönü gave financial support to various Bulgarian Turkish journalists, including M. Necmettin Deliorman, to ensure publications favorable to Turkey. However the political situation changed and in 1943, İnönü, now President, banned the circulation of a pamphlet *Bulgarya'daki 1,300,000 Türk* (1,300,000 Turks in Bulgaria) written by various Turkish Bulgarians including Deliorman.³ While Halil Yaver's anti-Bulgarian books, which even attracted the attention of the Bulgarian press, were circulated freely in Turkey, in 1937, on the request of the Ministry of Internal Affairs, his book, *Nereye Gidiyorsun Türkiye?* (Turkey, Where are You Going?) published by 'Götenberg Matbaası' in Galata, was banned by the Turkish government.⁴ In support of its request that the book be banned, the Ministry stated that the book 'includes a detrimental publication against Yugoslavia, which is an ally of Turkey, and against the Balkan Pact' and 'causes complications for Turkish foreign policy and for Turkey's internal position.'⁵ Images were thus not merely related to the historian's choice but also to the political circumstances of the time which dictated which country a particular image was applied to. In the 1920s', the image of brutality was applied to Greece, but in the 1930s', the recipient of that image was Bulgaria.

The Balkans and Europe

One of the central pillars of Ottoman and Turkish historiographical treatment of the Balkan region, which continued as a constant and unchanging factor, unbroken by the transformation from empire to Republic, is made up of Ottoman/Turkish responses to European claims of superiority over the East. Without understanding the centrality of the European civilization debate for the Ottomans and Turks, it is impossible to understand the reasons behind the image of the Balkans as a space of confrontation with Europe in Ottoman and Republican historiography, or Ottoman and Turkish sensibilities over the region.

For much of nineteenth-century Europe, there was an unbridgeable gap between the "rational Occident" and the "irrational Orient," a belief which was not merely imperialistic but was perceived to be based on sound reasoning.[6] Lord Cromer regarded the 'Turkish oriental mind' as something quite incomprehensible. Sir Edward Grey, British Foreign Secretary during the First World War, recalled Cromer's remarks:

> If it is important to you to know what an Oriental is going to do you must ask yourself three questions: (1) What would you yourself do under the same conditions? (2) What do you think the wisest man you know would do? (3) What do you think the Oriental will do? When you have answered these questions you will know three things that the Oriental certainly will not do. Nearer to his intention than that you cannot get.[7]

European self-confidence about the superiority of European civilization and belief that European civilization was destined to be the only "new" and "advanced" civilization, were the back-bone of the European intellectual paradigm, although according to Braudel, finding a clear definition of civilization in the nineteenth-century European intellectual realm is not possible.[8] Nevertheless, despite the lack of a coherent understanding of civilization or a clear definition of European civilization within Europe, the Ottoman empire was in comparison considered "barbarous" or "semi-barbarous." The Ottoman empire played the role of the "other" to European civilization whose image was fashioned to an extent by using the Ottoman empire and the world of Islam as a mirror to show what European civilization was certainly not. This was not new, for Machiavelli defined Europe by contrasting it with the Ottoman state, in effect arguing that 'we' are European because 'we' are not Ottoman.[9] The concept of the barbarous Ottoman, too, was not new. For Piccolomini, later Pope Pius II (1458-1464), the Turks were 'the most cruel among men, enemies of civilized living and learning.'[10] What was new, however, was the Ottoman response and the empire's desire and attempt to defend itself against the European claims of superiority and prove that, in fact, such claims were unfounded.

The Ottoman elite, which came increasingly to experience at first hand the European attitude to the Ottoman state and her culture as a result of travelling to Europe as exiles, students, tourists or government representatives, was very well informed about the European intellectual paradigm, established on the perception of European civilization as the only "civilization." These ideas disseminated through the European countries, were almost immediately transmitted into Ottoman domains both via European newspapers, books and journals,[11] and through the Ottoman press, which published both translations of these European ideas or responses to them. Such responses could also be published in book form.

These Ottoman responses to the European challenge over civilization are epitomised in the last quarter of the nineteenth century by the works of Namık Kemal. Namık Kemal did not in fact have any clear definition of what was meant by European civilization, something even the Europeans themselves had failed to define. He established a direct link between civilization and progress, to which humans were naturally inclined. For him, civilization was equal to technology, science and modern methods in business, none of which were restricted to Europe, while European lifestyle and culture did not form part of his understanding of civilization. For him, thus, there was no need to adopt European culture and lifestyle in order to be civilized:

> Now if we want to adopt civilization, wherever we find true public works of this kind, we shall take them. Just as we do not need to adopt the eating of leech *kebap* from the Chinese in order to be civilized, we are not under any obligation [to accept] European dancing or imitate their marriage practices.[12]

Parallel to this view, Namık Kemal argued strongly that Europe did not understand the Ottoman empire or the East. This was a response in part to the European charge of barbarity and irrationality. In response to Ernest Renan's claims over the incompatibility of Islam and education,[13] Namık Kemal defended Islam's role in education, arguing that Islam, in fact, paved the way for the development of education and attacked the European lack of information about it.[14] This was not the first time that Namık Kemal had attacked Europe over its ignorance of the East, for he had already published in 1872 an article, 'Avrupa Şarkı Bilmez' (Europe does not know the East).[15] Ahmed Cevdet Paşa, too, underlined in *Tezakir* the European lack of knowledge about Islam, an essential element of the Ottoman empire for Ahmed Cevdet Paşa who came from the *ulema*. Upon being corrected over his belief in the existence of clergy in Islam, the French ambassador commented 'I have lived in İstanbul for a long time, [but] I have not apparently been able sufficiently to learn about it.' Ahmed Cevdet Paşa noted this startling lack of knowledge of Islam exhibited even by a European representative in the Ottoman empire and went on to say:

> You lived in Beyoğlu.[16] You could not have learnt about the conditions of the Ottoman empire or even of the spirit of İstanbul properly. Beyoğlu is an isthmus between Europe and the Islamic lands. From here you see İstanbul through a telescope, but the telescopes which you used were always warped.[17]

Some argued that European civilization was not in fact from Europe but from the Arabs, i.e. from Islam. Akyiğitzade Musa, a migrant from Russia who had worked as a history teacher and a customs officer controlling the entry of books and newspapers in Sirkeci (İstanbul), argued in 1315/1897 that the roots of contemporary European civilization were Islamic. Contrary to the argument used, for example, by Hegel, giving Islamic civilization only the role of transmitter of ancient philosophy to Europe,[18] Akyiğitzade Musa attributed an integral role to Islamic civilization, in which 'Turks' also had a part, through which the Europeans both received civilization and as a result of which the 'vahşi' (wild, barbarous) Europeans became civilized.[19] In this way, the author not only reversed the European claims of superiority of their own civilization, but also legitimised the adoption of European civilization, whose roots lay in Islamic civilization. Şemseddin Sami, who was educated in a Greek school, blamed Christianity for the decline of Greek civilization. It was, however, Islam which had brought back Greek civilization, Europe thus receiving Greek civilization which the Europeans claimed as the root of the European civilization, from Islamic civilization.[20]

In a booklet published in İstanbul in 1302/1885 (1886), Gaspıralı İsmail (İsmail Gaspıranski), a journalist from the Crimea and a relative of Akçuraoğlu Yusuf, totally rejected any idea of adoption of European civilization. For him, European civilization was not something new but was rather 'Old Greek, New European' (Eski Yunanlı taze Avrupalı), an old civilization doomed to vanish due to the lack of 'justice' in European societies for the vast majority of the population. He equated

European civilization with 'Christian civilization' and likened it to a fine looking and well made up woman whose teeth were, in fact, false, whose hair was artificial, whose breasts were made bigger by the addition of cotton wool and whose body under her fine taffeta clothes was scarred.[21] Gaspıralı perceived Islamic civilization as an alternative to European civilization, which aspired through colonization to swallow up other parts of the world. However, Gaspıralı did not denounce European science and technology, since he did not perceive them as parts of European civilization, but advocated their adoption. In this respect, his understanding of European civilization, excluding science and technology and taking only the way of living and culture as a part of civilization, differed from that of Namık Kemal and Ziya Gökalp.

Contrary to Gaspıralı İsmail's total rejection of European civilization, another view advocating total adoption of European civilization, perceived not only as science and technology but also as life style and culture, found supporters among the Ottoman elite in the Abdülhamidian era. The followers of this view also attempted to demonstrate that the Ottomans were a part of European civilization and that the European accusation of Ottoman barbarity was groundless. The novel, *Salon Köşelerinde*, written in 1905 by Safveti Ziya, who was one of the *Edebiyat-ı Cedide* writers, displayed the struggle of the Ottoman elite with the European preconceptions of the Ottoman and the Turk. The novel, published in an İstanbul journal, *Servet-i Fünun*, told the story of a "Europeanized" Ottoman man who socialized in the foreign quarters of İstanbul and tried to prove by waltzing like a European that he was 'civilized' to an English girl with whom he had fallen in love:

> Instead of demented and childish behaviour giving way to feelings which, like love and desire, are temporary, forgettable, and leave behind them frustration, separation, and regret, and leaving to one side all that daydreaming, I changed my plan of action, thinking that it would be necessary to prove to an English girl and an English family that Turkishness within a society is not an example of barbarity, but an adornment, and that the Turks too are a civilized nation.[22]

Even in this non-political, romantic novel, the Europeanized character, who was ready to accommodate to European culture, exhibited a reactionary attitude to the European perception of the Turk and fought against this "misperception" by dancing, an activity which Namık Kemal did not regard as something necessary in order to be civilized.[23]

All these responses shaped in the late nineteenth and early twentieth centuries continued to exist in the ideologically uncertain atmosphere of the post-1908 period. As in the pre-1908 era, in this new era, too, the Ottoman elite was very receptive to European views on the Ottoman empire. Mehmed Bey complained to Ramsay about *The Times* newspaper because of its biased coverage of the Ottoman empire and contemporary developments within the empire.[24] After recounting his conversation with this Mehmed Bey, Ramsay noted: 'The whole matter shows how much importance is attached in Turkish circles to the opinions expressed in the foreign press, and how much harm may be done by the leading newspapers of Europe through unintelligent and harsh criticism of the internal affairs of other countries.'[25]

With the deposition of Abdülhamid II, a new era in the writing of history texts started. The recent history of the Ottoman empire was included in the new texts, unlike the practice prevalent in the Abdülhamidian era in which the history texts did not detail recent historical events or did not mention anything about the near past at all. This attempt at integration of recent events into school history texts was designed to legitimize the 'July 10 Revolution' (10 Temmuz İhtilali) as a just intervention and political turning point in Ottoman history, and to deligitimize the deposed sultan Abdülhamid and his practice of power in the eyes of the new generation. These new histories continued to use the internal organizations of sections followed by Ahmed Vefik's *Fezleke*, accepted as the first text book to adopt the European style of periodization of history, but also, unlike their predecessors, included sections on Ottoman civilization as a response to the ideological needs of the new regime.

Two history texts dated 1327/1911, written respectively by Ahmed Refik and jointly by Ali Reşad and Ali Seydi, all of whom were integral to history text book production and education in the last years of Abdülhamid, throughout the İttihad ve Terakki era and into the Republic, responded to all the requirements of the new regime: to demonize Abdülhamid, to present the 10th of July as the day of salvation and to prove the existence of an Ottoman civilization. The books, according to a statement printed on the cover pages, were prepared 'according to the programme' (programa göre) for the second year of the *rüşdiye*, presumably referring here to the curriculum issued by the Ministry of Education. Ali Reşad and Ali Seydi further underlined that their book was in accordance with the latest 'programme.' In his chapters on the periods 1003-1203/1594-1789 and 1203-1327/1789-1909, Ahmed Refik includes a section in each on Ottoman civilization subdivided into 'sultans,' 'statesmen,' 'army and navy,' 'finance,' 'art and industry' and 'foreign affairs.'[26] In each of these, he sets out to demonstrate, rather simplisticly, the presence of an Ottoman civilization, which, for him, apparently merely consists of having, for example, a good army, or an efficient navy. In contrast, Ali Reşad and Ali Seydi end their book with a section devoted to Ottoman civilization designed to prove an Ottoman contribution to "civilization" in, for example, army and architecture, and to negate the accusations of Ottoman barbarity. For the authors, 'the Ottomans were in any case from the beginning of their organization a civilized people. They did not destroy the works of the Romans, Byzantines and Seljuks which they found in the areas where they set up their governments. On the contrary they benefited from them.'[27] After implicitly negating the European image of the Ottoman empire and demonstrating the Ottoman contribution to "civilization" and the European debt to the Ottomans from whom they had in fact learned much, the authors responded to another accusation, that the Ottomans did not leave any trace of civilization on their lands. Ottoman domains were so vast that it was impossible to create 'works of civilization' (asar-ı medeniye) and even those which did exist remained unnoticed. The second reason for this scarcity of the signs of civilization was that the Ottomans were constantly forced to fight against their enemies making it impossible to concentrate on works of civilization:

> Yes, we were a military government, we spent our lives in war. But if Ottoman history is studied well, it will be seen that the wars we ourselves initiated were few, indeed very few. Our enemies always come against us, we are then forced to come against them.[28]

Further, for a century 'the whole world' had struggled with the Ottomans, and therefore the Ottoman government had been unable to focus on science and education. This had led to the corruption of public morality and supremacy of ignorance so that recently the people and soldiers had prevented everything, which the state wanted to do. These problems apart, however, the authors stressed the inherent civilization of the Ottomans: 'Otherwise, from the point of view of natural ability, there is no difference between us and the other civilized nations.'[29]

The response to European claims of superiority at the level of school text books, which inevitably reflected state requirements, formed part of a wider debate among the Ottoman elite. Under Abdülhamid, this debate within the Ottoman empire had tended to be defensive, either Ottoman civilization was presented as the best or, in the event of adoption from Europe, such adoption was presented as acceptable since European civilization in any case came from the Arab and Islamic world. In the post-Abdülhamidian era, there is a shift towards a more aggressive stand together with a sense of the victimization of the Islamic world in the face of European civilization, now equated with imperialism. While the challenge stays the same and while the responses too could be fundamentally the same, there is a sharper, more aggressive and more threatening attitude, which reflects the new harder-edged approach of the İttihad ve Terakki era in general.

One of the responses among the Ottoman elite was acceptance of the great danger in which the Ottoman empire found itself and, consequently, of the need to imitate European models in order to survive. Prens Sabahaddin, the nephew of Abdülhamid II, was extremely concerned about this threat to the Ottoman empire which he argued had already been expelled from Europe and would soon be expelled from Asia.[30] In contrast to Gaspıralı İsmail, for whom in 1885 British society was an example of the inequalities and decadence of Europe which would ultimately lead to its downfall,[31] Prens Sabahaddin in 1334/1916 advocated, as one of the ideas for ensuring the survival of the state, the creating of a landed aristocracy similar to that in Britain which would both share power with the centre and would also be economically effective in exploiting agricultural lands within the empire which were currently underused.[32]

By no means all advocated imitation, and the post-1908 period witnessed fierce and total rejection of European civilization. For one author, whose elderly father had been killed by the Bulgarians in Dimetoka during the Balkan Wars, 'the civilization of the twentieth century is anti-Muslim,' something which in any case 'we all knew and this time we understood it better and believed it more.'[33] The journal, *Sırat-ı Müstakim*, later called *Sebilürreşad*, was an important platform for the discussion of the Ottoman and Islamic confrontation with Europe over the subject of civilization. Although this journal was later labeled 'Islamist' by modern historians,[34] this kind of a categorization is somewhat misleading since among the writers of the journal were well-known "Turkists" such as Ağaoğlu Ahmed and Akçuraoğlu Yusuf. The journal, thus, was addressed to a wider readership with its wide range of writers from both within Ottoman domains and from outside. In a 1327/1911 article, the confrontation between the East and West was presented as a confrontation between the crescent and the cross, in which the crescent was victimized by the bloodthirsty European civilization:

> If we unite, let us be sure that no one can bend our arm. In an instant casting aside 'the oppression and tyranny' of the cross which we have borne on our shoulders for a thousand years and flinging it in the face of these false civilized ones, we will have performed our humane and Islamic duty.[35]

This concept of a false or fake civilization continues in the Republican era as a part of the representation of Europe in school texts. A history text from 1926 clearly shows Turkish resentment over the lack of European concern for the aggression of the Balkan states against the Muslim population during the Balkan War: 'Europe, falsely claiming civilization, remained merely a spectator of such oppression and previously unwitnessed barbarity.'[36] This statement also carries with it the implied criticism of double standards, a criticism explicitly underlined in the 1327/1911 text referred to above. Here the author contrasts European attitudes to barbarity, acceptable against Muslims, but not Christians:

> Nothing is left unwritten, nothing is left unsaid when a bandit who attacks our soldiers on the Bulgarian or Greek frontier is disposed off. But when they burn our villages and cut off the ears and noses of our wretched Muslim brothers, we remain silent. When we are about to send soldiers against our own ignorant subjects who are revolting only due to provocation, the big (!) English newspaper [*The*] *Times* seeks to say that we cannot do anything against the Christians, the Catholic Albanians, who have revolted, because of the Austrian right of protection over the Catholics. European

newspapers were applauding the [Ottoman] government for severely punishing the rebels during last year's Albanian revolt. This year, the same newspapers were defending the people from the same ethnic group, but only because they were Christian, and were talking about our soldiers' barbarous treatment of them. So this is how European civilization behaves![37]

This image of a monstrous, imperialistic and fake European civilization is visible also in the Turkish National anthem, the words of which were written during the National Liberation War by Mehmed Akif (Ersoy), one of the prolific and important writers of *Sırat-ı Müstakim-Sebilürreşad*. In his poem, chosen to form the Turkish national anthem, the first two verses of which were then put to music, one of the verses which technically forms part of the national anthem but is not sung, depicts civilization, here meaning European, as a single-toothed monster.[38]

These discussions over the place of the Ottoman empire vis-à-vis Europe went on during the Republican era. One way of fighting against Europe was to be perceived as part of it, part of its "superior" civilization, thus circumventing any criticism of the new Turkish state or justification for imperialism.[39] This approach was advocated by Celal Nuri (İleri) in 1926. From the circle of Abdullah Cevdet, who was a well-known positivist writer of the era and the publisher of the journal *İctihad*, Celal Nuri considered the issue from a very positivist perspective while being well aware of the on-going discussions in Europe which envisaged the end of European civilization.[40] Apart from this line of thinking based on the inevitability of embracing Western civilization by renouncing Eastern civilization, there was an attempt to reconcile the West and the East, such as that by Ziya Gökalp who described civilization as 'knowledge, science and industry [or technology].'[41] Here, accepting European civilization in fact meant appropriating modern science and technology without renouncing native culture. In that sense Ziya Gökalp echoed Namık Kemal's view concerning western civilization in the twentieth century.

This confrontation with Europe was inevitably carried on into state-sponsored national history-writing. History-writing was perceived as a means of demonstrating the Turkish contributions not only to the eastern but also to the western civilizations.[42] In the opening speech of the first Turkish History Congress, the platform for the introduction of the national history thesis, the Minister of Education, Esad Bey, summarized the aim of the new history thesis, quoting from *Tarih I*:

> We are fearful of going down in history as a people, a nation who will be remembered with hatred by future generations. Whereas in fact we are determined to be the possessors of the most august and honourable place in history as an entity which individually and nationally produced the highest works for civilization, which worked hard for the progress of humanity, which left valuable, perpetual works of knowledge and art which will be beneficial for generations to come. For this reason we will raise our children with this thought, this upbringing and this conviction.[43]

Within this discourse on the place of civilization, the superiority of European civilization and the Ottoman responses, from the era of Abdülhamid through the İttihad ve Terakki period and on into the Republic, the Balkans formed a key arena for this European-Ottoman confrontation. In 1877, Edward Freeman[44] ended his book on Ottoman power in Europe with a description of the Ottoman place there. For Freeman, the Turk in South-eastern Europe 'can shew [sic.] no memorials of cultivation; he can show only memorials of destruction. His history for the five hundred years during which he has been encamped on European soil is best summed up in the proverbial saying, "Where the Sultan's horse-hoof treads, grass never grows again."'[45] The Ottoman was an alien presence in Europe. 'The Turk came into Europe as a stranger and an oppressor, and after five hundred years he is a stranger and oppressor still.'[46] Forty years later, this image of tyranny and 'incapacity' for civilization inherent in the Ottoman character formed part of the practical information given in *A Handbook of Turkey in Europe* prepared by the British Admiralty War Staff Intelligence Division during the First World War. In a section entitled 'Defects of Turks as a ruling race,' the text states:

> The Turk succeeded in orientalizing and proselytizing and reducing to practical servitude a considerable part of the Balkans because he found there no unity of race or religion, but he has never succeeded in assimilating the conquered people here or elsewhere. It is most unfortunate that owing to his inherent incapacity for art or science or business or political life the

energies of the Turk are prone to find their outlet mainly in works of destruction. Wherever he rules we find squalor and decay, and the suggestion of the distracting temporary settlement of a migratory race.[47]

This general attitude towards Ottoman existence in Europe was not limited only to the British, for other Europeans also expressed similar negative attitudes.[48] Even the well-known Prussian historian Ranke, well before Freeman, summed up the Ottoman contribution to the lands which they had conquered using the proverb which Freeman too repeats: 'Un proverbe dit: «L'herbe ne croît plus là où un cheval ottoman a posé son pied.» Le dévastation des plus beaux pays de la terre, dont ils ont fait la conquête, paraît le confirmer suffisamment.' For Ranke, the Ottomans, although many of them showed virtues such as humanity, loyalty and generous hospitability, nevertheless 'sont toujours restés barbares.' In fact, the Ottomans 'ont toujours repoussé l'action bienfaisante de la civilization.'[49]

Ottoman culpability was not limited to material destruction and the lack of any signs of civilization in the European parts of her territory or any other of her domains, but Ottoman dominance, according to the European outlook, was responsible from the "negative" characteristics of her enslaved Christian subjects, such as the Greeks or Armenians, who consequently lost their virtue. After discussing the hospitality of the Turks, Francis Beaufort, sent to Anatolia to make a survey by the Lords Commissioners of the Admirality in 1811-1812, moves on to the Greeks:

> In this point of view, the character of the modern Greeks would ill bear a comparison with that of their oppressors; such a comparison, however, would be unfair, for slavery necessarily entails a peculiar train of vices; but it may be hoped, that the growing energy, which one day will free them from political slavery, will also emancipate them from its moral effects.[50]

In 1916, on the back cover of *Armenia: Past and Present* written by W. Llew. Williams, the former editor of *The Sunday Strand*, the Armenian inclination to intrigue was credited to the Turkish oppression: 'There in the heart of Asia Minor will be a Christian people, virile, intelligent, prolific, with an abnormally developed capacity for intrigue - the result of centuries of oppression and suppression.'[51]

In the 1930s', this view of the Balkan peoples' loss of virtue under Ottoman rule was echoed in a cover letter sent by the Turkish Ministry of Foreign Affairs to the Prime Minister's Office together with an article from the Bulgarian French language newspaper, *La Bulgarie*. This article, 'Un portrait français du peuple bulgare,' reported on the views of the French *chargé d'affaires* M. Georges Picot and others on the 'qualitiés de labeur du peuple bulgare,' a people who, with the Ottoman conquest, had slipped into oblivion. 'C'est la nuit de l'histoire. Il y a toujours une Bulgarie, mais ce n'est que le nom d'une province turque.' Certain lines in the article had been underlined: 'Il est bien vrai que la chance, les vicissitudes de la politique internationale et les hasards des guerres ont pu, dans le passé, donner à des peuples favorisés par le sort un pouvoir disproportionné à leurs qualités et une grandeur apparente defiant l'équité.' The cover letter interprets these lines in the following way: 'Since the subject [of the article] consists of repeating that the Bulgarian nation was hardworking and then forgotten under the Ottoman yoke, it may be concluded that the underlined phrases implied an allusion which was the production of hatred and jealousy of the past of the Turkish nation.'[52] Thus Ottoman success was due to chance and Bulgarian remained unrewarded. In a 1945 history text book, Samih Nafiz Tansu reverses the European claims of Ottoman corruption of virtues of its subjects by attributing the responsibility for the deterioration of the Ottoman governance in the Balkans to the people of these conquered lands:

> The Ottoman administration, which had been the symbol of law and justice in the fifteenth, sixteenth and the seventeenth centuries, became corrupted under the affects of the corrupted morals of the people of the countries which it had occupied, bribery, corruption, and patronage became very widespread and the leaders began to oppress the people.[53]

The European alienation of the Ottomans from their European lands led not only to resistance and reaction on the part of the Ottoman central elite, who defined their interest according to the state's, but also emboldened the non-Muslim subjects of the Ottoman empire in the Balkans to resist Ottoman sovereignty and strive for independence. In the twentieth century, this alienation forced the Muslim population of the empire in the Balkans to look for other references of identification in order to keep their lands. Mehmet Ali Ayni, who was at that time government inspector, related his conversation with a group of young Muslim Albanians in Yanya (Ioannina) in 1912. These Albanians wanted to dis-identify themselves from the Ottoman element and to prove that, unlike the Ottomans who were destined to be expelled from Europe, Albanian Muslims were the autochthon people of the Albanian lands and therefore, unlike the Ottomans, had the right to live there: 'The European states will drive the Turks from Europe. But we are 'autochthon' and if we unite with you, they will drive us out as well. Therefore we want to stay in our homeland.'[54] This Albanian line of thinking developed as a response to European alienation of the Ottoman and Muslim element from the Balkan territories and resulted in an Albanian claim of being an inalienable part of the soil on which they lived and had been living for time immemorial. This creation of a rooting in the soil as a response to the European threat of expulsion was similarly used by the Turkish national historians for their claims over the Anatolian lands, expressed in the first state-sponsored Turkish History Congress. Afet İnan sought to prove in her paper that the Turks were the 'autochthon people of Anatolia' and that therefore the Turks had an eternal and inalienable right of ownership over the Anatolian soil.[55]

The Ottoman/Turkish elite in some cases adopted the European approach over the Ottoman empire in connection with the civilization of the Ottoman periphery, perceiving the periphery as something which needed to be civilized. The journalist Ahmed Şerif, writing about his travels in the Ottoman provinces for *Tanin*, a newspaper which had a close connection with the İttihad ve Terakki, conceived the Ottoman government's use of force against the rebels in Albania as an important part of a mission of civilising the periphery:

> But the amunition which falls from the rifles and cannons plants the seeds of humanity and civilization in the places where it falls. This is in essence an exalted obligation, but a bitter one in the face of Albanian ignorance, and will be the final obligation in the pages of the fate of Albania.[56]

All the elements discussed so far, the European claim to superiority of civilization and the Ottoman/Turkish responses to this, the centrality of the Balkans within this discourse and the terminology used, can be seen clearly in two particular case studies, those of Greece and Bulgaria.

In the third volume of the history text *Tarih*, prepared for high schools as a part of the nationalistic project of re-writing history according to the needs of the Turkish nation-state, the European support for the Greeks was explained as follows:

> Classical Greek language and literature had been taught for a long time in middle and high schools in European countries such as England, France and Germany. The life of Ancient Greece, dressed up and embellished, was presented as more brilliant and more civilized than it actually was. Ancient Greek philosophers, poets, orators and historians were read and expounded and the exaggerated stories of the Ancient Greek wars were thought of as if true. *In short, most of the literate westerners were lovers of and respectful of Ancient Greece.* While the connection of those calling themselves Greek or *Rum* to Greece and Rome in the nineteenth century was limited to their living in those countries, the western Christians, saturated in hatred of the Turks and the Muslims, showed these rebellious *Rum* as the grandchildren of Plato, Aristotle, Homer, and Demosthenes, but the Ottomans as remnants of barbarians, and an exhilarating, favourable and loving wind blew in favour of the rebels in the whole of western and central Europe; everywhere *Helinosları sevenler* (philhelènes) societies were established; these societies included many priests, poets, politicians, soldiers, conservative or pretentious women, and vagabonds; much aid too was collected. Even the great English poet Byron, after various unseemly events which made it impossible for him to stay in his own country, went to Greece to save the Greeks, and joined the rebels. The famous French poet Victor Hugo wrote a collection of poems praising and eulogizing the Greeks and calumniating the Turks. Some worthless English and French officers even attached themselves to the rebels. In short, throughout Europe various social classes were captivated by philhellenism. This current of thought had its effect on European men of state.[57]

This bitter and sarcastic view of the European perception of the Greeks and the Greek uprising cannot be considered merely as a reaction to Great Power intervention in Ottoman affairs. Although, as discussed earlier, there was an element of resentment over the direct intervention of Europe in the Ottoman territories,[58] here the reference point was not direct intervention, but the European categorization of the Ottomans as barbarians vis-à-vis the Greeks who were considered the representatives of civilization, and therefore a part of Europe. This reaction to the European 'love' for the Greek, which found a reflection in this history text book, was the culmination of the Ottoman, later the Republican, reaction to the European perception of Greeks and Ottomans/Turks within the civilization discourse.

Lord Byron became for the Ottomans and later for the Republican elite, a symbol of blindness and injustice towards Ottoman/Turkish Muslims. His works were regarded as dangerous during the reign of Abdülhamid II, for in 1310/1892, the *Zaptiye Nezareti* (the Ministry of Internal Security) considered three volumes of his works published in 1850 and 1859, to be against the Ottoman empire.[59] Byron, together with Victor Hugo, appeared as the quintessential European reference points for discussion of European inhumanity and hypocrisy in the post-World War I memoirs of Cemal Paşa, the Naval Minister and Commander of the Fourth Army in Syria. In a section on the 'Ermeni Meselesi' (the Armenian Question), in which he sought to justify his own conduct, Cemal Paşa attacked European disinterest in the Armenian massacres of Muslims, a disinterest mirrored in the European disinterest in the Greek massacres of Muslims, both specifically during the Morean uprising and in general: 'The Lord Byrons and Victor Hugos who should recite dirges for those deaths, did not appear for those wretched people because they were Turks and Muslims. These bloody events left no trace other than a few pages in the history books written only by the Ottomans.'[60]

This resentment over the double-standards of the Europeans was also expressed by Ali Reşad: 'The defects and crimes of the [Greek] rebels were not seen: all kinds of virtues were attributed to them because the Europeans regarded the Ottomans as barbarians and they looked on the uprising of the Greeks as if it were the battle of civilization against barbarity.'[61]

Mustafa Kemal himself said in speech in June 1922 that for Europe Turkey was barbarous, brutal and incapable of functioning as a civilized state. This perception justified for European politicians their incitement of the Greek attack and subsequent atrocities against the Turkish population. 'We are' he concluded 'a most wretched people faced by the indifference of the whole civilized world as it watches this bloody struggle in which we are fighting for our lives and for our independence.'[62]

A further aspect of the European representation of Greeks was the connection between the modern inhabitants of the country and the ancient Greeks. This became a target in the Ottoman and Republican response. In 1316/1898, Şemseddin Sami tried to prove that the modern Greeks had very little connection with the ancient Greeks, the founders of "civilization." For him, the contemporary Greek population was an 'intermingling of the descendants of the ancient Greek people and those from the Macedonian, Roman, Avar, Slav, Albanian and other tribes who through the ages had passed through these lands,'[63] while 'the Greek language, famous in the world for its perfection, has, as a result of being mixed with various foreign tongues, and having lost all its eloquence in the process, become the language we today call *Rumca*, a crude and irregular language of imperfection.'[64]

Şemseddin Sami's challenge to the European constructed link between Ancient and modern Greece through his discussion of the impurity of the modern Greek population was repeated by Celal Nuri in his book *Rum ve Bizans*, which he published in 1917.[65] This representation of the modern Greek population became an accepted "fact" in Republican historiography. Nearly 40 years after Şemseddin Sami wrote his description of the modern Greek population, two retired officers, Fahrettin and Seyfi, in a history text on the Morean uprising, defined the Greeks as being 'a nation of mixed-race born of the intermingling of the ancient Greeks, Macedonians, Romans, Avars, Slavs and Albanians.'[66] This mixed-race character of the Greek nation was underlined in the first volume of *Tarih*: 'The people who are today called Greeks are the creation of a later mixing of various races.'[67]

Not only were the Greek race and the establishment of the Greek state evaluated within a civilization paradigm, but so too were later confrontations with the Greek army. Girid Resmolu Mavnahoyuzade Ahmet bin Kasım drew attention to Ottoman soldiers' transporting of injured Greek soldiers to hospitals in the 1897 Ottoman-Greek war as showing the Ottoman soldiers' "Ottoman' (*milli*) virtues which would illuminate the brightest page of the history of civilization.' He added

'The Greeks reacted very barbarously to this generous treatment. But their barbarity of thought could not break even to the slighest degree the civilized propensity of the Ottomans. Every individual acted according to his own character.'[68] Fifteen years later, in another account of the war with the Greeks, Bekir Fikri, an Ottoman officer who took part in the Balkan Wars, emphasized the tyranny of 'the so-called civilized, barbarous Greeks' in the introduction to his translation of what he claimed to be the diary of a Greek sergeant and which he incorporated into his own memoirs.[69] Here, both Girid Resmolu Mavnahoyuzade Ahmet bin Kasım and Bekir Fikri reversed the European paradigm and represented the Greeks as barbarous and uncivilized.

While Greece, in the role of "the other," was used by the Europeans to denote the degradation of Ottoman civilization, the Bulgarian uprising and the Ottoman handling of the issue were used as proof of Ottoman barbarism in practice. In Britain the 'Bulgarian atrocities' became an important issue for the depiction of the Turkish 'barbarities.' In an open air meeting on Summer House Hill, Blaydon-on-Tyne on 30 September 1876, Joseph Cowen, a Liberal Party MP, described the brutality of the Turks, 'the monsters that have created such scenes,' to his audience by comparing the scenes of violence in Lord Byron's well-known poem 'Siege of Corinth' with the 'Bulgarian atrocities,' and concluding that from time to time the latter surpassed the former.[70] Some weeks before Cowen's speech, William Gladstone, the leader of the Liberal Party, then in opposition, published a pamphlet, which was described as an 'indigestible book with a malicious tongue' (garezkâr bir lisanla ağır bir kitap).[71] In it he condemned the Ottoman empire because of the 'Bulgarian atrocities,' which he defined as 'the basest and blackest outrages upon record within the present century, if not within the memory of man.'[72] He also drew a direct correlation between the character of the Turk and these atrocities, beginning his essay by locating the Turk in civilization:

> Let me endeavour very briefly to sketch, in the rudest outline, what the Turkish race was and what it is. It is not a question of Mahometanism simply, but of Mahometanism compounded with the peculiar character of a race. They are not the mild Mahometans of India, nor the chivalrous Saladins of Syria, nor the cultured Moors of Spain. They were, upon the whole, from the black day when they first entered Europe, the one great anti-

human specimen of humanity. Wherever they went, a broad line of blood marked track behind them; and, as far as their dominion reached, civilisation disappeared from view. They represented everywhere government by force, as opposed to government by law. For the guide of this life they had a relentless fatalism: for its reward hereafter, a sensual paradise.[73]

Gladstone's rhetoric was very much related to the needs of internal British politics, and to the relations between the Conservative government under Disraeli and the opposition.[74] During these events, support appeared in various circles for the Bulgarian cause. Lady Strangford, described by George Washburn, who taught for many years in Robert College, as 'especially interested in the people of the Balkan Peninsula,'[75] collected money for the Bulgarians who were the victims of atrocities. Similar support continued after the establishment of the Bulgarian Principality on a political level. A 1907-document from the Ottoman embassy in London lists the names and addresses of 78 members of the Balkan Committee, aiming at 'the annexation to Bulgaria of the *vilayet* of Rumeli which was inhabited by people of Bulgarian origin' (Bulgar unsuruyla meskun Rumeli vilayeti şahanesinin Bulgaristan'a ilhakı). According to this list, 12 of the 78 Committee members were MPs, whose posts were underlined and translated into Ottoman.[76]

There was bitter reaction among Ottomans in the region to this savage criticism. In his memoirs in which he described the Russian-supported Bulgarian atrocities and the forced migration of the Muslims, the *müftü* of Zagora, Hüseyin Raci Efendi asked the European societies for the protection of animals 'when they take the Bulgarian barbarians, who are more abominable than wild beasts, under their protection, in what group of rapacious animals do they classify them?'[77]

British reaction to the Bulgarian events was carefully watched in İstanbul and the government responded accordingly.[78] Moreover, trying to correct this "misinformation" in British public opinion became an important mission for the Young Turks in Europe. In 1903, Ali Haydar Midhat wrote the biography of his father Midhat Paşa, which he first published in English in London. The book had an appendix devoted to 'the Bulgarian Massacres,' based on the correspondence of the British official witnesses to the events, which aimed to demonstrate how the issue was exaggerated and manipulated in the British press which barely mentioned the Muslim victims of the uprising.[79] The same book was later published in both Ottoman and French. In neither version was there a separate appendix on the Bulgarian massacres, demonstrating that the issue became more important within Britain than in France and that the author tailored his narration accordingly.

The late nineteenth-century Ottoman historians did not focus on the European reaction to the 'Bulgarian atrocities.' Ahmet Cevdet Paşa did not touch upon it in his accounts and his explanation for the lack of European support of the Ottoman empire during the Bulgarian uprising was that the Ottoman Sadrazam Mahmud Nedim Paşa, who was under the bad influence of the Russian ambassador, Nicholas Pavlovich Ignatiev, decided not to pay the interest on the Ottoman bonds which were sold on the European market thus causing the decline of support for the Ottoman government.[80] However, in the later period, the Ottoman and Republican historians focused more on the European, especially the British misperception and misrepsentation of the Bulgarian case. Ahmed Rasim summarized the echo of the Bulgarian uprising in Europe: 'The Turks butcher the Christians' (Türkler Hristiyanları kesiyorlar). He wrote that 'the (unjust suffering of the Bulgarians) is being spoken about throughout the whole civilized world' (Bütün cihan medeniyetde (Bulgarların mağduriyeti) nden bahs ediliyordu). He explained this European reaction to such misinformation as being the result both of the Russian conspiracy which revolved round misinforming the European press at the expense of the Ottoman empire, and of the incompetence of the Sadrazam Mahmud Nedim Paşa. According to him, the Europeans were already 'angry' (dilgir) with the Ottoman government due to its decision not to pay the interest on the Ottoman bonds and this helped European acceptance of the Russian propaganda.[81] Later, Gladstone became the symbol of the British and European reaction and emnity against the Ottoman empire, and referring to him automatically brought to mind the 'Bulgarian atrocities' and the European reaction, as is clear from İbrahim Rafet's comment in his 1913 book on Bulgaria: 'Moving the Circassians and Pomaks against the comitadjis, the Ottoman government began to punish them and the Balkans ran with blood. It is thought that the enmity of the Englishman Gladstone began at this time.'[82]

In the 1930s', with the deterioration of relations with Bulgaria, the conflict between the two countries continued at an intellectual level.

Now the discussion did not take place between Turkey and the western powers, but with Bulgaria itself. We can see traces of this discussion among the Turks in the Bulgarian lands, as for example in a 1924 history school text book published in Şumnu (Šumen) in Bulgaria. The author, Osman Nuri (Peremeci) sought to demonstrate the Turkish contribution to civilization. He claimed Arab men of learning as Turks, underlined the existence of a pre-Islamic Turkish literature and set out to explain why the Turks, after accepting Islam, gave up their script and chose Arabic letters and why they chose to write in Arabic and Persian in attempt to prove that this was not due to any Turkish lack of civilization.[83] Eighteen years later, Osman Nuri Peremeci, now a teacher in Edirne, attempted in his book *Tuna Boyu Tarihi* to show how the Bulgarians manipulated the massacres in order to convince the Europeans of the barbarity of the Ottoman government. The only European "villain" to appear in his accounts was Gladstone: 'the famous enemy of Turks and Muslims.'[84]

Ten years before the appearance of Osman Nuri Peremeci's book on Bulgarian history, Halil Yaver, a lawyer who described himself on the cover of his 1938 book, *Balkan Sulhunu Kim Tehdid Ediyor? Bulgarların Balkanları İstilâ Planları* (Who Threatens the Balkan Peace? The Bulgarian Balkan Invasion Plans), as being from the village of Dolna Banya, in the *kaza* of Samakov, in the *sancak* of Sofia in the Danube *vilayet*, published a book entitled *Bugünkü Bulgaristan'da Türk Düşmanlığı. Bulgar Sefiri G. Pavlofa Bir Cevap* (Emnity to the Turk in Today's Bulgaria. An Answer to the Bulgarian Ambassador G. Pavlov). Halil Yaver claimed that in Bulgaria, insulting Turkey had become a tradition. He further attacked the Bulgarian national anthem in which, according to Halil Yaver, the Turks were depicted as 'les hordes farouches.' He then accused the Bulgarian government of being hypocritical since on the one hand it pretended to friendly relations with Turkey, and on the other made plans to insinuate a Bulgarian population into Eastern Thrace.[85] These allegations found echoes in the Bulgarian press. The Turkish embassy in Bulgaria sent summaries and translations of the articles about the book and the author to the Ministry of Foreign Affairs and the Ministry then informed the Prime Minister's Office, sending on the translations with a cover letter which singled out certain points in these articles, one of which was from the newspaper of the Society of Thrace, *Trakia*: 'Tout ceci a laissé des traces profondes dans les âmes du turc peu civilisé et il n'oubliera jamais que c'est le bulgare qui l'a chasse de l'Europe.'[86]

This Bulgarian press coverage seemed to provoke yet a further Turkish response and in 1934, the Edirne MP, Mehmet Şeref, unleashed a vicious and impassioned attack on the Bulgarians:

> This nation, with its crude, unworked, and unrefined soul, without fine arts, with no power of creativity, with hatred of the Turk as the only national culture, raised constantly memorizing poems which explained how the eyes of an Anatolian Turkish soldier crucified on Mahya hill were gouged out, how his nails were pulled out, how his fingers were broken, how his penis was cut off, raised giving constantly fallacious and wrong lessons of this enmity towards the Turks to Bulgarian children in all the books of culture such as reading, history and geography in the schools, never able to add a single brick, a single tile to the great civilized work of humanity in the Balkans, this nation remained as something Medieval in modern civilization, only burning, destructive, tyrannical, narrow minded, of limited mentality, dull of soul, senseless.[87]

As can be seen from these two case studies, the images of these two different uprisings which led to the establishment of nation-states in Ottoman territories carried different weight and importance in late Ottoman and Republican historiography. However, the place of the two cases in the civilization discourse demonstrated that the representation of the establishment of the Balkan nation states became a part of the Ottoman and Republican confrontation with Europe. Every European perception of the Ottoman empire found a reaction among the Ottoman elite, in particular among the Ottoman historians. This "reaction" was carried on into the Republican era as a starting point for the writing of the history of the establishment of the Balkan nation states as well as their consolidation of power at the expense of the Ottoman state. In these cases there was no break in presentation between the empire and the Republic, the historiography of the Republic functioning as if it was the direct inheritor of that of the empire.

The Balkans and Russia

A well-known Turkish proverb says 'You can not have a hide from a bear nor a Russian as a friend.'[88] Although the date of this proverb is unknown, it encapsulates nicely the place of Russia in Ottoman/Turkish historiography on the establishment of nation-states in the Ottoman European territories. The Ottoman-Russian confrontation was, from the eighteenth century onwards, one of the most important topics on which the Ottoman and Turkish historians had inevitably to focus. Direct or indirect Russian involvement in the uprisings and separatist movements which developed in the Ottoman territories in Europe made Russia one of the main actors on the Balkan scene in Ottoman and Republican history-writing. Russia was defined as the number one enemy of the Ottoman empire in Republican historiography.[89]

Russia was not automatically considered as a natural part of European civilization by the Ottoman and Republican elite. Gaspıralı İsmail made a clear distinction between the European and Russian way of life (*maişet*), a term which he used together with civilization (*medeniyet*) as the essential component of his concept of civilization. According to this distinction, Russia was not considered a part of European civilization, and Russian Panslavists contended that European civilization was not desirable for the Russian world.[90] This attitude to Russia's position being outside Europe carried on into the Republican era. In a school text of 1926, Russia was treated not as an intrinsic part of, but rather as a late comer to, European civilization.[91] In the third volume of *Tarih*, the Russian location within Europe was still unclear: on page 217, Russia was considered one of the five European states which had interfered in the internal affairs of the Ottoman empire, while on page 242, Russia was considered separately from Europe.[92] This inconsistency about the place of Russia among the European states may be accounted for by the fact that *Tarih* was the production not of an individual historian but a group of authors. This led, as has been pointed out by Osman Nuri Ergin, to a lack of homogenity and variety of styles throughout the volumes.[93] The end result was that there was no unity of interpretation of Russia's position within or without Europe among the Turkish historians of the 1930s'.

Although the Republican historians were not united over the place of Russia in European civilization, they were agreed on the importance of Russian involvement in the Balkans. Early historians, such as Ahmed Cevdet Paşa, Ahmed Vefik and Lütfiye Hanım, or those who followed their works such as Ali Cevad, regarded Russian involvement in provoking uprisings in the Balkans as paramount. The influence of the Russian ambassador in İstanbul, Ignatiev, for example, on the Ottoman approach to the uprisings in Bosnia-Herzegovina and Bulgaria in 1875 was very much emphasized by Ahmed Cevdet Paşa who also heavily criticized the Sadrazam Mahmud Nedim Paşa for his pro-Russian leanings. Mahmud Nedim Paşa, called 'Nedimof' by his political opponents, submitted so completely to Russian demands that 'he gave his beard into the hands of Russian ambassador Ignatiev.'[94]

While Ignatiev remains a "traditional" representative of Russian political interference and intrigue for Ahmed Cevdet Paşa, for other historians he became a figure rather of Panslavism, of the ideological threat of the Russian empire.[95] Although Russia occupied within the centre-periphery paradigm a position similar to that of the other states involved in Balkan politics, it, unlike the other extra-regional states, developed a powerful ideological bond with the Slavic population of Ottoman Europe through Panslavism which nurtured the idea of unity among all Slavic peoples. Panslavism became the image of Russian infiltration into Ottoman European lands through ideas.

In his history of the late Ottoman empire which was published a few years after his death in 1326-1327/1910, Mahmud Celaleddin Paşa, a minister during Abdülhamid's reign, drew a direct link between the aim of the unification of Slavs and the uprisings in Bulgaria:

> The society founded in Moscow and its branches elsewhere, following their ideas and desire to bring about the establishment of Slav unity, left nothing undone by word or deed in the regions of Bulgaria, Serbia, Bosnia and Montenegro in pursuit of the dreams of establishing a great Southern Slav state on the ruins of Austria and the Ottoman empire whose established governments they strove to topple and obliterate. With that aim, the hearts and minds of the Slavs dependent on Austria were also aroused.[96]

Mahmud Celaleddin Paşa's understanding of Russian policy in the Balkans was very influential on the work of Ahmed Rasim.[97]

The centrality of Russian-sponsored Panslavism in the historians' narration of the position of Russia within the Balkans continued in the later period. In 1337/1921, Köprülüzade Mehmed Fuad wrote:

Russians worked thoroughly using schools, churches, books and newspapers to strengthen the idea of Slavism among Serbs and Bulgarians in the Balkans. These nations living under the Turkish yoke remembered that they had their own past, their own state in the past. Upon finding an opportunity, and with Russian provocation, they revolted.[98]

After the establishment of the Republic, Ali Reşad too, in a more sophisticated style, stressed the importance of Russian Panslavist ambitions.

After the conclusion of the Paris Treaty, the officials of the Slav Union Society, which was established in Russia in 1857 with the aim of stirring up the Slavs in the Balkans into revolt against Turkey, provoked the Bosnian and Herzegovinan Christians and gave a great deal of money for works such as the building of churches and schools. The same propaganda was made among the Bulgarians.[99]

Panslavism continued to be a reference point in the historiography of the 1930s', but the concept of "Turkishness" was also added to the historian's depiction of Russian policy in the Balkans. In the section on the Russians in the Balkans, *Tarih* explains that the Russians

adding a new propaganda of "racial brotherhood" and "Slavism" to the old Christian propaganda, began to stir up the true Slavs such as the Serbs and Montenegrins who were in the majority in the Balkans, and the Bosnians and Bulgarians who although "actually Turks" counted themselves as Slavs due to Russian inculcation against the Ottoman government.[100]

The concept of Panslavism continued to be used as a conceptual tool for narrating not only the nineteenth-century Russian policy in the Balkans but also for analysing the 1930s' developments in the region. The concept now had an interregional significance while the central role of Russia/the Soviet Union had declined. In 1934, the Turkish ambassador in Bucharest, Hamdullah Suphi (Tanrıöver) sent a report to the General Secretary of the Cumhuriyet Halk Partisi, Recep (Peker) on the latest *coup d'état* in Bulgaria. Hamdullah Suphi, after evaluating this event as a victory for Yugoslav and French policy in the region, underlined what was a very important point from the perspective of Turkey, that the political group *Zveno*, which had seized power, was supporting a policy of unification of the Southern Slavs. The leader of this group, Kazanov, declared, while on a visit to Serbia just prior to the coup, that 'the dawn of the ideal of Slav unity in the Balkans is about to break.'[101] This new Panslavist policy led to the decline of Bulgarian claims in Macedonia and created a rapprochement between Yugoslavia and Bulgaria. However, the main target of the new government was now, according to Hamdullah Suphi, the Maritsa valley, which was considered by the Bulgarian authorities as 'a natural area of expansion' for Bulgaria.[102]

Within or without Europe, Russia became a source of a Panslavist image of the Balkans in Ottoman, later Republican, representation. In the 1930s', this idea of Panslavism further took on a regional character and Panslavism became the ideology of the Slav nations in the Balkans. By the 1930s', two different kinds of Panslavism coexisted in the perception of the Republican elite.

Barbarity and Violence

Narrating violence as an inherent part of the image of "the enemy" and portraying this violence, enacted against a group of which the narrator was a member, is one method of creating group unity, which may, in turn, result in a united reaction against the common enemy. Such use of violence narration was not in itself new and indeed was very much present, for example, in fifteenth-century Latin calls for a crusade against the Turkish menace, perceived as threatening the very survival of the Christian world.[103] In the late Ottoman and early Republican era, too, violence narration was important in the Ottoman/Turkish image of the Balkans. Nurturing fear, disgust and hatred through graphic narrations of rape, torture, massacre and assault on the holy places created an image of the Balkans and those elements which formed it, the Bulgarians, Greeks, Montenegrins and Serbians, as an agent of evil in Ottoman/Turkish histories, literary works and memoirs.

Targets of such narration, aimed at canalizing feelings of revenge, varied according to the enemy of the moment. Mahmud Celaleddin Paşa targeted his violence narration on the Bulgarians and in his section on the Bulgarian uprisings of 1876 in *Mirat-ı Hakikat*, he gives many graphic descriptions of torture, massacre and rape in the Muslim villages as well as in those Bulgarian villages which rejected the demands of the Bulgarian rebels. Ahmed Rasim, who continuously referred to *Mirat-ı Hakikat* for the late nineteenth-century events in the empire, focused much less on the Bulgarians and much more on Crete, graphically describing scenes of violence to show the sufferings of the Muslims on the island. He was writing at a period when the discussions over the sovereignty of Crete had reached peak-point. The hot issue now was Crete, not Bulgaria.

The Balkan Wars represented a huge psychological blow for the Ottoman elite. The Ottoman despair, the level of violence associated with these wars and the acute sense of alienation from the Balkans are all expressed in a poem written in that period by Mehmed Akif (Ersoy), himself an Albanian:

> Let the Montenegrin bandit, the Serbian donkey, the Bulgarian snake
> And then the Greek dog encircle our fatherland completely...
> Let them scatter our whole army
> Let them drive us out, taking our lands from us
> Let those without friends or family, fall under the knife,
> Let those who have suffered a thousand calamities be violated...
> One looses honour (*ırz*), one blood.[104]

In the short period during and just after the Balkan Wars, popular journals designed for a wider readership which advocated the strengthening of Turkishness, such as *Genç Kalemler*, *Halka Doğru* and *Türk Yurdu*, all used themes of violence within a religious framework as a symbol of differentiation from the Balkan nations which had formed an alliance against the Ottoman empire.[105] Anger over the defeat in the Balkans spurred such journals on to attempt to draw the people together and wield the Turkish masses into a common unity in the face of this Balkan enemy in order to galvanize and mobilize them to re-conquer the lost lands. One of the ways in which they sought to do this was to stress the violence and, together with this, to underline violence within a religious context. Certain metaphors such as 'crescent' (hilal) versus 'cross' (salib/haç), the victimized Turkish or Muslim girl whose honour was the honour of Muslims, Turks or Ottomans, and the 'imperialistic Christian West' were used repeatedly.

These representations which were used during the Balkan Wars were never forgotten and were reused for individual Balkan states such as Greece in the time of the Turkish National Liberation War. The report prepared by the Ankara government in English on 'Greek Atrocities in Asia Minor' for the international audience describes the atrocities against the Muslim population after the Greek invasion of Anatolia as follows:

> The atrocities perpetrated by the Greeks, since they landed in Smyrna exceed all similar crimes recorded up to now in the annals of history. The Greek soldiery have even violated little girls under eight and old women above seventy years of age. Great is the number of villages which have been burnt down by them, without any military necessity.
> All the sacred institutions and objects of worship which all nations, not excepting the most savages [sic.], are taught and wont to respect, have been polluted by them. The Koran, the sacred book of Mohammedans, has been torn to pieces and its leaves used for the filthiest and most disgusting purposes before the very eyes of Turkish peasants.[106]

The report talks of a 'policy of extermination which Greece has consistently being pursuing, for a very long time, against Turkey' and described 'ferocity' as the 'outstanding feature of Greek policy towards Turkey.'[107] To support this and create a narrative continuity in the Greek position against the Turkish existence in the Balkans and Anatolia and a continuum from the Balkan wars to the Turkish National Liberation War, the report referred to the book written by Bekir Fikri, *Batı Ordusunda Kuvva-i Seyyare yahut Grebene*, on the Balkan Wars and published shortly after the wars in which, according to this report, 'it has been proved by authentic documents that King Constantin, who at the time was Crown Prince, issued an order for the extermination of Turks.'[108] In the post-Liberation War period and on into the 1930s', this narration of violence continued, using much the same imagery as before.

The theme of the suffering Ottoman/Turkish Muslim woman, as both the bearer of the honour (*namus*) of the "community" and the feeble victim of the bloothirstiness of the enemy, was an important part of the image of the Balkans as the barbarous and savage aggressor in

Ottoman/Turkish written memory. Woman was always a very important and powerful metaphor for the honour of the community defined in a sexual sense. Infiltration of the female space was in fact infiltration of the sacred space of the community, defined by its male members. The sexual accesibility of a woman for her husband alone was the main factor in the honour of the community within its religious and traditional system. The fundamental importance of sexual exclusivity is clear from Akyiğitzade's disgust at the right of a feudal lord to spend the first night with his serf's new bride (ilk koca hakkı) practiced in Medieval Europe, which he used to demostrate the decadence of European society.[109]

This honour differed from that of the state which could be lost as a result of the loss of legitimacy and perceived power, leading to the loss of respect of its subjects, and thus its honour. This 'state honour' (devletin namusu) appears in both Ahmed Cevdet Paşa and later in Ahmed Rasim.[110] Although in the real world, the loss of honour for a woman ended with her being ostracized by the community, rendering her "untouchable," in these historical accounts, the woman became the bearer and protector of the honour of the community in spite of her honour having being violated. The "ideal" woman, who was the embodiment of the honour of her Muslim community, becomes a heroine in these accounts by resisting, either successfully or unsuccessfully, and then dying. The actual reality of the situation is thus "purified out," a reality which appears much more starkly, for example, in the memoirs of Falih Rıfkı (Atay), a journalist writing for the newspaper *Akşam* and who in 1922 travelled from İzmir to Bursa with Halide Edib (Adıvar), Yakup Kadri (Karaosmanoğlu), and Mehmed Asım (Us) to investigate the effects of the Greek invasion and withdrawal. In his account of the destruction of Manisa, he discusses the impact of rape on the community:

> And what about the disaster of honour (ırz faciaları)? When it comes to this subject, all the townspeople and villagers remain silent. This disaster of honour is not like a bayonet wound for the women and girls who remain alive. It remains a stain on the lives of those who were virgins, of the widows, and of the married women. We spoke on the road with a 13 or 14 year old village boy. We asked 'Do you have a fiancée?'
> - I did, but...

- Don't you now?
- My fiancée was touched by an infidel.
That is why women and girls try not to talk about their suffering but to strive to have it forgotten.[111]

The reality of the situation is also apparent from the details given in official documents, where the aim was to report events to the government in formulaic terms as in, for example, the account in a document of May 1337/1921 which reported the rape of a 13-year old girl and assault of young village women.[112] Women were not so much forgotten as "reinvented." Heroeification of the victim and the demonization of the enemy go hand in hand in the creation of the "Balkan barbarian."

The narration of sexual violence appears in two forms, one by implication and one graphic and direct. In narration by implication, the author left much to the imagination of the reader. Ahmed Rasim, in his account of the fleeing of the Muslims in Crete into the Ottoman castles, refers to four Muslim girls being seized and taken to the mountains by bandits: 'Only one of these girls was rescued' (Bu kızlardan ancak biri kurtarılabildi). The fate of the three other girls is left unexplained as is the condition of the girl who was rescued.[113] This implication rather than graphic narration of violation was used widely in poems such as Mehmed Emin (Yurdakul)'s 1921 poem, 'Vur' (Strike!), in which the poet called on the 'National Army' to kill those who had violated Muslim women: 'Oh Turk, strike the ones who fashion the shirt of sin for the virgins of the fatherland.'[114] The absence of blatant imagery and use of implication had a very powerful impact on the minds of people in creating a "barbarous Balkans."

Another way of narration was very graphic and did not leave any space for imagination. This narration was much more personal in approach giving often the names of the individual assaulted and the names of their villages and towns:

Three of these [Bulgarian soldiers] entered the home of Hüseyin Bey. They bound the arms of this poor trembling man and his trembling son-in-law, Yusuf Bey, and raped Hüseyin Bey's wife and daughter before their very eyes. Then cutting of their ears and their fingers one by one, they killed the two women in front of their husbands.[115]

In this narration, sexual violence did not finish with the death of the victim: 'They [the Bulgarian rebels] executed the director (müdür) of the district (nahiye) of Avratalan, his wife and children, his scribe and his guards and after the murder of the director's daughter, cutting off her genitalia, they exhibited them like a bracelet.'[116] In a 1933 book, the Montenegrins were depicted as conducting similar practices on the corpses of the Ottoman soldiers: 'They [the Montenegrins] put the fingers of martyrs, which they cut off, on their chests two by two like a cross and cut off the penises of some and placed them in their mouths.'[117]

A woman might be penetrated but what made her more honourable was that she resisted, even if such resistance was futile. Bekir Fikri, who uses what he claims to be the diary of a Greek sergeant in which the sergeant narrated his sexual assaults on Muslim women and girls, underlined his admiration for the resistance put up by the Muslim women in order to 'remain honourable' even in the worst conditions.[118] In Halide Edib's story 'Emine'nin Şahadeti' (The Martyrdom of Emine), based on an investigation in the region between Bursa and İzmir conducted in 1922 by a group of Turkish journalists and writers in which Halide Edib took part, Emine, who died while fighting back to protect her husband and her honour, becomes the symbol of the Muslim-Turkish woman who resisted the violation of the enemy. Her husband described her tragic death: 'Emine saved me and her honour, but for that I was left, and she died.'[119] Resistance was not to be limited only to rape but was to be applied to any kind of exposure of the body or any activity which would carry sexual connotations, such as dancing. In 1920, Mehmed Emin (Yurdakul) in his poem, 'Aydın Kızları' (The Maidens of Aydın), described the Greek invasion and the sexual offences carried out by the Greek soldiers against the girls and women of Aydın. In this poem, sexual offence was not only penetration but also forcing the girls to dance in front of the soldiers: 'In these nights of chaos, they demanded disgusting sex from us, in the bloody gardens of death, they said to us 'dance, play!''[120] Mehmed Şeref, in his depiction of the torture of young Turkish women and girls by putting cats into their shalwars, felt pride for these women who did not take off their shalwars since they were ashamed of showing their bodies.[121]

Ömer Seyfeddin, who took part as an officer in the Balkan Wars and was taken prisoner by the Greeks, wrote a story 'Beyaz Lale,' published in 1330/1914 in *Donanma Mecmuası*,[122] utilizes graphically all the symbolism of violence. Such violence was familiar to an Ottoman audience who had either witnessed the effects of such violence or had read about it in newspapers or other publications about the atrocities perpetrated on the Muslim population of the Balkans during and just after the Balkan Wars. Such publications included books published by the Rumeli Muhacirin-i İslamiye Cemiyet-i Hayriyesi (The Charitable Organization for Migrants from Rumeli) on the atrocities commited by the Bulgarians and their allies in Bulgaria and Macedonia. These books gave very vivid descriptions of violence and torture - extending from ripping fezes from the heads of Muslims to plundering, forced conversion and rape.[123] One book published in 1329/1913 included pictures depicting various scenes of violence narrated in the text. One picture was of the public exhibition of a Muslim man in Kavala whose eyes had been gauged out and whose lips and nose cut off.[124]

Ömer Seyfeddin's story, which brings together many such accounts of violence, tells of the obsessive and futile attempt of a Bulgarian officer, Radko Balkaneski, sexually to possess Turkish-Muslim Lale, 'the most beautiful girl of Serez (Siroz),' called 'Beyaz Lale' (White Tulip) because of her beautiful white skin.[125] Lale resisted Balkaneski in order to protect her honour at the expense of her own life. Balkaneski represents the Balkans, the symbol of blind imitation of the West, of western materialism and clinical rationalism[126] and of imitation of a European life style in which it had no place.[127] Balkaneski was also alien to the Orient, despite his "Orientalist" dream of Lale as a concubine in his harem, the space which for him symbolizes both sexual fantasy and mystic peace.[128]

In the story, both Lale and her father display a willingness to trust Balkaneski. Believing that the Balkan armies would bring democracy and civilization to Serez (Siroz) - which did not in fact offer much resistance to the Bulgarian forces[129] - the father decided to stay rather than join the retreating Ottoman army, and was subsequently killed by Balkaneski. Lale, trusting Balkaneski's reassurances that no harm would come to her, opened the door of the house to him. During her struggle with him, she thinks:

What should she do? What should she do now? The disgusting spittle of this enemy who held nothing sacred was smeared over every part of her body. Her honour was being stripped away by force. Her cries went unanswered, no help could reach her. So she was to be the object of the most filthy, most disgusting enjoyment of this wild animal. No, no, no...[130]

Lale decided to commit suicide rather than accept penetration by the enemy. However, even in death she was not spared as the 'devil' Balkaneski raped her corpse. Lale, who in death resembled 'an angel in heaven who had fallen asleep while praying to God,'[131] paid for naiveness and belief in the sweet words of Balkaneski, opening the door to him, but saved her honour in death. Balkaneski's rape of Lale's dead body symbolizes the Balkan rape of the Ottoman empire in Europe and its futility. Balkaneski's portrayal is of a Balkans with no moral boundaries, only uncurbed and uncontrollable desire. This story also carries an admonition for the Turks: they should not be fooled into forgetting who they were. Although school texts from the 1930s' onwards avoided using open depictions of violence, Ömer Seyfeddin's stories, including 'Beyaz Lale' were among the readings suggested for school children by the Ministry of Education.

In a more general sense, violence, as in torture and brutality, was in itself essential to these narrations. The impact of such descriptions of violence was enormous in particular when it involved children. The graphicness of such descriptions was overwhelming in, for example, Mehmet Şeref's 1934 account of the violence of the Bulgarians against Muslim children during the Bulgarian uprising:

> They impaled up to 150 little ones, only six months old, or one or two years old, on objects such as long bayonets, knives, stakes... As their tiny bodies were in the throes of death, while trembling, their blood flowed, these hordes of barbarians held them up in the air, jigging around, dancing, and these little ones died under a sky stained blood red.[132]

This level of violence narration is evident also in the writings of Ahmed Rasim in the earlier part of the century. Writing about Crete in 1284/1867, Ahmed Rasim described how 'in one of these battles, bandits seized a soldier, Çilingir Mustafa, alive and first cut off his hands, and cut open his chest and tore out his heart and then they scalped him and he became a martyr.'[133]

Ahmed Rasim's book was written as a school text book. This kind of graphic imagery in the school texts was used in the later period as a powerful tool to convey the sufferings and injustices inflicted on the Turks by their enemies. İhsan Şeref wrote a primary school text book in 1926 which included the following account of Greek violence during the National Liberation War:

> Cursed [Greek soldiers] incinerated our beautiful villages on the shores of the Marmara. They plucked out the eyes of the innocent villagers not sparing the women, the girls or even the babes in swaddling clothes, they cut off their ears, their noses, their breasts, they ripped open their stomaches, and all that in the world can be called barbarous they did.[134]

Well before İhsan Şeref, Kamil Paşa used similar imagery to describe the brutality of Serbian rebels under the leadership of Kara Yorgi: 'Serbian bandits who were not satisfied by attacking the Muslims in the town of Belgrade and killing [all] males, perpetrated barbarous actions such as ripping open the stomachs of pregnant women and taking their babies out.'[135] By the 1920s', the narration of violence perpetrated against the Turks had become normal in school text books. The essential element was Turk/Muslim as innocent victim, regardless of time or enemy. In a school history text book published in 1929 for the fifth year of primary school, the authors use similar simplistic descriptions of violence, regardless of the period discussed. While the Greeks 'cut the Turks to pieces and plundered their homes and property' during the Morean uprising,[136] the Bulgarians, Greeks, Serbians and Montenegrins 'burned and destroyed the places they entered. They strangled people without pity' in the First Balkan War.[137] The same authors, in their school history text book for the fourth year of primary school, also describe the Greek invasion of İzmir. Having invaded İzmir and joined up with the Armenians and indigenous Greeks, '[the Greeks] unjustly killed the Turkish youths and plundered their shops and houses.'[138]

Injustice and innocence became an integral part of this violence narration which stressed the inhuman barbarity perpetrated on an innocent victim. Victimization and innocence of individuals was now much more prominent than in the nineteenth-century accounts in which injustice is seen as being against the state rather than against the innocent individual. This contrasts with the 1930s' when such graphic violence narrations were largely absent from school text books: the state was now interested in ensuring that the population forgot the violence of the recent past, but not the injustices.

Another major theme in violence narration was the assault on the Muslim holy places. These holy places were considered an integral part of the very identity of the Muslims/Turks and they tied the Muslim/Turkish population to their land. The existence of such holy places signified the right of Muslim existence on this Muslim soil. Fear and terror of infidel contamination of places held sacred by the community is a universal theme. In the fifteenth century, the fall of Constantinople was seen by many Latin contemporaries in terms of horror at the Muslim dominance of Christian holy places. Piccolomini, later Pope Pius II, wrote of his suffering at 'the thought that the church of Santa Sofia, most famous in all the world, has been destroyed and desecrated, that the numerous basilicas dedicated to the saints, true works of art, have been reduced to ruins and contaminated by the filth of Muhammad.'[139] This revulsion was reversed in the twentieth-century Ottoman/Turkish-Muslim popular culture, historiography and literature as the Muslims wept for the desacration of their holy places in the Balkans. Kazım Nami Duru, a member of the İttihad ve Terakki who became an important educationist and school text book writer in the Republican era, quoted popular folk songs from the 1910s', telling of the grief of the Muslim people over the loss of the Balkan lands, and the conversion of mosques to churches.[140] Mosques were sometimes defiled in more dramatic ways. In Ömer Seyfeddin's short story 'Beyaz Lale,' Balkaneski ordered his men to convert the Gazi Evrenos mosque into a stable for army packhorses and the Halil Paşa mosque into a depot for 'pork pastrami' (domuz pastırmaları),[141] echoing here Piccolomini who lamented the use of the sanctuaries and abodes of monks as brothels.[142]

Mosques and graveyards were the material proof of the existence of the Muslims and Ottomans in the Balkans, and their destruction was perceived as a conscious attempt to erase this proof. The Republican government watched the assaults on the Muslim holy places carefully. A letter dated September 1933 from the Turkish embassy to the Ministry of Foreign Affairs informing Ankara of the assault on a shrine in Deliorman in Bulgaria by a group of Bulgarian youths, interpreted the event as a demonstration of the Bulgarian feeling of alienation from the newly conquered territory:

We have already informed you of the attacks perpetrated from time to time on this shrine (türbe) and of searches for skeletons made by digging inside it. Bulgarians, who still feel themselves foreigners after 50 years of Bulgarian rule in the region of Deliorman, are trying to take revenge by destroying any traces left of Turkish sovereignty and of the Turkish majority.[143]

İhsan Şeref sums up the totality of violence: 'No soul remained in Rumeli no honour (namus), bells were hung above our mosques and our 1,000-year old graves had been opened.'[144]

The Intellectual Contribution of the Balkans

A less violent image of the Balkans which appears in Ottoman/Turkish history-writing was that of being a source of ideas. Such ideas could be perceived both as dangerous and seditious, and as a source of inspiration for nationalist policies for some of the Ottoman and Republican elite.[145] In *Tarih-i Siyasiye-i Devlet-i Aliye-i Osmaniye* (The Political History of the Ottoman State), Kamil Paşa underlines the importance of books for the dissemination of ideas of "independence" in the Greek schools and their significance in the creation of support among the Orthodox population of the empire for a Greek uprising. He also points to the failure of the Ottoman state to control these publications:

> On account of both the government's failure to take the Greeks seriously and the bigotry of the times preventing education in a foreign language, there was no one among the people of Islam able to examine and understand the detrimental books and pamphlets which were being studied in the Greek schools, and therefore the officials of the state were unaware of the Greek plans.[146]

The Abdülhamidian government of which Kamil Paşa was a member, was not, however, unaware as its predecessors had been, and control of publications from outside the borders of the Ottoman empire was an important part of the attempt to control the flow of dangerous ideas. Kamil Paşa, as the governor of the *vilayet* of Aydın, was actively involved in this process. A coded telegram dated 1322/1906 from the Babıali contained the order of the Minister of Internal Affairs, Memduh

Paşa, to Kamil Paşa, concerning the banning of all Greek (Yunan) newspapers from entering the Ottoman empire, since these newspapers were publishing articles aimed at inciting the Greek (Rum) subjects of the Ottoman empire.[147] Not only political issues but also economic matters were sometimes conceived of as a threat to the interests of the Ottoman empire. The French newspaper, '*Economist*' was banned because it was seen as containing articles against the sultanate.[148]

The perception of threat was not limited to publications from outside the Ottoman borders or in foreign languages within the empire. The real threat from the Balkans, however, stemmed from newspapers published in Turkish by Ottoman and Turkish subjects there.[149] The Abdülhamidian government both used a wide-ranging spy system to collect information and to keep the opposition under surveillance in the Balkans, and tried to control the entrance of these anti-regime publications into Ottoman domains. *Uhuvvet*, a newspaper published in Rusçuk (Ruse) by Rusçuklu Mehmed Teftiş, was banned, and, according to the order of the Minister of Internal Affairs, Memduh Paşa, to the governor of Aydın, Kamil Paşa, its dissemination was never to be allowed and any copies already received were to be collected and destroyed.[150] Another newspaper *Sada-i Millet*, published in Sofia, was banned even before its copies arrived in Ottoman controlled lands by a telegram from the Ministry of Internal Affairs to Kamil Paşa stressing that no copies should be allowed to cross the Ottoman borders.[151]

Fear of the danger presented by published material from the Balkans continued during the İttihad ve Terakki government. The entry of the newspaper, *Balkan*, published in Turkish in Filibe (Plovdiv), was banned by the cabinet, Meclis-i Vükela, since the content of the newspaper was found to be 'unsuitable' (gayr-i münasib).[152]

The Ankara government also banned publications from neighbouring Balkan countries which were considered a threat. In the event of any such banned publications continuing to be brought into the country, those involved in bringing them in were, on occasion, to be taken to the İstiklal Mahkemesi (Independence Tribunal). *Politiki Erena* [*sic*.], which was published in Greece and brought into İstanbul, was thus threatened with court action.[153] The newspaper *Rizospastis* was another publication from Greece which was banned from Turkey on the pretext that it spread communism.[154]

Despite all these precautions, the Balkans continued, for the Turkish Republic, to be a threat to the very survival of the state, due to its ability to act as a haven for anti-regime and anti-reform Turkish opposition. Certain Turkish and Muslim elements in the Balkans, either from the region or those who had escaped or been exiled to it, were perceived as threats to the reforms undertaken in Turkey because of their publications. The Cabinet banned entry into Turkey of the Turkish language newspapers *Posta* from Gümülcine (Komotene),[155] *Hakikat* and *İmdad* from Selanik (Thessaloniki)[156] and *İ'tilâ* from İskeçe (Xanthi) due to their detrimental contents.[157] Another newspaper, *Koca Balkan*, published in Filibe (Plovdiv) in Bulgaria, was banned entry into Turkey due to an article, 'Yaşasın Şapka' (Long Live the Hat), which was against wearing the hat in Turkey and was considered by Turkish authorities as 'total incitement' (serapâ ifsadât).[158]

The attention of the Turkish embassy in Bucharest was drawn to a pamphlet entitled 'Kuranımızı Bağrımıza Basarak Geliriz' (We come holding our Kuran to our breast), written by Hafız Latif who was a preacher at the Hünkar Cami in Mecidiye in Romania, since its content was considered to be against the Turkish regime. According to a document dated 3 December 1932, the embassy contacted the Romanian Ministry of Foreign Affairs whereupon the Minister himself expressed his regret over this incident and assured the Turkish embassy that all necessary steps to deal with the situation would be taken.[159] Seven months later, according to another document, the Turkish embassy was still trying to take action against Hafız Latif. The embassy especially wished to prevent his publishing a newspaper called *Doğru Yol* (The Right Path), and to stop his propaganda against the use of the Latin script in Turkey.[160]

Not only was any campaign against Latin letters conceived of as a threat to the Turkishness propagated by the Kemalist regime, but this applied too to merely rejecting their use. In a petition submitted to the Prime Minister İsmet İnönü requesting an increase in the amount of aid from the Turkish government for their newspapers, three Turkish journalists and newspaper owners in Bulgaria, Mehmet Lütfi Takanoğlu, the owner of newspaper *Rodop*, Mahmut Necmettin Deliorman, the owner of the newspaper *Deliorman*, and A. Hilmi Turgut from the newspaper *Halk Sesi* drew the Prime Minister's attention to the danger posed by a certain printing house which was publishing in Arabic script. This printing house had been established by Hüseyin Hüsnü Hoca, whose 'position as head *müftü* made him an extremely useful tool of the government' (hükümetin müthiş bir aleti olan başmüftülük makamı), Arif Hikmet, Arif Oruç and others, who were referred to as 'traitors' (hainler), and was regarded as particularly threatening since its aim was to print school texts.[161] In 1936, Yaşar Nabi (Nayır), an important writer and publisher of the Republican era, expressed his anger towards Hüseyin Hüsnü, whom he described as a loyal servant of the Bulgarian government,[162] over his policies, including readopting the Arabic script for Turkish schools in Bulgaria. According to Yaşar Nabi, this further created a division between the Turks living in villages and those in towns, since the schools in towns continued to use the Latin alphabet, while those in villages re-adopted the Arabic script. This division within the Turkish minority served the Bulgarian policy of assimilating the Turks by providing education in Bulgarian as an alternative.[163] Indeed, the Bulgarian authorities used this rift among the Turkish minority in order to counter Kemalist propaganda in Bulgaria.[164] For this purpose the Bulgarian government supported the use of the Arabic alphabet in the Turkish schools and it was only in 1938 that the Bulgarian government took the decision to make the use of the Latin alphabet in Turkish schools compulsary.[165] This decision, however, did not solve this problem over the Latin alphabet.[166] The Turkish authorities adopted different methods in order to spread the Latin alphabet among the Turkish minority in Bulgaria, sending Turkish type faces, for example, for newspapers such as *Rodop* and *Turan*. In 1933, the Turkish ambassador in Sofia, Tevfik Kamil Bey, wrote to the Prime Minister's Office asking for the type faces requested by the newspaper *Turan* to be put in two boxes, each weighing 40 kilos. The boxes should be labelled 'furniture' so as not to 'attract the attention' of the Bulgarian authorities and to avoid any problems over the quota assigned to the embassy for the amount of material it was able send.[167]

The Turkish authorities constantly perceived anti-Kemalist publications outside the Turkish borders as a threat and kept them under continous surveillance as they did, for example, with the newspaper *Balkan*, published in Gümülcine (Komotene), which, in a Turkish document, was defined as 'the centre of activity of the '150'likler' [i.e. those expelled by the Turkish authorities] and the fugitives,'[168] and banned by the cabinet in 1341/1925 'due to its detrimental content' (münderecât-ı muzırrasına binâen).[169] In 1932, a copy of the newspaper dated 4 October 1932 was sent to the Prime Minister's office with a cover letter stipulating that *Balkan* was published by 'fugitives' (firariler). This issue contained an article, 'Ankaracılar Okusun' (Let those supporters of Ankara read this), about elections in Greece. In this article, while Greece was praised and all Greeks were regarded as victors due to the fact that their election system had functioned successfully, the Kemalist regime was criticized as being autocratic.[170] Concern about and awareness of anti-Kemalist propaganda was not restricted to official circles. Yaşar Nabi also drew attention to this propaganda and to the Greek government's turning a blind eye to it: 'The traitors who had fled from Turkey, even up until recently, found opportunities to spread their seditious propaganda freely among the Turks of western Thrace.'[171]

While the Balkans were then perceived as a constant source of dangerous propaganda, for some of the Ottoman/Turkish elite, on the other hand, they provided inspiration for their idea of national identity and nationalist policies. The end of the Balkan wars ushered in a period of questioning of beliefs, ideas and policies, all of which had failed to prevent the dissolution of the empire, and the enemy was examined in an attempt to find out what had gone wrong with the Ottoman empire. The traumatic experience of the war paved the way for serious questioning of the idea of Ottomanism. In a story called 'Hürriyet Bayrakları' dated 1913, Ömer Seyfeddin questioned the viability of Ottomanism by narrating the apathy of the Bulgarian villagers to the celebration of the "civic" festival of 10 Temmuz (10 July) in 1910, taken as the beginning of the second constitutional period and the end of the "Abdülhamidian tyranny."[172] Three years before the publication of this story, Ahmed Şerif wrote in *Tanin*, an important pro-İttihad ve Terakki newspaper published by Hüseyin Cahit (Yalçın), Tevfik Fikret and Hüseyin Kazım in the post-1908 period, about the disinterest of the Christian Serbs and Muslim Bosnians living in the village of Berane and Tergovişte over celebrating 10 Temmuz.[173] Despite the similarity of these two scenes, the approaches to this apathy of the villagers to the 10 Temmuz reflected the different convictions of these two authors about Ottomanism. While Ömer Seyfeddin wondered why the Bulgarian villagers should have a reason to celebrate something which did not mean anything to them, and thus condoned their apathy, Ahmed Şerif was unhappy with this apathy and angry over this 'ignorance' of the villagers who did not understand the importance of this Ottoman day of 'liberation.'[174]

In Ömer Seyfeddin's stories, the Bulgarian national consciousness was an important example which the Turks should imitate. Although in these stories the Bulgarian characters were generally depicted as evil and heartless, as in the case of 'Beyaz Lale,' they were also admired due to their patriotism and excessive conviction, which could even lead them to death. His 1918 story, 'Nakarat,' was an important example of using a Bulgarian character as an antithesis to the Ottoman character who did not have national feelings. In this story, a young Ottoman officer in Macedonia in 1903-1904 felt a burning desire and love for a Bulgarian girl, the daughter of a dead priest. The girl seemed to be responding to his love by continuously singing a song, 'Naş naş Çarigrad naş.' The officer imagined that this was a love song for him, and he started to repeat the rhyme to himself. He later learnt, however, that it in fact meant 'İstanbul will be ours.' The officer was shaken by this and led to the realization of the futility of his life in comparison with that of the Bulgarian girl, who was more nationally conscious than him although she was Bulgarian and a woman. The story ended with his self-examination:

> So, for one week I have been lying thinking about the difference between me and the bold daughter of the priest of the revolutionary committee (komita) who died in the forest of Vehelmefçe for an idea he held sacred.
> So (İşte), for one week... [175]

While Bulgaria was an example of national consciousness for the nationalists, it was also an example of rationality for the positivists. For Abdullah Cevdet, the Bulgarians were winning the Balkan War because

> they had worked 30-odd years, they had strengthened their race, they had been busy with reorganization and carrying out good administration, they had prepared the conditions for victory and independence. They had faith in the fatherland (vatan), liberty and in their country having a future.

In contrast, Turkish school children were instructed by order of the Bab-ı Meşihat (the Office of the Şeyhülislam) to repeat a prayer 4,444 times in order to ensure the success of the Ottoman army: 'Our skulls' he wrote 'have been emptied. Within our skins no flesh, no bone or blood remained. No villager remained in our villages, no village remained for our villagers. Anatolia has been emptied. Anatolia is ill, Anatolia is dying.'[176]

In the Republican era, too, the Balkan countries continued to be examples referred to by the Republican elite. In 1928, Tekin Alp (Moise Cohen) in his book *Türkleştirme* (Turkification) in which he attempted to develop a methodological approach to the Turkification policies which the state should implement, conceived of the Balkan countries as successful examples of 'nationalization' (millileştirme), that is making their inhabitants adopt one state-imposed national identity regardless of their ethnic origins:

> Shining and decisive examples for "adaptation" were found in all the Balkan countries such as Bulgaria, Greece and Romania. I myself know many people in Greece who are in origin Vlach, Bulgarian or Albanian and who have been completely "Greekified" by means of nationalization. They speak Greek as their mother tongue but at home they can only speak with their old mothers and fathers in Vlach or Bulgarian. Such men can often be met among the heads of the financial and economic institutions, and even among the high officials of state. There are many around them who know their genealogical tree, but no one looks down on them. They see no need to hide their origins.[177]

Eight years later, Yaşar Nabi, an important figure of the Republican intellectual elite, seemed to accept *a priori* the naturalness of national homogenisation policies in the Balkan countries. What he proposed was to further these policies in both the Balkan countries and in Turkey by encouraging the Turkish and Muslim minority groups to migrate to Turkey while proposing the exchange of the Greeks living in İstanbul with the Turks in Western Thrace.[178] The Balkans thus created a positive and a negative image, or sometimes both, depending on the self-perception of the Ottoman/Republican elite whose perceptions were determined according to their own needs and priorities.

Vatan and the Danube

'Dying for the *vatan* (fatherland)'(vatan uğruna can vermek) became one of the well-repeated clichés of history-writing in the last quarter of the nineteenth century, used by Ahmed Vefik Paşa and Ali Cevad.[179]

Ahmed Cevdet Paşa discussed the concept of *vatan* in connection with European usage of the fatherland and compared its power with the power of religion over the Muslim soldiers. He approached the concept of *vatan* very pragmatically, arguing that *vatan* for the Muslim soldier was the 'square' (meydan) in his village, and he concluded that the idea of fatherland could provide neither the motivation nor the belief necessary to inspire soldiers to fight and die which Islam did.[180] For Namık Kemal, however, later known as 'the poet of the fatherland' (vatan şairi), the love for *vatan* was the dominant love throughout the history of mankind, in every religion, every *millet*, every system of upbringing and education (terbiye), and every civilization, and, for him, what made a land a *vatan* was the corpses of those who had died for it: 'We gave one precious soul for every stone of the land in which we live. For us every handfull of its soil is a reminder of the body of a hero who was sacrificed for it. For us our land is beyond comparison with the *vatan* of China or Siberia.'[181]

Namık Kemal's vagueness of definition of *vatan* provides a kind of elusiveness that was transferred to the later period and paved the way for the different interpretations of the term. What was the *vatan*, where were its borders, what made a land a *vatan*, were all questions the answers to which changed from period to period, from individual to individual. But what was sure was that *vatan* was not limited to the political borders of the state; it might coincide with them in some cases, but the imagination of the *vatan* was not circumscribed by them.

For the historian Murad Bey, who migrated in 1873 from Dagistan to the Ottoman empire in his youth, the *vatan* of the Muslims was not bordered by 'mountains and streams' as depicted, according to him, in the history books, but that land inhabited by Muslims and especially the centre of the caliphate, that is İstanbul.[182] Ziya Gökalp, in his nationalist phase after the defeat of the First World War, idealized *vatan* in his 1918 poem,'Vatan,' as a Turkified and homogenized place where the Quran was recited in Turkish in the mosques and where capital, technology and science were all in the hands of the Turks.[183]

The borders of an imagined fatherland often exceeded the legal borders of the states, such as in the vision of a Greater Greece, Bulgaria or Serbia. In the Ottoman/Turkish case the imagined fatherland, exceeding the borders of the state was very well exemplified by the concept of Turan, "sloganized" in 1326/1911: '*Vatan* for the Turks is neither Turkey nor Turkistan/ *Vatan* is a big and limitless country:

Turan.'[184] However, in some cases, contrary to the idea of expansion, the *vatan* was smaller than the existing boundaries of the state in the minds of the early twentieth-century public and elite. *Vatan* was clearly an important concept for Mahmud Şevket Paşa, the Sadrazam and Minister of War who lectured Said Paşa in 1913 on the need to sacrifice everything for it when trying to persuade Said Paşa not resign from the Cabinet.[185] Yet his *vatan* was smaller than the actual Ottoman state for he was willing to hand over Kuwait and Qatar to the British, defining them as useless desert: 'We could not quarrel with England because of two districts (kaza) consisting only of desert like Kuwait and Qatar. What kind of benefit could we receive from these insignificant lands?'[186] His pragmatic approach, which was based not on the idea of the integrity of the fatherland but on the calculation of profit and loss, can be seen also in his attitude to Albania and Edirne.[187]

The shrinkable or expandable character of the borders of the *vatan* can be seen during the period in which the İttihad ve Terakki was in power after 1913. The Ottoman government entered into negotiations with Bulgaria in 1915 to try and persuade the Bulgarian government to declare war on the side of the Axis powers. Enver Paşa, who hoped for the expansion of Ottoman lands as a result of the war, contemplated giving Kırkkilise (modern Kırklareli), then part of Ottoman territory, to Bulgaria in return for her entry into the war.[188] In the same period, the people questioned the relevance of Yemen to their *vatan*. Many Anatolian and Balkan folk songs mourned the futile deaths of their soldiers in Yemen and questioned the reason for such dying. In a folk song from Erzincan, the woman who sent her husband to Yemen asks: 'What is Yemen to us?' (Yemen bizim neyimize?)[189]

With the creation of the Republic, the concept of the *vatan* was made to coincide with the political borders. The new state was anxious to give out a message of being contented with the existing state frontier and of their being no Turkish wish for expansion. *Vatandaş İçin Medenî Bilgiler* (Civil Knowledge for the Citizens), written by Afet [İnan] who relied heavily on the notes of Mustafa Kemal, describes how the Turkish *vatan* had been very large but was now enclosed, contently, within the contemporary state boundaries: 'there was no continent which did not become part of the Turkish *vatan*. The whole world, Asia, Europe, Africa became the homeland (yurt) of the ancestors of the Turks... But the modern Turkish nation (millet) is content with the homeland (yurt) it now has... Our fatherland (vatanımız) is the homeland within the present political boundaries.'[190] On 19 May 1944, the anniversary of Mustafa Kemal's landing in Samsun and the date accepted as the beginning of the Turkish National Liberation War and later celebrated as 'Gençlik ve Spor Bayramı' (The Festival of Youth and Sports), the President İsmet İnönü, in need of distancing the regime from every fascist tendency within the country due to the imminent end of the war, addressed Turkish relations with its neighbouring countries and underlined Turkey's contentment with its existing borders:

> On the day on which the national liberation came about we were friends only with the Soviets and all our neighbours kept alive in their minds all the memories of old hatreds. In everybody's mind was the thought that if we regained a little strength we would give ourselves up to an adventurist and aggressive policy. The Republic perceived one of the fundamental conditions for a strong civilized way of living as being the existence of an atmosphere of security within the family of nations. It counted the ensuring of good and sincere neighbourly relations with its neighbours which had recently separated from the empire as necessary for the happiness of the nation.[191]

This approach enabled the state to give up Mosul. It was, however, very much the result not of an ideological conviction about *vatan* but a pragmatic realization of the realities of political power. This too can be seen in the annexation of Hatay. But whether this was in reality a reflection of what the elite emotively felt about their *vatan* is another matter. Certainly, some of the elite had a vision of *vatan* which was not necessarily bounded by the political borders of the new state. An important minister under İsmet İnönü, Hasan Âli Yücel, revealed his yearning for the Danube in his poem, 'Tuna Türküsü' (The song of the Danube) in which he spoke of 'my beautiful homeland' (güzel yurdum) and his constant pain of seperation.[192]

The flexibility of the concept of *vatan* allowed the Danube to become an integral part of the imagination of the *vatan* regardless of the geo-political borders of the late Ottoman empire or Turkish Republic. The Danube, for Braudel one of the double frontiers of Europe, the other being the Rhine,[193] obtained a pivotal position in the Ottoman/Republican imagination of *vatan*. İslam Bey, the heroic character of Namık Kemal's well-known first play *Vatan Yahut Silistre*

(Fatherland or Silistria) of 1873 made a speech to boost the spirits of his compatriots who were going to fight in Silistre (Silistria in northeast Bulgaria) against the Russians:

> Friends, we are going to the banks of the Danube! The Danube is for us the water of life. If the Danube were to go, our *vatan* could not live. If our *vatan* does not live, no one can live in the *vatan*...God orders us to love the *vatan*. Our *vatan* means the Danube. Because, if the Danube is lost, *vatan* will not remain... Wherever the earth is turned on the banks of the Danube, a bone of your father or your brothers is found. The soil which rises through the churning waters of the Danube is the chemical essence of the bodies of those who have died to protect it. [194]

Although the Danube was part of Ottoman territory when this play was written, it was lost with the establishment of the Bulgarian state and never formed part of the territory of the Turkish Republic. However the longed-for and idealized Danube continued to be a part of the imagined Turkish fatherland into the 1930s' and unlike any other geographical location, mountain or river, became an extension of the Turkish fatherland in literary works, memoirs, and histories of the period. *Vatan Yahut Silistre* was republished in 1931. The Ottoman play remained unchanged, except for sometimes replacing the word Ottoman with Turk, and the Danube kept its central place as the 'water of life' in the now Turkish *vatan*.[195]

Ahmed İhsan (Tokgöz), the well-known publisher of the late Ottoman and early Republican era, wrote in the introduction to his book about his week long journey along the Danube: 'It is impossible for our hearts not to tremble when we recall the name of the Danube which was the scene of very important and terrible events in the history of our existence.'[196] The deep significance of the Danube in the late Ottoman empire and the early Republican era comes out clearly in the memoirs of Yahya Kemal Beyatlı, the well-known Turkish poet and MP in the Republican parliament, who was originally from Üsküp (Skoplje). In an article published in 1337/1921, he wrote:

> If a river exists in the heart of a Turk, that river is the Danube, if there is a mountain, it is the Balkan range. Forty three years have elapsed since the separation from the banks of the Danube and the

foothills of the Balkan range. But can even long centuries wipe from our hearts those waters and those snow caped foothills? I do not know. Do you think this longing exists only in the hearts of the children of Rumeli? Does not a Turk from Diyarbakır who has never set foot on the soil of Rumeli sing this folk song with the same longing?

The mist of [the Balkan mountains of Şıpka (Shipka in Bulgaria)] are yearned for, look the red blood of the Balkan mountains of Şıpka still oozes, we left 30 years ago and now we have come again to Şıpka. [197]

This intensity of feeling is also evident in 'Tuna Üstündeki Ses' (Voice over the Danube), which İsmail Habib Sevük wrote from notes dictated by Mustafa Kemal Atatürk in 1932.[198] 'Ignoramus! Which three centuries, which ten centuries?/ The banks of the Danube are the lands of the Turks/...Over the Danube, under the Danube/ it has always been the Turkish fatherland.'[199]

In 1938, Halil Yaver, another émigré, referred to the murmur of the beautiful Danube, which seaped into 'our national consciousness' (milli benliğimiz).[200] Another émigré from the Balkans, Osman Nuri Peremeci, took the Danube as the centre of his book, *Tuna Boyu Tarihi* (The History of the Banks of the Danube), in which he narrated the history of Bulgaria, of which part of the modern state was included in the 'Tuna vilayeti,' the Danube province under the Ottomans.[201] The Danube became a central reference point for Turkishness in the Republican era: Behçet Kemal Çağlar, a well-known Republican poet, asks the Danube to call out whenever it sees a Turk, and to remain proud of its Turkishness.[202] Bülent Ecevit, the Prime Minister until 2002, too, perceived the Danube as Turkish and in his poem, 'Tuna,' published in 1986, he grieves for the desolation of the Danube, left by the Turks: 'Ask the Danube why it weeps when in its dreams it sees the reflection of a Turk.'[203]

Vatan was thus an amorphous term. While it could coincide with the physical borders of state, it could also represent an imagined fatherland. The Balkans both in the late Ottoman period and in the early Republic played a role in the fluctuating concept of *vatan* and an idealized image of the Balkan lands, from time to time, appeared in the imagination of the Turkish fatherland in the Republican mind-set.

Migration

Another image of the Balkans in the Ottoman/Turkish collective memory as witnessed in what one might call the written memory, what society chooses to recall and record for posterity, was that of migration. The phenomenon of migration of population from or to Ottoman territories was not new in Ottoman historiography. The Ottoman government applied a policy of forced migration within its territories throughout its history.

With the 1877-1878 Russian-Ottoman war, the perception of population movement as something hitherto normal in Ottoman historiography changed and such movements became seen as abnormal and traumatic. The war, which resulted in a considerable loss of Ottoman territory and the forced migration of the Muslim population into the empire, changed the population map of Anatolia and Rumeli and changed also the perception of migration in the minds of people. The scenes of migration and the pain caused by this event became an important memory for later generations who became the elite of the new Turkish Republic. Yahya Kemal (Beyatlı), writing in 1921 of his travels in the Balkans, referred in his account of Zağra (Zagora), to *Tarihçe-i Vak'a-i Zağra*, written by Raci Efendi, the *müftü* of Zağra, in which Raci Efendi narrated his memoirs of the events of 1876.[204] Summarising this account, Yahya Kemal, who was deeply affected by this memoir, stressed two tragic aspects of the events in Zagora in 1876, the violence and the forced migration which he described as 'the second and the last disaster.'[205] Writing a year later, in 1922, Falih Rıfkı (Atay) referred to the impact this same book of Raci Efendi had had on him when he read it during 'the bloody days of the Balkan war' and which left him carrying 'an incurable wound in my heart.'[206] The migration as a result of this war was defined in relation to Bulgarian violence: 'The Bulgarians began barbaric atrocities against the Muslim people. Despite the harshness of the winter, group by group the people migrated and the number of migrants in İstanbul was almost the same as the number of its inhabitants. Further, their pitiable condition increased feelings [for their plight].'[207]

Although the Congress of Berlin led to a great loss of Ottoman territory and considerable movement of population, it was the Balkan migrations that had a significant psychological impact on the Ottoman elite, for it was this migration that they themselves witnessed as the Muslim population, in a pitiful condition, fled to İstanbul. Migration in the East, occasioned by the loss of Kars, Batum, Ardahan and Beyazıt, did not have the same impact as it was not so visible to the elite in the capital. The newspapers of the period gave accounts of the miserable conditions of those Muslims who fled to İstanbul before the Russian and Bulgarian forces. In *Basiret*, an İstanbul newspaper, Ali Efendi describes the situation of these 'guests of God' (Allah misafirleri):

> The hearts of those who go to Sirkeci station and see the condition of these poor people melt even if they are of stone. Especially the violent trembling and moaning of the bare headed and bare footed little children and the women weeping, without thought for themselves, asking help in the name of God from their fellow citizens for the protection of their beloved children, and the soul-rending condition of the sick and the powerlessness of the old make us feel that this places a great duty both legal and humane on the men of state.[208]

While the Balkan migrations of 1877-1878 were remembered, it was the migrations of the Balkan Wars which were fresh in the minds of the Republican elite and represented more vividly the trauma of migration which was for them essentially a Balkan phenomenon. This created a mental dislocation for the contemporary elite who was shocked by the defeat which, according to a member of the İttihad ve Terakki at the time, was the worst defeat of the Turk since the legendary 'Ergenekon,' the mythical account of the entrampment of the Turks in a place surrounded by iron mountains and of their escape, guided by a grey wolf.[209] The frustration and desperation felt by the Ottoman elite at the end of the Balkan Wars is clear from the words of the main character in Ömer Seyfeddin's short story 'Rûznâme' (Diary). The main character, an army officer, wrote in his diary: 'Rumeli cannot take back its old form. Now Rumeli has been broken off from Turkish land never to be re-attached. Even if the European armies come, they can never now drive the Serbs and the Bulgarians from here!'[210]

Şevket Süreyya Aydemir, an important member of the Kadro movement of the 1930s' and an important writer, who was from Edirne, summarized this frustration, disbelief, and loss of faith in the past created by the defeat in the Balkan Wars:

This means that up to that date we were living in a dream world. It means that all the things we believed were an illusion. In fact this empire had perhaps died a long time ago. Perhaps we only lived it through our illusions. Perhaps that lost Ottoman Africa was never ours. Perhaps that Ottoman Europe had not been counted as ours for a long time. It means that Crete, Eastern Rumeli, Bosnia-Herzegovina, which was the Danube provinces, had become for us a thing of the past long ago.[211]

This pragmatic realization of reality resulted in a more political response and in engineering a population policy. The İstanbul Agreement signed in 1913 by the İttihad ve Terakki government included an appendix which includes a clause on the optional exchange of population between Bulgaria and the Ottoman empire which, according to Cemal Paşa, was successfully carried out.[212] This exchange was considered useful for decreasing tension between the two states.[213] In the same period, the İttihad ve Terakki government also attempted to initiate negotiations with the Greek government over the issue of the exchange of the Greek population in the coastal area of the province of Aydın with those Muslims of Macedonia who were willing to leave.[214] Galip Kemalî Söylemezoğlu, who in 1946 wrote his memoirs of his time in the Ottoman embassy in Athens between 1913-1916, explained how he had put forward a proposal for such an exchange of population:

Since the signing in 1878 of the Berlin Agreement, it has been known and proven by various and unparalled events what happened in every Balkan country to the ill-fated Muslim population which met the catastrophe of being separated from the empire. For this reason, I suggested to Monsieur Venizelos, merely as my personal opinion, that an agreement be made for the exchange of the Muslims in Macedonia with the settled Greek (Rum) population in the province of Aydın, that the property which they would leave behind would be given to those [coming] by means of exchange and the difference between the value would be indemnified by the governments. My proposition, as will be seen later, was considered acceptable and finally, after the Ayvalık incident in July, it was officially adopted and two different commissions were set up, one in İzmir and one in

Thessaloniki, but unfortunately, with the outbreak of the First World War, neither time nor possibility remained for the application of this mutual agreement which would have saved us from such great afflictions.[215]

The policy of exchange of population became central with the creation of the Turkish Republic and the signing of the Lausanne Treaty. In 1926 the exchange of population between Greece and Turkey, as set out in the Lausanne Treaty, was carried out. A joint commission was set up to decide who had the right to stay, who had to be exchanged, and to settle issues of property. The Muslims who were living in Greece, with the exception of Western Thrace, would be exchanged with the Orthodox-Greek (*Rum*) population living in Turkey, except İstanbul. The main identifier in deciding who would be considered "Turkish" or "Greek" was religion. This was not a merely political decision based just on political convenience, for religion was a main reference point for self-identification, as is clear in the petitions submitted to the Exchange of Population Commissions about the violence against the Muslim population in Greece and their wish to migrate to Turkey in which the main reference point was *being Muslim*.[216] Although there were discussions about the identity of the Orthodox population in Anatolia and some circles considered these people 'Christianized Turks' since they spoke Turkish as their native tongue and shared a common origin,[217] the religion was the main official reference point for the definition of the identity as was clear from a government decree ordering authorities not to accept any request of conversion until the end of the war in order to prevent any further security problem, despite the fact that there was no legal obstacle to conversion.[218] After the war, during the Lausanne talks, the Turkish government, concerned about the possibility of failing to reach an agreement over the exchange of population, went so far as to establish a Turkish Orthodox Church[219] in order to divert the allegiance of the non-Muslim Turkish subjects from the Greek Patriarchate in İstanbul which became a target of anti-Greek feelings during the war and was considered an extension of the Greek government.[220] From this point onwards, the Greek Patriarchate came to be represented in very negative terms, and, together with the Phanariots, was portrayed as pursuing only personal interests and exploiting not only the "master," the Ottomans, but also the Orthodox population which it had under its charge. This negative representation appeared in the first edition of *Tarih III*.[221] In his report on *Tarih III* which was written on the request of Türk Tarihi Tetkik Cemiyeti, Mehmet Ali Ayni, then professor of the history of religions in the Darülfünun, drew attention to this overgeneralized representation applied to the Phanariots and suggested that a more balanced approach would have been better: 'Again on this page [page 95] while discussing the Greek Beys of Fener, it would have been more objective had the loyal service given by some of them to the state been referred to.'[222] However, this suggestion was ignored in the second edition of *Tarih III* which was published a couple of months after this report.[223]

With the definition of who would be exchanged with whom in the agreement of the *mübadele* (exchange of population), the existing identifications were used in order to create homogenous states in which a limited minority might be acceptable. Thus religion, for the new Turkish state, was the main identifier that distinguished the Turk from the others, at least within the region of the Balkans.

In the school history texts of the 1920s', this exchange of population was justified by presenting this event as if it was the exchange of "evil" people of Anatolia, the Orthodox population, with "good" people of Greece, Turks/Muslims: 'The Anatolian Greeks who were living like a snake within us, were exchanged with our Turkish brothers in Greece.'[224] This hostility is also evident in the 1339/1923 book, *Tarihimizde Rumlar, Patrikhane ve Yunancılık* (Greeks, the Patriarchate and Pro-Greekness in Our History):

> The [Lausanne] Conference still seems to persist over the need for the minorities to live as they are accustomed. To live as they are accustomed, that is to teach being an enemy of the Turk in the schools and that the blood of the Turk is legitimate, to pray in the churches for the safety of the Greek nation and for victory in battles which aim at our destruction, to collect quantities of aid for the Greek army through philanthropic organizations (!) ... History and even events which are not yet part of history show that this style of action had become natural for the *Rum*. They have always thought like Greeks, they have always been proud of Greekness, at the moment when clouds appeared on the horizon, slobbering streams of *rakı* [induced] saliva, they, in total grossness, ripped open their blue and white hearts in front of us. After so many

events, above all, after this Greek defeat, this element, which manifests Greekness more here than in Athens, can never be a friend of the Turk. Why should we knowingly protect and nourish this enemy among us? Why should we see the faces of the Greek King Yorgi [George] and Queen Sophia of wherever in the shop of the milkman Pauli? If the civilized governments accept certain rights for minorities, such rights should not include that of being able to be openly hostile to the owner of the country.[225]

Despite the fact that the narration of the exchange of population with Greece did not appear in such a hostile way the 1930s' school texts, a period of friendly relations with Greece, nevertheless, the perception of the threat which might be posed by possible Greek resettlement in the lands from which they had migrated was reflected in these texts. In *Tarih IV*, the permanence of the exchange of population was stressed: 'The resettlement on their old lands of the Greeks and the Turks who had been exchanged was forbidden under any circumstances.'[226] The preoccupation with any potential resettlement is evident in a book on Greece issued to military personal in 1930 in which, after noting how the position of the Morea during the time of Evliya Çelebi, when half its population was Albanian Christian recalled that of İzmir now, the writer went on to stress the need to prevent any Greek return to İzmir or the surrounding coastal district: 'It should be regarded as a most important national duty to prevent the Greeks who have been expelled under the Treaty of Lausanne from insinuating themselves in any way into İzmir and the coastal areas at any price.'[227]

While the army was entrusted with the duty of preventing the Greeks resettling on the Aegean coast, the Turkish government watched every move and word of the Greek authorities concerning any possible resettlement in Anatolia. The Turkish Ministry of Foreign Affairs was very agitated in 1933 by the speech of the Greek Prime Minister, Tsaldaris, which he delivered to the Greek parliament setting out his government's programme. The Prime Minister stated that his government would work to facilitate the migration of Greeks to suitable countries, especially to the areas which they had recently left. This remark worried the Turkish authorities in Ankara and they demanded a clarification of this statement via the Turkish embassy in Athens from the Greek Minister of Foreign Affairs, who then explained that the Greek Prime Minister had here meant various places in South America and Africa. However, the Turkish Ministry of Foreign Affairs still regarded it as necessary to inform the Turkish Prime Minister's Office about the situation.[228]

According to the protocol of settlement annexed to the Treaty of Friendship signed by the Turkish and Bulgarian governments in Ankara on 18 October 1925, both sides guaranteed minority rights, as granted by Bulgaria to the Muslims in Bulgaria under the Treaty of Neuilly, and by Turkey to the Bulgarians, defined as non-Muslim and Bulgarian-speaking, in Turkey under the Treaty of Lausanne. Thus, while religion, as in the case of the exchange of population agreement with Greece, became the basic identifier of Turkish national identity, that of being Bulgarian in Turkey depended not only on being non-Muslim but also on speaking Bulgarian.[229] In contrast, the Turkish-speaking Orthodox population of Karaman moved to Greece since it was loyal to the Greek Patriarchate.

The use of religion as the main identifier went on during the 1930s', usually taken as the peak point of secularisation in the contemporary historiography of the era. The official discourse of the 1930s' underlined the importance of secularism and the policy of decreasing the role of religion, at least in public life. Religion was not considered one of the factors that had led to the creation of the Turkish nation as defined by Afet (İnan) in her book, *Vatandaş İçin Medenî Bilgiler*, written using Mustafa Kemal's notes, and secularism was regarded as one of the main tenants of the Turkish state: every person who attained the age of majority was free to choose his religion.[230] Afet saw religion as a positive obstacle to the formation of the nation:

> Turks were a great nation even before they accepted Islam. After accepting this religion, this religion did not bring about a union of the Turks either with the Arabs, or the Persians or any others of the same religion, to form a nation together. On the contrary, it weakened the national bonds of the Turkish nation. It numbed the national sentiments, the national emotion. This was very natural, because the aim of the religion which was founded by Muhammed was a comprehensive policy of community above all nations.[231]

Similarly a 1934 definition of Turk openly excludes religion as a compenent of Turkishness: 'In the Turkish Republic, a Turk is a person who speaks Turkish, is raised in Turkish culture and who makes the Turkish ideal his own, regardless of religion.'[232]

However, despite this open secularisation, religion continued in practice to be one of the most important identifiers of Turkishness, and as a reference point of identification in relation to the neighbouring countries. The practical repercussions of the use of religion as a pragmatic and natural, non-artificial identifier became apparent in relation to the reality of migration from the Balkans. The decline of the role of religion in the public life of the members of the nation as represented in Afet's text, written for schools, was not clearly reflected in the *İskan Kanunu*, the law of settlement, enacted in 1934, which gave wide executive power to the government to distribute the population of the state in accordance with the homogenization policy of Turkification. The third clause of this law defined *muhacir*s (migrants): 'Individuals or tribes, settled or nomadic, of Turkish lineage who want to come, individually or together from outside in order to settle in Turkey, and those who are settled and tied to Turkish culture are accepted by order of the Ministry of Interior in accordance with the statutes of this law.' The law leaves an open door for interpretation by adding 'who and the people of which countries will be counted as tied to Turkish culture is to be determined by order of the Cabinet.'[233]

The documents concerning migration of population from the Balkan countries, and other documents demonstrating the concern of the Turkish government over the situation of the Muslim population in the Balkans prove that, contrary to the official discourse disseminated through official and semi-official channels, such as schools, journals and the libraries of the Halkevleri, religion as an identifier was an important factor in deciding who was eligible to migrate to Turkey and who within the Balkans could potentially be considered a useful asset in extending the influence of the Turkish state. During the 1930s', we see two kinds of publications defending different stand-points on the migration from the Balkans. The first approach was very much in accord with the official discourse of the government, defining "Turk" by language and ethnicity. This idea found supporters among well-known figures in the Cumhuriyet Halk Partisi such as the Turkish ambassador to Romania, Hamdullah Suphi (Tanrıöver).

In contrast to the official discourse and the ideas of people such as Hamdullah Suphi, religion in practice was a significant factor. Muslims were seen as easily assimilative within Turkey. For this reason, the

Gagauz, although Turkish according to the criteria of Hamdullah Suphi, were, for Halil Yaver, on the contrary, a danger to the security of the state and should not be allowed to settle in Thrace since they were Orthodox and culturally Bulgarian, and their presence would encourage Bulgarian intervention in the region.[234] Halil Yaver had earlier, in April 1936, sent a report to the Prime Minister's Office in which he expressed his deep concerns over Bulgarian hostility towards Turkey.[235] Such concerns over a Bulgarian presence in Thrace were also evident in the earlier protocol signed in 1925 between Bulgaria and Turkey.[236]

In 1933, the Turkish embassy in Sofia wrote to the Ministry of Foreign Affairs, which in turn sent on a report to the Prime Minister's Office, about the migration to Turkey of the Pomaks, the Turks, and the gypsies who had been 'accommodating to Turkishness' (Türklüğe temessül etmiş), spoke Turkish and had settled in the cities. If these populations were not moved to Turkey, they would, in the view of the Turkish embassy, be in danger of accommodating to Bulgarianness (Bulgarlığa temessüllerine imkân bırakılması) which would constitute 'a national mistake' (millî bir hata) for the Turkish government.[237]

While for Halil Yaver, the Gagauz were not suitable candidates for migration to Turkey, since they were Orthodox, the Pomaks, for the Turkish embassy in Sofia, on the other hand, should be encouraged to emigrate to Turkey since, although ethnically Bulgarian, they were Muslims. However, since the Bulgarian government did not accept Pomak migration to Turkey, any such migration would have to be by Pomaks, who in any case wished to leave for Turkey, seeking asylum for religious reasons. Under these circumstances and in view of the repression suffered by the Pomaks, the embassy urged that the Turkish authorities ease the entry of these people into the country.[238] Concern over the situation of the Pomaks had in fact been expressed much earlier under the İttihad ve Terakki government when there were deep concerns over the position of the Muslim population in Western Thrace and the Bulgarian attempt at forced conversion of Pomaks to Christianity just after the Balkan Wars.[239]

Turkish authorities were always very sensitive to any attempt by Balkan governments to convert Muslims in their territories, and followed any such attempts keenly. The Turkish ambassador in Berlin, for example, reported a rumour circulating about the conversion of 'Turkish Muslims' in Prizren to Christianity. This rumour caused considerable agitation among the Turkish authorities, although it was later discovered that the 'Turkish Muslims' concerned were in fact Albanians who had converted to Islam 50 years earlier and had Muslim names, but held masses in the Catholic church at night and had declared their Catholicism the previous year.[240]

Turkish-Albanian relations in this period were strained for religious reasons. In Kosovo, the authorities followed a policy of encouraging the Albanians to leave. For this reason, the Turkish authorities began to issue visas for Turkey to these Albanians. This was not viewed well by the Albanian government which was not happy to see Albanians leaving Kosovo, and in consequence complained to the Turkish government over the issuing of visas.[241] Although the government was prepared to consider this issue, it remained concerned about the position of the Turkish language and culture (*hars*). A letter from the Turkish embassy in Tirana in 1933 discussed the necessity of accepting Albanian students in Turkish schools in order to revive the declining Turkish language and *hars* in Albania. The letter noted that there were 70 Albanian students in Italy, 23 in Greece, 11 in Romania, eight in Yugoslavia, three in Bulgaria and three in France. The letter went on to state: 'My evaluation is that it would be appropriate in particular for the children of the martyred soldiers and officials who gave their lives for our country (memleket), even if they are Albanian, exceptionally to be accepted in our schools.'[242]

This idea of keeping a Turkish cultural presence alive in the Balkans was an important part of Turkish policy. Such cultural presence was to be that defined and supported by the Turkish authorities which provided funds to newspapers and schools for this purpose.[243] In this context, Islam was seen as a positive asset for Turkey in that it prevented the assimilation of Muslim minorities. Yaşar Nabi, an important writer and publisher and very much part of the Republican intellectual elite, for whom Islam was not important for the development of Turkish national consciousness, could not avoid realizing that Islam was a core reference point for the Muslim population in the Balkans which would keep them resisting any assimilation policies. He quoted the experience of one of his acquaintances:

> An acquaintance of mine explained to me, with tears in his eyes, how, while travelling in Bulgaria, he had seen little children, who were playing in the garden of a school, cross themselves, pray in

Bulgarian and sing [Bulgarian] national songs. Upon realizing that they were Turkish, he felt a deep pain in his heart.[244]

Continous migration to Turkey from the Balkans kept the image of the Balkans as a constant source of migrants in the forefront of popular perception, and the word *muhacir* (migrant) came to mean in modern Turkish, Turkish citizens who had immigrated from a Balkan country.

The existence of the multiple images of the Balkans demonstrates the centrality of the Balkans in the late Ottoman and early Republican mentality. The region came to symbolize the injustices, losses, yearnings, and failures suffered by the Ottomans and the Turks. These images were constantly reproduced in the history texts and the literature well into the Republican era and the vivid impact and emotive power of the Balkans still remains strong in the Turkish psyche.

CONCLUSION

From olden days, we Turks, in whatever place we stepped, with whatever peoples (kavim) we took under our rule, we interfered neither in their languages nor their religions, [*] nor did we even touch their social organizations.
In this way they lived excellently among us like an independent government, a nation. Because they did not send soldiers and did not go to war, their populations increased. Thanks to their schools, their knowledge increased. Because trade and crafts were in their hands, their pockets were full of our money. Then, incited by the Europeans, they discovered a new word, "nationalism". This was a trend. Due to this trend, they exposed their hatred of the Turk which they had hidden in their hearts until now. Our enemies also helped them. Thus each one of our subject [peoples] emerged as an individual state, such as Montenegro, Serbia, Romania, Bulgaria, Greece.
[*] We understood how bad a mistake this had been when the English invaded İstanbul and our Greek and Armenian subjects tore everything from us even down to the fezes on our heads. But what use was [such understanding]![1]

The central feature of this depiction, written in 1926 for primary school children, is the good Turk wronged. While the Ottomans ruled justly, fought and suffered, the peoples of the Balkans, left to live without interference, prospered in peace. But these ungrateful peoples had always harboured hatred in their hearts and, stirred up by the Europeans, turned to nationalism.

This perception of being a victim, unjustly wronged and misunderstood, formed a fundamental element in Ottoman/Turkish mentality, and was important in developing a sense of unity among the Turks. The Balkans played a major role in the creation of this victim mentality, for it was here in particular that the Turks felt themselves to have been betrayed. The continuous references in the history texts, as well as in other writings, to the injustices, violence and betrayal inflicted on the Ottomans by their Balkan subjects, the graphic scenes of violence and descriptions of migration, together with the expressions of an acute sense of alienation from what had been their soil, of expulsion from what had formed part of their mental *vatan*, from the bone-strewn banks of the river of life, the Danube, all fed into the creation of the victim as part of national identity. The Ottomans/Turks felt too that, unjustly, the Balkan peoples had always 'hidden hatred in their hearts,' and that they were faced constantly with an implacable hostility from the Balkan states. It was this common hostility that, according to Yusuf Hikmet Bayur, united a deeply divided Balkans and made a Balkan alliance possible.[2] Ahmed Hasır and Mustafa Muhsin argued that the hostility and betrayal of the non-Turkish elements caused the Ottoman loss of the Balkan Wars.[3]

In the 1930s', official government policy always emphasized peace among the Balkan states, including Turkey and underlined that Turkey, like the other Balkan states, had emerged with the dissolution of the Ottoman empire. All Balkan states thus had a common history. But the Turks were anxious to stress that in this shared past they themselves had suffered as much as any other Balkan nation, they were not oppressors but equal victims. In the Balkan Conference of 1931, Mustafa Kemal said: 'If this history has painful memories, then all the Balkan peoples share them. The Turkish part is no less bitter.'[4] Despite his support for Balkan rapprochement, Falih Rıfkı Atay was also bitter about the denial of Turkish suffering. 'The Turks,' he wrote, 'felt the pain of the Ottoman deterioration and fall as much as the others.'[5]

For the Ottomans/Turks, the Europeans too were totally unjust in their approach. The Ottomans/Turks bitterly resented the European failure ever to see the Ottomans as victims or to accept the Ottoman empire as part of the civilized world. This perception of Europe is made clear in a text written during the Turkish National Liberation War:

> If the Greek government had attempted to revive the Byzantine empire and to invade Anatolia a year before, this was not a new plan. Twenty-five years before, they had prepared to come from

Rumeli to İstanbul. According to this calculation, the Rum in the empire (memleket) would again have raised rebellions, would again have led the Greek army, would again have hanged and mutilated [the people]. Indeed, they had painted Crete in blood. They killed the Muslims with a barbarity which even animals slaughtered in a slaughterhouse are safe from. What happened? One or two commissions and five or ten communications! In the end it came to war. We thrashed the Greeks. But the esteemed Europeans said the Turk had no right according to the system. In Rumeli murders by brigands continued for 20 years. Only the Turks were blamed. For Europe, Turkish blood is lawful. In the face of this naked reality, all the sentences which contain the words humanity and civilization are nothing more than the grinning of a masquerade which holds all the filth of hypocrisy and deceit.[6]

In the 1940s' this European attitude still rankled. Yakup Kadri Karaosmanoğlu attacked those, like the German historian Ranke, who had presented the Ottomans/Turks as nothing more than a destructive force outside the bounds of civilisation. 'What fool said 'in the place where Turkish armies have passed grass does not grow'?' he asked. 'Wherever Turkish armies went they brought order, organization and tranquility. At a stroke, countries which had for centuries been in anarchical turmoil found peace and calm. The Turks took over these foreign nations which were incapable of governing themselves and put them on the road to independence and stability.'[7]

This anger at such injustice and betrayal was also evident in the frustration over the physical loss of territory: 'Harvested grapes are sour/ The rebellious slave stopped paying the old poll tax/ Seven kings were again crowned/ The crows occupied the nest of the falcon.'[8] For Mehmed Fuad Köprülü, the well-known historian and Republican politician, thus, the conquered lands, now undeservedly in the hands of slaves who had revolted, produced a bitter crop and the once glorious eyrie of the high-flying falcon had become the nest of base crows.

With the loss of the Balkans, the Ottomans, or more particularly the Turks of the Republic, were faced also with the struggle to save their past, and to preserve it from the again unjust assaults of the various Balkan nations. The glorious past of the Ottomans in the Balkans was under constant attack from the historians of the Balkans, for whom the

Ottoman past represented tyranny, oppression and stagnation. In 1938, Falih Rıfkı Atay, in his very positive book on Yugoslavia, *Tuna Kıyıları* (The Banks of the Danube), still felt the need to defend the Ottoman past: 'The Ottomans neither undertook a barbarian invasion or a crusade against the Balkans or Hungary.'[9] In his seminal article, 'Osmanlı İmparatorluğunda Çiftçi Sınıflarının Hukukî Statüsü' (The legal status of peasant classes in the Ottoman empire) written in 1937, the well-known Turkish historian, Ömer Lütfi Barkan heavily criticised the Balkan historical representation of the Ottoman occupation of the Balkans and claimed that 'to regard the past under Turkish rule as a "Babylonian captivity" for the Balkan nations is nothing other than malicious propaganda in the service of a strange nationalism which feels the need to take its strength from the feelings of hatred and revenge which are nourished against Turkishness.'[10] The need to defend the Ottoman past from unjust representation even led in some cases to Republican historians choosing their research topics especially in order to refute such allegations against the empire.

For the Republican elite, who perceived history as a part of the national identity, this attack on the Turkish past was an attack on its very being. Turkish concern over negative representation of the Ottoman past by the Balkan states exhibited itself in Turkish diplomatic relations with their Balkan neighbours. In 1933, the Bulgarian director and actor Vassil Gendov made a film, *Бунтът на робите* (The Slaves' Revolt), about the Bulgarian independence struggle, the main character of which was Vasil Levski, a leading figure of the Bulgarian uprising in 1873.[11] The Turkish Ministry of Foreign Affairs was alarmed by the film which 'depicts and demonstrates the imagined tyranny which the Bulgarians experienced under 500 hundred years of Turkish rule,' and whose 'crude and ugly depiction' would 'offend ... the feelings of our nation as well as instigate Bulgarian ideas against us.' The Ministry demanded an explanation from the Bulgarian government as to why it had given permission for the circulation of such a film.[12]

The Bulgarian government did not accept the Turkish view that the film was anti-Turkish, pointing out that 'since the imagined events in the film concerned the Ottoman period, [the film] could not be perceived as being against the new Turkish government and nation.'[13] However, despite the Bulgarian government's stress on the lack of connection between the film and modern Turkey, the Turkish authorities tracked closely the development of the film in Bulgaria. Two months later, the Ministry of Foreign Affairs contacted the Prime Minister's Office over the film, whose title was translated into Turkish as '*Esirler İsyanı*,' informing the Prime Minister's Office of the report written by the Turkish consulate in Varna. In this report, the film was described as 'a Bulgarian national propaganda film' and was, according to the report, being shown in schools upon the request of the Bulgarian education authority in Varna. The film juxtaposed Turk versus Bulgarian, not Ottoman versus Bulgarian, and, in the report, the film was considered to be a depiction of the Turk as a brutal oppressor rather than a representation of Bulgarian independence. In an attempt to express how base the film was, the report noted that the main female character in the film, Hristina, was played by Vassil Gendov's wife Zhana Gendova, who was, according to rumour, 'a former prostitute in the brothels of Paris.'[14]

The anger over the loss of the Balkans drove the Turks to reconsider their past in an attempt to explain what had happened. This resulted in a deep sense of regret and bitterness for what had been a terrible, and pointless, sacrifice. In contrast to Balkan histories, those of the early Turkish Republic regarded Ottoman policy in the Balkans as not having been firm enough, and failure to deal effectively with the problems of the Balkans was a source of regret for some of the Turkish historians.[15] The poet Yahya Kemal, himself from Üsküp (Skolpje), expressed his deep regret over the loss of his birth-place: 'When at one time it was ours, part of our true *vatan*/ why is Üsküp not ours today? I felt this deeply.'[16]

The loss of the Balkans forced the Turkish elite to look towards Anatolia. Halide Edib regarded this as a positive development:

> That the Balkan defeat leading to the final withdrawal of Turkey from the Balkans was a blessing in disguise, no one realized at the moment. Consciousness that all the Anatolian manhood, the energy, and the resources of the empire spent hitherto on the Balkans would now be spared, dawned only gradually upon Turkish minds. Perhaps the early withdrawal of Turkey from the Balkans is one of the fundamental reasons for hope in a firmer future development of New Turkey.[17]

The loss of the Balkans forced the Turkish intellectuals to focus on Anatolia, the only territory which was left to them. Anatolia was therefore presented as the spiritual homeland, 'the source of our power,'[18] and withdrawal into Anatolia as a return to their native soil. The great territorial loss of the empire was not significant because Anatolia, the 'soul' of the Turks remained.[19]

The bitterness of loss, however, remained. Falih Rıfkı Atay, writing just after the World War I, graphically expressed the sense of grief and anger he felt over the price Anatolia had paid both in the Balkans and in the other lands of the empire. 'Anatolia looks at us all with hatred, suspicion and mistrust. We are bringing ourselves and our regret to this mother from whose breast we have torn hundreds of thousands of children and carried them away.'[20] This invoked a sense of shame among the ruling elite: 'As if ashamed before Anatolia, wagons, carts, trucks, all crossed Anatolia secretly and quickly on the way to İstanbul with their curtains closed, their tarpaulins drawn down, their lights out.'[21]

Such regret in turn fed into anger over the enormous suffering and sacrifice squandered on the ungrateful lands of the empire. Falih Rıfkı Atay's *Zeytindağı*, his memoirs of the four years he spent in the Ottoman army in Syria and Palestine with Cemal Paşa during World War I, are a vivid expression of this resentment over such cruel waste. Crossing Anatolia by train to İstanbul after the war, he heard a woman at a station asking 'have you seen my Ahmed?' Her question made the author reflect on all the Anatolian soldiers wasted in the war and he asked himself 'which Ahmed? Which of the hundreds of thousands of Ahmeds?.. Was he destroyed by ice, by sand, by water, by scurvy, by typhus? If he escaped from all these, if you see your Ahmed, you too will ask 'have you seen my Ahmed?'[22] With bitterness, Falih Rıfkı Atay thought:

> No... Not one of us has seen your Ahmed. But Ahmed has seen everything. He has seen a hell which even Allah could not explain to Muhammed.
> Now all the winds from the West and East, right and left blow towards Anatolia screaming destruction. Stopping at the railway tracks, highways, khans and fountains, and squatting down, Anatolia searches for her son.

Anatolia asks for her Ahmed. Ahmed who yesterday was cheaper than a pile of bullets, now we are reading his value in the eyes of a mother eagle who is looking straight at us, her wings folded back and her claws clenched.

If we could only say why we wasted Ahmed, if we could explain to one mother what we had gained by this, if we could give news that would make her proud... But we lost Ahmed in a gamble.[23]

NOTES

Introduction

1 Rumeli Muhacirin-i İslamiye Cemiyet-i Hayriyesi, *Alam-ı İslam. Rumeli Mezalimi ve Bulgar Vahşetleri. İslamiyetin Enzar-ı Basiretine ve Alem-i İnsaniyet ve Medeniyetin Nazar-ı Dikkatine* (İstanbul, 1329), p. 70: 'Dedemin sürdüğü, can ektiği toprak gitdi../ Öyle bir gitdi ki hem: bir daha gelmez idi!'

2 İbn ül-Haşim Nureddin Fikri, *Dimetokada Kanlı Bir Levha. Bulgar Vahşetlerinden* (Dersaadet, n.d.), pp. 30-1: 'Altıyüz bu kadar senedenberi dünyanın üç büyük kıtasında kemal-i satvetle hükümran oldukdansonra akıbet Rum elinden de çıkarıldık. Hem de dünkü çobanlarımız, dünkü uşaklarımız çıkardılar. Yediğimiz sille-i hakaretin acısını kıyamete kadar kalbimizden çıkarmamaklımız [*sic.*] lazımdır.'

3 [Tanrıöver], Hamdullah Suphi, 'İstila Önünde Türk Halkı. 1920-1336 da İzmir Kız Muallim Mektebinde' in *Dağyolu, 2inci Kitap* (Ankara, 1931), pp. 191-2: 'Balkan milliyetperverliği başka milletlerin milliyetperverliğine benzemez. Balkan milliyetperverliği baskın, suikast, bomba ve çete hareketlerile dolu hususî, kızıl bir tarihe maliktir. Balkan milliyetperverliği yırtıcıdır, vahşidir. Balkan memleketleri hayvanatı vahşiye bahçelerine benzer, her hududun arkasında birbirinden demir parmaklıklarla ayrılmış diş ve tırnaktan ibaret kan içici bir milliyetperverlik vardır. Bu milliyetperverlikler hudutların demirleri arasında mütemadi birbirine pençelerini uzatırlar ve yekdiğerini yırtarlar. Müştereken bizim üzerimize saldırdıkları zaman ne kadar vahşi iseler, Balkan muharebesinden sonra gördüğümüz üzere kendi aralarında boğuşmaya başladıkları zaman da o kadar vahşidirler.'

4 Karpat, Kemal H., *Turkey's Politics: The Transition to a Multi-Party System* (Princeton, 1959), *passim*.

Chapter One

1 Carr, E. H., *What is History*, with a New Introduction by Richard J. Evans (Basingstoke, 2001), p. 2.
2 Tanpınar, Ahmet Hamdi, *Beş Şehir* (İstanbul, 2001), p. 24: 'Sade millet ve cemiyetlerin değil, şahsiyetlerin de asıl mana ve hüviyetini, çekirdeğini tarihilik denen şeyin yaptığı düşünülürse, bu iç didişme hiç de yadırganmaz. Mazi daima mevcuttur. Kendimiz olarak yaşayabilmek için, onunla her an hesaplaşmaya ve anlaşmaya mecburuz.'
3 Akçura, Yusuf, *Osmanlı İmparatorluğunun Dağılma Devri, "Türk Tarihinin Ana Hatları" Eserinin Müsveddeleri* (İstanbul, n. d.), p. 23: 'Dil ve tarih, bir milletin hüviyetini muhafaza ve inkişaf ettirmekte en mühim amillerdir.'
4 Baymur, A. Fuat, *Tarih Öğretimi* (Ankara, 1945), p. 1: 'Ulusal kimliğin uyanmasında, beslenip kökleşmesinde tarihin mühim bir rolü vardır. Tarih için haklı olarak «kök duygusu» kazandırır derler. Gerçekten bu sayede ecdadımızla aramızda münasebet kurulmuş olur. Onların yaşayış, düşünüş ve duyuş tarzları, mücadeleleri hakkında fikir edinir; onlara neler borçlu olduğumuzu anlar, gelecek nesle karşı olan ödevlerimizi öğrenmiş bulunuruz. Schopenhauer'in dediği gibi, bir millet benlik şuuruna, ancak tarihi vasıtasiyle varabilir. Sonra yine haklı olarak söylenildiği gibi, geçmiş bizim içimizde yaşadığı takdirde milletimiz bir isrikbale [*sic*.] sahip olabilir.'
5 Akçuraoğlu Yusuf (ed.), *Türk Yılı* (İstanbul, 1928), pp. 319-25.
6 Togan, A. Zeki Velidi, *Tarihde Usul* (İstanbul, 1950), pp. 182-3.
7 Namık Kemal, *Külliyat-ı Kemal, Üçüncü Tertib 1 - Osmanlı Tarihi, Cild 1, Cüz 1* (İstanbul, 1326), pp. 18-19.
8 Yinanç, Mükrimin Halil, 'Tanzimattan Meşrutiyete Kadar Bizde Tarihçilik' in *Tanzimat I* (İstanbul, 1940), pp. 576-7 and Kaplan, Mehmed, *Namık Kemal Hayatı ve Eserleri* (İstanbul, 1948), p. 158.
9 Ahmed Vefik Paşa, *Fezleke-i Tarih-i Osmani* ([İstanbul], 1286).
10 Akçura: *Osmanlı İmparatorluğunun Dağılma Devri*, passim.
11 [Ahmed], Cevdet Paşa, *Tezâkir 40-Tetimme*, edited by Cavid Baysun (Ankara, 1991), correspondence with Ahmed Mithad Efendi, pp. 236-44.
12 Halaçoğlu, Yusuf, in Ahmed Cevdet Paşa, *Ma'rûzât*, edited by Yusuf Halaçoğlu (İstanbul, 1980), p. xii.
13 Namık Kemal: *Osmanlı Tarihi*, 'İfade-i Meram', pp. 3-34. The introduction was reprinted in the early Republican era in 'Tahrib-i Harabat' in Uraz, Murad, *Namık Kemal* (İstanbul, 1938), pp. 68-9 and 'Namık Kemal, Tarih

Nedir?' in [Sevük], İsmail Habib, *Tanzimattanberi II - Edebiyat Antolojisi* (İstanbul, 1943), pp. 163-4.

14 For a discussion of the meaning of the term *millet*, often translated as nation, see Chapter 3.

15 Namık Kemal: *Osmanlı Tarihi*, p. 3: 'Bir milletin tarihi bilinmezse bekasına terakkisine lazım olan esbabın mevcudi, mefkudi nereden okunabilecek?' Mizancı Murad perceived history as a useful and practical tool for the statesmen. Mehmed Murad, *Tarih-i Umumi*. Vol. I (İstanbul, 1307), pp. 5-6.

16 For a discussion of Abdülhamidian censorship, see Boyar, Ebru, 'Engelhardt from censorship to icon: the use of a European diplomat's history in Ottoman and Turkish historiography on the *Tanzimat*', *Eurasian Studies*, III/1 (2004), pp. 81-8 and 'The press and the palace: the two-way relationship between Abdülhamid II and the press, 1876-1908,' *Bulletin of the School of Oriental and African Studies*, LXIX/3 (2006), pp. 417-32.

17 Adnan, A., 'Türk İnkılâp Tarihi [Yusuf Hikmet Bayur],' *Türkiyat Mecmuası*, VII-VIII (1940-1942), p. 337, footnote 3.

18 Akçuraoğlu Yusuf: *Türk Yılı*, pp. 319-25.

19 For example, see [Altınay], Ahmed Refik, *Hilminin Mektep Kitapları: Küçük Tarih-i Osmani. Mekatib-i Rüşdiye İkinci Senelerine Mahsus Proğrama Tevfikan Tertib Edilmiştir. 32 Resim ile 8 Haritaya Camidir* (İstanbul, 1327), p. 120; İhsan Şeref, *Cumhuriyet Çocuklarına Tarih Dersleri. Üçüncü Sınıf* (İstanbul, 1926), p. 61 and Süleyman Edip and Ali Tevfik, *İlkmektep Çocuklarına Yeni Tarih Dersleri, Beşinci Sınıf* (İstanbul, 1929), p. 120. This view is repeated by modern Turkish historians, for example, see Tekeli, İlhan and Selim İlkin, *Osmanlı İmparatorluğu'nda Eğitim ve Bilgi Üretim Sisteminin Oluşumu ve Dönüşümü* (Ankara, 1999), p. 179.

20 Although the curriculum prepared for primary schools in 1891 did not include history lessons, history was in the curriculum of town primary schools in 1902. The curriculum of middle (*rüştiye*) and secondary schools (*idadi*) and higher education (*mülkiye*) prepared between 1891 and 1902 also listed history lessons. Zengin, Zcki Salih, *II. Abdülhamit Dönemi Örgün Eğitim Kurumlarında Din Eğitimi ve Öğretimi 1876-1908* (Adana, 2003), tables 2-16.

21 This one dimensional and heavily tailored history-teaching was later regarded as responsible for creating ignorance of the plight of the Ottoman empire and of the situation in the world among the Ottoman educated elite.

For example, see the memoirs of Ahmed Rasim who was a student in that period (Ahmed Rasim, *Matbuat Hatıralarından. Muharrir, Şair, Edib* (İstanbul, 1342-1924), pp. 82-4).

22 Abdurrahman Şeref, *Tarih-i Devlet-i Osmaniye*, Vol. II (İstanbul, 1318), pp. 256-7 and 371, and Ali Cevad, *Mükemmel Osmanlı Tarihi* (İstanbul, 1316), p. 211.

23 See the memoirs of Falih Rıfkı Atay who was an *idadi* student in the late Abdülhamidian era. Atay, Falih Rıfkı, *Batış Yılları* (İstanbul, 1963), p. 26.

24 For example, a history book about the French Revolution was seized at the customs of Golos (Volos in south-east Thessaly) among 13 books which were detrimental (efkar-ı muzırraya müteallik). 18 Şaban 1315 and 30 Kanun-u evvel 1313: Başbakanlık Osmanlı Arşivi, İstanbul (hereafter BOA), Y. PRK. ASK. 135-74.

25 '909. Sultân 'Abdül-Hamīd'e,' in Tansel, Abdullah Fevziye (ed.), *Nâmık Kemal'in Husûsî Mektupları*, IV, *VII.-VIII. Rodos ve Sakız Mektupları* (Ankara, 1986), pp. 467-8.

26 Namık Kemal: *Osmanlı Tarihi*, p. 1. The banning of *Osmanlı Tarihi* became the subject of discussion. The book was said to have been banned as a result of a spy report (*jurnal*) submitted to Abdülhamid. See M. Salah Aldin, *Merhum Kemal Bey'in Tarihi Meselesi ve Mevad-ı Saire* (İstanbul, 1327).

27 Mehmed Memduh, 'İki Arîza,' *Müteferrika*, 1 (1993), p. 137. See also Tansel's discussion of the banning of the book by the palace in Tansel: *Nâmık Kemal'in Husûsî Mektupları, IV. VII. - VIII. Rodos ve Sakız Mektupları*, pp. 509-13.

28 Özgül, Metin Kayahan (ed.), *Ali Ekrem Bolayır'ın Hâtıraları* (Ankara, 1991), pp. 318, 323.

29 Kuran, Ercüment, 'Ottoman historiography of the Tanzimat period,' in Lewis, Bernard and P. M. Holt (eds.), *Historians of the Middle East* (London, 1962), p. 423.

30 Nihat Sami Banarlı describes Namık Kemal as a 'Turkish nationalist' (Türk milliyetçisi). See for example Banarlı, Nihat Sami, *Namık Kemal ve Türk-Osmanlı Milliyetçiliği* (İstanbul, 1947), p. 4.

31 Key, Kerim K., *An Outline of Modern Turkish Historiography* (İstanbul, 1954), p. 4, footnote 7. This commission was considered the nucleus of the Türk Tarihi Tetkik Cemiyeti which was established in 1931. The difference between Tarih-i Osmani Encümeni and Türk Tarihi Tetkik Cemiyeti was that the latter was directly controlled by the government, particularly by

Mustafa Kemal Atatürk himself, since it was considered one of the "revolutionary" tools.
32 Necib Asım and Mehmed Arif, *Osmanlı Tarihi,* Vol. I (İstanbul, 1335), p. d. The section 'Türkler' (Turks) is 288 pages long.
33 Köprülüzade Mehmed Fuad, 'Bizde Milli Tarih Yazılabilir mi?' *Yeni Mecmua,* I/22 (6 December 1917), pp. 427-8.
34 Emin Ali, 'Tarih Usulüne Dair,' *Yeni Mecmua,* II/52 (31 July 1918), pp. 514-6: 'Vesika yoksa tarih de yok' (p. 516).
35 Köprülü, Fuad, 'Türk Edebiyatı Tarihi'nde Usûl' in *Edebiyat Araştırmaları* (Ankara, 1966), pp. 3-47: 'Türkler'in yalnız şiirini değil, bütün fikrî ve medenî tezâhürlerini asırlar boyunca tam ve vâzıh bir sûrette yaşatacak böyle bir eser, yalnız millî değil, ayni zamanda beşerî ve ilmî bir âbide olacaktır' (pp. 22-3). This article was originally published in *Bilgi Mecmuası,* I /1 (1329), pp. 3-52.
36 Köprülü: 'Türk Edebiyatı Tarihi'nde Usûl,' p. 13: 'İyi bir tarihçi, tabiî ilimlerin dar käidelerini değil, bu ilimlerin tedkikinde hâkim olan ilmî rûhu almaya çalışmalıdır.'
37 *Birinci Türk Tarih Kongresi, Konferanslar, Münakaşalar* (n. p. p., n.d.), p. 320. This speech was republished in Köprülüzade M. Fuat, *Türk Dili ve Edebiyatı Hakkında Araştırmalar* (İstanbul, 1934), pp. 1-25.
38 Köprülü: 'Türk Edebiyatı Tarihi'nde Usûl', p. 47: 'Edebiyat tarihine hevesli her Türk genci, henüz inşâ malzemesinden hiçbiri hazır bulunmıyan bu büyük millî ve ilmî âbide için, izah edilen usûller dairesinde hiç olmazsa birer taş getirmeye çalışmalıdır; çünkü, vücûde gelecek bu muhteşem abide, büyük ve şerefli Türk milletinin asırlar boyunca muhtelif safhalarda kendini gösteren Türk millî dehâsının vahdetini göstererek, istikbâldeki nesilleri ayni vahdet gâyesine sevkedecektir. Türk edebiyatı tarihçisi için bundan daha asil ve mukaddes bir hedef nasıl tasavvur olunabilir!' See also pp. 9-10, 13.
39 [Altınay], Ahmed Refik, 'Tarih ve Müverrihler: 4 - Tarih Bir İlimdir,' *Hayat,* III/63 (9 February 1928), pp. 6-7: 'Tarih ilmi sair ilimlere benzemez; o sayılamayan şeyleri sayar, ruhların temevvücünden mütehassis olur; onun ruhundan her şey ihtizaz eder; o, dehanın, «faal zeka» nın, mutevasıtın serine temas ederek Rabdan aldığı emri icra eder.'
40 Birgen, Muhittin, 'Tarihimiz, Tarihçilerimiz ve Cumhuriyet,' in Arıkan, Zeki (ed.), *Tarihimiz ve Cumhuriyet, Muhittin Birgen (1885-1951)* (İstanbul, 1997), p. 104: 'Çünkü, Türk için Osmanlı tarihi demek, yedi asırlık bir zulmün tarihi demekti.'

41 Birgen: 'Tarihimiz, Tarihçilerimiz ve Cumhuriyet,' pp. 103-5; and 'Kapıkulunun Tasvifi. Kapıkulu Edebiyatı,' in Arıkan, *Tarihimiz ve Cumhuriyet,* pp. 130-4: 'Osmanlı ve Türk tarihleri meselesinin halli "Osmanlı" kelimesinin kuyruğuna bir "Türk" kelimesi yapıştırmak suretiyle temin edilemez' (p. 134).

42 [İnan], Afet, 'Türk Osmanlı Tarihinin Karakteristik Noktalarına Bir Bakış,' in *İkinci Türk Tarih Kurumu Kongresi. İstanbul 20-25 Eylül 1937. Kongrenin Çalışmaları, Kongreye Sunulan Tebliğler* (İstanbul, 1943), pp. 756-65.

43 The Halkevleri were established in order to encourage the spread of national consciousness and understanding of the ideals of the Republic among the population.

44 Ali Necip, 'Halkevleri Yıldönümü Nutku,' *Ülkü Halkevleri Mecmuası,* III/13 (March 1934), p. 7: 'Başka milletler bizi Küçük Asya'da ve Avrupa'da yerleşmiş sarı ırka mensup yabancı ve düşman bir millet tanmak istediler.'

45 Ünaydın, Ruşen Eşref, 'Tarih Kurumu'nun Kuruluş Hazırlığı,' in *Atatürk Tarih ve Dil Kurumları. Hâtıralar* (Ankara, 1954), p. 59.

46 Ali Reşat, *Umumi Tarih* (İstanbul, 1929).

47 Akçuraoğlu Yusuf Bey, 'Tarih Yazmak ve Tarih Okutmak Usullerine Dair,' in *Birinci Türk Tarih Kongresi,* pp. 577-607.

48 Atay, Falih Rıfkı, 'Tarih Kongresi,' *Ülkü Halkevleri Mecmuası,* X/55 (September 1937), p. 1: 'Renkli ve barbar Türk telâkkisi Osmanlı gafleti içinde ve terceme yolu ile, Türk mekteplerine kadar girmiştir.'

49 Togan: *Tarihde Usul.*

50 Togan, Zeki Velidi, *Scientific Collaboration of the Islamic Orient and the Occident. A Lecture Delivered in the Faculty of Law on 17th May 1950* (İstanbul, 1951).

51 Peyami Safa, *Türk İnkılâbına Bakışlar (Cumhuriyetin 15 inci yılı münasebetile)* ([İstanbul], [1938]), p. 224: 'Bütün bu millî şeref ve iddia kabarışları önünde, kendini geri bir Asya ırkının küçülmüş, iğrilmiş ve kurumuş bir dalı sanan Osmanlı çocuğunun Bosna-Hersek, Trablusgarb, Balkan ve Sevr felâketlerinden sonra yarımyamalak uyanmış millî şuurunun dibini kemiren kendini aşağı görme kompleksini parçalamak, ona Avrupa medeniyeti manzumesine girebileceğini bir çırpıda ispat ettikten sonra, insan kadar eski tarihinin zaman içindeki yekpare ve heybetli kitlesinden mekân içindeki büyük taazzuva geçişin imkânlarını sezdirerek, ruhunu koskoca ve ebedî Türkiye hakikatinin damgasını basmak... İşte

milliyetçi ve medeniyetçi Atatürk inkılâbının en esaslı temellerinden biri.' For the continuation of this idea into the 1970s', see Baykal, Bekir Sıtkı, 'Atatürk Devrimlerinde Tarihin Rolü,' in *Atatürk ve Devrim. Atatürkçü Düşünce Üzerine Denemeler* (Ankara, 1973), pp. 71-7.

52 Karaosmanoğlu, Yakup Kadri, *Atatürk* (Ankara, 1981), p. 87.
53 Karaosmanoğlu: *Atatürk*, p. 88: 'ne Dumlupınar zaferi; ne Lozan sulh muahedesi, ne onu takip eden bir sürü politik, sosyal, kültürel ve ekonomik inkılâplar cihanın, Türk milleti aleyhindeki kötü zannını ve bedbaht kanaatlerini hâlâ sarsamamıştı! Kendi yurdunda kök salmış bütün asırlık hurafeleri bir hamlede söküp atan bu adam, objektif ilmin, hak ve hakikatın öz kaynağı telâkki edilen garb âleminin kafasından bu kara cehalet beneğini bir türlü silemiyordu.'
54 This term is used when referring to both the Ottoman and the early Republican periods (treated as a continuum) when neither the word Ottoman nor the word Turkish can be used alone.
55 Gramsci, Antonio, 'The intellectuals,' in *Selections from the Prison Notebooks*, edited and translated by Quintin Hoare and Geoffrey Nowell Smith (London, 1998), p. 12.
56 Bursalı Mehmet Tahir Efendi, *Osmanlı Müellifleri 1299-1915*, Vol. III (İstanbul, 1975), p. 30.
57 Baysun, M. Cavid, 'Cevdet Paşa'nın İşkodra'ya Memûriyetine Âid Vesîkalar,' *Tarih Dergisi*, XVI/21 (1966), pp. 39-52.
58 For a biography of Abdurrahman Şeref, see Efdal Aldin, *Abdurrahman Şeref Efendi Tercüme-i Hali. Hayat-ı Resmiye ve Hususiyesi* (İstanbul, 1345-1927).
59 Emil, Birol, *Mizancı Murad Bey Hayatı ve Eserleri* (İstanbul, 1979), pp. 36-55; 63-4.
60 Hürmen, F. Rezan (ed.), *"Bir Devlet Adamının" Mehmet Tevfik Beyin (Biren) II. Abdülhamid, Meşrutiyet ve Mütareke Devri Hatıraları* (İstanbul, 1993), I, p. 463.
61 Mizancı Murad, *Mücahede-i Milliye. Gurbet ve Avdet Devirleri* (İstanbul, 1994), pp. 41-72. For a transliterated text of the *layiha*, see Kaplan, Mehmet, İnci Enginün, Birol Emil and Zeynep Kerman (eds.), *Yeni Türk Edebiyatı Antolojisi*, Vol. III (İstanbul, 1979), pp. 496-508.
62 Kuran, Ahmet Bedevî, *İnkılâp Tarihimiz ve "Jön Türkler"* (İstanbul, 1945), pp. 40-62. For a more negative picture of Mizancı Murad's character and history-writing, see Yinanç: 'Tanzimattan Meşrutiyete Kadar Bizde Tarihçilik', pp. 579-81.

63 Namık Kemal, '980. Menemenli Rif'at Bey'e (30 Haziran 1304),' in Tansel: *Nâmık Kemal'in Husûsî Mektupları, IV. VII.-VIII. Rodos ve Sakız Mektupları*, pp. 559-61.
64 *II. Abdülhamid'in Hatıra Defteri* (İstanbul, 1960), p. 106: 'Ben edebiyata düşman olsaydım, Kemal Bey'e, vefâtı gününe kadar kesemden maaş vermez ve oğlunu hizmetime almazdım. Ben edebiyata düşman olsaydım, Ekrem ve Ebüzziya Beylerin o kadar cev rü [*sic.*] nâzını çekmezdim. Ben edebiyata düşman olsaydım, Abdülhak Hâmit Bey'i dolgun maaşlarla terfih ettikten başka arasıra, borçlarını da vermek gibi hayırhaklıklarda bulunmazdım. Ben edebiyata ve fenn-i tarihe düşman olsaydım, bir aralık tac ü tahtımla da uğraşmak istemiş olan Murat Bey'in her münâsebetsizliğine katlanarak saltanatımın son demine kadar mustevfi maaş ile hizmeti devlette kalmasına kâil olmazdım. Hayır, tekrar ederim ki, ben üdebânın hakiki ve müşfik dostu idim. Eğer onlara düşman olsaydım, benim de sokak ortalarında edip ve muharrir öldürecek adamlarım yok değildi.'
65 Karal, Enver Ziya, 'Atatürk'ün Türk Tarih Tezi' in *Atatürk Hakkında Konferanslar* (Ankara, 1946), p. 56.
66 Maliye Nazırı Cavid Bey, *Felaket Günleri. Mütareke Devrinin Feci Tarihi*, edited by Osman Selim Kocahanoğlu (İstanbul, 2000), I, pp. 191-2.
67 *Kapıkulu* (slave of the Port) is the term used for a palace servant employed in the administration or the army.
68 Birgen pointed out that he did not use 'class' in the Marxist sense, he meant rather 'eta' which he defined at length in 'Kapıkulu'nun Tavsifi. Kapıkulu Edebiyatı' in Arıkan: *Tarihimiz ve Cumhuriyet*, pp. 130-1.
69 Reşit Galip, 'Türk Tarih İnkılâbı ve Yabancı Tezler,' *Ülkü Halkevleri Mecmuası*, II/9 (October 1933), pp. 164-6.
70 See Türkeş, Mustafa, *Ulusçu Bir Sol Akım: Kadro Hareketi (1932-1934)* (Ankara, 1999).
71 B. A. [Burhan Asaf], 'Kronikler: Arkada Kalan Darülfünun,' *Kadro Aylık Fikir Mecmuası*, I/8 (August 1932) [reprinted in Ankara, 1978], I, pp. 47-8.
72 [Aydemir], Şevket Süreyya, 'Millî Kurtuluş Hareketleri Hakkında Bizim Tezimiz,' *Kadro Aylık Fikir Mecmuası*, I/12 (December 1932) [reprinted in Ankara, 1978], I, p. 44: 'Biz yeni hayat şartları için yeni fikir ve yeni insan arıyoruz. Hasretimiz ve teveccühümüz ancak yeniyedir.'
73 Bilsel, Cemil, *İstanbul Üniversitesi Tarihi* (İstanbul, 1943), pp. 31-4.
74 Başgöz, İlhan and Howard E. Wilson, *Educational Problems in Turkey 1920-1940* (Bloomington, 1968), p. 166. The Minister of Education, Reşit

Galip said 'yeni bir tarih telâkkisi, milli bir hareket halinde bütün ülkeyi sardı, Darülfününda buna bir alâka uyandırabilmek için üç yıl kadar uğraşmak lâzım geldi.' In Bilsel: *İstanbul Üniversitesi Tarihi*, p. 34.

75 T. T. T. Cemiyeti, *Tarih I- Tarihtenevvelki Zamanlar ve Eski Zamanlar* (İstanbul, 1932), p. 2: 'How is a nation a state, and, therefore, the source of laws and the power which executes them. But at the same time it is itself subject to these laws.' (Nasıl ki, millet devlettir; bu itibarla kanunların sahibidir ve onları infaz eden kuvvettir; fakat aynı zamanda kendi de bu kanunlara tabidir.)

76 Kaplan: *Namık Kemal*, pp. 151-2.

77 Ahmed Refik Altınay continued to produce similar books in the Republican era, such as *Kızlar Ağası* (İstanbul, 1926).

78 25.v.1942: Başbakanlık Cumhuriyet Arşivi, Ankara (hereafter BCA), 490 01 869 4231.

79 The full reference of the book is Peremeci, Osman Nuri, *Tuna Boyu Tarihi* (İstanbul, 1942). Günaltay asked the author to change the statement 'The first Bulgarians lived by shepherding and by plundering' (İlk Bulgarların geçinmesi çobanlık ve yağmacılık ile idi) (on p. 11 of the manuscript). The author changed it to 'The first Bulgarians lived by shepherding' (İlk Bulgarların geçinmesi çobanlık ile idi) (on p. 21 of the book).

80 For Halkevleri and their functions see *Atatürk ve Halkevleri. Atatürkçü Düşünce Üzerine Denemeler* (Ankara, 1974) and Şimşek, Sefa, *Bir İdeolojik Seferberlik Deneyimi Halkevleri 1932-1951* (İstanbul, 2002).

81 See, for instance 27.xii.1936: BCA, 490 01 850 361 1, for the list of the books to be bought and sent to the Halkevleri by the party.

82 [Altınay], Ahmed Refik: *Küçük Tarih-i Osmani*, p. 128: 'Osmanlı namı anıldığı zaman bu okuduğun şeyleri, milletimizin eski halini, Osmanlılığın eski parlaklığını askerlerimizin eski şerefini daima gözünün önüne getir! Bu şerefi muhafaza etmeğe bütün kuvvetinle çalış! Milletine muhabbetini, vatanına sadakatini ancak böyle ispat edebilirsin. Sana bu dersleri ancak tarih öğretebilir; onun için vatanının halini, milletinin büyüklüğünü sana öğreten Osmanlı tarihini seve seve, düşüne düşüne okumalısın.'

83 İhsan Şeref: *Cumhuriyet Çocuklarına Tarih Dersleri*, p. 10: 'Bizimde tarihimiz vardır. Hem de pek şanlıdır. Adı Anadolu Türklerinin tarihi» [*sic.*] dir. Herkes kendi milletinin tarihini mutlaka bilmelidir. Eğer tarihimizi bilmez isek bizde milliyet duygusu olmaz [.] Böyle millet, milliyet duygusu olmayan insanların sana bana, hiç kimseye bir faidesi dokunmaz.' İhsan Şeref attended the first Historical Congress and gave an

emotional speech there. For this speech, see *Birinci Türk Tarih Kongresi*, pp. 14-6.

84 *Türk Çocuklarına Tarih Notları* (Ankara, 1929), pp. 22-3. 'Tarih bu mühim vazifeyi ifa ederken, yalnız, bugünün insanlarını, tenvir ve irşat etmekle kalmıyor, bundan sonra gelecek insanlara da faideli bir mürebbi oluyor.' This understanding of history as being a mirror for the future and providing moral lessons extracted from the history of their forefathers appears in a school text book written by a Turkish teacher in Bulgaria published for minority schools there. [Peremeci], Osman Nuri, *Ecdad Tarihi* (Şumnu, 1340-1924), pp. a-c.

85 T. T. T. Cemiyeti: *Tarih I* (1932), p. 8. The same role was attributed to history by Şemsettin Günaltay using the same words in 1939. Günaltay, Şemsettin, *Lise Kitapları. Tarih I* (İstanbul, 1939), p. 2.

86 Karal: 'Atatürk'ün Türk Tarih Tezi,' p. 60.

87 *Atatürk'ün Özdeyişleri* (Ankara, 1975), p. 28: 'Tarih bir milletin nelere müstait olduğunu ve neler başarmaya muktedir bulunduğunu gösteren en doğru bir kılavuzdur.'

88 İnan, Afet, 'İstiklâl Savaşında Tarih Bilgisinin Rolü' in *Atatürk Hakkında Konferanslar* (Ankara, 1946), p. 8. İnan's idea of history was very commonly accepted in the early forties, as evident in the definition of history given by A. Şükrü Esmer in the introduction to his book on political history prepared for the School of Political Science (Siyasal Bilgiler Okulu): 'Tarih denilen anahtar mevcut olmadıkça bugünü anlamak mümkün değildir.' See *Siyasi Tarih* (İstanbul, 1944), p. 1.

89 [Aykaç], Fâzıl Ahmet, *Gelecek Asırlarda Tarih Dersi* (n.p.p., 1928). For a popular publication in order to encourage interest in history see Sertelli, İskender Fahreddin, *Tarih Sevgisi, Yeni Vesikalar* (İstanbul, 1936).

Chapter Two

1 *The Times*, Wednesday, July 3, 1876, p. 5. Sir Edward S. Creasy used the term to denote the Balkan mountains, not a specific region. Creasy, Edward S., *History of the Ottoman Turks: From the Beginning of their Empire to the Present Time* (London, 1878), p. 65.

2 Mazower, Mark, *The Balkans* (London, 2001), pp. 3-4.

3 Todorova, Maria, *Imagining the Balkans* (New York and Oxford, 1997), p. 32.

4 Ahmed Vefik Paşa, *Lehçe-i Osmani* (Dersaadet, 1306), I, p. 193. The first edition of this dictionary was published in 1293/1876 and the second edition was published in 1306/1890.
5 Ş. Sami, *Kâmûs-ı Türkî* (Dersaadet, 1317, reprinted in İstanbul, 1999), p. 275: 'sarp ve müselsel veya ormanla mestur dağ, silsele-i cibal.'
6 Ş. Sami, *Kamus-i Fransevi. Fransızcadan Türkçeye Lugat. Dictionnaire Français-Turc* (İstanbul, 1299-1882), p. 229.
7 Ş. Sami, *Kamus ül-Alam. Tarih ve Coğrafya Lugatı*, Vol. II (İstanbul, 1316-1899), p. 1,211.
8 Kamil Kapudan, *Karadağ. Karadağ Hakkında Bazı Malumata Şamildir* (İstanbul, 1294), p. 26.
9 'Devr-i İstila' in Pala, İskender (ed.), *Namık Kemal'in Tarihi Biyografileri* (Ankara, 1989), p. 13.
10 [Ahmed Lütfi Efendi], *Vak'a-Nüvis Ahmed Lûtfî Efendi Tarihi C. XI*, edited by M. Münir Aktepe (Ankara, 1989), p. 43.
11 Ahmed Cemal, *Mefahir-i Milliye-i Osmaniyeden: Plevne Müdafası* (Kostantiniye, 1316), p. 11.
12 Kazım Bey Karabekir, *Edirne Mahfil-i Askeriyesinde Verilen Konferanslardan Sırb-Bulgar Seferi 1885* (Edirne, 1328), p. 43.
13 Ali Cevad, *Memalik-i Osmaniyenin Tarih ve Coğrafya Lugatı* (Dersaadet, 1313), p. 197: 'Balkan: Avrupa-i Osmaniyede Bulgaristan ile Şarki Rumeli arasında garbdan şarka doğru muvazatan imtidad eyleyen silsile-i cibalin ismidir ki bulunduğu şeb-i cezire namıyla müsemma olmuştur.'
14 Ş. Sami: *Kamus ül-Alam,* Vol. II, pp. 1,211-7: 'Balkan şeb-i cezıresi şimalen Avusturya ve Macaristanla, şimal-i şarki tarafından Rusya ile, şarken Karadenizle ve İstanbul Boğazıyla, cenuben Marmara Denizi, Kala-i Sultaniye Boğazı, Adalar Denizi ve Akdenizle, garben Yunan ve Adriyatik Deniziyle ve Dalmaçya ile mahdud ve muhat olub, ″30 ° 36 ile ″30 ° 47 arzı şimali ve ″20 ° 15 ile ´40 ° 29 tul-u şarki arasında mümted olur' (p. 1,211).
15 Ş. Sami: *Kamus ül-Alam,* Vol. II, p. 1,211.
16 Ali Rıza, *Atlaslı Memalik-i Osmaniye Coğrafyası, Kısm-ı Evvel* (İstanbul, 1318), p. 6.
17 İstanbul Belediyesi, *İstanbul Şehri Rehberi* (İstanbul, 1934), p. 154: 'The reason that the Greeks and Orthodox are still called *Rum* and the Balkan Peninsula, *Rumeli* in Turkish and that, in the past, the Arabs and Muslims called Anatolia *Diyarı rum* comes from [the fact] that these places had belonged to the ancient Romans and the people of these places were the subjects of the ancient Romans.' (Türkçede Yunanlılara ve Ortodokslara

halâ (Rum) ve Balkan yarımadasına (Rumeli) Anadoluya evvelcede Araplar ve İslâmlar tarafından (Diyarı rum) denilmesinin sebebi bu yerlerin eski Romalıların arazisi ve buralardaki halkın da eski Romalıların tebaası olmasından ileri gelir.)

18 T.T.T. Cemiyeti, *Tarih III. Yeni ve Yakın Zamanlar*, second edition (Ankara, 1941), pp. 18-9 and p. 20: 'İmparator, Osmanlı Türklerinin *Rumeli*ye geçip Bulgarlar ve Sırplar üzerine yürümesi halinde, bir müddet daha İstanbulun tehlikeyi atlatacağını zannediyordu [...] Gelibolu, Osmanlıların Balkanlarda yaptıkları seri fütuhatın ve harekâtın üssübahrisi oldu [...] Daha evel de söylendiği üzere Osmanlı Türkleri Balkanlara geçmeden önce, Balkan Yarımadası, milâttan evel Trak ve milâttan sora Hun, Avar ve Bulgar istilâ ve muhaceretlerine sahne olmuştur.'

19 Nahid Sırrı, *Bir Edirne Seyahatnamesi* (Ankara, 1941), p. 5: 'Trakya'nın ve hattâ daha uzakların, hemen bütün eski Rumeli'nin havasını.'

20 İnalcık, Halil, *Tanzimat ve Bulgar Meselesi* (Ankara, 1943), p. 84, footnote 1. This book was based on his PhD. dissertation.

21 İnalcık: *Tanzimat ve Bulgar Meselesi*, for example pp. 8, 16, 18, 24-5, 26, 109, 41, footnote 3.

22 İnalcık: *Tanzimat ve Bulgar Meselesi*, for example, p. 17.

23 İnalcık, Halil, 'Rumeli' in *The Encyclopaedia of Islam,* second edition, Vol. VIII (Leiden, 1995), pp. 608-9. Suraiya Faroqhi seems to use these two terms interchangeably in her 'Making a living: economic crisis and partial recovery' in İnalcık, Halil and Donald Quataert (eds.), *An Economic and Social History of the Ottoman Empire 1300-1914* (Cambridge, 1994), pp. 411-636. Karpat, Kemal H., *The Politicization of Islam. Reconstructing Identity, State, Faith, and the Community in the Late Ottoman State* (Oxford, 2001), p. 6; Georgeon, François, *Des Ottomans aux Turcs. Naissance d'une nation* (İstanbul, 1995), p. 1.

24 Quataert, Donald, *The Ottoman Empire, 1700-1922* (Cambridge, 2000), p. 204.

25 Fortna, Benjamin C., *Imperial Classroom, Islam, the State and Education in the Late Ottoman Empire* (Oxford, 2002), p. 155. See also Brubaker, Rogers, *Nationalism Reframed. Nationhood and the Nation Question in the New Europe* (Cambridge, 1996), p. 153.

26 Ş. Sami: *Kâmûs-ı Türkî*, p. 275: 'Rumeli = memalik-i Osmaniyenin Avrupada ki kısmı.' Rumeli is defined as 'Turkey in Europe' and 'the province of Macedonia' in Redhouse, James W., *A Turkish and English Lexicon* (Constantinople, 1890), p. 994. However, Ş. Sami underlines the

difficulty of defining the borders of Rumeli. See in *Kamus ül-Alam, Tarih ve Coğrafya Lugatı*, Vol. III (İstanbul, 1308-1891), p. 2,376.

27 Ahmed Nazmi, *Rumeli Haritası* (İstanbul, 1329).

28 Pakalın, Mehmet Zeki, *Osmanlı Tarih Deyimleri ve Terimleri Sözlüğü* (İstanbul, 1946): III, p. 56: 'Rumeli: Osmanlı İmparatorluğunun Avrupa kıt'asındaki kısmına verilen addır'; p. 57: 'Rumeli Eyaleti: Osmanlı İmparatorluğunun Avrupa kıt'asındaki büyük eyaletlerden birine verilen addır. Eyalet aşağıdaki yerleri ihtiva ediyordu: Selânik, Üsküp, Ohri, Köstendil, Delvina, Avlonya, Elbasan, Prizren, Dukagin, Alacahisar, Vilçetrin, Yanya, Semendre, Yanova.'

29 Marriott, J. A. R., *The Eastern Question. An Historical Study in European Diplomacy* (Oxford, 1917), p. 18.

30 'Diplomacy in the Balkans' by a former Eastern correspondent in *The Times*, Tuesday, October 27, 1885, p. 8. However, in the school atlas, *The World Wide Atlas of Modern Geography*, with an introduction by J. Scott Keltie, fifth edition (Edinburgh and London, 1902), the term 'the Balkans' refers only to the mountains. In a school atlas of 1938, published by the same publishing house, the Balkans appears as a regional designation. *W. & A. K. Johnston's Modern School Atlas*, edited by W. R. Kermarck, ninth edition (Edinburgh and London, 1938), 'Italy and the Balkans,' pp. 22-3.

31 1298 (date on the file): BOA, Y. PRK. TKM., 4-57.

32 *The Times*, Thursday, April 23, 1903, p. 4.

33 1298 (date on the file): BOA, Y. PRK. TKM., 4-57.

34 Tüccarzade İbrahim Hilmi, *Memalik-i Osmaniyenin Ceb Atlası* ([İstanbul], 1323), p. 1: 'Avrupa-i Osmani Balkan yarım adasının vastında vaki ve sathının nısfından ziyadesini camidir.'

35 Binbaşı Mehmed Nasrullah, Kol Ağası Mehmed Rüşdi, and Mülazım Mehmed Eşref, *Memalik-i Mahrusa-i Şahaneye Mahsus Mükemmel Mufassal Atlas* (İstanbul, 1325), p. 4. For an earlier example of an atlas which does not contain *balkan* as a name of a region, see Rıza, *Sevkül Ceyş Atlası* (İstanbul, 1306).

36 11 Teşrin-i sani 1305: BOA, Y. PRK. A. 5-50; for censoring newspapers published in İstanbul, 15 Teşrin-i sani 1305: BOA, Y. PRK. A. 5-52 and for a discussion of censorship, see 12 Teşrin-i sani 1305: BOA, Y. PRK. A. 5-51.

37 İnuğur, M. Nuri, *Basın ve Yayın Tarihi* (İstanbul, 1982), pp. 263-4; İrtem, Süleyman Kâni, *Abdülhamid Devrinde Hafiyelik ve Sansür, Abdülhamid'e*

Verilen Jurnaller, edited by Osman Selim Kocahanoğlu (İstanbul, 1999), pp. 217-30.
38 [Ergin], Osman Nuri, *Abdülhamid-i Sani ve Devri Saltanatı. Hayat-ı Hususiye ve Siyasiyesi* (İstanbul, 1327), p. 582: '«Ermenistan» kelimesi gibi tarih ve coğrafyaya müteallik esamiyenin zikri memnudur.'
39 İrtem: *Abdülhamid Devrinde Hafiyelik ve Sansür*, p. 217: 'Ermenistan gibi tarih ve coğrafyaya müteallik isimlerin zikri yasaktı.'
40 Fesch, Paul, *Constantinople aux derniers jours d'Abdul-Hamid* (Paris, [1907]), pp. 52-3.
41 Kabacalı, Alpay, *Başlangıçtan Günümüze Türkiye'de Basın Sansürü* (İstanbul, 1990), pp. 57-8; Koloğlu, Orhan, '"Muzır" Ararken Alay Konusu Olan Rejim: II. Abdülhamit Sansürü,' *Tarih ve Toplum*, 38 (January 1987), p. 18; Boyar: 'The press and the palace,' pp. 418-9.
42 Tüccarzade İbrahim Hilmi: *Memalik-i Osmaniyenin Ceb Atlası*, p. 1.
43 Mizancı Murad: *Mücahede-i Milliye*, p. 117: 'Mısır sözü bir aralık padişahın sinirine o kadar dokunmağa başlamıştı ki, hürriyet, vesayet, vatan sözleri gibi Mısır dahi yasak edilmiş idi.'; Yalçın, Hüseyin Cahit, *Siyasal Anılar* (İstanbul, 2000), pp. 35-6.
44 For a discussion of the meaning of the term *millet*, see Chapter 3.
45 İhsan Şeref: *Cumhuriyet Çocuklarına Tarih Dersleri*, pp. 57 and 61; Süleyman Edip ve Ali Tevfik, *İlk Mektep Çocuklarına Tarih Dersleri. Dördüncü Sınıf* (İstanbul, 1929), p. 117; Süleyman Edip and Ali Tevfik: *İlkmektep Çocuklarına Yeni Tarih Dersleri. Beşinci Sınıf*, p. 120.
46 Ahmed Vefik Paşa: *Fezleke*, p. 292 and Lütfiye Hanım, *Mirat-ı Tarih-i Osmani* (İstanbul, 1293), p. 407.
47 Kaplan, *et al.*: *Yeni Türk Edebiyatı Antolojisi*, III, p. 502.
48 Ali Cevad: *Mükemmel Osmanlı Tarihi*, 'millet' (pp. 286 and 296) and 'vatan' (p. 296).
49 'Albania' in *The Times*, Wednesday, September 14, 1881, p. 5; 'Armenia' and 'Turkey' in *The Times*, Tuesday, September 6, 1881, p. 6.
50 Ali Haydar Midhat Bey, *The Life of Midhat Pasha. A Record of His Services, Political Reforms, Banishment, and Judicial Murder* (London, 1903), p. 33.
51 Ali Haydar Midhat Bey, *Midhat Pacha. Sa vie - son ouvre* (Paris, 1908), p. 2.
52 Ali Haydar Midhat, *Midhat Paşa'nın Hayat-ı Siyasiyesi, Hizmatı ve Şahadeti* (Kahire, 1322), pp. 6-7 and Ali Haydar Midhat, *Midhat Paşa. Hayat-ı Siyasiyesi, Hidematı, Mena-i Hayatı* (İstanbul, 1325), I, p. 6: 'O

aralık Rumelinin sağ ve orta kollarında ve hususiyle büyük Balkan'ın her cihetinde zuhur eden haydudluk ve katl-i tarik maddeleri dahilen ve haricen pek ziyade ehemmiyet almış idüğünden bunun içün kuvvet ve şöhret ve şekime sahibi birinin intihabı lazım iken Babıali'den kimsenin haberi olmaksızın müşarün-ileyh [Kıbrıslı Mehmed Paşa] bu maslahata Midhat Efendi'nin memuriyetini ve kendüye icraat içün mezuniyyet-i fevkalade verilmesini arz ederek...'

53 Mehmed Arif, *Başımıza Gelenler. Rusya Muharebesi Ahiresinin Anadolu Kısmından ve Mısır Ahvalinden ve Bu Münasebetle Tenkidat-ı Mühimme-i Ahlakiyeden Bahseder* (Dersaadet, 1328), p. 3; Mehmed Arif, *Başımıza Gelenler. Bin İkiyüz Doksan Dört Tarih-i Hicriyesinde Vukubulan Rusya Muharebesinden Bahseder* (Mısır, 1321), p. 3: 'Romanyalıları, Sırblıları, Karadağlıları, Bulgarları birer hükümet-i müstakile heyetinde Balkan hükümetleri namıyla ihya eden yine tarihtir.'

54 Ragıb Rıfkı, *Musavver Bulgaristan. Ahval-i Coğrafiye ve Tarihiyesi, Etnoğrafya Nokta-ı Nazarından Tedkiki, Suret-i Teşkil ve İdare-i Dahiliyesi, Ahval-i Askeriyesi* (İstanbul, 1324), for example see p. 26.

55 Ragıb Rıfkı: *Musavver Bulgaristan*, p. 27.

56 [Altınay], Ahmed Refik: *Küçük Tarih-i Osmani*, p. 104.

57 Ahmed Rasim, *Resimli ve Haritalı Osmanlı Tarihi*, Vol. IV (Konstantiniye, 1330-1328).

58 Engelhardt, Ed., *La Turquie et le Tanzimat ou historie des réformes dans l'empire ottoman depuis 1826 jusqu'à nos jours* (Paris, 1882), two vols.; Engelhard, Ed., *Türkiye ve Tanzimat. Devlet-i Osmaniyenin Tarih-i Islahatı 1826-1882*, translated by Ali Reşad (İstanbul, 1328). For the subjectivity of translation of Engelhardt by Ali Reşad, see Boyar: 'Engelhardt from censorship to icon,' p. 94. In Ali Reşad's translation, 'population balkaniques' (p. 138) was translated as 'Balkan akvamı' (p. 328) and this term was used in Ahmed Rasim's *Resimli ve Haritalı Osmanlı Tarihi*, IV, p. 2,227.

59 Ahmed Rasim: *Resimli ve Haritalı Osmanlı Tarihi*, IV, p. 2,227. For further examples of the use of *balkan*, see pp. 2,166 and 2,209 for 'Balkan Şeb-i Ceziresi,' p. 2,140 for 'Balkanlar.'

60 Rumeli Muhacirin-i İslamiye Cemiyet-i Hayriyesi, *Alam-ı İslam. Bulgar Vahşetleri. İslamiyetin Enzar-ı Basiretine ve Alem-i İnsaniyet ve Medeniyetin Nazar-ı Dikkatine* (İstanbul, 1328), for example see p. 1 and p. 35. Rumeli Muhacirin-i İslamiye Cemiyet-i Hayriyesi: *Rumeli Mezalimi ve Bulgar Vahşetleri*, for example see p. 11 and p. 14.

61 Hüseyin Kazım, *Arnavutlar Ne Yaptılar?* (İstanbul, 1330), p. 4: 'Damn them [the Albanians] for they were the fundamental reason for the Quadruple Balkan alliance.' (Lanet onlara ki, Balkan ittifak-ı murebbanın sebeb-i asliyesi Arnavudlardır.)
62 Ahmed Salah Aldin, *Makedonya Meselesi ve Balkan Harbi Ahiri* (Dersaadet, 1331), pp. 5 and 10.
63 Ziya Gökalp, 'Balkanlar Destanı' in Tansel, Abdullah Fevziye (ed.), *Ziya Gökalp Külliyatı-1. Şiirler ve Halk Masalları* (Ankara, 1989). This poem was first published in 1912, in *Tanin* with the title 'Muharâbe Destanı-Karadağ'da' and, under the new title, it was published in 1914 in Ziya Gökalp's first book of poems, *Kızılelma*.
64 Mehmed Eşref, *32 Yafta 128 Parça Haritaya Havi Tarih-i Umumi ve Osmani Atlası* ([İstanbul], 1330).
65 Kelekyan, Diran (Kélékian, Diran), *Kamus-i Fransevi. Dictionnaire Turc-Français* (İstanbul, 1329-1911), p. 247. In the introduction to the dictionary, Kelekyan explains the reason for the publication of this dictionary as being the need to update Şemseddin Sami's dictionary according to the needs of the day stemming from developments in science, art and literature. He writes: 'Osmanlılarla Avrupalıların yekdiğerini tamamıyla anlamaları Şark ve Garb lisanlarındaki kelimeler arasında ahenk peydasına yani bir fikri efham eden lugata hatib ve muhatabın aynı manayı atf etmesine mütevakıf idi' ('Mukaddime,' p. 7); 'Pour bien se comprendre entre européens et ottomans, il fallait préciser la signification des mots, afin de leur attribuer exactement le même sens dans les deux langues' ('Introduction,' p. 10).
66 Ali Seydi, *Resimli Kamus-i Osmani* (Darülhilafe-i Aliye, 1330), I, p. 169: 'Rumeli-i Şahaneyi garbden şarka doğru kat eden cibal-i şahika-ı maruf.'
67 Ali Seydi, *Resimli Yeni Türkçe Lûgat* (İstanbul, 1929), p. 85: 'bundan dolayı o kıt'aya Balkan yarımadası denir.'
68 Ali Reşad, *Asr-ı Hazır Tarihi. Liselerin İkinci Devre Son Sınıflarına Mahsustur* (İstanbul, 1926).
69 Faik Sabri, *İlk Atlas. İlk Mekteplere Mahsus* (İstanbul, 1927), p. 1. The same author does not use the Balkans as a regional designation in his 1928 atlas prepared for secondary and high schools. See Faik Sabri, *Orta Atlas. Liselere ve Orta Mekteplere Mahsus* (İstanbul, 1928).
70 *Türk Tarihinin Ana Hatları Atlası* (Ankara, 1931), Section 24b.
71 'Projet Greco-Turc' in 9.i.1934: BCA, 030 10 227 526 9, f. 13.

Chapter Three

1 For example, see Namık Kemal, 'Bir Mülahaza' in Özön, Mustafa Nihat (ed.), *Ölümünün 50 nci Yılı Münasebetiyle Namık Kemal ve İbret Gazetesi* (İstanbul, 1938), p. 37, and Ahmed Cevdet Paşa: *Ma'rûzât*, p. 224. Ahmed Cevdet Paşa's *Tezâkir* is full of these kinds of references due to his missions in different parts of the empire as an inspector, and he himself witnessed these kinds of large and small scale of uprisings.

2 [Ahmed] Cevdet Paşa, *Tezakir 1-12*, edited by Cavid Baysun (Ankara, 1953), p. 139.

3 For the *Kuleli Vakası*, see [Ahmed] Cevdet Paşa, *Tezâkir 13-20*, edited by Cavid Baysun (Ankara, 1960), pp. 82-5.

4 [Ahmed] Cevdet Paşa: *Tezâkir 13-20*, p. 226.

5 Ahmed Cevdet, *Tarih-i Cevdet*, Vols. V-VI ([İstanbul], 1294), VI, p. 115: 'Fesüpanallah ne garibtir ki Fransızlar ihtilal çıkarmaktan meramları istiklal ve hürriyet ve müsavat ve serbesiyet istihsali iken onun yerine ehl-i arz üzerine erazilin hükümet-i mutlakiyesi ve suçsuz adamı katl etmek gibi cinayetin icrası kaide olmuştu.'

6 Kemalettin Şükrü, *Büyük Fransız İhtilâli* (İstanbul, 1931), p. 1: '(Büyük ihtilâl) ismini hakkile kazanan bu millet isyanı' and 'uzun zaman saray istipdadı ve asılzadeler zulmü altında inletilen aç bırakılan sefalete sürüklenen bir milletin nihayet birleşerek bütün boyunduruklardan kendisini nasıl kurtardığını göstermesi itibarile bir intibah dersi mahiyetini arzeder.'

7 Hancızade Mehmed Remzi, *Fikr-i İhtilal* ([İstanbul], 1331), p. 3: 'kin yekdiğerini çekememek, isnad ve iftira.' The author dates his work 26 Şubat 1328.

8 Hancızade Mehmed Remzi: *Fikr-i İhtilal*, p. 4: 'Ve işte his-i ihtilal, hep bu sefil izzet-i şahsiyeden, ahlak-ı reddiyenin bu tezahuratından tevlid ediyor.'

9 Hancızade Mehmed Remzi: *Fikr-i İhtilal*, p. 5: 'Bir zaman devlet ve millet-i Osmaniyenin bais-ı fevz-u felahı olan bazı hasais-i esasiye-i milliye vardı. Küçükler büyüklere azim bir his-i emniyet ve itimad, derin bir his-i etba ve inkıyad ile mütehassis bulunurlardı. Onun için idi ki bir hükümet uzun bir müddet mevkiini muhafaza edebilirdi. İntizamı muhafaza etmek, ahenk-i içtimai-i temin, muvazene-i siyasiye-i hüsn-ü idare eylemek kabil oluyordu; fakat bugün bizim çün bir anane-i hasene haline girmiş olan o ahlak tamamiyle zail oldu. Küçüğün büyüğe karşı büyük bir adam itimadı var. Fi elvaki bu neticeyi de husule getiren silsile-i vekai, mukadderat-ı hadisatdır; fakat bir noktaya kadar muhik ve tabi olan bu neticeyi lazım

gelen noktada tevkif etmek kabil olmadı: Kimse haddini bilmiyor, kimse hakkına razı göstermiyor, herkes kolayca ve süratle en büyük mevkilere nail olmak saadetine mazhar bulunmak isteyor.'

10 Hancızade Mehmed Remzi: *Fikr-i İhtilal*, p. 6. For a reflection of how 'ihtilal' and 'inkılap' were perceived negatively by the majority of the Ottoman society in this period, see Yakup Kadri Karaosmanoğlu's novel, *Hüküm Gecesi* (İstanbul, 2001), p. 152.

11 Ağaoğlu, Ahmet, *İhtilal mi İnkılap mı* (Ankara, 1942), pp. 7-18.

12 Ağaoğlu: *İhtilal mi İnkılap mı*, p. 17: 'isyan bir camianın ittehaz etmiş olduğu istikamete karşı hareket etmeğe denilirse'; 'Ankaradaki icmai ümmet.'

13 Ağaoğlu: *İhtilal mi İnkılap mı*, p. 18: 'İhtilâl, Revolte, isyan manâsında daima geçici, muayyen ve mahdut bir hâdiseyi ifade eder. İhtilâller daima anî olur ve mahdut gayesini istihsale ya muvaffak olur, ya olmaz ve lâkin daîma yine anî olarak söner.'

14 Ağaoğlu: *İhtilal mi İnkılap mı*, p. 19: 'İnkilâp ise, - revolution - mânasına gelen muayyen bir cemaâtın manen ve maddeten inkişaf ve teâli ettiği halde kendisinin tâbi olduğu tarzi idare, siyasî ve içtimaî müesseselerin tebdiline mani olan hailleri kaldırmak için icra ettiği kıyama denilir.'

15 Ağaoğlu: *İhtilal mi İnkılap mı*, pp. 20-3.

16 T.T.T. Cemiyeti, *Tarih IV. Türkiye Cümhuriyeti* (İstanbul, 1934), p. 57.

17 Karal, Enver Ziya, *Türkiye Cumhuriyeti Tarihi (1914-1944) [Lise Kitapları]* (İstanbul, 1945), p. 18.

18 Ahmed Cevdet, *Tarih-i Cevdet*, Vols. VII-VIII ([İstanbul], 1288), VII, pp. 404-5.

19 [Ahmed] Cevdet Paşa: *Tezakir 1-12*, p. 12.

20 Köprülüzade Mehmed Fuad, *Milli Tarih. Devre-i Mütevassıta - İkinci Sene* (İstanbul, 1337), *passim*.

21 T.T.T. Cemiyeti: *Tarih III*, pp. 200-1.

22 Ali Seydi: *Resimli Yeni Türkçe Lûgat*, p. 486: 'karışıklık çıkarma, fesat. Devlet kanunlarına muhalefetle karışıklık vücuda getirme. Ekşime, karışma.'

23 Ali Seydi: *Resimli Yeni Türkçe Lûgat*, p. 532: 'Âsi olma, serkeşlik, itaatsızlık. Günah.'

24 Tansu, Samih Nafiz, *Osmanlı Tarihi* (İstanbul, 1945), p. 59: 'Balkanlı milletlerin 19üncü asrın yarı evvelinde istiklâl ve hürriyetleri için yaptıkları kalkınmalara-Milli isyanlar-adı verilmiştir.'

25 Tansu: *Osmanlı Tarihi*, pp. 62-3.

26 Redhouse: *A Turkish and English Lexicon*, p. 1,364. The same meaning for the term *fetret* was given in the Ottoman dictionaries. See Kelekyan: *Kamus-i Fransevi*, p. 885; Ş. Sami: *Kâmûs-ı Türkî*, p. 981.
27 Ahmed Vefik Paşa: *Fezleke*, p. 288, Ali Cevad: *Mükemmel Osmanlı Tarihi*, p. 216 and Ahmed Cevdet, *Tarih-i Cevdet*, Vols. XI-XII ([İstanbul], [1301]), XI, p. 161 and *Ma'rûzât*: p. 1. Also see Mehmed Salahi, *Girid Meselesi (1866-1889)*, edited by Münir Aktepe (İstanbul, 1967), p. 76.
28 Ahmed Vefik Paşa: *Fezleke*, p. 281; Ali Cevad: *Mükemmel Osmanlı Tarihi*, p. 211.
29 For example see Abdurrahman Şeref, *Tarih-i Devlet-i Osmani*, Vol. II (İstanbul, 1318), p. 372.
30 See for example, İnalcık: *Tanzimat ve Bulgar Meselesi*, p. 2.
31 Ahmed Cevdet: *Tarih-i Cevdet*, Vols. V-VI, VI, pp. 101 and 108: 'ateş-i ihtilal alevlenmekte idi.'
32 Ahmed Rasim: *Resimli ve Haritalı Osmanlı Tarihi*, IV, p. 2,229.
33 M. Tevfik, *et al.*, *Tarih III. Yeni ve Yakın Zamanlarda Osmanlı - Türk Tarihi* (İstanbul, 1931), p. 101.
34 [Ahmed Lütfi Efendi]: *Vak'a-Nüvis Lütfi Efendi Tarihi C. XI*, pp. 57 and 93.
35 [Ahmed Lütfi Efendi]: *Vak'a-Nüvis Lütfi Efendi Tarihi C. XI*, p. 21.
36 [Ahmed Lütfi Efendi], *Vak'a-Nüvis Lütfi Efendi Tarihi C. XV*, edited by M. Münir Aktepe (Ankara, 1993), p. 77 and Ahmed Lûtfî Efendi, *Vak'anüvîs Ahmed Lûtfî Efendi Tarihi* (İstanbul, 1999), I, p. 6.
37 For this discussion over the purification of language see Ömer Seyfeddin, 'Yeni Lisan,' *Genç Kalemler*, II/1 (29 Mart 1327) in Parlatır, İsmail and Nurullah Çetin (eds.), *Genç Kalemler Dergisi* (Ankara, 1999), pp. 75-81. Ali Canip ve Ziya Gökalp, 'Yeni Lisan,' *Genç Kalemler*, II/2 (27 Nisan 1327) in Parlatır and Çetin: *Genç Kalemler Dergisi*, pp. 105-9. One of the main aims of the *Genç Kalemler* was to promote the 'new language' so that almost every issue of the journal had an article about this subject. Although this view of *Genç Kalemler* was challenged and polemics among the literary elite went on, the language of the historical texts as well as of the official documents had already begun to change.
38 For examples, see Ahmed Cevdet Paşa: *Ma'rûzât*, pp. 22-3 and p. 45; [Ahmed Lütfi Efendi]: *Vak'a-Nüvis Lütfi Efendi Tarihi C. XI*, p. 56.
39 [Ahmed] Cevdet Paşa: *Tezakir 1-12*, p. 12 and [Ahmed] Cevdet Paşa, *Tezâkir 21-39*, edited by Cavid Baysun (Ankara, 1963), p. 11. See the discussion of the term within the context of the late Ottoman education

system in Somel, Selçuk Akşin, *The Modernization of Public Education in the Ottoman Empire 1839-1908. Islamization, Autocracy and Discipline* (Leiden, 2001), pp. 58-9.

40 Mustafa Nuri Paşa, *Netayic ül-Vukuat*, Vol. IV (İstanbul, 1327), p. 68: 'Sırb reayası tahsil-i istiklal sevdasına düşüp.'

41 [Ahmed] Cemal Paşa, *Hatırat 1913-1922* (Dersaadet, 1922), p. 59: 'en şımarık Balkan devleti sırasına geçen Sırplar.' For further use of the term *şımarmak*, see Ahmed Rasim: *Resimli ve Haritalı Osmanlı Tarihi*, IV, p. 1,854: 'the Greeks who were spoilt by the Navarino incident' ((Navarin) vakası üzerine şımaran Rumlar) The allied Balkan states were referred to as 'Europe's spoilt vagabonds and the Balkan's tramps' (Avrupanın şımarık, Balkanın derbeder serserileri) in M. Şemseddin, 'Balkanlılar İttihad Etmiş, Osmanlılar Sizde Meydan-ı Şehamete Koşunuz' (With the Balkan nations united, run, oh Ottomans, to the valour of the battlefield), *Sebilürreşad*, IX-II/216-34 (14 Zilkade 1330 and 11 Teşrin-i evvel 1328), p. 145. The Balkan people were referred to as 'those spoilt people of the Balkans' (Balkanların o şımarık halkı) in Rumeli Muhacirin-i İslamiye Cemiyet-i Hayriyesi: *Bulgar Vahşetleri*, p. 36. This term was also used in the Republican texts. See for example Sedes, İ. Halil, *1875-1878 Osmanlı Ordusu Seferleri. 1876-1877 Osmanlı-Karadağ Seferi* (İstanbul, 1936), p. 35; Külçe, Süleyman, *Osmanlı Tarihinde Arnavudluk* (İzmir, 1944), p. 333.

42 Ş. Sami: *Kâmûs-ı Türkî*, p. 446: 'uzaklaştırma, tebid: eşkiyayı def ve tenkil etti.'

43 Ş. Sami: *Kâmûs-ı Türkî*, p. 371: 'muhalif-i kanun-u hareket edenler hakkında ahkam-ı lazimenin tatbiki.'

44 Ş. Sami: *Kâmûs-ı Türkî*, p. 446: (tenkil) 'emsaline ibret olacak bir mücazat verme'; *ibid*, p. 371: (tedib): 'edeb ve terbiye öğretme, terbiye verme.'

45 Simpson, J. A. and E. S. C. Weiner, *The Oxford English Dictionary*, second edition, Vol. X (Oxford, 1989), p. 35.

46 See footnote 103 in Sungu, İhsan, 'Tanzimat ve Yeni Osmanlılar' in *Tanzimat I* (İstanbul, 1940), p. 847. Sungu also mentions Namık Kemal's reaction to the Babıali's translation of 'nation' as 'millet.'

47 Ş. Sami: *Kâmûs-ı Türkî*, p. 484: (cins): 'kavm, kabile: Arnavud, Çerkes cinsi'; (cinsiyet): 'Bir kavm ve kabileye mensubiyet, mensub bulunulan kavm ve kabile: Arab cinsiyeti; beyinlerinde cinsiyet iştirakı vardır.'

48 Ş. Sami: *Kâmûs-ı Türkî*, p. 1,570: (Yunani): 'Yunan memleketine mensub ve müteallik veya memleket ahalisinden olan'; (Yunanlı): 'Yunan ahalisinden adam.'
49 Mehmed Salahi: *Girid Meselesi*, p. 73: 'yunânîliğin büyük bir gayret ve himmetle neşr ve tevsi'ine çalışılmakda olduğunu ve bu yoldaki himmet ve gayretlerin işte böyle insana cinsiyyet ve milliyyetini bile red ve tahkîr etdirecek ve başka bir milliyyete intisabla müftehir edecek derecede te'sirât-ı ciddiyyesi bulunduğunu düşündüm.'
50 Mehmed Salahi: *Girid Meselesi*, p. 77: 'Yunanlılık illeti ile bî-huzûr olan bu sersemin dallandıra ballandıra verdiği îzâhâtı kâh gülerek kâh redderek dinledim.'
51 Ş. Sami: *Kâmûs-ı Türkî*, p. 1,400: (millet): 'Bir din ve mezhebde bulunan cemaat: millet-i İslam.'
52 Namık Kemal, 'İstikbal' in Özön: *Namık Kemal ve İbret Gazetesi*, pp. 32-3 and also see Sungu: 'Tanzimat ve Yeni Osmanlılar,' pp. 805-6 for his similar understanding of the role of Islam in the empire in his article which he wrote before he went to Europe.
53 [Ahmed] Cevdet Paşa: 'Tezkire 18' in *Tezâkir 13-20*, pp. 157-226.
54 [Ahmed Lütfi Efendi]: *Vak'a-Nüvis Lütfi Efendi Tarihi C. XI*, p. 59 and [Ahmed Lütfi Efendi], *Vak'a-Nüvis Lütfi Efendi Tarihi, C. X*, edited by M. Münir Aktepe (Ankara, 1988), p. 61.
55 'Ibn Khaldun used the concept of this term as the basis of his interpretation of history and his doctrine of the state; for him it is the fundamental bond of human society and the basic motive force of history,' in *The Encyclopaedia of Islam, New Edition - Glossary and Index of Technical Terms; to Volumes I-VII and to the Supplement, Fascicules 1-6*, compiled by J. van Lent and H. U. Qureshi (Leiden, 1995), p. 23.
56 [Ahmed] Cevdet Paşa: *Tezâkir 13-20*, pp. 166-7.
57 [Ahmed Lütfi Efendi], *Vak'a-Nüvis Lütfi Efendi Tarihi C. XII*, edited by M. Münir Aktepe (Ankara, 1989), pp. 65 and 43.
58 Ahmed Cevdet Paşa: *Ma'rûzât*, pp. 42-5.
59 Ahmed Cevdet Paşa: *Ma'rûzât*, pp. 43-4.
60 [Ahmed Lütfi Efendi]: *Vak'a-Nüvis Lütfi Efendi Tarihi C. XI*, pp. 63-71, and *Vak'a-Nüvis Lütfi Efendi Tarihi C. XV*, p. 39.
61 Akçuraoğlu Yusuf, *Zamanımız Avrupa Siyasi Tarihi* (Ankara, 1933), p. 179.
62 Ahmed Rasim: *Resimli ve Haritalı Osmanlı Tarihi*, IV, p. 2,179.

63 Ahmed Cevdet Paşa: *Ma'rûzât*, pp. 2; 22-3, 113-5 and Sungu: 'Tanzimat ve Yeni Osmanlılar,' pp. 783-4.
64 Sungu: 'Tanzimat ve Yeni Osmanlılar', p. 782.
65 Ş. Sami: *Kâmûs-ı Türkî*, p. 171: 'uyanma, uyanıklık; gafletin zıddı, göz açıklığı, teyakkuz.' The most well-known usage of the term originated from one of Namık Kemal's novels, *İntibah* which was first published in 1876. In this novel, Namık Kemal tells the story of Ali Bey who had been the "prey" of a prostitute. *İntibah*, as a term, symbolizes the process of Ali Bey's self-realization. Namık Kemal, *İntibah (Ali Bey'in Sergüzeşti)*, edited by Mehmet Kaplan (Ankara, 1984).
66 Mahmud Celaleddin Paşa, *Mirat-ı Hakikat. Tarih-i Mahmud Celaleddin Paşa* (Dersaadet, 1326-1327), I, p. 80.
67 Kamil Paşa, *Tarih-i Siyasiye-i Devlet-i Aliye-i Osmaniye*, Vol. III ([İstanbul], 1327-1325), p. 56: 'hem mezheplerinin ezhanına ihtilal efkarını ilkaya bezl-i mesai etmişlerdir.'
68 [Altınay], Ahmed Refik: *Küçük Tarih-i Osmani*, p. 128.
69 Ali Canip and Ziya Gökalp, 'Yeni Lisan' in Parlatır and Çetin: *Genç Kalemler Dergisi*, pp. 105-9. The section from which the definition of *millet* comes, was written by Ziya Gökalp on p. 108: 'Bizce millet siyasî bir nüfuza, yani bir "devlet kuvveti" ne malik bir cemaattir. Binaenaleyh "Osmanlılık" mutlaka bir millettir. Fakat Türk, Rum, Kürt, Arnavut, Bulgar, Ermeni, unsurları gibi Osmanlı milletinin içtimaî bünyesine dahil olunan heyetler birer millet değil, bir "kavim" den ibarettir.'
70 [Altınay], Ahmed Refik: *Küçük Tarih-i Osmani*, p. 105: 'Balkanlardaki hükümetler hep Yeniçerilerin zorbalıklarından bıkıp usanmış olduklarından birer birer isyan etdiler. Bunlardan Sırplar bir kaç defa ayaklandılar.'
71 Ziya Gökalp, 'Millet Nedir' from *Küçük Mecmua*, 28 (25.12.1923) quoted in Göksel, Ali Nüzhet (ed.), *Ziya Gökalp. Hayatı, Sanatı, Eseri* (İstanbul, 1952), p. 79: 'Millet, salisen bir imparatorluk dahilinde müşterek bir siyasî hayat yaşayanların mecmuu da değildir. Meselâ eski Osmanlı imparatorluğunun umum tebaasına Osmanlı milleti namını vermek hatâydı. Çünkü bu halitanın içinde müteaddit milletler vardı.'
72 Ziya Gökalp: 'Millet Nedir,' pp. 79-80: 'bu rabıta, terbiyede, harste, yani duygularda iştiraktır.'
73 Ziya Gök Alp, *Türk Medeniyet Tarihi. Birinci Kısım* (İstanbul, 1341), p. 7: 'Bir medeniyetin, her milletde aldığı hususi şekilleri vardır ki bunlara hars adı verilir.'

74 See The text of *Ahd-ı Milli Beyannamesi* in Tunaya, Tarık Z., 'Osmanlı İmparatorluğundan Türkiye Büyük Millet Meclisi Hükümeti Rejimine Geçiş' in *İstanbul Üniversitesi Hukuk Fakültesi Devletler Hususî Hukuku Ord. Profesörü Muammer Raşit Seviğ'e Armağan* (İstanbul, 1956), p. 19: 'dinen, ırkan, emelen müttehit ve yekdiğerine karşı hürmeti mütekabile ve fedakârlık hissayatıyla meşhun ve hukuku ırkiye ve içtimaiyeleriyle şeraiti muhitiyelerine tamamiyle riayetkâr Osmanlı İslâm ekseriyetiyle meskûn.'

75 [İnan], Afet, *Yurt Bilgisi Notlarından: Vatandaş İçin Medenî Bilgiler. I. Kitap* (İstanbul, 1931), p. 7: 'Millet, dil, kültür ve mefkûre birliği ile biribirine bağlı vatandaşların teşkil ettiği siyasî ve içtimaî heyettir.'

76 T.T.T. Cemiyeti: *Tarih III*, p. 213: '...dil, yahut fikir ve his itibarile bir olan ve kendilerine millet adı verilen birtakım insan kütlelerinin, hürriyetlerini ve birliklerini, inkişaflarına lâzım olan hayatî şartları temin için yaptıkları mücadelelerdir.'

77 Köprülüzade Mehmed Fuad: *Milli Tarih*, p. 38: 'Denizcilik vasıtasıyla Avrupa milletleriyle münasebette bulunan Moralılar, 'mekteb' ve 'kilise' sayesinde, kendilerinin 'esir' olduklarını ve bundan kurtulmak içün isyan lazım geldiğini öğrendiler. Mektebleriyle kiliseleri onlara «Yunanlı» olduklarını öğretdi. Rusyada ve Avrupanın sair yerlerinde okuyan Moralı gençler, milletdaşlarının istiklaline çalışıyorlardı. Osmanlı devletini zayıf düşürerek parçalamak isteyen Ruslar da bunlara dehşetli yardımlarda bulunuyorlardı. «Etniki Eterya» denilen Rum istiklal cemaati işte bu suretle vücuda gelmiş, İstanbuldaki Rum patrikhanesi bu hususda çok gayret göstermişdir.' See also Ahmed Hasır and Mustafa Muhsin, *Türkiye Tarihi* (İstanbul, 1930), pp. 440-1 and Ahmed Hasır and Mustafa Muhsin, *Kurun-u Cedidde ve Asr-ı Hazırda Türkiye Tarihi. İstanbul'un Fethinden Zamanımıza Kadar* (İstanbul, 1924), pp. 424-6.

78 Akçura: *Osmanlı İmparatorluğunun Dağılma Devri*, p. 20.

79 Ahmed Hasır and Mustafa Muhsin: *Türkiye Tarihi*, p. 435: 'Kezalik bazı yerlerde eski fermanlara istinaden teşkilâtlarını muhafaza etmiş olan sırp manastırları mevcuttu. Bunlar millî emeller ve an'aneleri yeni nesillere naklediyorlar, bu suretle millî bir intibah hareketi için müsait bir zemin hazırlıyorlardı.' See also Ahmed Hasır and Mustafa Muhsin: *Kurun-u Cedidde ve Asr-ı Hazırda Türkiye Tarihi*, p. 420. For keeping religion, language and traditions alive see [Sedes], İ. Halil Paşa, *1876-1878 Osmanlı-Sırp Seferi* (İstanbul, 1934), I, pp. 23-4.

80 Ahmed Hasır and Mustafa Muhsin: *Türkiye Tarihi*, p. 440: 'Fransız ihtilâli ile Avrupada başlıyan milliyet hareketi çok geçmeden gemicilik ve ticaret

dolayısııle Avrupa ile sıkı temasta bulunan Mora Rumlarında da tesirini göstermişti.'
81 M. Tevfik, *et al.*: *Tarih III*, p. 99: '1789 fransız ihtilâlinin ortaya attığı, *hürriyet ve müsavat, milliyet ve istiklâl idealleri* de, şehirlerde yaşıyan ve Avrupa ile ticarî münasebette bulunan hıristiyan tebaanın kulağına geldi; ve onlar tarafından yavaş yavaş başka hıristiyan reayaya da neşrolundu. Müslüman Osmanlılar, Fransa ihtilâline dair hiçbir sarih fikir edinmedikleri zamanlarda bile, Galatanın, Fenerin, Bükreşin ve Adalar Denizinin Avrupa ile münasebette bulunan Rumları, bu vakıanın mahiyetini az çok öğrenmiş bulunuyorlardı.' See also Akçura, *Osmanlı İmparatorluğunun Dağılma Devri*, for the influence of the French Revolution on the development of Romanian national ideas: p. 16; for the French policy of disseminating 'nationalist and revolutionary ideas which had begun to be forgotten in their countries or which the authorities were striving to make the people forget' (memleketlerinde artık unutulmaya başlayan ve unutulmasına uğraşılan ihtilâl fikirlerini, miliyet fikrini) among the Greeks for their own interests (p. 19), and for the influence of these ideas on the Greeks of the empire, p. 20. For the usage of this cliché in the later period, see for example, Işın, Mithat, *Tarihte Girit ve Türkler* (n.p.p., 1945), p. 49.
82 As reported in [Ahmed] Cevdet Paşa: *Tezakir 1-12*, p. 85: 'Devlet-i aliyye dört esas üzere müesses olup bunlar ile her nasıl istenilir ise idaresi ve ilerlemesi kabil olur ve bunlardan her kangısı nakıs olur ise idâre kabil olmaz. Dört esas budur. Millet-i islâmiyye devlet-i türkiyye salâtîn- i osmaniyye pâyitaht-ı İstanbul.'
83 For the discussion of the Ottoman empire's loosing its honour in the eyes of its subjects see Ahmed Cevdet: *Tarih-i Cevdet*, Vols. VII-VIII, VII, pp. 233-4 and Ahmed Rasim: *Resimli ve Haritalı Osmanlı Tarihi*, IV, p. 2,093. For the reflection of this line of thinking in Republican historiography, see M. Tevfik, *et al.*: *Tarih III*, p. 96.
84 Kamil Kapudan: *Karadağ*, *passim*.
85 Mehmed Salahi: *Girit Meselesi*, p. 35.
86 Mehmed Salahi: *Girit Meselesi*, pp. 32-3, 35-8.
87 K. N. [Kazım Nami Duru], 'Siyasî Notlar,' *Genç Kalemler*, I/11-(3) (undated) in Parlatır and Çetin: *Genç Kalemler Dergisi*, p. 26: 'Komite kuklalarının ipi Sofya'dan oynatıldıkça ittihaz olunacak tedabirin daha mükemmel olması kabil olamayacak gibidir.'

88 İnalcık: *Tanzimat ve Bulgar Meselesi*, p. 26: 'Bulgarların, diğer Balkan milletleri gibi, etraflarında yardıma gelebilecek mustakil, medenî seviyesi yüksek hiç bir devlet yoktu.'
89 Andrić, Ivo, *Bosnian Chronicle or The Days of the Consuls* (London, 1996), p. 2.
90 27 Safer 1292 and 23 Mart 1291: The National Library of St. Cyril and St. Methodious, Sofia (hereafter NLCM), OAK 3-64: 'Gerek merkum papas Alfonso ve gerek sair düvel-i mütehabbe tebaası Memalik-i Mahsusa-i Şahanenin her tarafında seyr ve seyahat ve hatta ihtiyar-i ikamet edebileceğinden rahib merkuma dahi istediği mahale gitmekden asla mani edilmez.'
91 Uzunçarşılı, İsmail Hakkı, 'İkinci Abdülhamid'in Alman İmparatoruna Çekmiş Olduğu Bir Telgraf,' *Türkiyat Mecmuası*, XII (1955), p. 138: 'biçare müslüman ahalinin hiç bir vechile mağdur olmamasına.'
92 İrtem, Süleyman Kâni, *Osmanlı Devleti'nin Makedonya Meselesi, Balkanlar'ın Kördüğümü*, edited by Osman Selim Kocahanoğlu (İstanbul, 1999), p. 120. For a brief narration of Albanian "national" ideas revolving around the Prizren League, see a Republican text published by the Turkish Military, Ferik Abdurrahman Nafiz and Mirliva Kiramettin, *1912-1913 Balkan Harbinde İşkodra Müdaafası* (İstanbul, 1933), I, p. 15.
93 *Girid İhtilali. Ahiren Girid Ceziresinde Serzede-i Zuhur Olan İhtilale Dair Evrak-ı Mühimmeyi ve Pariste Fransızca Tab ve Neşr Olunan Risalenin Tercümesine Şamildir* (Hanya, 1314), pp. 90-100.
94 *Girid İhtilali*, p. 51.
95 [Ahmed] Cevdet Paşa: *Tezâkir 13-20*, p. 196.
96 [Ahmed Lütfi Efendi]: *Vak'a-Nüvis Ahmed Lûtfî Efendi Tarihi C. XI*, pp. 56-7 and [Ahmed] Cevdet Paşa: *Tezâkir 13-20*, pp. 161-8.
97 1298 (date given on the file): BOA, Y. PRK. AZJ. 4-108, p. 2: 'Çünki yirmi bin familyadan ibaret olan mezkur Ulah ve Arnavudun celebkeş misallu koyun sürüleri ile beraber Teselyaya gidemeyeceklerinden çobanlığı terk eyletişleri içün başka bir sanatın icrasına muktedir olamadıklarından Teselya'nın Yunanistan'a terkine karşu durabilirler. Hatta ittifak ve tecemmü edeceklerdir ve muvaffak olmadıkları halde eşkiyalığa mübaşeret eyleyeceklerdir. Buhalde Şarkda asayiş berkemal olacak iken merkumenin ahvali bir çok müşkilat ve fenalığa mucib olacaktır. Herhalde gerek İslam ve gerek Hıristiyan olan Arnavudun [?] Ulahların mahvından asla ve katiyyen mesrur olamazlar. Çünki Ulahların başına gelen fenalığın ilerude onların da başına gelebileceğini

düşüneceklerdir. Ve bu sebebden bunların dahi Ulahlar ile beraber silaha sarılarak Teselya'nın Yunanistan'a terkine karşu duracakları karine-i hatırdır.'

98 See Ahmed Rasim: *Resimli ve Haritalı Osmanlı Tarihi*, IV, pp. 2,167 and 2,177-8.

99 Yasamee, F. A. K., *Ottoman Diplomacy. Abdülhamid II and the Great Powers 1878-1888* (İstanbul, 1996), pp. 153-79.

100 Ragıb Rıfkı: *Musavver Bulgaristan*, p. 47: 'Burada garib bir mesele var: Biz, onlara anlaşılmayan bir fikir ile dost-u muavenetimizi uzatdık, niçin?.. Çünkü Bulgarlar bizim tabiamız idi ve onlara haricden vukubulacak bir taarruz hukuk-u Osmaniyeye tecavüz demek oluyordu. Bu doğru bir şey; fakat bizim hukukumuza doğrudan doğruya taarruz eden bir mütecasiri tedib eylemek ve çiğnediği toprağımızı loş vücudundan tathir etmek muhak ve meşru bir vazifemiz değil miydi?'

101 Kazım Bey Karabekir: *Sırb-Bulgar Seferi-1885*, p. 8: 'Teşrin-i evvel nihayetine doğru Dersaadet'den Sofya'ya bir nota geldi: «Sırbiye'nin Bulgaristan'a tecavüzü Memalik-i Osmaniye'ye tecavüz gibi ad olunacakdır. Bu babda Sırbiye hükümetine de bir nota verilmiştir!» Yolunu şaşırmış bir tehdid! Koca bir vilayetimizi istila eden Bulgarlar'a biz ses çıkarmadığımız gibi ses çıkarana da ilanı harbe kalktık. Güya bu tarz hareketle biz Bulgaristan'ın istiklaline mani oluyorduk! Bulgarlar bu ümid olunmaz mürüvvete fiilan da teşekkürde kusur etmediler: Rumeli-i Şarki'yi bu notanın kefaletine bağlayarak ordularını garbe, Sırbiye'ye karşı nakle başladılar.'

102 It could be argued that Greece was the only nation-state in the European territories of the Ottoman empire which received its independence without even having an autonomous status, if the short-lived conditions of the Treaty of Edirne between the Ottoman state and Russia, which granted autonomous status to Greece and the Principalities under Russian protection on 14 September 1829, are not considered.

103 'Etniki Eterya' or 'Etniki Heterya' are the Ottoman Turkish counterparts of the *Philiki Etairia* in most of the studied texts. However, although this corrupted name refers to *Philiki Etairia,* the meaning is not identical (For 'Etniki Heterya,' see M. Tevfik, *et al.*: *Tarih III*, pp. 101-2 and T.T.T. Cemiyeti: *Tarih III*, p. 201 and p. 203. For 'Etniki Herterya,' see Işın: *Tarihte Girit ve Türkler*, p. 50. For 'Etniki Eterya' or 'Etniki Eteriya,' see Köprülüzade Mehmed Fuad: *Milli Tarih*, p. 38; Ahmed Hasır and Mustafa Muhsin: *Türkiye Tarihi*, p. 441).

104 For example see Jelavich, Barbara, *History of the Balkans. Eighteenth and Nineteenth Centuries* (Cambridge, 1997), pp. 214-29.
105 Ahmed Vefik Paşa: *Fezleke*, pp. 287-8.
106 Lütfiye Hanım: *Mirat-ı Tarih-i Osmani*, pp. 398-9, 413, 416-7.
107 Ali Cevad: *Mükemmel Osmanlı Tarihi*, pp. 212, 215, 217.
108 Kashani-Sabet, Firoozeh, 'Cultures of Iranianness: the evolving polemic of Iranian nationalism' in Keddie, N. and R. Matthee (eds.), *Iran and the Surrounding World: Interactions in Culture and Cultural Politics* (Seattle, 2002), p. 174.
109 Ahmed Cevdet: *Tarih-i Cevdet*, Vols. VII-VIII, VII, pp. 233-4.
110 Mustafa Nuri Paşa: *Netayic ül-Vukuat*, IV, p. 74.
111 Mustafa Nuri Paşa: *Netayic ül-Vukuat*, IV, p. 72: 'mustaid-i fesad olan Mora ahalisi.'
112 Mustafa Nuri Paşa: *Netayic ül-Vukuat*, IV, pp. 73-4.
113 [Altınay], Ahmed Refik: *Küçük Tarih-i Osmani*, p. 104.
114 Ali Reşad and Ali Seydi, *Tarih-i Osmani. Resimli ve Haritalı. Mekteb-i Rüştiyenin İkinci Senesi İçin Kabul Edilen Son Proğrama Tevfikan Tertib Edilmiştir* (İstanbul, 1327), p. 108.
115 Ali Reşad and Ali Seydi: *Tarih-i Osmani*, p. 107: 'Şimdiki Yunanistan kıtası (Mora) eyaleti namıyla Devlet-i Osmaniyenin bir vilayeti idi. Ahalisi gayet azgın ve şımarık olduğundan aralık aralık fırsat buldukça isyan ederler ve fakat üzerlerine asker sevkiyle tedib ediliyorlardı.'
116 M. Tevfik, *et al.*: *Tarih III*, p. 100.
117 E. Yzb. Fahrettin and E. Yzb. Seyfi, *1820-1827 Mora İsyanı* (İstanbul, 1934), p. 4.
118 Ahmed Vefik Paşa: *Fezleke*, p. 287; Ali Cevad: *Osmanlı Tarihi*, p. 215; Lütfiye Hanım: *Mirat- i Tarih-i Osmani*, p. 413.
119 Ahmed Müfid, *Tepedelenli Ali Paşa. 1744-1822* (İstanbul, 1324). Ahmed Müfid first published this text in 1903 in Cairo when he was the first secretary of the Ottoman embassy in Brussels. This text has also been translated into Greek by the Association of Epirotic Studies in Ioannina. Ahmet Moufit, *Ali Pasas o Tepenenlis (1744-1822)*, translated by A. N. Iordanoglou with introduction and commentary by K. P. Vlahos (Ioannina, 1980). I should like to thank Professor Angeliki Konstantakopoulou for providing me with this translation. Ferik Abdurrahman Nafiz and Mirliva Kiramettin: *İşkodra Müdaafası*, p. 10.
120 For vilification of the sultans see Ali Reşad and Ali Seydi: *Tarih-i Osmani*, pp. 129-30; Ahmed Refik: *Küçük Tarih-i Osmani*, pp. 112, 120-1.

121 Ahmed Cevdet: *Tarih-i Cevdet*, Vol. XI, p. 165. See also Abdurrahman Şeref, 'Hâlet Efendi' in *Tarih Konuşmaları (Tarih Musahabeleri)*, edited by Eşref Eşrefoğlu (İstanbul, 1978), p. 28.

122 In the history texts from the Republican era, Halet Efendi was described very negatively for example as 'müfsid' (intriguer, seditious) in Ahmed Hasır and Mustafa Muhsin: *Türkiye Tarihi*, p. 439. See also a very negative portrait of Halet Efendi, Abdurrahman Şeref, 'Hâlet Efendi' in Eşrefoğlu: *Tarih Konuşmaları*, pp. 23-31.

123 Although the distinction between state and private interest is very obvious in these texts, it is not the same for that between public and state, both of which can be read as synonymous in these texts. However, this should not be taken as a generalization which can be applied to any understanding of this distinction in the era under examination. For a more liberal understanding of the distinction between public and state interests displayed by the Ottoman MP Rıza Bey, see Boyar, Ebru, 'Public good and private exploitation: Criticism of the tobacco Régie in 1909', in Boyar, Ebru and Kate Fleet (eds.), *Ottomans and Trade* (Oriente Moderno, XXV (LXXXVI)) (Rome, 2006), pp. 193-200.

124 Ahmed Müfid: *Tepedelenli Ali Paşa*, p. 219: 'Rum isyanı sırf Ali Paşa'nın eser-i ifsadı zan edülüp ehemmiyet-i mesele vakti zamanıyla anlaşılamadı. Devlet-i Aliye-i Osmaniye'ye bu yüzden iras olunan mazarrat Tepedelenli Ali Paşa'nın şerinden şüphesiz kat ender kat büyüktür.' Ferik Abdurrahman Nafiz and Mirliva Kiramettin: *İşkodra Müdaafası*, p. 10.

125 M. Tevfik, *et al.*: *Tarih III*, p. 100.

126 Ahmed Vefik Paşa: *Fezleke*, p. 289.

127 Lütfiye Hanım: *Mirat-ı Tarih-i Osmani*, pp. 416-7: '1243 de düşman devletin şu intizamını çekemeyup Yunan vakası müşkülatı daha bitmezden Rusyalu Yunanlıların istiklaliyet iddiasını iltizam ile İngiltere ve Fransa devletlerini dahi her nasılsa daire-i ittifakına aldı.'

128 Abdurrahman Şeref: *Tarih-i Devlet-i Osmani*, II, pp. 371-2 and Akçuraoğlu Yusuf, *Tarih-i Siyasi* (n. p.p., 1927), pp. 4-13.

129 [Altınay], Ahmed Refik: *Küçük Tarih-i Osmani*, p. 105.

130 Ali Reşad and Ali Seydi: *Tarih-i Osmani*, p. 110: 'Osmanlılarca ilelebet unudulmuyacak olan (Navarin) vakası.'

131 Ahmed Hasır and Mustafa Muhsin: *Türkiye Tarihi*, p. 455: 'hukuku [*sic.*] düveli payimal eden ve tarihi medeniyette silinmez lekelerden olan.'

132 Akçuraoğlu Yusuf: *Tarih-i Siyasi*, p. 7: '[The Greeks] requested that England help them and appoint a king over them.' ([Yunanlılar]

İngiltere'nin kendilerine yardım etmesini ve başlarına bir kral tayin etmesini rica ediyorlardı.)

133 Köprülüzade Mehmed Fuad: *Milli Tarih*, p. 45: 'Geçen asrın ibtidasında çıkan «milliyet» fikri, «her milletin müstakil bir devlet olması» nazariyesi, sırf Avrupa devletlerinin yardımıyla, az zamanda «Yunanistan» ı doğurmuşdu.'

134 Süleyman Edip and Ali Tevfik: *İlkmektep Çocuklarına Yeni Tarih Dersleri, Beşinci Sınıf*, pp. 78-9.

Chapter Four

1 Kadare, Ismail, *Three Elegies for Kosovo*, translated from the Albanian by Peter Constantine (London, 2000), pp. 16-7.
2 Kadare: *Three Elegies for Kosovo*, p. 78.
3 Mehmed Salahi: *Girid Meselesi*, pp. 31-5, 100-1 and Kamil Kapudan: *Karadağ*, pp. 28-30. See also Ahmed Cevdet Paşa's *Tezâkir 13-20* (pp. 166-7) for the fluidity of boundaries based on his personal experience as a government inspector in İşkodra (Škodra).
4 Mehmed Salahi: *Girid Meselesi*, p. 32.
5 E. Yzb. Ziya and E. Yzb. Rahmi, *Girit Seferi (Mart-1645: 6-Eylûl-1669)* (İstanbul, 1933), p. 3.
6 Işın: *Tarihte Girit ve Türkler*, p. 44.
7 Kamil Kapudan: *Karadağ*, p. 15.
8 Ahmed Cevdet Paşa: *Ma'rûzât*, pp. 43-4: 'Karadağlular vahşî âdemlerdir.'
9 Ahmed Rasim: *Resimli ve Haritalı Osmanlı Tarihi*, IV, pp. 2,138-9: 'Karadağlıların üsera-ı Osmaniyeye reva gördükleri vahşet, calib-i nefret bir halde idi. Burunlarını, kulaklarını kesub salıyorlardı.' For a similar narration see [Ahmed] Cevdet Paşa: *Tezâkir 13-20*, p. 175.
10 Akçuraoğlu Yusuf: *Zamanımız Avrupa Siyasi Tarihi*, p. 149.
11 Sedes: *1876-1877 Osmanlı-Karadağ Seferi*, p. 23: 'Umran, refah ve saadet velhâsıl hayatın lezzetinden mahrum ve yarım vahşet halinde yaşayan bu halk için; savaş adeta tatlı bir meşguliyet sayılırdı'; 'ülkelerinin tabiî teşekkülâtı iktızası güçlü kuvvetli yaratılmış olan,' 'yaşayışları icabı umumiyetle silâhları omuzlarında çobanlık eder ve gezerlerdi. Avcılık ve hattâ haydutlukla geçinen bu halk, ayrı ayrı askerî bir kıymet kazanmışlardı.'
12 'Balkanlar Destanı' in Tansel: *Şiirler ve Halk Masalları*, p. 88: 'Demiş ki: Nereye girmişse Hilâl,/ Orası Turân'dır onu geri al,/ Domuz çobanları olamaz kıral,/ Tanrı'nın ülkesi: Turân içinde.' In his 1927-novel, *Hüküm*

Gecesi, Yakup Kadri Karaosmanoğlu used the metaphor of 'pig herder' to refer to the Balkan states: 'We want war; we want war. Our national honour cannot be a toy of pig herders.' (Harp istiyoruz; harp istiyoruz. Millî namusumuz domuz çobanlarının oyuncağı olamaz) (p. 185).

13 [Sedes], İ. Halil Paşa: *1876-1878 Osmanlı-Sırp Seferi*, I, p. 4, footnote 1: 'Şimdiki Yugoslavyadaki Kıral hanedanının dedesi olan bu Kara Yorginin asıl meslek ve san'ati domuz çobanlığı idi.'

14 Akçura: *Osmanlı İmparatorluğunun Dağılma Devri*, p. 17: 'Bu Sırb isyanlarının başında Avusturyada küçük zabitlik ederek biraz askerlik öğrenmiş Kara Yorgi adlı bir domuz çobanı bulunuyordu. Etrafına toplanan çete, dağlarda ve ormanlarda domuz güden ve meslekleri iktizası daima müsellâh gezinen ve serbestliğe alışkın bulunan domuz çobanlarile, Sırb şarkılarında âdeta birer millî kahraman gibi gösterilip alkışlanan yol kesici, köy basıcı haydutlardan (Haiduk) ibaretti.'

15 Ahmed Hasır and Mustafa Muhsin: *Türkiye Tarihi*, p. 434: 'Fatih zamanında istiklâllerine nihayet verilmiş olan Sırplar ekseriyetle Mısır [*sic.*] ziraatı veya domuz çobanlığı yaparak köylü halinde yaşamakta idiler.' *Ibid*, p. 436: 'Bunun üzerine öteden beri Kara Yorginin mualif ve rakibi bulunan (Miloş Obrenoviç) isminde eski bir domuz taciri Sırplara başknez (reis) oldu.'

16 9 and 10.v.1883 (the date on the telegrams): BOA, Y. A. HUS. 173-74.

17 9.v.1883 (the date on the report from the Ottoman *chargé d'affaires* in Athens): BOA, Y. A. HUS. 173-84.

18 9 and 10.v.1883 (the date on the telegrams): BOA, Y. A. HUS. 173-74.

19 22.v.1883 (the date on the telegram): BOA, Y. A. HUS. 173-94, 9 and 14.v.1883 (the date on the telegrams): BOA, Y. A. HUS. 173-80.

20 23.v.1883 (the date on the telegram): BOA, Y. A. HUS. 173-98.

21 For example, for a report on the Bulgarian military activities see 15.v.1882: BOA, Y. PRK. ASK. 12-38.

22 However, Abdülhamid II seemed not to have forgotten the Serbian threat, see his memoirs written in 1917, *İkinci Abdülhamid'in Hatıra Defteri*, pp. 108-9.

23 19.ix.1886 (the date of the report from the Ottoman embassy in Belgrade): BOA, Y.PRK. HR. 10-12.

24 'Diplomacy in the Balkans' in *The Times*, Tuesday, October 27, 1885, p. 8. See also Marriott: *The Eastern Question*, p. 31.

25 For the term "archaelogical traveller" coined by Ramsay himself, see Boyar, Ebru, 'British archaelogical travellers in nineteenth-century Anatolia: Anatolia 'without' Turks,' *Eurasian Studies*, I/1 (2002), p. 97.
26 Ramsay, W. M., *The Revolution in Constantinople and Turkey. A Diary, with Episodes and Photographs by Lady Ramsay* (London, 1909), pp. 26-7.
27 Girid Resmolu Mavnahoyuzâde Kasım bin Ahmet, 'Teselya Tarihi 1313' in Kodaman, Bayram (ed.), *1897 Türk-Yunan Savaşı (Tesalya Tarihi)* (Ankara, 1993), p. 61: 'Daha dün aldın a Yunan bu kraliyeti sen / Arslana karşı durur mu acaba yavru köpek.'
28 Âkil Koyuncu, 'Girit İçin (7 Ağustos 1326), *Genç Kalemler*, II/3 (6 Mayıs 1327) in Parlatır and Çetin: *Genç Kalemler Dergisi*, p. 135: 'Of course do not believe because I exist; and oh Greek/ Take care! The Cross defiles the tomb of Islam/ Take care! Do not mock my religion; wake up a little/ Since the crown on your head is a present from me.' (Elbet inanma, çünkü varım ben; ve ey Yunan/ Dikkat! Salîp makber-i İslâm'ı kirletir./ Dinimle dikkat! Oynama artık; biraz uyan,/ Tâcın da çünkü re'sine benden hediyedir.)
29 Ahmed Râsim, 'Hem Muammâ Hem Parola,' in *Eşkâl-i Zamân*, edited by Orhan Şaik Gökyay (İstanbul, 1969), p. 164: 'İşte, şunun bunun koltuğu altında büyümenin böyle sonuçları vardır. Vakit olur ki, koruyucunun eli insanın ensesinde boza pişirir.'
30 [Ahmed] Cemal Paşa: *Hatırat*, p. 59: 'Islahat-ı dahiliyede temin-i muvaffakiyet için Balkan hükümat-ı sagiresinin ikide birde yaygara koparmalarına sebebiyet veren anasır-ı muhtelife meselesine bir nihayet vermek icab ediyordu.'
31 Tansu: *Osmanlı Tarihi*, p. 80.
32 İnalcık: *Tanzimat ve Bulgar Meselesi*, p. 38: 'Rus yardımı ile Osmanlı hakimiyetinden çıkmış.'
33 Quoted in Berkes, Niyazi, *The Development of Secularism in Turkey* (London, 1998), p. 358.
34 İbn ül-Haşim Nureddin Fikri: *Dimetokada Kanlı Bir Levha*, pp. 30-1: 'Altıyüz bu kadar senedenberi dünyanın üç büyük kıtasında kemal-i satvetle hükümran olduktansonra akıbet Rum elinden de çıkarıldık. Hem de dünkü çobanlarımız, dünkü uşaklarımız çıkardılar. Yediğimiz sille-i hakaretin acısını kıyamete kadar kalbimizden çıkarmamaklımız [sic.] lazımdır.'
35 Bayur, Yusuf Hikmet, *Türk İnkılâbı Tarihi, Cilt: II, Kısım: I* (İstanbul, 1943), p. 421: 'Balkanlılar da Büyük Devletlerle birlikte "mahkemeye,, üye

olmaya ve Osmanlıya buyruklar vermeye ve "hüküm,, giymeye kalkışmaktadırlar.'

36 9.xi.1932: BCA, 030 10 226 523 30, p. ii. A copy of this report by the Turkish ambassador in Athens was forwarded to the Prime Minister's Office with an introductory letter written by the Minister of Foreign Affairs, Tevfik Rüştü.

37 1.iii.1934: BCA, 030 10 242 632 18: 'Anka kuşu gibi külünden yeniden doğırmağa başlıyan bulgar milletine karşı olan adaletsizliklerin.' This translation from a Bulgarian newspaper, *Borba*, published in Filibe (Plovdiv) was sent to the Prime Minister's Office by the Ministry of Foreign Affairs. For Ormanjiyev, see also 20.iii.1932: BCA, 030 10 240 621 7.

38 Ali Reşad: *Asr-ı Hazır Tarihi*, p. 193: 'Avusturya-Macaristan Bosna ve Hersek'i işgal ederek bir Balkan devleti oldu.'

39 Bayur, Yusuf Hikmet, *Yeni Türkiye Devletinin Haricî Siyaseti* (İstanbul, 1935), pp. 161-2.

40 Rumeli Muhacirin-i İslamiye Cemiyet-i Hayriyesi: *Rumeli Mezalimi ve Bulgar Vahşetleri*, p. 14; Ahmed Hasır and Mustafa Muhsin: *Türkiye Tarihi*, pp. 710-1; M. Tevfik, *et al.*: *Tarih III*, pp. 145 and 148, and T.T.T. Cemiyeti: *Tarih III*, pp. 302 and 305; Bayur: *Türk İnkılâbı Tarihi, Cilt: II, Kısım: I*, pp. 64, 197, 210, 220.

41 *Atatürk'ün Söylev ve Demeçleri. II (1906-1938)* (Ankara, 1959), pp. 272-3: 'Balkan Milletleri içtimai ve siyasi ne çehre arzederlerse etsinler, onların Orta-Asya'dan gelmiş aynı kandan, yakın soylardan müşterek cedleri olduğunu unutmamak lâzımdır.

Karadeniz'in şimal ve cenup yollariyle, binlerce seneler deniz dalgaları gibi birbiri ardınca gelip Balkanlarda yerleşmiş olan insane kitleleri, başka başka adlar taşımış olmalarına rağmen, hakikatte bir tek beşikten çıkan ve damarlarında aynı kan deveran eden kardeş kavimlerden başka bir şey değildirler.'

42 Karal: 'Atatürk'ün Türk Tarih Tezi,' p. 64: 'milliyet ile insanlığın uzlaşacağı.'

43 4.vi.1933: BCA, 030 10 241 629 1.

Chapter Five

1 Halil Yaver, *Bugünkü Bulgaristan'da Türk Düşmanlığı. Bulgar Sefiri G. Pavlofa Bir Cevap* (İstanbul, 1932), pp. 4-16. Halil Yaver's agitation over the Bulgarian national anthem in his book found a reaction in the Bulgarian

press and the newspaper *La Bulgarie* wrote: 'Aussi, s'est-il rabattu sur l'hymne national, datant de la guerre russo-turque, lequel hymne cependant, par une attention délicate et spontanée envers nos amis Turcs, a été complément modifié depuis assez longtemps déjà, ce que le bulgarophobe susmentionné aurait dû savoir' in 30.iii.1933: BCA, 030 10 241 627 2, p. 4. For the reflection of the Bulgarian national anthem in the late Ottoman era, see Ömer Seyfeddin, 'Nakarat,' *Yeni Mecmua*, 63/III (3 October 1918), pp. 216-20.

2   25.xii.1935: BCA, 030 10 255 719 29.
3   4.xii.1933: BCA, 030 10 241 631 10 and 2.vi.1943: BCA, 030 10 243 645 4. The names of the other journalists are Arif Necip Kaskatı and Gültekin Arda.
4   31.viii.1937: 030 18 2 78 75 13.
5   21.viii.1937: ek: 86/283, 31.viii.1937: 030 18 2 78 75 13: 'Türkiye'nin müttefiki olan Yugoslavya ve Balkan antantı aleyhinde zararlı neşriyatı ihtiva etmekte ve Türkiye'nin haricî seyasetini ve dahilî vaziyetini teşviş edecek mahiyette bulunmaktadır.'
6   Masur, Gerhard, 'Distinctive traits of western civilization: through the eyes of western historians,' *The American Historical Review*, LXVII/3 (1962), pp. 591-608; Rodinson, Maxime, *Europe and the Mystique of Islam*, translated by Roger Veinus (London, 2002), pp. 64-71.
7   Viscount Grey of Fallodon, *Twenty-Five Years 1892-1916*, Vol. I (New York, 1925), pp. 121-2.
8   Braudel, Fernand, 'The history of civilizations. The past explains the present' in *On History*, translated by Sarah Matthews (Chicago, 1982), pp. 184-202.
9   Bertelli, Sergio (ed.), *Niccolò Machiavelli, Il Principe e Discorsi sopra la prima deca di Tito Livio*, with an inroduction by Giuliano Procacci (Milan, 1960), pp. 26-7.
10 Enea Silvio Piccolomini, 'Lettera al Cardinale Nicola di Cues' in Pertusi, Agostino (ed.), *La caduta di Constantinopoli*. Vol. II. *L'eco nel mondo* (Milan, 1976), p. '54. I should like to thank Dr. Kate Fleet for drawing my attention to these sources.
11 Captain Burnaby, a British traveller who traveled in Anatolia before the Ottoman-Russian war of 1876, tells how European newspapers were sold freely in the streets of İstanbul, in Burnaby, Capt. Frederick, *On Horseback through Asia Minor*, with a new introduction by Peter Hopkirk (Oxford, 1996), p. 9.

12 Namık Kemal, 'Medeniyet,' *İbret*, no. 84, 1 January 1873 in Özön: *Namık Kemal ve İbret Gazetesi*, p. 216: 'Şimdi biz tervici medeniyeti arzu edersek bu kabîlden olan hakayıkı nafıayı nerede bulursak iktibas ederiz. Temeddün için Çinlilerden sülük kebabı ekletmeyi almaya muhtaç olmadığımız gibi Avrupalıların dansına, usulü münakehatını taklit etmeye de hiç mecbur değiliz.'

13 Renan, Ernest, *L'Islamisme et la science. Conférence faite a la Sorbonne le 29 mars 1883* (Paris, 1883). For example, according to Renan: 'Persuadé que Dieu donne la fortune et le pouvoir à qui bon lui semble, sans tenir compte de l'instruction ni du mérite personnel, le musulman a le plus profond mépris pour la science, pour tout ce qui constitue l'esprit européén' (p. 3). For Renan Islam was 'la chaîne la plus lourde que l'humanité ait jamais portée' (p. 17).

14 Namık Kemal, *Külliyat-ı Kemal, Birinci Tertib 1 - Renan Müdafaanamesi* (İstanbul, n.d.), p. 2. For a modernist approach, see Berkes: *The Development of Secularism in Turkey*, pp. 261-88.

15 Namık Kemal, 'Avrupa Şarkı Bilmez,' *İbret*, no. 7, 22 July 1872 in Özön: *Namık Kemal ve İbret Gazetesi*, pp. 54-9.

16 The quarter of İstanbul where the foreign embassies were located and where most of the Europeans lived.

17 [Ahmed] Cevdet Paşa: *Tezâkir 21-39*, pp. 103-4: 'Hayli vakit İstanbul'da oturdum. Buralara lâyıkiyle ma'lûmât alamamışım'; 'Siz Beyoğlu'nda oturdunuz. Değil memâlik-i osmâniyyenin nefs-i İstanbul'un bile ahvâlini lâyıkiyle öğrenemediniz. Beyoğlu Avrupa ile memâlik-i islâmiyye arasında bir berzahtır. Buradan İstanbul'u siz durbin ile görürsünüz. Lâkin kullandığınız durbinler hep çarpıktır.'

18 Brown, Robert F. (ed.), *Hegel Lectures on the History of Philosophy. The Lectures of 1825-1826*. Volume III. *Medieval and Modern Philosophy* (Berkeley, Los Angeles and Oxford, 1996), pp. 35-9.

19 Akyiğitzade Musa, *Avrupa Medeniyetinin Esasına Bir Nazar* (İstanbul, 1315), p. 6: 'Avrupalıyı hal-i cehaletden kurtaran madde medeniyet-i İslamiyedir.'

20 Ş. Sami, *Kamus ül-Alam. Tarih ve Coğrafya Lugatı*, Vol. VI (İstanbul, 1316-1898), pp. 4,826-7.

21 Gaspıranski, İsmail, *Avrupa Medeniyetine Bir Nazar-ı Muvazene* (Kostantiniye, 1302), p. 18: 'Velhasıl bir baktıkça Avrupa maişeti ve medeniyeti gayet süslü ziynetli ve yakışıklı bir kadına benzedebilir ve lakin birazda dikkat olunur ise şu kadının dişleri uydurma. Saçları takma. O, dolu

dolu göğüsleri kabartma pamuk ... ve birde o canfes elbiseleri taşladılur ise yaralara kuturlara tesadüf olunub çevrilmeden gayri mecal kalmaz.'

22 Safveti Ziya, *Salon Köşelerinde*, edited by Nuri Akbayar (İstanbul, 1998), p. 140: 'Aşk ve sevda gibi geçici, unutulucu, ardı sıra hüsranlar, hicranlar, pişmanlıklar bırakıcı hislere boyun eğerek mecnunca, çocukca hareket edecek yerde bütün o hayalperverliği bir tarafa bırakarak cemiyet içinde Türklüğün bir vahşet örneği değil bir ziynet, Türklerin de medeni bir millet olduğunu bir İngiliz kızına, bir İngiliz ailesine ispat eylemek lazım geleceğini düşünürek hareket tarzını değiştirdim.'

23 Namık Kemal: 'Medeniyet,' p. 216.

24 Ramsay: *The Revolution in Constantinople and Turkey*, pp. 28-35.

25 Ramsay: *The Revolution in Constantinople and Turkey*, p. 34. Murad Bey, the historian, also mentioned his attempt to attract the attention of his French guests to the mis-representation of eastern events in the French newspapers. Mizancı Murad: *Mücahede-i Milliye*, pp. 25-6.

26 [Altınay], Ahmed Refik: *Küçük Tarih-i Osmani*, pp. 90-4, 124-7.

27 Ali Reşad and Ali Seydi: *Tarih-i Osmani*, p. 132: 'Osmanlılar zaten bidayet-i teşekküllerinde medeni bir kavim idiler. Hükümetlerini teşekkül eyledikleri mevkiada buldukları Roma, Bizans, Selçuk esarini tahrib değil* [*sic.*] bilakis bunlardan istifade ettiler.'

28 Ali Reşad and Ali Seydi: *Tarih-i Osmani*, p. 136: 'Evet; biz hükümet-i askeriye idik, ömrümüzü harble geçirdik. Lakin tarih-i Osmani iyi okunacak olursa: görülürki bizim kendiliğimizden muharebe ettiğimiz pek, hemde pek azdır. Daima düşmanlarımız üzerimize gelir, biz de onlara karşı çıkmağa mecbur oluruz.'

29 Ali Reşad and Ali Seydi: *Tarih-i Osmani*, pp. 136-7: 'Yoksa istidad itibarıyla bizim diğer mütemeddin kavimlerden hiçbir farkımız yoktur.' Also see Mizancı Murad, *Mücahede-i Milliye* for the natural talent of the Ottomans for civilization.

30 Prens Sabahattin, *Türkiye Nasıl Kurtarılabilir ve İzâh'lar*, transliterated by Fahri Unan (Ankara, 1999), p. 9.

31 Gaspıranski: *Avrupa Medeniyetine Bir Nazar-ı Muvazene*, pp. 11-3.

32 Prens Sabahattin: *Türkiye Nasıl Kurtarılabilir ve İzâh'lar*, pp. 156-7 and 162-3.

33 İbn ül-Haşim Nureddin Fikri: *Dimetokada Kanlı Bir Levha*, p. 5: 'Zaten hepimiz biliyorduk ve bu sefer daha iyi anladık, daha kavi iman etdikki yirminci asrın medeniyeti Müslüman aleyhdarlığıdır.'

34 See for example Berkes: *The Development of Secularism in Turkey*, pp. 341-3. Niyazi Berkes's division of intellectuals, for example, into Islamists, Westernists and Turkists, can be misleading, for these intellectuals did not necessarily hold fixed ideological positions and their ideas could be reactive responses to European challenge at a particular moment rather than constant intellectual constructions.

35 Ömer (Darülfünun Mezunlarından), 'Hilal ve Salib,' *Sırat-ı Müstakim*, VI/137 (1327), p. 110: 'İttihad edersek emin olalım ki bizim kolumuzu hiç kimse bükemez. Bin seneden beri omuzlarımızda taşıdığımız "salibin zulmünü," ["]tahakkümünü" bir anda fırlatarak bu yalancı medenilerin yüzlerine çarparak vazife-i insaniye ve İslamiyemizi yapmış oluruz.'

36 İhsan Şeref: *Cumhuriyet Çocuklarına Tarih Dersleri*, p. 23: 'Medeniyet iddia eden yalancı Avrupa bu kadar zulümlere, bu görülmemiş vahşetlere seyirci kaldı.'

37 Ömer: 'Hilal ve Salib,' p. 110: 'Bulgaristan hududunda, Yunan hududunda askerlerimize hucüm eden bir eşkiya gebertiliyor da aleyhimizde söylenmedik laflar, yazılmadık yazılar kalmıyor. Sonra diğer taraftan köylerimizi yakıyorlar, zavallı İslam kardeşlerimizin kulaklarını, burunlarını kesiyorlarda yine sukut ediyoruz. Tabiayamızdan sırf eser-i teşvik ile isyan eden bir takım cühela üzerine asker sevk edecek oluruzda İngilterenin büyük (!) gazetesi Taymis Avusturyanın Katolikler üzerindeki hakkı himayesinden bahsederek Hıristiyanlara, isyan etmiş Katolik Arnavudlarına bir şey yapamayacağımızı söylemek istiyor. Geçen seneki Arnavudluk isyanında hükümeti usatı şiddetle tedib ettiğinden dolayı Avrupa gazeteleri alkışlıyordu. Aynı gazeteler bu sene aynı kavme mensub lakin Hıristiyan olduğundan himaye ediyor ve onlara askerimizin vahşiyane muamelesinden bahs ediyor. İşte medeni Avrupanın harekatı!'

38 'Medeniyet dediğin tek dişi kalmış canavar.'

39 See Ağaoğlu: *İhtilal mi İnkılap mı*, pp. 59-61 and also see Ağaoğlu Ahmet, 'Garp ve Şark,' *Vatan*, No. 158 (5 September 1923) in Kaplan, Mehmet, İnci Enginün, Zeynep Kerman, Necat Birinci and Abdullah Uçman (eds.), *Atatürk Devri Fikir Hayatı* (Ankara, 1981), I, pp. 83-7.

40 İleri, Celâl Nuri, *Türk İnkilabı*, edited by Recep Durmaz (İstanbul, 2000), pp. 59-78.

41 Ziya Gökalp, 'XLVIII Kızlarım Seniha, Hürriyet ve Türkân Hanımlara' in Tansel, Abdullah Fevziye (ed.), *Ziya Gökalp Külliyâtı – II. Limni ve Malta Mektupları* (Ankara, 1989), p. 79: 'ilimdir, fendir, sânayi'dir.'

42 Reşit Saffet [Atabinen], 'Millî Tarih' in *Türklük ve Türkçülük İzleri* (Ankara 1930), pp. 9-13, in Kaplan, *et al.*: *Atatürk Devri Fikir Hayatı*, II, p. 236. See also Mehmet Saffet [Engin], 'Anadolu'da En Eski Türk Medeniyeti ve Cihan Medeniyetlerine Hâkimiyeti', *Ülkü*, III/16 (June 1934), pp. 263-7 in Kaplan, *et al.*: *Atatürk Devri Fikir Hayatı*, II, pp. 265-72.

43 *Birinci Türk Tarih Kongresi*, p. 13: 'Gelecek nesillerin nefretle yadedeceği bir insan, bir millet olarak tarihe geçmekten hazer ederiz. Bilâkis fertçe ve milletçe medeniyete en yüksek işler görmüş, insanlığın yükselmesine çok çalışmış, gelecek nesillerin istifade edebileceği kıymetli, ölmez, ilmî ve san'atkârane eserler bırakmış bir varlık olarak tarihte en muhterem en şerefli bir yer sahibi olmak azmindeyiz. Bu sebeple çocuklarımızı da bu fikir, bu terbiye ve kanaat ile yetiştireceğiz.' This was the quotation given by Esad Bey himself, and taken from *Tarih I*, although there are in fact some differences from the original text. T. T. T. Cemiyeti: *Tarih I*, p. 9.

44 On the cover page of his book he is described as 'Knight Commander of the Greek Order of the Saviour, and the Servian Order of Takova, Corresponding Member of the Imperial Academy of Sciences of Saint Petersburg.'

45 Freeman, Edward A., *The Ottoman Power in Europe, its Nature, its Growth and its Decline* (London, 1877), p. 312.

46 Freeman: *The Ottoman Power in Europe*, p. 311.

47 *A Handbook of Turkey in Europe*. Prepared on behalf of the Admiralty (Admiralty War Staff Intelligence Division, January 1917), p. 57; for a similar evaluation see also The Historical Section of the Foreign Office, *Anatolia* (London, 1920), p. 16.

48 For example, for the French attitude, see Thiers, M. Henri, *La Serbie, sa passé et son avenir* (Paris, 1862).

49 Ranke, M. Leopold, *Histoire des Osmanlis et de la monarchie espagnole pendant les XVIe et XVIIe siècles,* accompanied notes by M. J.-B. Haiber (Paris, 1839), p. 105. Ahmed Refik interpreted this view of Ranke's about the Ottoman place within civilization as 'Although Ranke admits the honesty, humanity and hospitality of the Ottomans, he was convinced that their religious concerns distanced them from civilization.' (Ranke, Osmanlıların doğruluğunu, insaniyetini, mihmannevazlığını teslim etmekle beraber, dini endişelere irtibatın kendilerini medeniyetten uzak bulundurduğuna kanidir.) Apart from this, Ahmed Refik regards the section of this book on the Ottoman empire highly. [Altınay], Ahmed Refik,

'Alman Müverrihleri: Ranke', *Yeni Mecmua*, I/21 (29 November, 1917), pp. 404-5.
50 Beaufort, Francis, *Karamania, or a Brief Description of the South Coast of Asia Minor and of the Remains of Antiquity. With Plans, Views and & c. Collected during a Survey of that Coast, under the Orders of the Lords Commissioners of the Admirality, in the Years 1811 & 1812* (London, 1817), p. 51.
51 Williams, W. Llew, *Armenia: Past and Present. A Study and a Forecast*, with an introduction by T. P. O'Connor, MP (London, 1916).
52 20.ix.1933: BCA, 030 10 241 630 39. The underlined lines are 'Mevzu bulgar milletinin çalışkanlığını ve sonra Türk boyunduruğu altında ismi unutulduğunu tekrar anlatmaktan ibaret olduğu için altı çizili satırların Türk milletinin mazisi hakkında haset ve kinin mahsulü bir imayı tazammun ettiğine hükmedilebilir.'
53 Tansu: *Osmanlı Tarihi*, p. 61: '15-16-17 nci asırlarda hakkın ve adaletin timsali olan Osmanlı idaresi, işgal ettiği memleketler halkının tefessüh etmiş ahlâkının tesirleri altında bozulmuş, rüşvet, irtikâp, iltimas alabildiğine yürüdüğü gibi, baştakiler de halka zülum etmeye başlamışlardır.'
54 Aynî, Mehmed Ali, *Milliyetçilik* (İstanbul, 1943), p. 292. The author quotes: 'Avrupa devletleri Türkleri Avrupadan çıkaracaktır. Halbuki biz «otohton» uz eğer sizlerle birleşirsek bizi de çıkarırlar. Biz ise yurdumuzda kalmak isteyoruz.'
55 [İnan], Afet, 'Tarihten Evel ve Tarih Fecrinde' in *Birinci Türk Tarih Kongresi*, pp. 18-41.
56 Ahmet Şerif, *Arnavudluk'da, Sûriye'de, Trablusgarb'de Tanîn*, Vol. II, edited by Mehmed Çetin Börekçi (Ankara, 1999), p. 7: 'Fakat bu tüfeklerden, toplardan çıkan mermiler, düştükleri yere, insânlık ve medeniyyet tohumları ekiyor. Aslında yüce ve fakat, Arnavudların cehâletine karşı, acı olan bu mecbûriyyet, Arnavudluk'un kader sayfalarında, son bir mecbûriyyet olacaktır.'
57 T.T.T. Cemiyeti: *Tarih III*, p. 202: 'İngiltere, Fransa, Alamanya gibi Avrupa memleketlerinin orta ve yüksek mekteplerinde ötedenberi eski Yunan dili ve edebiyatı tedris olunurdu. Kadîm Yunanın hayatı süslenip bezenerek, olduğundan daha medenî ve parlak gösterilirdi. Kadîm Yunan filozofları, şairleri, hatipleri, müverrihleri okutulup tefsir edilir ve eski Yunan harplerinin mübalağalı hikâyeleri hakikat gibi öğretilirdi. *Hasılı okur yazar garplıların çoğu kadîm Yunan muhip ve hürmetkârı idi*. XIX.

asırda kendilerine Yunanlı veya Rum diyenlerin Yunan ve Romaya nispeti aynı memleketlerde yaşamaktan ibaret iken, Türklere ve Müslümanlara husumetle meşbu hıristiyan garplılar, bu ihtilâlci Rumları *Eflatun* ve *Aristo* ların, *Homer* ve *Demosten* lerin ahfadı, Osmanlıları ise barbarların bakayası gibi gösterdiler ve bütün Garbî ve Merkezî Avrupada ihtilâlciler lehine heyecanlı bir teveccüh ve muhabbet cereyanı hasıl oldu; her tarafta *Helinosları sevenler* (philhelènes) cemiyetleri teessüs etti; papazlardan, şairlerden, politikacılardan, askerlerden, mutaassıp veya ukalâ kadınlardan, serserilerden birçok adam bu cemiyetlere dahil oldu; bir hayli de iane toplandı. Hatta İngilizlerin büyük şairi *Bayrın* (Byron) kendi memleketinde oturamayacak kadar münasebetsizliklerde bulunduktan sora Yunanlıları kurtarmak için Yunanistana gidip ihtilâlciler arasına girdi. Fransızların meşhur şairi *Viktor Hügo* Yunanlıları medih ve sena, Türklere iftira ederek bir küme şiirler yazdı. Bazı serseri İngiliz ve Fransız zabitleri de ihtilâlcilere karıştılar. Hasılı bütün Avrupanın bazı içtimaî tabakalarını, bir Yunan muhipliğidir sardı. Bu fikir cereyanının Avrupa devlet adamlarına da az çok tesiri oldu.' For the continuation of a similar representation, see Işın: *Tarihte Girit ve Türkler*, p. 50. Işın makes the contrast between Turk and Greek explicit: 'Turks were represented as the remnants of barbarians.' (Türkler Barbarların bakayası gösterilir.)

58 The burning of the Ottoman fleet at Navarino was described as a 'barbarous action' by Ahmed Hasır and Mustafa Muhsin in *Türkiye Tarihi*, p. 455, footnote 1. See also Chapter 3 for further discussion of the Navarino incident within the context of the centre-periphery paradigm.

59 29 Zilhicce 1310 (date on file): BOA, Y. PRK. ZB. 11-104: 'Lord Byron'ın eserinden olub üç cildden ibaret ve Osmanlılar aleyhinedir.'

60 [Ahmed] Cemal Paşa: *Hatırat*, p. 242: 'Onlar Türk ve Müslüman oldukları için, o zavallılar namına mersiye han olacak Lord Byron'lar, Victor Hugo'lar zuhur etmemiş ve o hunin hadisat yalnız Osmanlılar tarafından yazılan tarih kitaplarında, bir kaç sahifa teşkil etmekten başka bir eser bırakmamıştır.' See [Ahmed] Cemal Paşa, *Hatıralar*, edited by Alpay Kabacalı (İstanbul, 2001), p. 381, in modern Turkish. See Ahmed Hasır and Mustafa Muhsin: *Türkiye Tarihi*, p. 448, footnote 1, for references to Lord Byron, Victor Hugo, and also to the French colonel Faviye (Fabvier) and a former minister of the Piedmont government, Santaroza, who both volunteered to fight in the Morean Uprising.

61 Ali Reşad, *Avrupa ile Münasebet-i Hariciyemiz Nokta-ı Nazarından Tarih-i Osmani* (Dersaadet, 1329), p. 640: 'Asilerin kusurları, cinayetleri

görülmüyor; her nevi fezail kendilerine atf olunuyordu. Çünkü Avrupalılar Osmanlıları barbar ad ediyorlar, Rumların kıyamına medeniyetin barbarlığa karşı mübarezesi nazarıyla bakıyorlardı.'

62 'Claude Farrère Şerefine Verilen Çay Ziyafetinde (18.VI.1922)' in *Atatürk'ün Söylev ve Demeçleri, II (1906-1938)*, pp. 33-38: 'Biz hayat ve istiklâl için mücadele eden ve bu kanlı mücadeleler manzarası karşısında bütün cihanı medeniyetin bîhis seyirci kaldığını görmekle dilhûn olmuş insanlarız' (p. 38).

63 Ş. Sami: *Kamus ül-Alam*, Vol. VI, p. 4,824: 'Yunan-ı Kadim ahalisinin ahfadıyla bu memleketi eskiden beri çiğneyüb geçmiş olan Makedonyalı, Romalı, Avar, Islav, Arnavud ve sair akvam efradının ihtilatından mütevellit olan Rum cinsiyeti.'

64 Ş. Sami: *Kamus ül-Alam*, Vol. VI, p. 4,827: 'Mükemmeliyetiyle dünyada meşhur olan lisan-ı Yunani elsine-i muhtelife-i ecnebiye ile karışmaktan, büsbütün fesahatını gayb ederek, elyevm Rumca dediğimiz kaba ve kaidesiz bir lisan-ı naks halini kesb etmiştir.'

65 [İleri], Celal Nuri, *Rum ve Bizans* (Kostantiniye, 1917), p. 10.

66 E. Yzb. Fahrettin and E. Yzb. Seyfi: *1820-1827 Mora İsyanı*, p. 2: 'Eski Yunanlılarla, Makedonyalı, Romalı, Avar ve Islav ve Arnavutların ihtilâtından doğma melez bir millettir.'

67 T.T.T. Cemiyeti, *Tarih I - Tarihtenevvelki Zamanlar ve Eski Zamanlar* (İstanbul, 1938), p. 186: 'Bugün Grek denilen kavim soraları [*sic.*] muhtelif ırktan birçoklarının karışmasından hasıl olmuştur.'

68 Kodaman: *1897 Türk-Yunan Savaşı*, p. 66: 'Yunanlılar bu mürüvvetkârâne mu'âmeleye karşı gâyet vahşiyâne mukabele ettiler. Lâkin onların fikr-i vahşeti Osmanlılar'ın meyl-i medeniyetini zerre kadar ihlâl edemez. Her bir ferd kendi mâhiyetine göre hareket eder.'

69 Bekir Fikri, *Balkanlarda Tedhiş ve Gerilla. Grebene* (İstanbul, 1976), p. 153.

70 'The Bulgarian Atrocities' in *Joseph Cowen's Speeches on the Near Eastern Question: Foreign and Imperial Affairs on the British Empire*, revised by His Daughter, Jane Cowen (London, 1909), pp. 9-10. George Washburn, an American teacher in Robert College, tells the story of how he and his colleague Dr. Long were instrumental in making the news about 'the Bulgarian Atrocities' known in Europe, especially in Britain. Washburn, George, *Fifty Years in Constantinople and Recollections of Robert College* (Boston and New York, 1909), pp. 100-26.

71 Ahmed Hasır and Mustafa Muhsin: *Türkiye Tarihi*, p. 665.

72 Gladstone, Right Hon. W.E., MP, *Bulgarian Horrors and the Question of the East* (London, 1876), p. 8.
73 Gladstone: *Bulgarian Horrors*, p. 9.
74 Burnaby: *On Horseback through Asia Minor*, pp. ix-x; In his speech, Cowen criticized government policy over the Ottoman empire, and the Bulgarian case was used as a means to enhance the position of the opposition on this issue. 'The Bulgarian Atrocities' in *Joseph Cowen's Speeches*, pp. 1-22. See also *The Times* editorial 'Mr. Gladstone's indictment of the Turkish' on Gladstone's allegations, *The Times*, September 8, 1876, p. 7.
75 Washburn: *Fifty Years in Constantinople and Recollections of Robert College*, p. 102.
76 28 Zilhicce 1325 and 19 Kanun-u sani 1323: BOA, Y.A. HUS. 517-197.
77 Hüseyin Raci, *Tarihçe-i Vaka-i Zağra* (İstanbul, 1326), p. 99: 'yabani canavardan eşna Bulgar vahşilerini hangi nevi hayvan-ı müfteris addiyle zir-i himayelerine alıyorlar.'
78 Küçük, Cevdet, 'Bulgar İhtilali'nin (1876) İngiliz Kamuoyunda Uyandırdığı Tepki ve Bunun Osmanlı-İngiliz İlişkilerine Tesiri,' *Güney-Doğu Avrupa Araştırmaları Dergisi*, 8-9 (1979-1980), pp. 117-66.
79 Ali Haydar Midhat Bey: *The Life of Midhat Pasha*, 'Appendix C,' pp. 285-92.
80 Ahmed Cevdet Paşa: *Ma'rûzât*, pp. 222-5 and [Ahmed] Cevdet Paşa: *Tezâkir 40-Tetimme*, pp. 146-8.
81 Ahmed Rasim: *Resimli ve Haritalı Osmanlı Tarihi*, Vol. IV, p. 2,239.
82 Doktor İbrahim Rafet, *Bulgaristan Ahvali* (İstanbul, 1329), p. 42: 'Hükümet-i Osmaniye Çerkesleri ve Pomakları komitacılar üzerine sevk ederek tedibe başlamış ve Balkanları kan bürümüştür. İngiliz Gladstone'un Türklere düşmanlığı bu vakitten başlıyor zan edilir.'
83 [Peremeci] Osman Nuri: *Ecdad Tarihi*, p. 9. Osman Nuri, who later took the surname Peremeci, was also one of the main contributers to an educational journal in Šumen, *Terbiye Ocağı* later called *Bulgaristan Türk Muallimleri Mecmuası*, which was published from 1921 to 1925. Karagöz, Âdem Ruhi, *Bulgaristan Türk Basını 1879-1945* (İstanbul, 1945), pp. 36-7. Osman Nuri Peremeci was also the author of *Tuna Boyu Tarihi* published in 1942. See also Chapter 2.
84 Peremeci: *Tuna Boyu Tarihi*, pp. 215-7. Gladstone was an important name which appeared in the narration of the Bulgarian uprising as the symbol of the European, especially British, lack of understanding and bias towards

Ottoman politics. For a further reference to Gladstone, see Ahmed Hasır and Mustafa Muhsin: *Türkiye Tarihi*, p. 665.
85 Halil Yaver: *Bugünkü Bulgaristan'da Türk Düşmanlığı*, passim.
86 30.iii.1933: BCA, 030 10 241 627 2. From the translation of the *Trakia* newspaper from the issue dated 2.ii.1933 in a file sent by the Ministry of the Foreign Affairs to the Prime Minister's Office. 'Trakya gazetesindeki makalelerin birinde kitap için yazılan cevapta: (az medenî Türk'lerin) kendilerini Avrupa'dan koğanların bulgarlar olduğunu unutmıyacakları" [*sic.*] yazılıdır.'
87 Mehmet Şeref, *Bulgarlar ve Bulgar Devleti* (Ankara, 1934), p. 55: 'Ruh kaba, yontulmamış, duygusu incelmemiş, güzel sanatlar yer bulmamış, yaratıcı kudret aralarında doğmamış, millî kültür yalnız Türk düşmanlığı şeklinde gösterilerek hep Mahya tepe üstünde çarmiha gerdiği bir Anadolu Türk askerinin nasıl gözlerini oyduğunu, nasıl tırnaklarını söktüğünü, nasıl parmaklarını kırdığını, nasıl tenasül aletini kestiğini, anlatan şiirleri ezberleye ezberleye mekteplerinde de bütün kıraat, tarih, çoğrafya gibi kültür kitaplarında Bulgar çocuklarına hep bu Türk düşmanlığı derslerini yalan yanlış vere vere yetişen bu millet balkanlarda aslâ insanlığın büyük medenî eserine bir tuğla, bir kiremit ilâve edemeyerek sade yakıcı, yıkıcı, zalim ve kalın kafalı, kalın ruhlu, kalın duygulu, muasır medeniyette orta devir adamı olarak kalmıştır.'
88 'Ayıdan post, Rus (Moskof)'dan dost olmaz.' Akçuraoğlu Yusuf compares Russia to a 'northern bear' in his narration of the outcome of the Crimean War for Russia: 'These assaults are like sticking a pocket knife into the tail and leg of a very thick-coated northern bear. In order to thrust a knife into its heart, it is necessary to cross Austria and use Austrian soldiers.' (Bu darbeler gayet kalın derili şimal ayısının kuyruğuna, bacağına çakı batırmak kabilindendir. Asıl kalbine hançer saplamak için Austuryadan geçmek ve Avusturya askerini kullanmak lâzımdır.) Akçuraoğlu Yusuf: *Zamanımız Avrupa Siyasi Tarihi*, p. 168.
89 E. Yzb. Fahrettin and E. Yzb. Seyfi: *1820-1827 Mora İsyanı*, p. 3: 'Osmanlı imparatorluğunun en birinci düşmanı.' For a personal reflection of this emnity, see Atay: *Batış Yılları*, p. 9: 'While we were still in the cradle, we were rocked by the fear of Russia. A giant like a ghost of death over our heads.' (Biz daha beşikte iken Moskof korkusu ile sallanmışız. Başımız üstünde ecel hayaleti gibi bir dev.)
90 Gaspıranski: *Avrupa Medeniyetine Bir Nazar-ı Muvazene*, p. 29 and also see p. 4, footnote 1.

91 İhsan Şeref: *Cumhuriyet Çocuklarına Tarih Dersleri*, p. 59.
92 T.T.T. Cemiyeti: *Tarih III*, pp. 217, 240-2.
93 Ergin, Osman, *İstanbul Mektepleri ve İlim, Terbiye ve San'at Müesseseleri Dolayısiyle. Türkiye Maarif Tarihi*, Vol. V (İstanbul, 1977), p. 1,795.
94 Ahmed Cevdet Paşa describes the "submission" of the Sadrazam Mahmud Nedim Paşa to Ignatiev as: 'sakalını Rusya elçisi İgnatief'in eline verdi' in *Ma'rûzât*, p. 222. Ignatiev became an integral figure in the representation of the Russian policy towards the Ottoman empire in the Republican histories. See for example, Ali Reşad: *Asr-ı Hazır Tarihi*, p. 203 and Ahmed Hasır and Mustafa Muhsin: *Türkiye Tarihi*, p. 665.
95 See for example, Ahmed Rasim: *Resimli ve Haritalı Osmanlı Tarihi*, Vol. IV, p. 2,196.
96 Mahmud Celaleddin Paşa: *Mirat-ı Hakikat*, Vol. I, p. 80: '«Islav-u İttihadı» maksadını istihsal eylemek için «Moskova» da tesis eden cemiyetin ve mahal-i sairede bulunan şuabatının fikr ve emelleri Devlet-i Aliye ile Avusturyanın bünyan hükümetlerince ika-ı tezelzül ve indirasa çalışarak bunların harabesi üzerine cenubi bir Islav devlet-i cesimesi tesis etmek gibi muhayyelata tabi olmasıyla Bulgaristan ve Sırbistan ve Bosna ve Karadağ kıtalarında kavlen ve fiilen sarf etmedikleri mesai kalmamış ve Avusturyaya merbut Islavların dahi o yolda zihin ve kalbleri uyandırılmış idi.'
97 Ahmed Rasim: *Resimli ve Haritalı Osmanlı Tarihi*, Vol. IV, for Panslavism, see pp. 2,135-6; 2,141; 2,166; 2,194-5.
98 Köprülüzade Mehmed Fuad: *Milli Tarih*, p. 45: 'Ruslar, Balkanlardaki Sırblarla Bulgarlar arasında «Islavlık» fikrinin kuvvetlenmesine mektebler, kiliseler, kitablar, gazetelerle adam akıllı çalıştılar. Türk boyunduruğu altında yaşayan bu milletler, kendilerinin bir mazisi, mazide bir devleti olduğunu hatırladılar. Rusların teşvikiyle fırsat buldukça ihtilaller çıkardılar.'
99 Ali Reşad: *Asr-ı Hazır Tarihi*, pp. 196-7: 'Paris muahedesinin akdinden sonra, 1857'de Rusyada teşkil eden Islav İttihadı Cemiyeti Balkanlardaki Islavları Türkiye aleyhine isyan etdirmek gayesini takib ettiğinden bu cemiyetin memurları Bosna ve Hersek Hıristiyanlarını teşvik ediyorlar; kilise ve mekteb inşası gibi işlere külliyetli paralar veriyorlardı. Aynı propaganda Bulgarlar arasında da yapılıyordu.' For the development and importance of Panslavism and Russian activities in Ottoman Europe, see Ahmed Hasır and Mustafa Muhsin: *Türkiye Tarihi*, pp. 660-3.

100 T.T.T. Cemiyeti: *Tarih III*, p. 257: 'Eski hıristiyanlık propagandasına yeni *ırkî kardaşlık, islavlık* propagandasını da ilâve ederek, Balkanlarda ekseriyet teşkil eden Sırp, Karadağlı gibi hakikî İslavları ve *esasen Türk* olmalarına rağmen Rusların telkini ile kendilerini İslav sayan Boşnak ve Bulgarları, Osmanlı Hükûmeti aleyhine tahrike koyuldu.'

101 22.v.1934: BCA, 490 01 607 105 9: 'Balkanlarda Islav birliği fikrinin şafağı doğmak üzeredir.'

102 'gayet tabii bir inkişaf sahası.' This quotation was later underlined by hand in the text.

103 Fleet, Kate, 'Italian perceptions of the Turks in the fourteenth and fifteenth centuries,' *Journal of Mediterranean Studies*, V/2 (1995), pp. 159-72.

104 Ersoy, M. Âkif, *Safahat* (İstanbul, 1958), p. 205: 'Karadağ haydudu, Sırb eşşeği, Bulgar yılanı,/ Sonra Yûnân iti çepçevre kuşatsın vatanı.../ Târ-ı mâr eyleyiversin de bütün ordumuzu,/ Bizi kovsun elimizden alarak yurdumuzu.../ Kimsesiz ailelerden kimi gitsin bıçağa:/ Kimi bin bir türlü fecaatle çekilsin kucağa.../ Birinin ırzı heder, birinin hûnu halâl.'

105 See Duman, Haluk Harun, *Balkanlara Veda. Basın ve Edebiyatta Balkan Savaşı (1912-1913)* (İstanbul, 2005) for a list of Ottoman literature concerning the Balkan Wars.

106 The Section of the General Staff of the Western Front, *Greek Atrocities in Asia Minor, First Part* (Constantinople, 1922), pp. 3-4.

107 The Section of the General Staff of the Western Front: *Greek Atrocities in Asia Minor*, p. 3.

108 The Section of the General Staff of the Western Front: *Greek Atrocities in Asia Minor*, p. 4, footnote x.

109 Akyiğitzade Musa: *Avrupa Medeniyetinin Esasına Bir Nazar*, pp. 4-5.

110 See Chapter 3. For the image of woman in the Ottoman Revolutionary press as a symbol of the honour of the nation in relation to Europe, see Brummett, Palmira, *Image and Imperialism in the Ottoman Revolutionary Press, 1908-1911* (Albany, 2000), pp. 232-47.

111 [Atay], Falih Rıfkı, 'Manisa Harabelerinde' in [Adıvar], Halide Edip, Yakup Kadri, Falih Rıfkı and Mehmet Asım, *İzmir'den Bursa'ya. Hikayeler, Mektuplar ve Yunan Ordusunun Sorumluluğuna Dair Bir İnceleme* (İstanbul, 1974), p. 62: 'Ya ırz faciaları? Bütün şehirler ve köyler bu bahis geldiği vakit susuyor. Zira yaşayan kadınlar ve kızlar için bu facia süngü yarası gibi değildir. Bakirenin, dulun veya zevcenin hayatında bir leke gibi kalıyor. Yolda on üç, on dört yaşında bir köylü çocuğu ile konuşuyorduk. «Nişanlın var mı?» diye sorduk.

_Vardı, ama...
_Şimdi yok mu?
_Nişanlıma gavur dokundu.
Onun için kadınlar ve kızlar bu ıstıraplarını anlatmağa değil, unutturmağa çalışıyor.'
Falih Rıfkı's point about how the women tried to have these rapes forgotten was noted in a document. 11 Haziran 1334: BOA, DH. EUM. 3 Şb. 26-11 in *Arşiv Belgelerine Göre Balkanlar'da ve Anadolu'da Yunan Mezâlimi II - Anadolu'da Yunan Mezâlimi* (Ankara, 1996), p. 21; facsimile on p. 394: 'Kızılcaterzi karyesinden bir kaç kadın ile İsmail Çavuş'un Gelibolu'ya hicretleri esnâsında Eksamel tarafından yolları kat´ ve başlarından Yeniköy Rumlarından teşhîs edemedikleri bir kaç kişi olduğu hâlde Bulgar askerleri tarafından der-dest olunarak tekrâr Kızılcaterzi karyesine getirildikleri ve ırza tecâvüz vukû'bulmadığı ifâde ediliyorsa da hâricen edilen arîz amîk tahkîkâta nazaran bunlardan birkaçının ırzlarına tecâvüz etdikleri anlaşılmıştır.'
112 14 Mayıs 1337: BOA, HR. SYS. 2624-80 in *II Anadolu'da Yunan Mezâlimi*, pp. 228-9; facsimile on p. 601: 'yine karye-i mezkûre ahâlîsinden Hasan oğlu Ali'nin on üç yaşındaki Şehriye nâm kızı cebren bikrini izâle etmek fi'l-i cinâyeti ikâ' ile karyeden genç kadınların kezâ ırz ve nâmûslarını cebren ta´arruzla fi'l-i şenâ'ati icrâdan sonra...'
113 Ahmed Rasim: *Resimli ve Haritalı Osmanlı Tarihi*, Vol. IV, p. 2,178.
114 Tansel, Abdullah Fevziye (ed.), *Mehmed Emin Yurdakul'un Eserleri 1. Şiirler* (Ankara, 1989), p. 289: 'Ey Türk vur, vatanın bâkirlerine/ Günahkâr gömleği biçenleri vur.'
115 Mehmet Şeref: *Bulgarlar ve Bulgar Devleti*, p. 47: 'Bundan üçü Hüseyin Beyin evine girmişti. Damadı Yusuf beyle evde titreşen zavallı adamı [*sic.*], damadiyle beraber kollarını bağladılar. Gözleri önünde kadını ile kızının ırzına geçtiler, sonra birer birer parmaklarını, kulaklarını keserek bu iki kadını kocalarının gözü önünde öldürdüler.'
116 Mahmud Celaleddin Paşa: *Mirat-ı Hakikat*. Vol. I, p. 84: '«Avratalan» nahiyesi müdirini ve evlad ve ailesi ve katib ve zaptiyelerini dahi idam etmişler ve müdirin kızını katl etdikten sonra fercini keserek bilezik resminde teşhir eylemişler idi.'
117 Ferik Abdurrahman Nafiz and Mirliva Kiramettin: *1912-1913 Balkan Harbinde İşkodra Müdaafası*, p. 29: 'Şehitlerin kestikleri parmaklarını ikişer ikişer salip şeklinde göğüslerine koyuyorlar, bazılarının da alâtı tenasüliyesini kesip ağızlarına veriyorlardı.'

118 Bekir Fikri: *Grebene*, p. 153.
119 [Adıvar], Halide Edip, *et al.*: *İzmir'den Bursa'ya*, p. 30: 'Emine beni ve namusunu kurtardı ama işte ben kaldım, o öldü.'
120 This poem was written on 15 Mayıs 1336. Tansel: *Mehmed Emin Yurdakul'un Eserleri 1. Şiirler*, pp. 279-88: 'Onlar da bu ma'siyet gecelerinde/ Bizden de bir iğrenç aşk istediler;/ Ölümün o kanlı bağçelerinde/ Bize de, 'Raksedin, çalın!' dediler' (p. 282).
121 Mehmet Şeref: *Bulgarlar ve Bulgar Devleti*, p. 28.
122 Ömer Seyfettin, *Ömer Seyfettin Külliyatı: 7- Beyaz Lâle* (İstanbul, 1942), pp. 3-31. The story was published in number 53-60 of the *Donanma Mecmuası*.
123 Rumeli Muhacirin-i İslamiye Cemiyet-i Hayriyesi: *Bulgar Vahşetleri* and *Rumeli Mezalimi ve Bulgar Vahşetleri, passim*.
124 Rumeli Muhacirin-i İslamiye Cemiyet-i Hayriyesi: *Rumeli Mezalimi ve Bulgar Vahşetleri*, p. 43.
125 Ömer Seyfettin: *Beyaz Lâle*, p. 21.
126 Ömer Seyfettin: *Beyaz Lâle*, pp. 17-18, 26.
127 Ömer Seyfettin: *Beyaz Lâle*, p. 23.
128 Ömer Seyfettin: *Beyaz Lale*, pp. 18, 22.
129 Rumeli Muhacirin-i İslamiye Cemiyet-i Hayriyesi: *Rumeli Mezalimi ve Bulgar Vahşetleri*, p. 17.
130 Ömer Seyfettin: *Beyaz Lale*, p. 28: 'Ne yapacaktı? Şimdi ne yapacaktı? İşte her yerine mukaddes tanımıyan düşmanının şenî tükürükleri sürülmüştü. Namusu zorla parçalanıyordu. Bağırmalarına hiçbir cevap aksetmiyor, imdadına hiç kimse yetişmiyordu. Demek o vahşî bir hayvanın en kirli, iğrenç eğlencelerine âlet olacaktı. Hayır, hayır, hayır...'
131 Ömer Seyfettin: *Beyaz Lale*, p. 30.
132 Mehmet Şeref: *Bulgarlar ve Bulgar Devleti*, p. 29.
133 Ahmed Rasim: *Resimli ve Haritalı Osmanlı Tarihi*, Vol. IV, p. 2,182: 'Bu muharabelerin birinde Çilingir (Mustafa) namında bir neferi eşkiya hayyan tutarak ibtida ellerini kesmişler, bağde göğsünü yarub kalbini çıkarmışlar, ondan sonra dahi başını yüzerek şehit etmişlerdir.'
134 İhsan Şeref: *Cumhuriyet Çocuklarına Tarih Dersleri*, p. 33: 'Melunlar, Marmara kenarındaki güzel köylerimizi cayır cayır yakdılar. Günahsız köylülerini karı demediler, kız demediler kundakdaki çocuklara kadar hepsinin gözlerini oydular, kulaklarını, burunlarını, memelerini kestiler, karınlarını yardılar dünyada vahşet namına ne varsa hepsini yapdılar.'

135 Kamil Paşa: *Tarih-i Siyasiye-i Devlet-i Aliye-i Osmaniye*, Vol. III, p. 34: 'Sırb eşkiyası Belgrad kasabasındaki İslam üzerine hücum ederek erkekleri öldürdüklerine kanaat etmeyerek gebe hatunların karınlarını yarub çocuklarını çıkarmak gibi muamelat-ı vahşiyaneye dahi irtikap etmişlerdir.'

136 Süleyman Edip and Ali Tevfik: *İlkmektep Çocuklarına Yeni Tarih Dersleri*. *Beşinci Sınıf*, p. 79: 'Türkleri kestiler; evlerini mallarını yağma ettiler.'

137 Süleyman Edip and Ali Tevfik: *İlkmektep Çocuklarına Yeni Tarih Dersleri*. *Beşinci Sınıf*, p. 125: 'Girdikleri yerleri yaktılar, yıktılar. Ahalisini insafsızca boğazladılar.'

138 Süleyman Edip and Ali Tevfik: *İlk Mektep Çocuklarına Tarih Dersleri*. *Dördüncü Sınıf*, p. 120: 'Rumlar, Ermeniler düşmanlarla birleştiler, haksız yere Türk gençlerini öldürdüler. Evleri, mağazaları yağma ettiler.'

139 Piccolomini: 'Lettera a Nicolò V' in Pertusi: *La caduta di Costantinopoli*, Vol. II, *L'eco nel mondo*, p. 46.

140 Duru, Kazım Nami, "*İttihat ve Terakki,, Hatıralarım* (İstanbul, 1957), p. 62: 'In 1320 Turkish honour was stained, Ah!/ Ah! Ah! Revenge! Revenge!/ Crosses were on mosques/ Minarets were demolished/ Mother, father, orphan, sick/ Were [all] cut [into pieces] perfidiously.' (1328'de Türk namusu lekelendi, of!/ Of! Of! İntikam! İntikam/ Camilere haç takıldı,/ Minareler hep yıkıldı,/ Anne, baba, öksüz alil/ Kahpecesine kesildi, of); p. 63: 'The sound of the *ezan* was not heard/ The cross was hung on the *mimbar* (pulpit)/ The infidel enemy hung flags on mosques and everywhere.' (Ezan sesi duyulmuyor/ Haç dikilmiş mimbere/ Kâfir düşman bayrak asmış/ Camilere, her yere.)

141 Ömer Seyfettin: *Beyaz Lâle*, p. 12: 'Gazi Evrenos camiine halkalar mıhlanarak ordu mekkârilerine ahır, Halil Paşa camii domuz pastırmalarına depo olacak.'

142 Piccolomini: "Lettera al Cardinale Nicola di Cues" in Pertusi: *La Caduta di Costantinopoli*, Vol. II, *L'eco nel mondo*, p. 52.

143 9.ix.1933: BCA, 030 10 241 630 35: 'Bu türbenin zaman zaman uğradığı tecavüzler ve içi kazılarak yapılan iskelet taharriyatı evvelce arzedilmiştir. Deli Orman muhitinde 50 senelik bir bulgar rejiminden sonra hala kendilerini yabancı hisseden bulgarlar, öçlerini Türk hakimiyyet ve ekseriyyetinin bıraktığı izleri yok ederek almağa çalışmaktadırlar Efendim.' Halil Yaver also wanted to draw the attention of the Prime Minister İsmet İnönü to the signs of the link between the soil and the people in his report sent to the Prime Minister's Office. See 24.iv.1936: BCA, 030 10 243 638 11.

144 İhsan Şeref: *Cumhuriyet Çocuklarına Tarih Dersleri*, p. 23: 'Rumeli'nde ne can kaldı, ne namus, camilerimize çanlar asıldı, bin senelik mezarlarımız açıldı.'
145 The extent to which the Balkan countries were significant in the development of political ideas within the Ottoman empire is open to discussion. For example, Hanioğlu underlines the lack of importance of Young Turk activities in the Balkans for the movement in general. Kemal Can, for instance, emphasises the influence of Balkan nationalism on the development of Turkish nationalism. Hanioğlu, Şükrü, *Preparation for a Revolution. The Young Turks, 1902-1908* (Oxford and New York, 2001), p. 78. Can, Kemal, 'Youth, Turkism and the extreme right. The "Idealist Hearths"' in Yerasimos, Stefanos, Günter Seufert and Karin Vorhoff (eds.), *Civil Society in the Grip of Nationalism* (İstanbul, 2000), pp. 353-4.
146 Kamil Paşa: *Tarih-i Siyasiye-i Devlet-i Aliye-i Osmaniye*, Vol. III, p. 57: 'Hükümet-i seniyece gerek Rumlara ehemmiyet verilmemesi ve gerek o zamanın taassubu ecnebi lisanı tahsiline mani olmasından dolayı ahali-i İslamdan Rum mekteblerinde okunan kitab ve risale-i muzırrayı teftiş ve tefhim edebilecek kimse olmaması cihetiyle memurin-i hükümet Rumların teşebbüsatından gafiller idi.'
147 3 Mayıs 1322: BOA, YEE. KP. 86-29/2862. The same file contains another telegram on the same subject dated 29 Nisan 1322.
148 10 Cemaziyelevvel 1292 and 1 Teşrin-i sani 1291: NLCM, OAK 6-15: 'hukuk-u saltanat-ı seniyeye dokunur suretde makalat görüldüğünden.'
149 [Temo, İbrahim], *İttihad ve Terakki Cemiyeti'nin Kurucusu ve 1/1 No'lu Üyesi İbrahim Temo'nun İttihad ve Terakki Anıları* (İstanbul, 2000), pp. 56-7.
150 19 Şubat 1320: BOA, YEE. KP. 86-23/2299. The order was in a coded telegram from the Minister of Internal Affairs, Memduh Paşa to the governor of Aydın, Kamil Paşa. The newspaper was published weekly and the first issue was published on 24 May 1904. Mehmet Teftiş became the editor of the newspaper after the 91st issue. According to the information given by Karagöz, the 90th issue was published on 21 November 1905. Karagöz: *Bulgaristan Türk Basını 1879-1945*, p. 25.
151 29 Kanun-u evvel 1320: BOA, YEE. KP. 86-23/2258. The order was in a coded telegram from the Minister of Internal Affairs, Memduh Paşa to the governor of Aydın, Kamil Paşa. This newspaper was apparently different from the one İbrahim Temo published in Bucharest. For this newspaper, see [Temo, İbrahim]: *İttihad ve Terakki Cemiyeti'nin Kurucusu*, pp. 105-9

and Hanioğlu, Şükrü, *The Young Turks in Opposition* (Oxford and New York, 1995), p. 123.

152 28 Mayıs 1330: BOA, MV, 189-37. According to Karagöz, during the First World War, Etem Ruhi (Balkan), the establisher and the owner of the newspaper, became an MP in the Radoslavov Party and moved the newspaper from Plovdiv to Sofia. This newspaper, which was started in 1905, was closed in 1920 when Etem Ruhi migrated to Turkey. Karagöz: *Bulgaristan Türk Basını 1879-1945*, pp. 23-4.

153 10 Mayıs 1341: BCA, 030 18 01 013 28 8.

154 13 Mayıs 1341: BCA, 030 18 01 013 29 4.

155 29 Nisan 1341: BCA, 030 18 01 013 25 17.

156 17 Teşrin-i evvel 1339: BCA, 030 18 01 07 37 14.

157 29 Teşrin-i sani 1341: BCA, 030 18 01 016 74 8.

158 22 Temmuz 1341: BCA, 030 18 01 014 14 44.

159 30.i.1932: BCA, 030 10 241 631 30.

160 3.vi.1932: BCA, 030 10 246 667 7.

161 1.xii.1933: BCA, 030 10 241 631 30.

162 [Nayır], Yaşar Nabi, *Balkanlar ve Türklük* (Ankara, 1936), p. 167: 'Türklüğün ve inkılabımızın sicilli düşmanı olan ve Bulgar hükûmetinin sırf bütün Bulgar emir ve menfaatlerine bir uşak sadıklığıyle hizmet ettiği için mevkiinde tuttuğu baş müftü.'

163 [Nayır], Yaşar Nabi: *Balkanlar ve Türklük*, p. 169.

164 'Bulgaristan'da Yabancı Propogandanın Önlenmesi Hakkında Hazırlanan 23.04.1934 Tarihli Komisyon Raporu. TsDA, F. 176K, op. 6, a.e. 2556, L. 1-23' in *Belgelerle Mustafa Kemal Atatürk ve Türk-Bulgar İlişkileri (1913-1938)* (Ankara, 2002), p. 334, for facsimile, see pp. 813-35.

165 For the Turkish translation of this document, see 'Belge 67. Türk Okullarında Eğitimin Latin Harfler ile Basılmış Kitaplarla Yapılmasına Dair Bulgaristan Milli Eğitim Bakanlığı'nın 12.04.1938 Tarihli Genelgesi. T.C. Cumhurbaşkanlığı Arş. A: IV-6, D: 53, f: 36-3' in *Belgelerle Mustafa Kemal Atatürk ve Türk-Bulgar İlişkileri*, p. 501, for facsimile, p. 918 and also see 'Belge 68. Bulgaristan Türk Okullarında Latin Alfabesine Geçiş İle İlgili Sofya Büyükelçiliği'nin 01.07.1938 Tarihli Raporu. BCA, 030.10.243-641-11' in *Belgelerle Mustafa Kemal Atatürk ve Türk-Bulgar İlişkileri*, p. 502-3, for facsimile, p. 919.

166 'Belge 69. Bulgaristan Türklerinin Eğitim Problemleri İle İlgili Bulgar Makamlarına Gönderdikleri 05.07.1939 Tarihli Dilekçe. TsDA, F. 166 K, op. 1 a.e. 890, L. 217-218' in *Belgelerle Mustafa Kemal Atatürk ve Türk-*

Bulgar İlişkileri, pp. 511-2, for facsimile of the whole document in Bulgarian, see pp. 921-4.
167 24.i.1933: BCA, 0 30 10 241 626 5.
168 13.x.1930: BCA, 030 10 107 697 5: 'yüzelliliklerle firarilerin merkezi fa'aliyeti olan Gümülcinede.'
169 23 Teşrin-i sani 1341: BCA, 030 18 01 016 72 4.
170 17.x.1932: BCA, 030 10 240 625 5. A letter from the Minister of Foreign Affairs to the Prime Minister's Office requested that 40,000 drachma be paid to support a political club established by the Turkish youth of Komotene in order to counter the anti-Kemalist propaganda of 'fugitives' and '150'likler.' 13.x.1930: BCA, 030 10 107 697 5.
171 [Nayır], Yaşar Nabi: *Balkanlar ve Türklük*, p. 225: 'Hatta, Türkiyeden kaçmış olan hainler yakın zamanlara kadar fesatçı propagandalarını serbestçe Garbi Trakya Türkleri arasında yaymak imkânlarını da bulmuşlardır.'
172 Ömer Seyfettin, 'Hürriyet Bayrakları' in *Bomba* (Ankara, 1998), pp. 101-12.
173 Ahmet Şerif: *Arnavudluk'da, Sûriye'de, Trablusgarb'de Tanîn*, pp. 91-5.
174 Yalçın: *Siyasal Anılar*, p. 34.
175 Ömer Seyfettin: 'Nakarat', pp. 216-20: 'İşte bir haftadır, Vehelmefçe Ormanlarında, kendince mukaddes bir fikir içün ölen komita papasının o cesur kızıyla aramdaki farkı düşünerek, yatıyorum.
İşte bir haftadır...' (p. 220)
176 Quoted from Abdullah Cevdet, *İctihad*, no. 54, p. 1,221 in Peyami Safa: *Türk İnkılâbına Bakışlar*, pp. 24-5: '[Bulgarlar] otuz bu kadar sene kadar çalıştılar, ırklarını kuvvetlendirdiler, bizzat tanzimi idare ve icrayi hüsnü idare ile meşgul oldular, zafer ve istiklâl esbabını hazırladılar: Vatana, hürriyete, memleketlerinin bir istikbale malik olduklarına iman ettiler.
Bizim kafataslarımız boşaldı. Derilerimiz içinde et, kemik, kan kalmadı. Köylerimizde köylü, köylülerimizde köy kalmadı. Anadolu boşaldı. Anadolu hastadır, Anadolu ölüyor.'
177 Tekin Alp, *Türkleştirme* (İstanbul, 1928), pp. 10-11: 'Bulgaristan, Yunanistan, Romanya gibi bütün Balkan memalikinde «intibak» içün pek parlak ve muganna misaller bulunuyor. Yunanistanda anasılı Ulah, Bulgar veya Arnavud olan bilzat pek çok zevat bilirim ki millileştirme suretiyle büsbütün Rumlaşmışlar. Kendileri Rumcayı anadili olmak üzere konuşuyor ve fakat evlerinde ihtiyar anaları ve babaları ilan Ulahca veya Bulgarcadan başka bir dil konuşmazlar. Bu gibi adamlara müessisat-ı maliye ve

iktisadiye ruusası ve hatta devlet ricali meyanında pek çok tesadüf olunur. Muhitlerinde bunların şecerelerini bilenler çoktur. Fakat hiç bir kimse onlara yan gözle bakmaz. Kendileri de şecerelerini ketm ve ihfaya asla lüzum görmezler.'

178 [Nayır], Yaşar Nabi: *Balkanlar ve Türklük*, pp. 226-8, 236-53.
179 Ahmed Vefik Paşa: *Fezleke*, p. 292 and Ali Cevad: *Mükemmel Osmanlı Tarihi*, p. 219.
180 Ahmed Cevdet Paşa: *Ma'rûzât*, pp. 113-5. For a summary of Cevdet's view on military service and translation of his views from *Ma'rûzât*, see Lewis, Bernard, *The Emergence of Modern Turkey*, second edition (London, Oxford and New York, 1968), pp. 331-2.
181 Namık Kemal, 'Vatan,' *İbret*, no. 121, 22 March 1873 in Özön: *Namık Kemal ve İbret Gazetesi*, pp. 266-7: 'Biz oturduğumuz yerin her taşı için bir cevheri can verdik. Her avuç toprağı nazarımızda o yola feda olmuş bir kahramanın yadigârı vücududur. Onu binaenaleyh bize göre vatanı Çin ile, Sibirya ile hemkıymet tutmak ihtimalin haricinde görünür.' Also see the same article in Namık Kemal, *Külliyat-ı Kemal, Birinci Tertib 3 - Makalat-ı Siyasiye ve Edebiye* (İstanbul, 1327), pp. 320-30.
182 Mizancı Murad: *Mücahede-i Milliye*, p. 16.
183 Tansel: *Ziya Gökalp Külliyatı-1. Şiirler ve Halk Masalları*, pp. 100-1.
184 Tansel: *Ziya Gökalp Külliyatı-1. Şiirler ve Halk Masalları*, p. 5: 'Vatan ne Türkiya'dır Türkler'ē, ne Türkistān;/ Vatan büyük ve müebbet bir ülkedir: Tūrān...'
185 Sarıgöl, Adem (ed.), *Harbiye Nazırı Sadrazam Mahmut Şevket Paşa'nın Günlüğü* (İstanbul, 2001), p. 69.
186 Sarıgöl: *Harbiye Nazırı Sadrazam Mahmut Şevket Paşa'nın Günlüğü*, p. 61; *Sadrazâm ve Harbiye Nazırı Mahmut Şevket Paşa'nın Günlüğü* (İstanbul, 1988), p. 45: 'Kuveyt ve Katar gibi çölden ibaret iki kaza yüzünden İngiltere ile ihtilaf çıkaramazdık. Bu ehemmiyetsiz topraklardan ne gibi bir istifademiz olabilirdi.'
187 Sarıgöl: *Harbiye Nazırı Sadrazam Mahmut Şevket Paşa'nın Günlüğü*, pp. 179-80, 34; *Sadrazâm ve Harbiye Nazırı Mahmut Şevket Paşa'nın Günlüğü*, pp. 133-4, 22-3.
188 9.viii.1915 (date in the document): BOA, Ali Fuad Türkgeldi Evrakı, 9-73.
189 This *türkü* (folk song) appears in a recent CD of Sabahat Akkiraz called *Konserler*. The *Yemen türküleri* (folk songs) are still very popular in Turkish music and sung both by folk singers and other musicians such as Zülfü Livaneli, Emel Sayın and Ferhat Göçer. In his depiction of Erzurum,

Ahmed Hamdi Tanpınar referred to a *Yemen türküsü*, one of the lines of which was 'Did you imagine that he who went to Yemen would come back?' ('Yemen'e gideni gelir mi sandın?' in *Beş Şehir*, p. 70). The most well-known *Yemen türküsü* is 'Burası Huştur' (Here is Huş), a mourning for those who went to Yemen. A story, 'Yemen Türküsü' (Yemen song) by Ferid C. Güven, appeared in *Ülkü Halkevleri Mecmuası*, VI/31 (September 1935), pp. 55-9. For an understanding of the place of Yemen for a Republican statesman, see the memoirs of İsmet İnönü, who spent two years there between 1911-1913 during the uprising. İnönü, İsmet, *Hatıralarım. Genç Subaylık Yılları (1884-1918)*, edited by Sabahattin Selek (İstanbul, 1969), pp. 87-115.

190 [İnan], Afet: *Yurt Bilgisi Notlarından: Vatandaş İçin Medenî Bilgiler. 1. Kitap*, pp. 8-9.

191 'Millî Şef ve Reisicumhur Büyük İsmet İnönü'nün 19 Mayıs 1944 Gençlik ve Spor Bayramı Günü Ankara 19 Mayıs Stadyumunda Verdikleri Söylev' in *Irkçılık-Turancılık* (Ankara, 1944), p. 7: 'Millî kurtuluş sona erdiği gün yalnız Sovyet'lerle dosttuk ve bütün komşularımız eski düşmanlıklarının bütün hâtıralarını canlı olarak zihinlerinde tutuyorlardı. Herkesin kafasında, biraz derman bulursak sergüzeştçi, saldırıcı bir siyasete kendimizi kaptıracağımız fikri yaşıyordu. Cumhuriyet, kuvvetli bir medeniyet yaşayışının şartlarından bir esaslısını, milletler ailesi içinde bir emniyet havasının mevcut olmasında görmüştür. İmparatorluktan son zamanlarda ayrılmış olan komşulariyle de iyi ve samimî komşuluk şartlarının temin edilmiş olmasını, Millelin [*sic.*] saadeti için lüzumlu saymıştır.'

192 Yücel, Hasan Âli, 'Tuna Türküsü' in Atasoy, Ahmet Emin (ed.), *XV. Yüzyıldan Bugüne Rumeli Motifli Türk Şiiri Antolojisi* (Bursa, 2001), p. 203: 'Hep seni özlüyorum,/ Yolunu gözlüyorum.'

193 Braudel: 'The history of the civilizations: the past explains the present' in *On History*, pp. 203-4.

194 Namık Kemal, *Vatan Yahut Silistre*, edited by Kenan Akyüz (Ankara, 1960), p. 21: 'Arkadaşlar, Tuna boyuna gideceğiz!.. Tuna, bizim için âb-ı hayattır. Tuna aradan kalkarsa vatan yaşamaz. Vatan yaşamazsa, vatanda hiçbir insan yaşamaz...Allah, vatana muhabbeti emrediyor. Bizim vatanımız Tuna demektir. Çünkü Tuna elden gidince vatan kalmıyor...Tuna kenarının neresini karıştırsanız, içinde ya babanızın, ya kardeşlerinizin bir kemiği bulunur...Tunanın suyu bulandıkça üzerine çıkan topraklar, muhafazası için ölen vücutların eczâsındandır.'

195 Kemalettin Şükrü, *Namık Kemal Hayatı ve Eserleri* ([İstanbul], 1931 in *Resimli Ansiklopedik Neşriyat* ([İstanbul], 1932)), p. 150. Compare this text with Namık Kemal: *Vatan Yahut Silistre*, edited by Kenan Akyüz.
196 Ahmed İhsan, *Tuna'da Bir Hafta* (İstanbul, 1327), p. 1: 'Tarih-i mevcudiyetimizin pek mühim ve feci vekayına sahne olmuş olan "Tuna" nın ismi yad edildiği zaman kalbimizin titrememesi kabil değildir.'
197 From 'Balkan'a Seyahat,' *Dergâh Mecmûası* (5 Teşrin-i sani 1337) in [Beyatlı], Yahya Kemal, *Çocukluğum, Gençliğim, Siyâsî ve Edebî Hâtıralarım* (İstanbul, 1973), p.146: 'Bir Türk gönlünde nehir varsa Tuna'dır, dağ varsa Balkan'dır. Vâkıâ Tuna'nın kıyılarından ve Balkan'ın eteklerinden ayrılalı kırk üç sene oluyor. Lâkin bilmem uzun asırlar bile o sularla kaplı karlı tepeleri gönlümüzden silebilecek mi? Zanneder misiniz ki bu hasret yalnız Rumeli'nin çocuklarının yüreğindedir? Rumeli toprağına ömründe ayak basmamış bir Diyarbekirli Türk de aynı hasretle bu türküyü söylemiyor mu?

Gözde tüter dumanları/ Bak Şıpka'nın Balkanları/ Hâlâ sızar al kanları/ Ayrılmıştık otuz sene/ İşte Şıpka geldik yine.'
198 Sevük, İsmail Habib, *Atatürk İçin* (Ankara, 1981), pp. 83-88.
199 Sevük: *Atatürk İçin*, pp. 132-7: 'Gafil! hangi üç asır, hangi on asır?/ Tuna yalıları Türk diyarıdır' (p. 135); 'Tuna'nın üstü Tuna'nın altı,/ Olmuştur daima Türk'ün vatanı' (p. 136).
200 Halil Yaver: *Balkan Sulhunu Kim Tehdid Ediyor? Bulgarların Balkanları İstilâ Planları* (İstanbul, 1938), pp. 42-3.
201 Peremeci: *Tuna Boyu Tarihi*, and also see his letter to the *Cumhuriyet Halk Partisi* concerning the publication of his book. 25.v.1942: BCA, 490 01 869 423 1.
202 Çağlar, Behçet Kemal, 'Hey Tuna Tuna' in Atasoy, *Rumeli Motifli Türk Şiiri Antolojisi*, p. 236: 'Türk'ü gördükçe seslen, Türklükle övün Tuna!'
203 Ecevit, Bülent, 'Tuna' in Atasoy, *Rumeli Motifli Türk Şiiri Antolojisi*, p. 294: 'Sor Tuna'ya nedendir bu ağlayışı/ Rüyasında bir Türk'ün aksi durunca.'
204 Hüseyin Raci: *Tarihçe-i Vaka-i Zağra*. This book was published by Hüseyin Raci Efendi's son after his father's death.
205 From 'Balkan'a Seyahat' in [Beyatlı], Yahya Kemal: *Çocukluğum, Gençliğim, Siyâsî ve Edebî Hâtıralarım*, p.149: 'ikinci ve son felâketi.'
206 [Atay], Falih Rıfkı, 'İzmir'den Bursa'ya Kadar; in [Adıvar], Halide Edip, *et al.*: *İzmir'den Bursa'ya*, p. 55: 'Balkan harbinin kanlı günlerindeydi'; 'içimde onulmaz bir gönül yarası gibi.'

207 Ahmed Hasır and Mustafa Muhsin: *Türkiye Tarihi*, p. 674: 'Bulgarlar da islâm ahaliye karşı vahşiyane mezalime başlamışlardı. Kışın şiddetine rağmen halk takım takım hicret etmekte, İstanbulda şehrin ahalisine yakın bir miktarda muhacir görülmekte idi. Bunların acıklı hali de ayrıca tesiri arttırıyordu.'

208 Basiretçi Ali Efendi, *İstanbul Mektupları*, edited by Nuri Sağlam (İstanbul, 2001), p. 661: 'Sirkeci İstasyonu'na gidip de bu fukaraların hâlini görenlerin yürekleri taş olsa eriyor. Hele o küçük çocukların baş açık yalın ayak, tiril tiril titreyip nalişleri ve kadınların nefislerini unutarak ciğerparelerinin muhafazaları için ağlaya ağlaya vatandaşlarından hasbetenlillâh istimdat eylemeleri, hastaların hâl-i cânhırâşı, ihtiyarların aczi zannederiz ki erbâb-ı iktidâra şer'an ve insaniyeten pek büyük vazifeler tahmil ediyor.'

209 Duru: *"İttihat ve Terakki,, Hatıralarım*, p. 62: 'Bu harp [Balkan] Türkü çok şaşırttı. Bütün tarihinde efsanevî (Ergenekon) dan sonra bu kadar ağır bir yenilgiye uğramamıştı.' The myth of 'Ergenekon' became a reference point for the Turkish nationalists during the Balkan War period. It was used by Ziya Gökalp, in his poem 'Türk An'anesi-Ergenekon' (*Türk Duygusu*, I/1 (25 Nisan 1329)) and Ömer Seyfettin in his poem, 'Ergenekon'dan Çıkış' (*Halka Doğru*, I/51 (27 Mart 1330)). For more details see Tansel: *Ziya Gökalp Külliyatı-1. Şiirler ve Halk Masalları*, pp. 336-7.

210 Ömer Seyfettin, 'Rûznâme (Balkan Savaşı Günlüğü)' in *Mahçupluk İmtihanı*, edited by Kemal Demiray (İstanbul, 1977), p. 186: 'Rumeli eski şeklini alamaz. Artık Rumeli bir daha yapışmamak üzere Türk ilinden kopmuştur. Avrupa'nın orduları gelip, Sırp ve Bulgarları buralardan çıkaramaz ya!...'

211 Aydemir, Şevket Süreyya, *Suyu Arayan Adam* (Ankara, 1959), p. 59: 'O güne kadar demek ki biz, bir hayal âleminde yaşamıştık. Bütün inandığımız şeyler demek ki bir vehimdi. Bu imparatorluk aslında belki çoktan ölmüştü. Biz onu belki de sadece, vehimimizle yaşatmıştık. Şu kaybolan Osmanlı Afrikası, belki hiçbir zaman bizim olmamıştı. Şu Osmanlı Avrupası, belki çoktan beri artık bizim sayılmazdı. Girit, Şarki Rumeli, Tuna eyâletleri olan Bosna-Hersek, demek ki çoktan beri, bizim için artık tarihe karışmıştı.'

212 'Belge 1. 1913 İstanbul, Bulgaristan-Türkiye Antlaşması. Düstur, 2. tertip, 7. cilt, pp. 15-45' in *Belgelerle Mustafa Kemal Atatürk ve Türk-Bulgar İlişkileri*, p. 20.

213 [Ahmed] Cemal Paşa: *Hatırat*, p. 59.

214 [Ahmed] Cemal Paşa: *Hatırat*, pp. 59-61.

215 Söylemezoğlu, Galip Kemalî, *Hatıraları. Atina Sefareti (1913-1916)* (n.p.p., 1946), p. 101: '...tâ Berlin ahitnamesinin imzası tarihi olan 1878 denberi İmparatorluğumuzdan ayrılmak felâketine uğramış bedbaht Müslüman halkın Balkanların her memleketinde başlarına gelen türlü malûm ve mücerrepti. Onun için Mösyö Venizelos'a sırf bir şahsi mülâhaza kabilinden "Makedonya'daki Müslümanlarla Aydın vilâyetinde meskûn Rumların" mübadele edilmesi, bunların bırakacağı emlâkin de "takas" suretiyle onlara verilmesi ve aradaki farkı fiatın Hükümetlerce tazmin edilmesi yolunda bir itilâf yapılmasını" [*sic.*] teklif ettim. İleride görüleceği veçhile bu teklifim muvafık görülmekle beraber, nihayet Temmuz'da çıkan "Ayvalık" hâdisesinden sonra resmen kabul edilmiş, biri İzmir, diğeri Selânik'te iki muhtelif komisyon teşekkül etmiş idiyse de, maalesef birinci cihan harbinin çıkması üzerine, bizi çok büyük elemlerden kurtaracak bu uyuşmanın tatbikine vakıt ve imkân kalmamıştır.'

216 22 Teşrin-i evvel 1339: BCA, 030 10 123 874 20.

217 Cami, *Osmanlı Ülkesinde Hıristiyan Türkler. Hicret Yolları*, second edition (İstanbul, 1932), pp. 6-8. The first edition of this book was published by the author Cami (Başkurt) during the Lausanne talks about the exchange of population with Greece. In the 1930s', well after the completion of this exchange, some still questioned the correctness of the decision. For example see [Sevük], İsmail Habib, *Tunadan Batıya. Tunadan Önce-Tuna Yolunda-Tunadan Sonra-Dönüş* (İstanbul, 1935), pp. 205-6.

218 22 Temmuz 1339: BCA, 030 18 01 07 25 17: 'Son zamanlarda gayri müslimlerin ihtidâ hakkındaki mürâca'atları çoğalmakta olup, gerçi kabûlünde bir mâni'-î ve kanûni yoksa da, idâreten ve hukûkan emniyet ve âsâyiş nokta-i nazarından ve Harb-i Umûmî esnasındaki emsâline nazaran mahzurdan sâlim olmadığından, Sulh'ün akdine ve hâl-i tabî'înin avdedine kadar ihtidâ taleblerinin hiçbir taraftan is'âf edilmemesi Dâhiliyye Vekâletinin 30 Haziran 39 târih ve Nüfûs Müdüriyyesi 471/21187 numaralu tezkiresi üzerine İcrâ Vekilleri Heyetinin 22.7.39 târihindeki içtimâlarında takarrür itmiştir. 22. 7. 1339.'

219 1 Mayıs 1337: BCA, 030 18 01 03 18 14 (Karar No. 825, eski defter C. No. 2, S. No. 504).

220 Behçet Kami, *Tarihimizde Rumlar, Patrikhane ve Yunancılık* (İstanbul, 1339), *passim*.

221 M. Tevfik, *et al.*: *Tarih III*, p. 97.

222 'VII Darülfünun Tasavvuf Tarihi (Dinler Tarihi) Müderrisi Mehmet Ali Ayni Beyin Mütaleanamesi,' p. 7 in *Darülfünun Müderrislerinin*

Mütalaaları (Türk Tarih Kurumu Library, Ankara, 15076-B/9521): 'Yine bu sayfada [sayfa 95] Fener Rum Beylerinden bahsedilirken onlardan bazılarının devlete sadakatle hizmet ettikleri de haber verilmiş olsaydı bitaraflık kaidesine muvafık olurdu.'

223 T.T.T. Cemiyeti: *Tarih III*, pp. 198-9.

224 Süleyman Edip and Ali Tevfik: *İlkmektep Çocuklarına Yeni Tarih Dersleri. Beşinci Sınıf*, pp. 145-6: 'İçimizde yılan gibi yaşıyan Anadolu Rumları, Yunanistandaki Türk kardeşlerimizle mübadeleye tutuldu.'

225 Behçet Kami: *Tarihimizde Rumlar, Patrikhane ve Yunancılık*, pp. 12-13: 'Hala Konferans, ekaliyetlerin bildikleri gibi yaşamaları lüzumunda musır görünüyor. Bildikleri gibi yaşamak. Yani mekteplerde Türke düşman olmayı, Türk'ün kanının helal olduğunu öğretmek, kiliselerde Yunan milletinin selametine, bizim makhuriyetizi istihdaf eden cidallarda zaferine dua etmek, cemiyet-i hayriyeler (!) vasıtasıylada Yunan ordusuna bol bol iane toplamak... Tarih ve henüz tarihe karışmayan vakalar gösteriyor ki Rumlar için bu tarz hareket tabi olmuştur. Onlar daima Yunanlı gibi düşünmüşler, Yunanlılıkla daima iftihar etmişler, havayı biraz dumanlı buldukları anda ağızlarından salkım salkım rakı salyaları kusarak mavi beyaz yüreklerini bütün gızletiyle önümüze açmışlardır. Bu kadar vakadan hele bu Yunan mağlubiyetinden sonra, Yunanlılığı Atina'dan ziyade burada temsile mazhar eden bu unsur Türk'e dost olamaz. İçimizde neden göz göre göre bu düşmanları saklayup beslemeliyiz? Neden südcü Pauli'nin dükkanında Yunan Kralı Yorgi'nin yok bilmem ne Kraliçesi Sofiya'nın suretlerini görmeliyiz? Eğer medeni hükümetler ekaliyetlere aid bir takım haklar kabul ediyorlarsa o hakların arasında memleketin sahibine alenen düşmanlık edebilmek şartı olmasa gerekdir.'

226 T.T.T. Cemiyeti: *Tarih IV. Türkiye Cümhuriyeti*, p. 127: 'Mübadele edilen Rumların ve Türklerin herne suretle olursa olsun tekrar eski yerlerine yerleşmeleri menolunmuştu.' The suspicion of Greek desires can be seen in Akçuraoğlu's interpretation of the meaning of Rigas's map of a Greater Greece which included many parts of Ottoman Anatolia: 'Yunanlılarca, - belki bugüne kadar - bu harita, eski Yunanistan haritası olmaktan ziyade müstakbel ve muhayyel bir Büyük Yunanistan siması sayılır.' In Akçura: *Osmanlı İmparatorluğunun Dağılma Devri*, p. 22.

227 *Yunanistan 1929-1930* (Hizmete Mahsus) (İstanbul, 1930), p. 28: 'Lozan muahedesiyle defedilen Rumların her ne pahasına olursa olsun İzmir ve sevahil mıntıkasına kat'iyyen sokulmamaları en mühim bir milli vazife addolunmalıdır.'

228 11.iv.1933: BCA, 030 10 255 716 11.
229 Hariciye Nezareti, *Türkiye Cumhuriyeti ile Bulgaristan Krallığı Arasında 18 Teşrin-i evvel 1925 Tarihinde Ankara'da Tanzim ve İmza Edilmiş Olan Muhadenet Muahede ve İkamet Mukavelenameleriyle Muhadenet Muahedenamesine Merbut Protokol*, pp. 4-5; protocol clauses A and B.
230 [İnan], Afet: *Vatandaş İçin Medenî Bilgiler. 1. Kitap*, pp. 13 and 7.
231 [İnan], Afet: *Vatandaş İçin Medenî Bilgiler. 1. Kitap*, p. 12: 'Türkler islâm dinini kabul etmeden evel de büyük bir millet idi. Bu dini kabul ettikten sora, bu din; ne Arapların; ne ayni dinde bulunan Acemlerin ve ne de sairenin Türklerle birleşip bir millet teşkil etmelerine tesir etmedi. Bilâkis, türk milletinin millî bağlarını gevşetti; millî hislerini, millî heyecanını uyuşturdu. Bu pek tabiî idi. Çünkü Muhammedin kurduğu dinin gayesi, bütün milliyetlerin fevkinde şamil bir ümmet siyaseti idi.'
232 T.T.T. Cemiyeti: *Tarih IV. Türkiye Cümhuriyeti*, p. 183: 'Türkiye Cumhuriyeti dahilinde Türk dili ile konuşan, Türk kültürü ile yetişen, Türk mefkûresini benimseyen her fert, hangi dinden olursa olsun Türktür.'
233 *İskân Kanunu. Resmi Gazetenin 21 Haziran 1934 Tarih ve 2733 Numaralı Nüshasından Alınmıştır* (İstanbul, 1934), p. 4: 'Türkiyede yerleşmek maksadile dışarıdan, münferiden veya müçtemian, gelmek istiyen Türk soyundan meskûn veya göçebe fertler ve aşiretler ve Türk kültürüne bağlı meskûn kimseler, işbu kanun hükümlerine göre Dahiliye Vekilliğinin emrile kabul olunurlar'; 'Kimlerin ve hangi memleketler halkının Türk kültürüne bağlı sayılacağı İcra Vekilleri Heyeti Kararile tespit olunur.'
234 Halil Yaver: *Balkan Sulhunu Kim Tehdid Ediyor?*, see the section 'Gagavuzlar Meselesi,' pp. 59-75.
235 24.iv.1936: BCA, 030 10 243 638 11.
236 Hariciye Nezareti: *Protokol*, p. 5, Section B.
237 17.vi.1933: BCA, 030 10 241 629 15.
238 17.vi.1933: BCA, 030 10 241 629 15; 20.v.1933: BCA, 030 10 241 628 10.
239 [Ahmed] Cemal Paşa: *Hatırat*, p. 43.
240 20.v.1933: BCA, 030 10 233 571 12.
241 2.ii.1933: BCA, 030 10 233 570 25.
242 20.v.1933: BCA, 030 10 233 571 11: 'Alelhusus babaları memleketimiz ugurunda [*sic.*] canlarını feda etmiş olan şehit zabit ve asker çocuklarının, arnavut irkindan [*sic.*] da olsalar her prensipe istisnaen mekteplerimize kabulleri pek münasip olacağı mütâlaasında bulunduğumu arz eylerim.' The report on this letter was sent from the Foreign Ministry to the Prime

Minister's Office, the Chief of General Staff, the Education Ministry and the Defense Ministry.

243 12.x.1933: BCA, 030 10 241 631 8. A letter thanking the Prime Minister İsmet İnönü for the sum of 6,500 leva (100 TL) given to the Turkish school in Plevne (Pleven). For the list of Turkish newspapers in Bulgaria and the amount of money provided by the Turkish government see 4.xii.1933: BCA, 030 10 241 631 30 and 16.iii.1934: BCA, 030 10 242 632 24. Also see 24.i.1933: BCA, 030 10 241 626 5 for an evaluation by the Turkish ambassador in Sofia, Tevfik Kamil Bey, of the usefulness of these journals for Turkish interests in Bulgaria.

244 [Nayır], Yaşar Nabi: *Balkanlar ve Türklük*, p. 169: 'Bir tanıdığım, Bulgaristanda seyahat ederken, bir mektep bahçesinde oynayan küçük yavruların haç çıkardıklarını, Bulgarca dualar ve millî marşlar söylediklerini gördükten sonra bunların Türk olduklarını anlayınca kalbinde ne derin bir ıztırap duyduğunu, gözlerinde yaşlarla bana anlattı.'

Conclusion

1 İhsan Şeref: *Cumhuriyet Çocuklarına Tarih Dersleri*, pp. 51-2: 'Biz Türkler, eskiden beri, hangi diyara inmiş, hangi kavmi idaremiz altına almış isek onların ne dillerine, ne de dinlerine hiç ilişmemişiz, [*] hatta cemaat teşlikatlarına bile dokunmamışız. Bir halde ki içimizde adeta başlı başına bir hükümet, bir millet gibi pek ala yaşıyorlardı. Asker vermedikleri, muharabelere gitmedikleri için nüfusları çoğalıyordu. Mektepleri sayesinde bilgileri artıyordu. Ticaret, sanat ellerinde olduğu için paralarımızla cebleri doluyordu. Bundan sonra Avrupalıların teşvikiyle ortaya bir «milliyet» lafı çıkardılar. Bu bir ceryan idi. Bu ceryan ile o zamana kadar yüreklerinde sakladıkları Türk düşmanlığını meydana çıkardılar. Düşmanlarımız da onlara yardım etdi. Böylece tebamızdan her biri birer devlet olarak ortaya çıkdı. Karadağ, Sırbistan, Romanya, Bulgaristan, Yunanistan gibi.

[*] Bunun ne yaman hata olduğunu İngilizler İstanbul'u işgal ettiği, Rum ve Ermeni tebamızın başımızdaki feslere kadar yırtdıkları zaman anladık. Ama ne faide!' See also p. 49.

2 Bayur: *Türk İnkılâbı Tarihi*, Cilt: II, Kısım: I, p. 227. Also see Ahmed Hasır and Mustafa Muhsin: *Türkiye Tarihi*, p. 710; İleri, Suphi Nuri, *Siyasî Tarih. XVIII inci Asırdan XX nci Asra Kadar* (İstanbul, 1940), p. 315.

3 Ahmed Hasır and Mustafa Muhsin: *Türkiye Tarihi*, p. 715: 'Türkün gayri anasırın Osmanlı vatanına sadakatsizliği.'

4   *Atatürk'ün Söylev ve Demeçleri I - T.B.M.M. ve C.H.P. Kurultaylarında (1919-1938)* (Ankara, 1961), p. 272: 'Bu tarihin elemli hâtıraları varsa, onlara sahip olmakta bütün Balkanlılar müşterektir. Türklerin hissesi ise daha az acı olmamıştır.'
5   Atay, Falih Rıfkı, *Tuna Kıyıları* (İstanbul, 1938), p. 29: 'Osmanlı sukut ve tereddisinin acısını Türkler de diğerleri kadar çekmişlerdir.'
6   Behçet Kami: *Tarihimizde Rumlar, Patrikhane ve Yunancılık*, p. 29: 'Yunan hükümeti bir sene evvel Anadolu'yu istila edub Rum imparatorluğunu ihyaya kalkdıysa bu teşebbüs yeni değildi. Yirmi beş sene evvel onlar İstanbul'a Rumeli'den gelmeğe hazırlanmışlardı. Hesabca memleketdeki Rumlar yine bu ihtilalleri çıkaracaklar yine Yunan ordusunda öne düşecekler yine asacaklar, yine keseceklerdi. Nitekim Girid'i kana boyadılar. İslamları mezbahanelerde kesilcn hayvanların bile masun kaldığı vahşetlerle öldürdüler. Ne oldu? Bir iki komisyon, beş on muhabere kağıdı! Netice harbe dayandı. Biz Yunanlıları tepeledik. Fakat muhterem Avrupalılar alelusul Türk'ün hakkı yok dediler. Rumeli'nde çete cinayetleri yirmi sene devam etdi. Yalnız Türkler kabahatli çıkarıldılar. Avrupa içün Türk kanı helaldir. Hakikatın bu çıplaklığı karşısında insaniyet medeniyet kelimeleri ihtiva eden bütün cümleler riyanın, hilekarlığın bütün pisliklerini ihtiva eden mashara sırıtmalarından başka birşey değildir.'
7   Karaosmanoğlu: *Atatürk*, p. 65: 'Hangi ahmak; «Türk ordularının geçtiği yerde ot bitmez» demiş? Türk orduları nereye gittiyse oraya nizam, intizam ve sükûn götürmüştür. Asırlardan beri anarşi içinde çalkalanan ülkeleri bir anda, huzur ve vikafa kavuşturmuştur. Kendi kendini idareden âciz nice yabancı milletlere baş olup onları istiklâl ve istikrar yoluna sokmuştur.'
8   Köprülü, Mehmet Fuat, 'Akıncı Türküleri' in Atasoy: *XV. Yüzyıldan Bugüne Rumeli Motifli Türk Şiiri Antolojisi*, pp. 193-4: 'Bozulan bağların üzümü acı;/ Âsi köle kesmiş eski haracı;/ Yine yedi kıral giymişler tacı/ Şahin yuvasını kargalar sarmış!' (p. 194)
9   Atay: *Tuna Kıyıları*, p. 25: 'Osmanlılar, Balkanlara ve Macaristana doğru, ne bir barbar istilâsı, ne de bir din seferi yapmadılar.'
10 Barkan, Ömer, 'Osmanlı İmparatorluğunda Çiftçi Sınıflarının Hukukî Statüsü', *Ülkü Halkevleri Mecmuası*, 56/X (October 1937), p. 154: 'Türk hâkimiyeti altında geçen zamanı Balkan milletleri için bir Babil Esareti telekki etmek ancak kuvvetini Türklüğe karşı beslenilecek bir kin ve intikam hissinden almak mecburiyetini hisseden garip milliyetperverliğin hizmetinde garazkâr bir propagandadan başka bir şey değildir.'

11 For a discussion of Gendov and Bulgarian cinema during the World War I, see Kelbetcheva, Evelina, 'Between apology and denial: Bulgarian culture during World War I' in Roshwald, Aviel and Richard Stites (eds.), *European Culture in the Great War. The Arts, Entertainment and Propaganda, 1914-1918* (Cambridge, 1999), pp. 215-42.
12 25.x.1933: BCA, 030 10 241 631 13: 'Bulgarların 500 yıl Türk idaresinden gördükleri muhayyel zulmu tasvir ve tespit'; 'Bulgar efkârını aleyhimize tahrik ettiği kadar milletimizin hissiyatını da bu kaba ve çirkin tasvirlerle rencide edecek.'
13 25.x.1933: BCA, 030 10 241 631 13: 'filimdeki muhayyel vukuatın Osmanlı devrine ait olması hasebi ile Yeni Türk hükûmeti ne Milleti aleyhine bir mana ifade edeceğinin tasavvur edilemediği.'
14 20.xii.1933 (Takdim): 030 10 241 631 37: 'Paris umumhanelerinin eski bir sermayesi olduğu.' For the importance of film for the Republican elite, see Boyar, Ebru and Kate Fleet, '"Making Turkey and the Turkish revolution known to foreign nations without any expense": Propaganda films in the early Turkish Republic,' *Oriente Moderno*, XXIV (LXXXV)/1 (2005), pp. 117-32.
15 See for example, İleri: *Siyasî Tarih*, p. 320: 'Bu Makidonyalılar âciz ve hafif Osmanlı idaresinde asırlarca rahat yaşayıp toprak ve mal sahibi olmuşlar ve papazları sayesinde kiliseleri etrafında birliklerini, dillerini ve teamüllerini muhafaza edebilmişlerdi. Makidonyalıları bedbaht eden Babıâlinin bu gayesiz siyaseti değil belki Ruslarla Avusturyalıların birbirne zıt tahrik ve teşvikleri oldu.'
16 [Beyatlı], Yahya Kemal, 'Kaybolan Şehir' in *Kendi Gök Kubbemiz* (İstanbul, 1961), pp. 73-4: 'Vaktiyle öz vatanda vaktiyle bizimken, bugün niçin/ Üsküp bizim değil? Bunu duydum, için için' (p. 74).
17 [Adıvar], Halidé Edib, *Turkey Faces West. A Turkish View of Recent Changes and Their Origin*, with a preface by Edward Mead Earle (New Haven, 1930, reprinted in New York, 1973), p. 109.
18 [Tanrıöver], Hamdullah Suphi, 'Niçin Mucadele Ediyoruz? Konya: Haziran 1920-336' in *Dağyolu, 2inci Kitap*, p. 182.
19 [Sevük], İsmail Habib: *Tunadan Batıya*, p. 88.
20 Atay, Falih Rıfkı, *Zeytindağı* (İstanbul, 1964): p. 128: 'Anadolu hepimize hınç, şüphe ve güvensizlikle bakıyor. Yüz binlerce çocuğunu memesinden sökerek alıp götürdüğümüz bu anaya, şimdi kendimizi ve pişmanlığımızı getiriyoruz.'

21 Atay: *Zeytindağı*, p. 129: 'Vagonlar, arabalar, kamyonlar, hepsi, ondan. [sic] Anadolu'dan utanır gibi, hepsi İstanbul'a doğru, perdelerini kapamış muşambalarını indirmiş, lâmbalarını söndürmüş, gizli ve çabuk geçiyor.'
22 Atay: *Zeytindağı*, pp. 128-9: 'Hangi Ahmed'i? Yüz bin Ahmed'in hangisini?... Ahmed'ini buz mu, kum mu, su mu, skorpit yarası mı, tifüs biti mi yedi? Eğer hepsinden kurtulmuşsa, Ahmed'ini görsen ona da soracaksın:
_ Ahmed'imi gördün mü?'
23 Atay: *Zeytindağı*, p. 129: 'Hayır... Hiç birimiz Ahmed'ini görmedik. Fakat Ahmed'in her şeyi gördü. Allah'ın Muhammed'e bile anlatamadığı cehennemi gördü. Şimdi Anadolu'ya, Batı'dan, Doğu'dan, sağdan, soldan bütün rüzgarlar bozgun haykırışarak esiyor. Anadolu, demiryoluna, şoseye, han ve çeşme başlarına inip çömelmiş, oğlunu arıyor.

Anadolu Ahmed'ini soruyor. Ahmed, o daha dün bir kurşun istifinden daha ucuzlaşan Ahmed, şimdi onun pahasını kanadını kısmış, tırnaklarını büzmüş, bize dimdik bakan ana kartalın gözlerinde okuyoruz. Ahmed'i ne için harcadığımızı bir söyleyebilsek, onunla ne kazandığımızı bir anaya anlatabilsek, onu övündürecek bir haber verebilsek... Fakat biz Ahmed'i kumarda kaybettik!'

BIBLIOGRAPHY

Primary Sources

Başbakanlık Osmanlı Arşivi, İstanbul (BOA)
Ali Fuad Türkgeldi Evrakı
Meclis-i Vükela Mazbataları - MV.
Yıldız Esas Evrakı, Sadrazam Kamil Paşa - Y.EE.KP.
Yıldız Sadaret Hususi Maruzat - Y.A.HUS.
Yıldız Tasnifi - Perakende Evrakı - Sadaret - Y.PRK.A.
Yıldız Tasnifi - Perakende Evrakı - Askeri Maruzat - Y.PRK.ASK.
Yıldız Tasnifi - Perakende Evrakı - Arzuhal ve Jurnaller - Y.PRK.AZJ.
Yıldız Tasnifi - Perakende Evrakı - Hariciye Nezareti Maruzatı - Y.PRK.HR.
Yıldız Tasnifi - Perakende Evrakı - Tahrirat-ı Ecnebiye ve Mabeyn Mütercimliği - Y.PRK.TKM.
Yıldız Tasnifi - Perakende Evrakı - Zabtiye Nezareti Evrakı - Y.PRK.ZB.

Başbakanlık Cumhuriyet Arşivi, Ankara (BCA)
Bakanlar Kurulu Kararları Fonu - 030 18
Başbakanlık Muamelat Evrakı Fonu - 030 10
Cumhuriyet Halk Partisi Fonu - 490 01

Saint Cyril and Methodious Library, Oriental Library, Sofia (NLCM)
Oriental Archive Collection- OAK

Darülfünun Müderrislerinin Mütalaaları (Türk Tarih Kurumu Library, Ankara, 15076-B/9521)

Newspapers
The Times
Cumhuriyet

Books and Articles

Abdurrahman Şeref, *Tarih-i Devlet-i Osmaniye*, Vol. II (İstanbul, 1318).

Abdurrahman Şeref, *Tarih-i Asr-ı Hazır*, Vol. I, edited by Mehmed Zekai and H. Mehmed Kamil (İstanbul, 1329).

Abdurrahman Şeref, *Tarih Konuşmaları (Tarih Musahabeleri)*, edited by Eşref Eşrefoğlu (İstanbul, 1978).

Abdurrahman Şeref, *Son Vak'anüvis Abdurrahman Şeref Efendi Tarihi. II. Meşrutiyet Olayları*, edited by Bayram Kodaman and Mehmet Ali Ünal (Ankara 1996).

Abdurrahman Şeref and Ahmed Refik [Altınay], *Sultan Abdülhamid Saniye Dair* (İstanbul, 1918).

[Adıvar], Halidé Edib, *Turkey Faces West. A Turkish View of Recent Changes and Their Origin*, with a preface by Edward Mead Earle (New Haven, 1930 reprinted in New York, 1973).

[Adıvar], Halide Edip, Yakup Kadri, Falih Rıfkı and Mehmet Asım, *İzmir'den Bursa'ya. Hikayeler, Mektuplar ve Yunan Ordusunun Sorumluluğuna Dair Bir İnceleme* (İstanbul, 1974).

Adnan, A., 'Türk İnkılâp Tarihi [Yusuf Hikmet Bayur],' *Türkiyat Mecmuası*, VII-VIII (1940-1942), pp. 335-40.

Adnan-Adıvar, A., 'Tarih Anlayışı' in *60. Doğum Yılı Münasebetiyle Fuad Köprülü Armağanı* (İstanbul, 1953), pp. 1-3.

Ağaoğlu, Ahmet, *İhtilal mi İnkılap mı* (Ankara, 1942).

Ağaoğlu, Ahmet, *Üç Medeniyet* (İstanbul, 1972).

Ahmed Cemal, *Mefahir-i Milliye-i Osmaniyeden: Plevne Müdafası* (Kostantiniye, 1316).

[Ahmed] Cemal Paşa, *Hatırat 1913-1922* (Dersaadet, 1922).

[Ahmed] Cemal Paşa, *Hatıralar, «İttihat-Terakki ve Birinci Dünya Harbi»*, edited by Behçet Cemal (n. p. p., 1959).

[Ahmed] Cemal Paşa, *Hatıralar*, edited by Alpay Kabacalı (İstanbul, 2001).

Ahmed Cevdet, *Tarih-i Cevdet* (İstanbul, 1292-1301).

[Ahmed] Cevdet Paşa, *Tezakir 1-12*, edited by Cavid Baysun (Ankara, 1953).

[Ahmed] Cevdet Paşa, *Tezâkir 13-20*, edited by Cavid Baysun (Ankara, 1960).

[Ahmed] Cevdet Paşa, *Tezâkir 21-39*, edited by Cavid Baysun (Ankara, 1963).

[Ahmed] Cevdet Paşa, *Tezâkir 40-Tetimme*, edited by Cavid Baysun (Ankara, 1991).

Ahmed Cevdet Paşa, *Ma'rûzât*, edited by Yusuf Halaçoğlu (İstanbul, 1980).

Ahmed Hasır and Mustafa Muhsin, *Kurun-u Cedidde ve Asr-ı Hazırda Türkiye Tarihi. İstanbul'un Fethinden Zamanımıza Kadar* (İstanbul, 1924).

Ahmed Hasır and Mustafa Muhsin, *Türkiye Tarihi* (İstanbul, 1930).

Ahmed İhsan, *Tuna'da Bir Hafta* (İstanbul, 1327).
[Ahmed Lütfi Efendi], *Vak'a-Nüvis Ahmed Lûtfî Efendi Tarihi*. Vols. X-XV, edited by M. Münir Aktepe (Ankara, 1988-1993).
Ahmed Lûtfî Efendi, *Vak'anüvîs Ahmed Lûtfî Efendi Tarihi*. Vols. I-VIII (İstanbul, 1999).
Ahmed Müfid, *Tepedelenli Ali Paşa. 1744-1822* (Kahire, 1903).
Ahmed Müfid, *Tepedelenli Ali Paşa. 1744-1822* (İstanbul, 1324).
Ahmed Nazmi, *Rumeli Haritası* (İstanbul, 1329).
Ahmed Rasim, *Resimli ve Haritalı Osmanlı Tarihi*, Vol. IV (Konstantiniye, 1330-1328).
Ahmed Rasim, *Matbuat Hatıralarından. Muharrir, Şair, Edib* (İstanbul, 1342-1924).
Ahmed Râsim, *Osmanlı Tarihi (Seçmeler)*, edited by İsmet Parmaksızoğlu (İstanbul, 1968).
Ahmed Râsim, *Eşkâl-i Zamân*, edited by Orhan Şaik Gökyay (İstanbul, 1969).
Ahmed Salah Aldin, *Makedonya Meselesi ve Balkan Harbi Ahiri* (Dersaadet, 1331).
Ahmet Şerif, *Arnavudluk'da, Sûriye'de, Trablusgarb'de Tanîn*, Vol. II, edited by Mehmed Çetin Börekçi (Ankara, 1999).
Ahmed Vefik Paşa, *Fezleke-i Tarih-i Osmani* ([İstanbul], 1286).
Ahmed Vefik Paşa, *Lehçe-i Osmani* (Dersaadet, 1306).
Akçuraoğlu, Y., *Ulum ve Tarih* (Kazan, 1906).
Akçuraoğlu Yusuf, *Tarih-i Siyasi* (n.p.p., 1927).
Akçuraoğlu Yusuf (ed.), *Türk Yılı* (İstanbul, 1928).
Akçuraoğlu Yusuf, *Zamanımız Avrupa Siyasi Tarihi* (Ankara, 1933).
Akçura, Yusuf, *Osmanlı İmparatorluğunun Dağılma Devri, "Türk Tarihinin Ana Hatları" Eserinin Müsveddeleri* (İstanbul, n.d.).
Akkaya, Şükrü, *Ankara Tarih-Dil-Coğrafya Fakültesi Tarih Metodu ve Felsefesi Notları. II. Kısım. Tarih İlminin Tarihi* (Ankara, 1938).
Akkaya, Şükrü, *Tarihin Tarihine Kuşbakışı* ([Ankara], 1938).
Akyiğitzade Musa, *Avrupa Medeniyetinin Esasına Bir Nazar* (İstanbul, 1315).
Ali Cevad, *Memalik-i Osmaniyenin Tarih ve Coğrafya Lugatı* (Dersaadet, 1313).
Ali Cevad, *Mükemmel Osmanlı Tarihi* (İstanbul, 1316).
Ali Fıtri, *(91-92) Hersek Seferi, 292-293 Osmanlı-Karadağ Seferi* (Dersaadet, 1337).
Ali Fuad, 'Rumeli-i Şarki Meselesi,' *Darülfünun Edebiyat Fakültesi Mecmuası*, VI/1 (January 1928), pp. 1-51.

Ali Haydar Midhat, *The Life of Midhat Pasha. A Record of His Services, Political Reforms, Banishment, and Judicial Murder* (London, 1903).

Ali Haydar Midhat Bey, *Midhat Pacha. Sa vie - son ouvre* (Paris, 1908).

Ali Haydar Midhat, *Midhat Paşa'nın Hayat-ı Siyasiyesi, Hizmatı ve Şahadeti* (Kahire, 1322).

Ali Haydar Midhat, *Midhat Paşa. Hayat-ı Siyasiyesi, Hidematı, Mena-i Hayatı* (İstanbul, 1325), 2 vols.

Ali Necip, 'Halkevleri Yıldönümü Nutku,' *Ülkü Halkevleri Mecmuası*, III/13 (March 1934), pp. 5-15.

Ali Reşad, *Avrupa ile Münasebet-i Hariciyemiz Nokta-ı Nazarından Tarih-i Osmani* (Dersaadet, 1329).

Ali Reşad, *Asr-ı Hazır Tarihi. Liselerin İkinci Devre Son Sınıflarına Mahsustur* (İstanbul, 1926).

Ali Reşat, *Umumi Tarih* (İstanbul, 1929).

Ali Reşad and Ali Seydi, *Tarih-i Osmani. Resimli ve Haritalı. Mekteb-i Rüştiyenin İkinci Senesi İçin Kabul Edilen Son Proğrama Tevfikan Tertib Edilmiştir* (İstanbul, 1327).

Ali Rıza, *Atlaslı Memalik-i Osmaniye Coğrafyası, Kısm-ı Evvel* (İstanbul, 1318).

Ali Seydi, *Resimli Kamus-i Osmani* (Darülhilafe-i Aliye, 1330).

Ali Seydi, *Resimli Yeni Türkçe Lûgat* (İstanbul, 1929).

[Altınay], Ahmed Refik, *Hilminin Mektep Kitapları: Küçük Tarih-i Osmani. Mekateb-i Rüşdiye İkinci Senelerine Mahsus Proğrama Tevfikan Tertib Edilmiştir. 32 Resim ile 8 Haritaya Camidir* (İstanbul, 1327).

[Altınay], Ahmed Refik, *Kadınlar Saltanatı* (İstanbul, 1332 [Vols I and II]; 1923-1924 [Vols III and IV]).

[Altınay], Ahmed Refik, *Kızlar Ağası* (İstanbul, 1926).

[Altınay], Ahmed Refik, 'Alman Müverrihleri: Ranke,' *Yeni Mecmua*, I/20 (22 November 1917), pp. 392-5 and I/21 (29 November 1917), pp. 403-6.

[Altınay], Ahmed Refik, 'Tarih ve Müverrihler: 4 - Tarih Bir İlimdir,' *Hayat*, III/63 (9 February 1928), pp. 6-7.

[Altınay], Ahmed Refik, *Türk İdaresinde Bulgaristan (973-1255)* (İstanbul, 1933).

Arıkan, Zeki (ed.), *Tarihimiz ve Cumhuriyet, Muhittin Birgen (1885-1951)* (İstanbul, 1997).

Arşiv Belgelerine Göre Balkanlar'da ve Anadolu'da Yunan Mezâlimi - I Balkanlar'da Yunan Mezâlimi (Ankara, 1995).

Arşiv Belgelerine Göre Balkanlar'da ve Anadolu'da Yunan Mezâlimi - II Anadolu'da Yunan Mezâlimi (Ankara, 1996).

Atabinen, Reşid Safvet, *Les apports Turcs dans le peuplement et la civilisation de l'Europe orientale* (İstanbul, 1952).

Atasoy, Ahmet Emin (ed.), *XV. Yüzyıldan Bugüne Rumeli Motifli Türk Şiiri Antolojisi* (Bursa, 2001).

Atatürk'ün Özdeyişleri (Ankara, 1975).

Atatürk'ün Söylev ve Demeçleri II (1906-1938) (Ankara, 1959).

Atatürk'ün Söylev ve Demeçleri I. T.B.M.M. ve C.H.P. Kurultaylarında (1919-1938) (Ankara, 1961).

Atay, Falih Rıfkı, 'Tarih Kongresi,' *Ülkü Halkevleri Mecmuası*, X/55 (September 1937), pp. 1-2.

Atay, Falih Rıfkı, *Tuna Kıyıları* (İstanbul, 1938).

Atay, Falih Rıfkı, *Batış Yılları* (İstanbul, 1963).

Atay, Falih Rıfkı, *Zeytindağı* (İstanbul, 1964).

Atay, Falih Rıfkı, *Çankaya* (İstanbul, 1969).

Aybar, Celal, *Bulgaristan Nüfusu* (Ankara, 1935).

[Aydemir], Şevket Süreyya, 'Millî Kurtuluş Hareketleri Hakkında Bizim Tezimiz,' *Kadro Aylık Fikir Mecmuası*, I/12 (December 1932) [reprinted in Ankara, 1978], I, pp. 38-44.

Aydemir, Şevket Süreyya, *Suyu Arayan Adam* (Ankara, 1959).

[Aykaç], Fâzıl Ahmet, *Gelecek Asırlarda Tarih Dersi* (n.p.p., 1928).

Aykaç, Fazıl Ahmet, *Kırpıntı* (İstanbul, 1991).

Aynî, Mehmed Ali, *Milliyetçilik* (İstanbul, 1943).

B. A. [Burhan Asaf], 'Kronikler: Arkada Kalan Darülfünun,' *Kadro Aylık Fikir Mecmuası*, I/8 (August 1932) [reprinted in Ankara, 1978], I, pp. 47-8.

Baltacıoğlu, İsmail Hakkı, 'Biz Türkler Nereden Geliyoruz, Nereye Gidiyoruz ve Biz Neyiz' in *Konuşmalar* [CHP Halkevi Neşriyatı] (Ankara, October 1940), pp. 25-9.

Barkan, Ömer, 'Osmanlı İmparatorluğunda Çiftçi Sınıflarının Hukukî Statüsü,' *Ülkü Halkevleri Mecmuası*, 56/X (October 1937), pp. 147-58.

Barkan, Ömer Lûtfi, 'Osmanlı Tarihinde Rumelinin İskânı İçin Yapılan Sürgünler Meselesi' in *CHP Konferanslar Serisi. Kitap: 16* (1940), pp. 55-72.

Basiretçi Ali Efendi, *İstanbul Mektupları*, edited by Nuri Sağlam (İstanbul, 2001).

Baymur, A. Fuat, *Tarih Öğretimi* (Ankara, 1945).

Baysun, M. Cavid, 'Cevdet Paşa'nın İşkodra'ya Memûriyetine Âid Vesîkalar,' *Tarih Dergisi*, XVI/21 (1966), pp. 39-52.

Bayur, Yusuf Hikmet, *Yeni Türkiye Devletinin Haricî Siyaseti* (İstanbul, 1935).

Bayur, Yusuf Hikmet, *Türk İnkılâbı Tarihi, Cilt: I* (İstanbul, 1940).

Bayur, Yusuf Hikmet, *Türk İnkılâbı Tarihi, Cilt: II, Kısım: I* (İstanbul, 1943).
Beaufort, Francis, *Karamania, or a Brief Description of the South Coast of Asia Minor and of the Remains of Antiquity. With Plans, Views and & c. Collected during a Survey of that Coast, under the Orders of the Lords Commissioners of the Admirality, in the Years 1811 & 1812* (London, 1817).
Behçet Kami, *Tarihimizde Rumlar, Patrikhane ve Yunancılık* (İstanbul, 1339).
Bekir Fikri, *Balkanlarda Tedhiş ve Gerilla. Grebene* (İstanbul, 1976).
Belgelerle Mustafa Kemal Atatürk ve Türk-Bulgar İlişkileri (1913-1938) (Ankara, 2002).
Berkes, Niyazi (ed.), *Turkish Nationalism and Western Civilization. Selected Essays of Ziya Gökalp* (New York, 1959).
Bertelli, Sergio (ed.), *Niccolò Machiavelli, Il Principe e Discorsi sopra la prima deca di Tito Livio*, with an introduction by Giuliano Procacci (Milan, 1960).
[Beyatlı], Yahya Kemal, *Kendi Gök Kubbemiz* (İstanbul, 1961).
[Beyatlı], Yahya Kemal, *Siyâsî ve Edebî Portreler* (İstanbul, 1968).
[Beyatlı], Yahya Kemal, *Çocukluğum, Gençliğim, Siyâsî ve Edebî Hâtıralarım* (İstanbul, 1973).
Bilsel, Cemil, *İstanbul Üniversitesi Tarihi* (İstanbul, 1943).
Binbaşı Mehmed Nasrullah, Kol Ağası Mehmed Rüşdi, and Mülazım Mehmed Eşref, *Memalik-i Mahrusa-i Şahaneye Mahsus Mükemmel Mufassal Atlas* (İstanbul, 1325).
Birinci Türk Tarih Kongresi, Konferanslar, Münakaşalar (n.p.p., n.d.).
Brown, Robert F. (ed.), *Hegel Lectures on the History of Philosophy. The Lectures of 1825-1826.* Volume III. *Medieval and Modern Philosophy* (Berkeley, Los Angeles and Oxford, 1996).
Burnaby, Capt. Frederick, *On Horseback through Asia Minor*, with a new introduction by Peter Hopkirk (Oxford, 1996).
Cami, *Osmanlı Ülkesinde Hıristiyan Türkler. Hicret Yolları*, second edition (İstanbul, 1932).
Cebesoy, Ali Fuat, *Büyük Harpte Osmanlı İmparatorluğunun 1916-1917 Yılındaki Vaziyeti. Brüssebi-Gazze Meydan Muharebesi ve Yirminci Kolordu* (İstanbul, 1938).
Creasy, Edward S., *History of the Ottoman Turks: From the Beginning of Their Empire to the Present Time* (London, 1878).
Çambel, Hasan Cemil, *Makaleler Hâtıralar* (Ankara, 1964).
Doktor İbrahim Rafet, *Bulgaristan Ahvali* (İstanbul, 1329).
Durham, Edith, *High Albania. A Victorian Traveller's Balkan Odyssey* (London, 2000).

Durham, M. Edith, 'The Contemporary Review, November 1908. Constitution in Albania' in M. Edith Durham, *Albania and the Albanians. Selected Articles and Letters 1903-1944*, edited by Bejtullah Destani (London, 2001).

Duru, Kâzım Nami, *"İttihat ve Terakki,, Hatıralarım* (İstanbul, 1957).

E. Yzb. Fahrettin and E. Yzb. Seyfi, *1820-1827 Mora İsyanı* (İstanbul, 1934).

E. Yzb. Ziya and E. Yzb. Rahmi, *Girit Seferi (Mart-1645: 6-Eylûl-1669)* (İstanbul, 1933).

Edip-Adıvar, Halide, *Türkün Ateşle İmtihanı. Kurtuluş Savaşı Anıları* (n.p.p., n.d.).

Efdal Aldin, *Abdurrahman Şeref Efendi Tercüme-i Hali. Hayat-ı Resmiye ve Hususiyesi* (İstanbul, 1345-1927).

Emin Ali, 'Tarih Usulüne Dair,' *Yeni Mecmua*, II/52 (31 July 1918), pp. 514-7.

Engelhardt, Ed., *La Turquie et le Tanzimat ou historie des réformes dans l'empire ottoman depuis 1826 jusqu'a nos jours* (Paris, 1882), two vols.

Engelhard, Ed., *Türkiye ve Tanzimat. Devlet-i Osmaniyenin Tarih-i Islahatı 1826-1882*, translated by Ali Reşad (İstanbul, 1328).

Engelhardt, *Tanzimat ve Türkiye,* translated by Ali Reşad (İstanbul, 1999).

Erem, Mustafa, *Büyük Harpte Osmanlı Rumeli Müfrezesi [Takviyeli 177. Piyade Alayı]* (İstanbul, 1940).

[Ergin], Osman Nuri, *Abdülhamid-i Sani ve Devr-i Saltanatı. Hayat-ı Hususiye ve Siyasiyesi* (İstanbul, 1327).

Ergin, Osman Nuri, *Mecelle-î Umûr-ı Belediyye* (İstanbul, 1995), nine vols.

Ersoy, M. Âkif, *Safahat* (İstanbul, 1958).

Esmer, A. Şükrü, *Siyasi Tarih* (İstanbul, 1944).

Faik Sabri, *İlk Atlas. İlk Mekteblere Mahsus* (İstanbul, 1927).

Faik Sabri, *Orta Atlas. Liselere ve Orta Mekteblere Mahsus* (İstanbul, 1928).

Fatma Aliye Hanım, *Ahmet Cevdet Paşa ve Zamanı* (İstanbul, 1994).

Ferik Abdurrahman Nafiz and Mirliva Kiramettin, *1912-1913 Balkan Harbinde İşkodra Müdaafası* (İstanbul, 1933), two vols.

Fesch, Paul, *Constantinople aux derniers jours d'Abdul-Hamid* (Paris, [1907]).

Freeman, Edward A., *The Ottoman Power in Europe, Its Nature, Its Growth and Its Decline* (London, 1877).

Gaspıranski, İsmail, *Avrupa Medeniyetine Bir Nazar-ı Muvazene* (Kostantiniye, 1302).

Gazi Ahmed Muhtar Paşa, *Anılar. Sergüzeşt-i Hayatım'ın Cild-i Evveli* and *Anılar-2- Sergüzeşt-i Hayatım'ın Cild-i Sanisi*, edited by Nuri Akbayar (İstanbul, 1996).

Girid İhtilali. Ahiren Girid Ceziresinde Serzede-i Zuhur Olan İhtilale Dair Evrak-ı Mühimmeyi ve Parisde Fransızca Tab ve Neşr Olunan Risalenin Tercümesine Şamildir (Hanya, 1314).

Gladstone, Right Hon. W. E., MP, *Bulgarian Horrors and the Question of the East* (London, 1876).

Göksel, Ali Nüzhet (ed.), *Ziya Gökalp. Hayatı, Sanatı, Eseri* (İstanbul, 1952).

Günaltay, Şemsettin, *Lise Kitapları. Tarih I* (İstanbul, 1939).

Güven, Ferid C., 'Yemen Türküsü,' *Ülkü Halkevleri Mecmuası*, VI/31 (September 1935), pp. 55-9.

Halil Yaver, *Bugünkü Bulgaristan'da Türk Düşmanlığı. Bulgar Sefiri G. Pavlofa Bir Cevap* (İstanbul, 1932).

Halil Yaver, *Balkan Sulhunu Kim Tehdid Ediyor? Bulgarların Balkanları İstilâ Planları* (İstanbul, 1938).

Hancızade Mehmed Remzi, *Fikr-i İhtilal* ([İstanbul], 1331).

A Handbook of Turkey in Europe. Prepared on behalf of the Admiralty (Admiralty War Staff Intelligence Division, January 1917).

Hariciye Nezareti, *Türkiye Cumhuriyeti ile Bulgaristan Krallığı Arasında 18 Teşrin-i Evvel 1925 Tarihinde Ankara'da Tanzim ve İmza Edilmiş Olan Muhadenet-i Muahede ve İkamet Mukavelenameleriyle Muhadenet Muahedenamesine Merbut Protokol.*

The Historical Section of the Foreign Office, *Anatolia* (London, 1920).

Hürmen, F. Rezan (ed.), *"Bir Devlet Adamının" Mehmet Tevfik Beyin (Biren) II. Abdülhamid, Meşrutiyet ve Mütareke Devri Hatıraları* (İstanbul, 1993), two vols.

Hüseyin Kazım, *Arnavudlar Ne Yaptılar?* (İstanbul, 1330).

Hüseyin Kazım Kadri, *Büyük Türk Lugatı* (İstanbul, 1928).

Hüseyin Raci, *Tarihçe-i Vaka-i Zağra* (İstanbul, 1326).

Irkçılık-Turancılık (Ankara, 1944).

Işın, Mithat, *Tarihte Girit ve Türkler* (n.p.p., 1945).

İ. Hakkı, *Yunanlılarla İstiklâl Harbi. Tabiye ve Sevkülceyş Noktai Nazarından Tetkik* (İstanbul, 1934).

İbn ül-Haşim Nureddin Fikri, *Dimetokada Kanlı Bir Levha. Bulgar Vahşetlerinden* (Dersaadet, n.d.).

İğdemir, Uluğ (ed.), *Heyet-i Temsiliye Tutanakları* (Ankara, 1975).

İhsan Şeref, *Cumhuriyet Çocuklarına Tarih Dersleri. Üçüncü Sınıf* (İstanbul, 1926).

II. Abdülhamid'in Hatıra Defteri (İstanbul, 1960).

İkinci Türk Tarih Kurumu Kongresi. İstanbul 20-25 Eylül 1937. Kongrenin Çalışmaları, Kongreye Sunulan Tebliğler (İstanbul, 1943).

[İleri], Celal Nuri, *Tarih-i Tedenniyat-ı Osmaniye. Mukadderat Tarihi* (n.p.p., 1331).
[İleri], Celal Nuri, *Rum ve Bizans* (Kostantiniye, 1917).
İleri, Celâl Nuri, *Türk İnkilabı*, edited by Recep Durmaz (İstanbul, 2000).
İleri, Suphi Nuri, *Siyasî Tarih. XVIII inci Asırdan XX nci Asra Kadar* (İstanbul, 1940).
İnalcık, Halil, *Tanzimat ve Bulgar Meselesi* (Ankara, 1943).
[İnan], Afet, *Yurt Bilgisi Notlarından: Vatandaş İçin Medenî Bilgiler. 1. Kitap* (İstanbul, 1931).
İnan, Afet, 'İstiklâl Savaşında Tarih Bilgisinin Rolü' in *Atatürk Hakkında Konferanslar* (Ankara, 1946), pp. 8-19.
İnan, Arı (ed.), *Prof. Dr. Afet İnan* (İstanbul, 2005).
İnönü, İsmet, *Hatıralarım. Genç Subaylık Yılları (1884-1918)*, edited by Sabahattin Selek (İstanbul, 1969).
İrtem, Süleyman Kâni, *Abdülhamid Devrinde Hafiyelik ve Sansür, Abdülhamid'e Verilen Jurnaller*, edited by Osman Selim Kocahanoğlu (İstanbul, 1999).
İrtem, Süleyman Kâni, *Osmanlı Devleti'nin Makedonya Meselesi, Balkanlar'ın Kördüğümü*, edited by Osman Selim Kocahanoğlu (İstanbul, 1999).
İskân Kanunu. Resmi Gazetenin 21 Haziran 1934 Tarih ve 2733 Numaralı Nüshasından Alınmıştır (İstanbul, 1934).
İstanbul Belediyesi, *İstanbul Şehri Rehberi* (İstanbul, 1934).
Joseph Cowen's Speeches on the Near Eastern Question: Foreign and Imperial Affairs on the British Empire, revised by His Daughter, Jane Cowen (London, 1909).
Kamil Kapudan, *Karadağ. Karadağ Hakkında Bazı Malumata Şamildir* (İstanbul, 1294).
Kamil Paşa, *Tarih-i Siyasiye-i Devlet-i Aliye-i Osmaniye*, Vol. III ([İstanbul], 1327-1325).
Kaplan, Mehmet, İnci Enginün, Birol Emil and Zeynep Kerman (eds.), *Yeni Türk Edebiyatı Antolojisi*. Vol. III (İstanbul, 1979).
Kaplan, Mehmet, İnci Enginün, Zeynep Kerman, Necat Birinci and Abdullah Uçman (eds.), *Atatürk Devri Fikir Hayatı* (Ankara, 1981), two vols.
Karal, Enver Ziya, *Halet Efendinin Paris Büyük Elçiliği (1802-1806)* (İstanbul, 1940).
Karal, Enver Ziya, *Türkiye Cumhuriyeti Tarihi (1914-1944) [Lise Kitapları]* (İstanbul, 1945).
Karal, Enver Ziya, 'Atatürk'ün Türk Tarih Tezi' in *Atatürk Hakkında Konferanslar* (Ankara, 1946), pp. 55-65.

Karaosmanoğlu, Yakup Kadri, *Zoraki Diplomat (Hâtıra ve Müşahede)* (İstanbul, 1955).

Karaosmanoğlu, Yakup Kadri, *Atatürk* (Ankara, 1981).

Karaosmanoğlu, Yakup Kadri, *Vatan Yolunda Milli Mücadele Hatıraları*, edited by Atilla Özkırımlı (İstanbul, 1999).

Karaosmanoğlu, Yakup Kadri, *Hüküm Gecesi* (İstanbul, 2001).

Karay, Refik Halit, *Memleket Hikayeleri* (İstanbul, 1964).

Kazım Bey Karabekir, *Edirne Mahfil-i Askeriyesinde Verilen Konferanslardan Sırb-Bulgar Seferi-1885* (Edirne, 1328).

Kelekyan, Diran (Kélékian, Diran), *Kamus-i Fransevi. Dictionnaire Turc-Français* (İstanbul, 1329-1911).

Kemalettin Şükrü, *Büyük Fransız İhtilâli* (İstanbul, 1931).

Kemalettin Şükrü, *Namık Kemal Hayatı ve Eserleri* ([İstanbul], 1931 in *Resimli Ansiklopedik Neşriyat* ([İstanbul], 1931)).

Kıbrıs İsyanı Meselesi ve Yunanistan (n.p.p., 1931).

Kodaman, Bayram (ed.), *1897 Türk-Yunan Savaşı (Tesalya Tarihi)* (Ankara, 1993).

Kohn, Hans, *Türk Milliyetçiliği*, translated by Ali Çetinkaya (İstanbul, 1944).

Köprülüzade Mehmed Fuad, 'Bizde Milli Tarih Yazılabilir mi?,' *Yeni Mecmua*, I/22 (6 December 1917), pp. 427-8.

Köprülüzade Mehmed Fuad, *Milli Tarih. Devre-i Mütevassıta - İkinci Sene* (İstanbul, 1337).

Köprülüzade M. Fuat, *Türk Dili ve Edebiyatı Hakkında Araştırmalar* (İstanbul, 1934).

Köprülü, Fuad, *Edebiyat Araştırmaları* (Ankara, 1966).

Köprülüzade Mehmed Fuad and Şahab Aldin Süleyman, *Yeni Osmanlı Edebiyatı Tarihi,* Vol. I (İstanbul, 1332).

Kuran, Ahmet Bedevî, *İnkılâp Tarihimiz ve "Jön Türkler"* (İstanbul, 1945).

Kurtoğlu, Fevzi, *Yunan İstiklal Harbi ve Navarin Muharebesi (Çengeloğlu Tahir Paşa)*, Vol. I (n.p.p., 1944).

Külçe, Süleyman, *Firzovik Toplantısı ve Meşrutiyet* (İzmir, 1944).

Külçe, Süleyman, *Osmanlı Tarihinde Arnavudluk* (İzmir, 1944).

Lise ve Orta Mektepler İçin Tarih Soruları (İstanbul, 1935).

Lütfiye Hanım, *Mirat-ı Tarih-i Osmani* (İstanbul, 1293).

Lyautey, Pierre, *Le drama oriental et le rôle de la France,* preface by M. Maurice Barrès, second edition (Paris, 1924).

M. Salahaddin, *Merhum Kemal Bey'in Tarihi Meselesi ve Mevad-ı Saire* (İstanbul, 1327).

M. Şemseddin, 'Balkanlılar İttihad Etmiş, Osmanlılar Sizde Meydan-ı Şehamete Koşunuz,' *Sebilürreşad*, IX-II/216-34 (14 Zilkade 1330 and 11 Teşrin-i evvel 1328), pp. 144-6.

M. Tevfik, *et al.*, *Tarih II - Orta Zamanlar* (İstanbul, 1931).

M. Tevfik, *et al.*, *Tarih III - Yeni ve Yakın Zamanlarda Osmanlı-Türk Tarihi* (İstanbul, 1931).

Mahmud Celaleddin Paşa, *Mirat-ı Hakikat. Tarih-i Mahmud Celaleddin Paşa* (Dersaadet, 1326-1327), three vols.

Mahmud Muhtar Paşa, *Balkan Savaşı. Üçüncü Kolordu'nun ve İkinci Doğu Ordusu'nun Muharebeleri* (İstanbul, 2003).

Maliye Nazırı Cavid Bey, *Felaket Günleri. Mütareke Devrinin Feci Tarihi*, edited by Osman Selim Kocahanoğlu (İstanbul, 2000), two vols.

Marriott, J. A. R., *The Eastern Question. An Historical Study in European Diplomacy* (Oxford, 1917).

Mears, Eliot Grinnell, *Modern Turkey. A Politico-Economic Interpretation, 1908-1923*, inclusive, with Selected Chapters by Representative Authorities (New York, 1924).

Mehmed Arif, *Başımıza Gelenler. Bin İkiyüz Doksan Dört Tarih-i Hicriyesinde Vukubulan Rusya Muharebesinden Bahseder* (Mısır, 1321).

Mehmed Arif, *Başımıza Gelenler. Rusya Muharebesi Ahiresinin Anadolu Kısmından ve Mısır Ahvalinden ve Bu Münasebetle Tenkidat Mühimme-i Ahlakiyeden Bahseder* (Dersaadet, 1328).

Mehmed Eşref, *32 Yafta 128 Parça Haritaya Havi Tarih-i Umumi ve Osmani Atlası* ([İstanbul], 1330).

Mehmed Memduh, 'İki Arîza,' *Müteferrika*, no. 1 (1993), pp. 137-8.

Mehmed Murad, *Tarih-i Umumi*, Vol. I (İstanbul, 1307).

Mehmed Murad, *Tarih-i Ebulfaruk*, Vol. I ([İstanbul], 1325).

Mehmed Salahi, *Girid Meselesi* (1866-1889), edited by Münir Aktepe (İstanbul, 1967).

Mehmed Subhi, *Karadağ ve Ordusu. Karadağ'ın Ahval-i Tarihiye ve Coğrafyasıyla Kuvva-i Askeriyesinden Bahseder* (Kostantiniye, 1318).

Mehmet Şeref, *Bulgarlar ve Bulgar Devleti* (Ankara, 1934).

Mizancı Murad, *Mücahede-i Milliye. Gurbet ve Avdet Devirleri* (İstanbul, 1994).

Mustafa Nuri Paşa, *Netayic ül-Vukuat*, Vol. IV (İstanbul, 1327).

Namık Kemal, *Külliyat-ı Kemal, Birinci Tertib 1 - Renan Müdafaanamesi* (İstanbul, n.d.).

Namık Kemal, *Külliyat-ı Kemal, Birinci Tertib 3 - Makalat-ı Siyasiye ve Edebiye* (İstanbul, 1327).

Namık Kemal, *Külliyat-ı Kemal, Üçüncü Tertib 1 - Osmanlı Tarihi, Cild 1, Cüz 1* (İstanbul, 1326).

Namık Kemal, *Vatan Yahut Silistre*, edited by Kenan Akyüz (Ankara, 1960).

Namık Kemal, *İntibah (Ali Bey'in Sergüzeşti)*, edited by Mehmet Kaplan (Ankara, 1984).

Nahid Sırrı, *Bir Edirne Seyahatnamesi* (Ankara, 1941).

[Nayır], Yaşar Nabi, *Balkanlar ve Türklük* (Ankara, 1936).

Necib Asım and Mehmed Arif, *Osmanlı Tarihi*, Vol. I (İstanbul, 1335).

Ömer (Darülfünun Mezunlarından), 'Hilal ve Salib,' *Sırat-ı Müstakim*, VI/137 (1327), pp. 109-10.

Ömer Seyfeddin, 'Nakarat,' *Yeni Mecmua*, 63/III (3 October 1918), pp. 216-20.

Ömer Seyfeddin, 'Tuhaf Bir Zulüm,' *Yeni Mecmua*, 66/III (26 October 1918), pp. 278-80.

Ömer Seyfettin, *Ömer Seyfettin Külliyatı: 5 - Asılzadeler* (İstanbul, 1938).

Ömer Seyfettin, *Ömer Seyfettin Külliyatı: 7 - Beyaz Lâle* (İstanbul, 1942).

Ömer Seyfettin, *Mahçupluk İmtihanı*, edited by Kemal Demiray (İstanbul, 1977).

Ömer Seyfettin, *Bomba* (Ankara, 1998).

Özgül, Metin Kayahan (ed.), *Ali Ekrem Bolayır'ın Hâtıraları* (Ankara, 1991).

Özön, Mustafa Nihat (ed.), *Ölümünün 50 nci Yılı Münasebetiyle Namık Kemal ve İbret Gazetesi* (İstanbul, 1938).

Pakalın, Mehmet Zeki, *Osmanlı Tarih Deyimleri ve Terimleri Sözlüğü* (İstanbul, 1946), three vols.

Pala, İskender (ed.), *Namık Kemal'in Tarihi Biyografileri* (Ankara, 1989).

Parlatır, İsmail and Nurullah Çetin (eds.), *Genç Kalemler Dergisi* (Ankara, 1999).

[Peremeci], Osman Nuri, *Ecdad Tarihi* (Şumnu, 1340-1924).

Peremeci, Osman Nuri, *Tuna Boyu Tarihi* (İstanbul, 1942).

The Permanent Bureau of the Turkish Congress at Lausanne, *Greek Atrocities in the Vilayet of Smyrna (May to July 1991)* (Lausanne, 1919).

Pertusi, Agostino (ed.), *La caduta di Costantinopoli*. Vol. I. *Le testimonianze dei contemporanei*, Vol. II. *L'eco nel mondo* (Milan, 1976).

Peyami Safa, *Türk İnkılâbına Bakışlar (Cumhuriyetin 15 inci yılı münasebetile)* ([İstanbul], [1938]).

Prens Sabahattin, *Türkiye Nasıl Kurtarılabilir ve İzâh'lar*, transliterated by Fahri Unan (Ankara, 1999).

Ragıb Rıfkı, *Musavver Bulgaristan. Ahval-i Coğrafiye ve Tarihiyesi, Etnoğrafya Nokta-ı Nazarından Tedkiki, Suret-i Teşkil ve İdare-i Dahiliyesi, Ahval-i Askeriyesi* (İstanbul, 1324).

Ranke, M. Leopold, *Histoire des Osmanlis et de la monarchie espagnole pendant les XVIe et XVIIe siècles*, accompanied notes by M. J.-B. Haiber (Paris, 1839).

Ramsay, W. M., *The Revolution in Constantinople and Turkey. A Diary, with Episodes and Photographs by Lady Ramsay* (London, 1909).

Renan, Ernest, *Qu'est-ce qu'une nation? Conférence faite en Sorbonne, le 11 mars 1882* (Paris, 1882).

Renan, Ernest, *L'Islamisme et la science. Conférence faite a la Sorbonne le 29 mars 1883* (Paris, 1883).

Reşit Galip, 'Türk Tarih İnkılâbı ve Yabancı Tezler,' *Ülkü Halkevleri Mecmuası*, II/9 (October 1933), pp. 164-77.

Rıza, *Sevkül Ceyş Atlası* (İstanbul, 1306).

Rumeli Muhacirin-i İslamiye Cemiyet-i Hayriyesi, *Alam-ı İslam. Bulgar Vahşetleri. İslamiyetin Enzar-ı Basiretine ve Alem-i İnsaniyet ve Medeniyetin Nazar-ı Dikkatine* (İstanbul, 1328).

Rumeli Muhacirin-i İslamiye Cemiyet-i Hayriyesi, *Alam-ı İslam. Rumeli Mezalimi ve Bulgar Vahşetleri. İslamiyetin Enzar-ı Basiretine ve Alem-i İnsaniyet ve Medeniyetin Nazar-ı Dikkatine* (İstanbul, 1329).

Sadrazâm ve Harbiye Nazırı Mahmut Şevket Paşa'nın Günlüğü (İstanbul, 1988).

Safveti Ziya, *Salon Köşelerinde*, edited by Nuri Akbayar (İstanbul, 1998).

Sarıgöl, Adem (ed.), *Harbiye Nazırı Sadrazam Mahmut Şevket Paşa'nın Günlüğü* (İstanbul, 2001).

The Section of the General Staff of the Western Front, *Greek Atrocities in Asia Minor, First Part* (Constantinople, 1922).

[Sedes], İ. Halil Paşa, *1876-1878 Osmanlı-Sırp Seferi* (İstanbul, 1934), two vols.

Sedes, İ. Halil, *1875-1878 Osmanlı Ordusu Seferleri. 1876-1877 Osmanlı-Karadağ Seferi* (İstanbul, 1936).

Sedes, Halil, *1875-1878 Osmanlı Ordusu Seferleri. 1875-1876 Bosna-Hersek ve Bulgaristan İhtilâlleri ve Siyasî Olaylar* ([İstanbul], 1946).

Sertelli, İskender Fahreddin, *Tarih Sevgisi, Yeni Vesikalar* (İstanbul, 1936).

Sertelli, İskender F., *Karakurumdan Tunaya Türk Akını. Tarihi Çocuk Romanı* (İstanbul, 1939).

[Sevük], İsmail Habib, *Tunadan Batıya. Tunadan Önce - Tuna Yolunda - Tunadan Sonra - Dönüş* (İstanbul, 1935).

[Sevük], İsmail Habib, *Tanzimattanberi II - Edebiyat Antolojisi* (İstanbul, 1943).

Sevük, İsmail Habib, *Atatürk İçin* (Ankara, 1981).

Söylemezoğlu, Galip Kemalî, *Hatıraları. Atina Sefareti (1913-1916)* (n.p.p., 1946).

Story, Sommerville (ed.), *The Memoirs of Ismail Kemal Bey*, with a preface by William Morton Fullerton (London, 1920).

Sungu, İhsan, 'Tanzimat ve Yeni Osmanlılar' in *Tanzimat I* (İstanbul, 1940), pp. 777-857.

Süleyman Edip ve Ali Tevfik, *İlk Mektep Çocuklarına Tarih Dersleri. Dördüncü Sınıf* (İstanbul, 1929).

Süleyman Edip and Ali Tevfik, *İlkmektep Çocuklarına Yeni Tarih Dersleri, Beşinci Sınıf* (İstanbul, 1929).

Ş. Sami, *Kamus-i Fransevi. Fransızcadan Türkçeye Lugat. Dictionnaire Français-Turc* (İstanbul, 1299-1882).

Ş. Sami, *Kamus-i Fransevi. Türkçeden Fransızcaya Lugat. Dictionnaire Turc-Français* (İstanbul, 1302-1885).

Ş. Sami, *Kamus ül-Alam. Tarih ve Coğrafya Lugatı* (İstanbul, 1306-1316-1889-1898), six vols.

Ş. Sami, *Kâmûs-ı Türkî* (Dersaadet, 1317 reprinted in İstanbul, 1999).

T. T. T. Cemiyeti, *Tarih I - Tarihtenevvelki Zamanlar ve Eski Zamanlar* (İstanbul, 1932).

T. T. T. Cemiyeti, *Tarih I - Tarihtenevelki Zamanlar ve Eski Zamanlar* (İstanbul, 1938).

T.T.T. Cemiyeti, *Tarih III - Yeni ve Yakın Zamanlar*, second edition (Ankara, 1941).

T.T.T. Cemiyeti, *Tarih IV - Türkiye Cümhuriyeti* (İstanbul, 1934).

Tanpınar, Ahmet Hamdi, *Beş Şehir* (İstanbul, 2001).

Tansel, Abdullah Fevziye (ed.), *Namık Kemal'in Husûsî Mektupları III. VI. Midilli Mektupları - II* (Ankara, 1973).

Tansel, Abdullah Fevziye (ed.), *Nâmık Kemal'in Husûsî Mektupları IV. VII.-VIII. Rodos ve Sakız Mektupları* (Ankara, 1986).

Tansel, Abdullah Fevziye (ed.), *Ziya Gökalp Külliyatı- I. Şiirler ve Halk Masalları* (Ankara, 1989).

Tansel, Abdullah Fevziye (ed.), *Ziya Gökalp Külliyâtı- II. Limni ve Malta Mektupları* (Ankara, 1989).

Tansel, Abdullah Fevziye (ed.), *Mehmed Emin Yurdakul'un Eserleri- I. Şiirler* (Ankara, 1989).

Tansu, Samih Nafiz, *Osmanlı Tarihi* (İstanbul, 1945).

[Tanrıöver], Hamdullah Suphi, *Dağ Yolu, Birinci Kitap* (İstanbul, 1929).

[Tanrıöver], Hamdullah Suphi, *Dağyolu, 2inci Kitap* (Ankara, 1931).

Tekin Alp, *Türkleştirme* (İstanbul, 1928).

[Temo, İbrahim], *İttihad ve Terakki Cemiyeti'nin Kurucusu ve 1/1 No'lu Üyesi İbrahim Temo'nun İttihad ve Terakki Anıları* (İstanbul, 2000).

Tengirşenk, Yusuf Kemal, *Türk İnkılâbı Dersleri, Ekonomik Değişmeler (Talebe Tarafından Derslerde Tutulan Notlarıdır)* (İstanbul, 1935).

[Tevfik Fikret], *Rübâb-ı Şikeste - Halûk'un Defteri ve Tevfik Fikret'in Diğer Eserleri*, edited by Fahri Uzun (İstanbul, 1962).

Thiers, M. Henri, *La Serbie, sa passé et son avenir* (Paris, 1862).

Togan, A. Zeki Velidi, *Tarihde Usul* (İstanbul, 1950).

Togan, Zeki Velidi, *Scientific Collaboration of the Islamic Orient and the Occident. A Lecture Delivered in the Faculty of Law on 17th May 1950* (İstanbul, 1951).

Tukin, Cemal, 'Balkan Harbinin Teşekkülü ve Bu Harbin Zuhuru' in *CHP Konferanslar Serisi Kitap: 5* (Ankara, 1939), pp. 21-41.

Tüccarzade İbrahim Hilmi, *Memalik-i Osmaniyenin Ceb Atlası* ([İstanbul], 1323).

Türk Çocuklarına Tarih Notları (Ankara, 1929).

Türk Tarihinin Ana Hatları Atlası (Ankara, 1931).

Uraz, Murad, *Namık Kemal* (İstanbul, 1938).

Uzunçarşılı, İsmail Hakkı, 'İkinci Abdülhamid'in Alman İmparatoruna Çekmiş Olduğu Bir Telgraf,' *Türkiyat Mecmuası*, XII (1955), pp. 135-44.

Ülken, Ziya, 'Tanzimattan Sonra Fikir Haraketleri' in *Tanzimat I* (İstanbul, 1940), pp. 757-75.

Ünaydın, Ruşen Eşref, *Atatürk Tarih ve Dil Kurumları. Hâtıralar* (Ankara, 1954).

Viscount Grey of Fallodon, *Twenty-Five Years 1892-1916*, Vol. I (New York, 1925).

W. & A. K. Johnston's Modern School Atlas, edited by W. R. Kermarck, ninth edition (Edinburgh and London, 1938).

Washburn, George, *Fifty Years in Constantinople and Recollections of Robert College* (Boston and New York, 1909).

Williams, W. Llew, *Armenia: Past and Present. A Study and a Forecast,* with an introduction by T.P. O'Connor, MP (London, 1916).

The World Wide Atlas of Modern Geography Political and Physical Containing One Hundred and Twenty-Eight Plates and Complete Index, with an introduction by J. Scott Keltie, fifth edition (Edinburgh and London, 1902).

Yalçın, Hüseyin Cahit, *Siyasal Anılar* (İstanbul, 2000).

Yinanç, Mükrimin Halil, 'Tanzimattan Meşrutiyete Kadar Bizde Tarihçilik' in *Tanzimat I* (İstanbul, 1940), pp. 573-95.

Yunanistan 1929-1930 (Hizmete Mahsus) (İstanbul, 1930).

Yusuf Fehmi, *Paris'te Türkler, Casusluk ve Karşıcasusluk*, edited by Ergun Hiçyılmaz (İstanbul, n.d.).

Ziya Gök Alp, *Türk Medeniyet Tarihi. Birinci Kısım* (İstanbul, 1341).

Secondary Sources

Abou-El-Haj, Rifa'at 'Ali, *Formation of the Modern State. The Ottoman Empire Sixteenth to Eighteenth Centuries* (New York, 1991).

Abou al Haj, R. A., 'The social uses of the past: recent Arab historiography of Ottoman rule,' *International Journal of Middle East Studies*, 14 (1982), pp. 185-201.

Abu-Manneh, Butrus, 'The Islamic roots of the Gülhane Rescript' in *Studies on Islam and the Ottoman Empire in the 19th Century (1826-1876)* (İstanbul, 2001), pp. 72-97.

Adanır, Fikret, *Makedonya Sorunu. Oluşumu ve 1908'e Kadar Gelişimi* (İstanbul, 1996).

Adanır, Fikret, 'Balkan historiography related to the Ottoman empire since 1945' in Karpat, Kemal H. (ed.), *Ottoman Past and Today's Turkey* (Leiden, 2000), pp. 236-52.

Adnan-Adıvar, Abdülhak, *Osmanlı Türklerinde İlim*, second edition (İstanbul, 1943).

Aktepe, M. Münir, 'Mehmed Salâhî Bey ve Mecmuasından Bâzı Kısımlar,' *Tarih Dergisi*, XVI/21 (1966), pp. 15-38.

Akün, Ömer Faruk, 'Namık Kemal'in Kitap Halindeki Eserlerinin İlk Neşirleri,' *Türkiyat Mecmuası*, XVIII (1973-1975), pp. 1-78.

Akyüz, Yahya, *Türk Eğitim Tarihi (Başlangıçtan 1982'ye)* (Ankara, 1982).

Alangu, Tahir, *Serveti Fünun Edebiyatı Antolojisi* (İstanbul, 1958).

Anderson, Benedict, *Imagined Communities, Reflections on the Origin and Spread of Nationalism* (London and New York, 2000).

And, Metin, *Tanzimat ve İstibdat Döneminde Türk Tiyatrosu (1839-1908)* (Ankara, 1972).

Anderson, Lisa, 'Legitimacy, identity and writing of history in Libya' in Davis, Eric, and Nicolas Gavrielides (eds.), *Statecraft in the Middle East. Oil, Historical Memory and Popular Culture* (Miami, 1991), pp. 71-91.

Andrić, Ivo, *Bosnian Chronicle or The Days of the Consuls* (London, 1996).

Anzulovic, Branimir, *Heavenly Serbia, From Myth to Genocide* (London, 1999).

Arai, Masami, *Turkish Nationalism in the Young Turk Era* (Leiden, 1992).
Arıkan, Zeki, 'Tanzimat'tan Cumhuriyet'e Tarihçilik' in *Tanzimat'tan Cumhuriyet'e Türkiye Ansiklopedisi* (İstanbul, 1985), VI, pp. 1584-94.
Arıkan, Zeki, 'Fransız İhtilâli ve Osmanlı Tarihçiliği' in Bacqué-Grammont, Jean-Louis and Edhem Eldem (eds.), *De la révolution française à la Turquie d'Atatürk. La modernisation politique et sociale. Les lettres, les sciences et les arts. Actes des colloques d'Istanbul (10-12 mai 1989)* (İstanbul and Paris, 1990), pp. 85-100.
Arnakin, George, 'The role of the religion in the development of Balkan nationalism' in Jelavich, Charles and Barbara (eds.), *The Balkans in Transition: Essays on the Development of Balkan Life and Politics Since the Eighteenth Century* (Berkeley, 1963), pp. 115-44.
Atatürk ve Halkevleri. Atatürkçü Düşünce Üzerine Denemeler (Ankara, 1974).
Atauz, Sevil (ed.), *Türkiye'de Sosyal Bilimler Araştırmalarının Gelişimi* (Ankara, 1986).
Babinger, Franz, *Die Geschichtsschreiber der Osmanen und Ihre Werke* (Leipzig, 1927).
Banarlı, Nihat Sami, *Namık Kemal ve Türk-Osmanlı Milliyetçiliği* (İstanbul, 1947).
Barbir, Karl K., 'Arab studies in Ottoman history since 1945' in Karpat, Kemal H (ed.), *Ottoman Past and Today's Turkey* (Leiden, 2000), pp. 272- 81.
Barker, Rodney, *Legitimating Identities. The Self-Presentations of Rulers and Subjects* (Cambridge, 2001).
Barkey, Karen and Mark von Hagen, *After Empire: Multiethnic Societies and Nation Building The Soviet Union and The Russian, Ottoman, and Habsburg Empires* (Boulder, Colerado and Oxford, 1997).
Başgöz, İlhan and Howard E. Wilson, *Educational Problems in Turkey 1920-1940* (Bloomington, 1968).
Bazin, Louis, 'Censure ottomane et lexicographie: Le Kamus-i Fransevî de Sâmî Bey' in Bacoqué-Grammont, Jean-Louis and Paul Dumont (eds.), *Économie et sociétés dans l'empire ottoman (fin du XVIIIe – début du XXe siècle)* (Paris, 1983), pp. 203-6.
Baykal, Bekir Sıtkı, 'Atatürk Devrimlerinde Tarihin Rolü' in *Atatürk ve Devrim. Atatürkçü Düşünce Üzerine Denemeler* (Ankara, 1973), pp. 71-7.
Baykara, Tuncer, *Osmanlılarda Medeniyet Kavramı ve Ondokuzuncu Yüzyıla Dair Araştırmalar* (İzmir, 1992).
Berkes, Niyazi, *Türkiye'de Çağdaşlaşma* (Ankara, 1973).
Berkes, Niyazi, 'The two facets of the Kemalist Revolution' offprint from *The Muslim World*, Hartford Seminary Foundation, LXIV/4 (1974), pp. 292-306.

Berkes, Niyazi, 'Unutulan Adam' offprint from *Sosyoloji Konferansları, Kitap 14* (İstanbul, 1976), pp. 194-205.

Berkes, Niyazi, *The Development of Secularism in Turkey* (London, 1998).

Berktay, Halil, *Cumhuriyet İdeolojisi ve Fuat Köprülü* (İstanbul, 1983).

Berktay, Halil, 'Dört Tarihçinin Sosyal Portresi,' *Toplum ve Bilim* (Summer/ Autumn 1991), pp. 19-45.

Bora, Tanıl, 'Turkish national identity, Turkish nationalism, and the Balkan problem' in *Balkans. A Mirror of the New International Order* (İstanbul, 1995), pp. 101-20.

Boyar, Ebru, 'British archaeological travellers in nineteenth-century Anatolia: Anatolia 'without' Turks,' *Eurasian Studies*, I/1 (2002), pp. 97-113.

Boyar, Ebru, 'Engelhardt from censorship to icon: the use of a European diplomat's history in Ottoman and Turkish historiography on the *Tanzimat*,' *Eurasian Studies*, 1/III (2004), pp. 81-8.

Boyar, Ebru, 'Public good and private exploitation: criticism of the tobacco Régie in 1909,' in Boyar, Ebru and Kate Fleet (eds.), *Ottomans and Trade (Oriente Moderno*, XXV (LXXXVI)) (Rome, 2006), pp. 193-200.

Boyar, Ebru, 'The press and the palace: the two-way relationship between Abdülhamid II and the press, 1876-1908,' *Bulletin of the School of Oriental and African Studies*, LXIX/3 (2006), pp. 417-32.

Boyar, Ebru and Kate Fleet, '"Making Turkey and the Turkish revolution known to foreign nations without any expense": Propaganda films in the early Turkish Republic,' *Oriente Moderno*, XXIV (LXXXV)/1 (2005), pp. 117-32.

Bozbora, Nuray, *Osmanlı Yönetiminde Arnavutluk ve Arnavut Ulusculuğu'nun Gelişimi* (İstanbul, 1997).

Börekçi, Mehmet Çetin, *Osmanlı İmparatorluğu'nda Sırp Meselesi* (İstanbul, 2001).

Braudel, Fernand, *On History*, translated by Sarah Matthews (Chicago, 1982).

Breuilly, John, *Nationalism and the State* (Manchester, 1998).

Brown, L. Carl (ed.), *Imperial Legacy: The Ottoman Imprint on the Balkans and the Middle East* (New York, 1996).

Brubaker, Rogers, *Nationalism Reframed. Nationhood and the Nation Question in the New Europe* (Cambridge, 1996).

Brummett, Palmira, *Image and Imperialism in the Ottoman Revolutionary Press, 1908-1911* (New York, 2000).

Caferoğlu, A., 'Hakikî Köprülü,' *Türkiyat Mecmuası*, XVIII (1968), pp. 1-10.

Can, Kemal, 'Youth, Turkism and the extreme right. The "Idealist Hearths"' in Yerasimos, Stefanos, Günter Seufert and Karin Vorhoff (eds.), *Civil Society in the Grip of Nationalism* (İstanbul, 2000), pp. 335-73.

Carr, E. H., *What is History*, with a new introduction by Richard J. Evans (Basingstoke, 2001).
Chatterjee, Partha, *Nationalist Thought and the Colonial World - A Derivative Discourse?* (London, 1986).
Chatterjee, Partha, *The Nation and Its Fragments: Colonial and Postcolonial Histories* (Princeton, N.J., 1993).
Choueiri, Youssef M., *Modern Arab Historiography. Historical Discourse and the Nation-State* (London and New York, 2003).
Clogg, Richard, *A Short History of Modern Greece* (Cambridge, 1979).
Clogg, Richard, 'The Greek Millet in the Ottoman empire' in Braude, Benjamin and Bernard Lewis (eds.), *Christians and Jews in the Ottoman Empire. Volume I. The Central Lands* (New York and London, 1982), pp. 185-207.
Cohen, Myron L., 'Being Chinese: the peripheralization of traditional identity,' *Daedalus*, 120 (1991), pp. 113-34.
Collingwood, R. G., *The Idea of History* (Oxford and Hong Kong, 1986).
Crampton, R. J., *A Short History of Bulgaria* (Cambridge, 1993).
Çelik, Bilgin, *İttihatçılar ve Arnavutlar. II. Meşrutiyet Döneminde Arnavut Ulusçuluğu ve Arnavut Sorunu* (İstanbul, 2004).
Davison, H. Roderic, *Essays in Ottoman and Turkish History, 1774-1923, The Impact of the West* (London, 1990).
De Certeau, Michel, *The Writing of History*, translated by Tom Conley (New York, 1988).
De Certeau, Michel, 'Writings and histories' in Spargo, Tamsin (ed.), *Reading of the Past* (Basingstoke, 2000), pp. 156-67.
Deringil, Selim, *The Well- Protected Domains. Ideology and the Legitimation of Power in the Ottoman Empire* (London, 1998).
Deringil, Selim, 'Legitimacy structures in the Ottoman state: reign of Abdülhamid II,' *International Journal of Middle Eastern Studies*, XXIII/3 (1991), pp. 345-59.
Deringil, Selim, 'The invention of tradition as public image in the late Ottoman Empire, 1808 to 1908,' *Comparative Studies in Society and History*, XXXV/1 (1993), pp. 3-29.
Deringil, Selim, 'The Ottoman origins of Kemalist nationalism: Namık Kemal to Mustafa Kemal,' *European History Quarterly*, XXIII/2 (1993), pp. 165-91.
Dizdaroğlu, Hikmet, *Ömer Seyfettin* (Ankara, 1964).
Djordjevic, Dimitrije and Stephen Fischer-Galati, *The Balkan Revolutionary Tradition* (New York, 1981).

Duara, Pransenjit, *Rescuing History from the Nation: Questioning Narratives of Modern China* (Chicago and London, 1995).

Duman, Haluk Harun, *Balkanlara Veda. Basın ve Edebiyatta Balkan Savaşı (1912-1913)* (İstanbul, 2005).

Duman, Hasan, 'Atatürk ve Kitap' in *Boğaziçi Üniversitesi Atatürk Konferansları Dizisi* (İstanbul, 1986), pp. 33-47.

Dündar, Fuat, *İttihat ve Terakki'nin Müslümanları İskân Politikası (1913-1918)* (İstanbul, 2001).

Emil, Birol, *Mizancı Murad Bey Hayatı ve Eserleri* (İstanbul, 1979).

Enginün, İnci, 'Turkish literature and self-identity: from Ottoman to modern Turkish' in Karpat, Kemal H. (ed.), *Ottoman Past and Today's Turkey* (Leiden, 2000), pp. 212-35.

Ergin, Osman, *İstanbul Mektepleri ve İlim, Terbiye ve San'at Müesseseleri Dolayısiyle. Türkiye Maarif Tarihi*, Vol. V (İstanbul, 1977).

Ersanlı-Behar, Büşra, *İktidar ve Tarih: Türkiye'de "Resmi Tarih" Tezinin Oluşumu. 1929-1937* (İstanbul, 1992).

Ersanlı, Büşra, 'History textbooks as reflections of the political self: Turkey (1930s and 1990s) and Uzbekistan (1990s),' *International Journal of Middle East Studies*, XXXIV/2 (2002), pp. 337-49.

Evans, Richard J., 'From historicism to postmodernism: historiography in the twentieth century,' *History and Theory*, 41 (February 2002), pp. 79-87.

Fleet, Kate, 'Italian perceptions of the Turks in the fourteenth and fifteenth centuries,' *Journal of Mediterranean Studies*, V/2 (1995), pp. 159-72.

Fleming, K. H., 'Athens, Constantinople, "Istambol": Urban paradigms and nineteenth-century Greek national 'identity,' *New Perspectives on Turkey*, 22 (2000), pp. 1-23.

Fortna, Benjamin C., *Imperial Classroom. Islam, the State and Education in the Late Ottoman Empire* (Oxford, 2002).

Foucault, Michel, *The Will to Knowledge, The History of Sexuality*. Vol. I, translated from French by Robert Hurley (London, 1998).

Foucault, Michel, *The Order of Things. An Archaeology of the Human Sciences* (London, 2000).

Foucault, Michel, *The Archaeology of Knowledge*, translated from French by A. M. Sheridan Smith (London, 2001).

Georgeon, François, *Des Ottomans aux Turcs. Naissance d'une nation* (İstanbul, 1995).

Ginio, Eyal, 'Mobilizing the Ottoman nation during the Balkan Wars (1912-1913): Awakening from the Ottoman dream,' *War in History*, XII/2 (2005), 156-77.

Glenny, Misha, *The Balkans 1804-1999, Nationalism, War and the Great Powers* (London, 2000).

Gökman, Muzaffer, *Ahmet Rasim. İstanbul'u Yaşayan ve Yaşatan Adam. Hayatı ve Eserleri* (İstanbul, 1989), two vols.

Gramsci, Antonio, *Pre-Prison Writings*, edited by Richard Bellamy and translated by Virginia Cox (Cambridge, 1994).

Gramsci, Antonio, *Prison Letters*, translated and introduced by Hamish Henderson (London and Chicago, 1996).

Gramsci, Antonio, *Selections from the Prison Notebooks*, edited and translated by Quintin Hoare and Geoffrey Nowell Smith (London, 1998).

Green, Anna and Kathleen Troup (eds.), *The Houses of History - A Critical Reader in Twentieth-Century History and Theory* (Manchester, 1999).

Hale, William, *Turkish Foreign Policy, 1774-2000* (London and Portland, 2000).

Hanioğlu, Şükrü, *The Young Turks in Opposition* (Oxford and New York, 1995).

Hanioğlu, Şükrü, *Preparation for a Revolution. The Young Turks, 1902-1908* (Oxford and New York, 2001).

Haarmann, Ulrich W., 'Ideology and history, identity and alterity: The Arab image of the Turk from the °Abbasids to modern Egypt,' *International Journal of Middle Eastern Studies*, XX/2 (1988), pp. 175-96.

Heinzelmann, Tobias, *Osmanlı Karikatüründe Balkan Sorunu 1908-1914* (İstanbul, 2004).

Heper, Metin, *The State Tradition in Turkey* (Beverley, 1985).

Heper, Metin, 'Atatürk'ün Devlet Düşüncesi' in *Boğaziçi Üniversitesi Atatürk Konferansları Dizisi* (İstanbul, 1986), pp. 61-5.

Hirschon, Renée, 'Knowledge of diversity: Towards a more differentiated set of 'Greek' perceptions of 'Turks',' *South European Society and Politics*, XI/1 (2006), pp. 61-78.

Hobsbawn, Eric, *On History* (London, 1998).

Hobsbawn, E. J., *Nations and Nationalism since 1780. Programme, Myth, Reality* (Cambridge, 2000).

Hobsbawn, Eric and Terence Ranger (eds.), *The Invention of Tradition* (Cambridge, 2000).

Hosking, Geoffrey, 'The Second World War and Russian national consciousness,' *Past and Present*, 175 (May 2002), pp. 162-87.

Innes, C. L., ''Forging the conscience of their race': Nationalist writers' in King, Bruce (ed.), *New National and Post-Colonial Literatures. An Introduction* (Oxford, 2000), pp. 120-39.

İnalcık, Halil and Donald Quataert (eds.), *An Economic and Social History of the Ottoman Empire 1300-1914* (Cambridge, 1994).
İnuğur, M. Nuri, *Basın ve Yayın Tarihi* (İstanbul, 1982).
İskit, Server R., *Türkiye'de Neşriyat Tarihi Hareketleri Tarihine Bir Bakış* (İstanbul, 1939).
İskit, Server, *Türkiye'de Matbuat İdareleri ve Politikaları* (İstanbul, 1943).
İskit, Server, *Türkiye'de Matbuat Rejimleri* (İstanbul, 1939).
Kabacalı, Alpay, *Başlangıçtan Günümüze Türkiye'de Basın Sansürü* (İstanbul, 1990).
Kadare, Ismail, *Three Elegies for Kosovo*, translated from the Albanian by Peter Constantine (London, 2000).
Kaplan, Mehmed, *Namık Kemal Hayatı ve Eserleri* (İstanbul, 1948).
Karagöz, Âdem Ruhi, *Bulgaristan Türk Basını 1879-1945* (İstanbul, 1945).
Karpat, Kemal H., *Turkey's Politics: The Transition to A Multi-Party System* (Princeton, N. J., 1959).
Karpat, Kemal H., *The Politicization of Islam. Reconstructing Identity, State, Faith, and the Community in the Late Ottoman State* (Oxford, 2001).
Kasaba, Reşat, 'A time and a place for the nonstate: Social change in the Ottoman empire during the "long nineteenth century"' in Migdal, Joel S., Atul Kohli and Vivienne Shue (eds.), *State Power and Social Forces, Domination and Transformation in the Third World* (Cambridge, 1994), pp. 207-30.
Kashani-Sabet, Firoozeh, 'Cultures of Iranianness: the evolving polemic of Iranian nationalism' in Keddie, N., and R. Matthee (eds.), *Iran and the Surrounding World: Interactions in Culture and Cultural Politics* (Seattle, 2002), pp. 162-81.
Kelbetcheva, Evelina, 'Between apology and denial: Bulgarian culture during World War I' in Roshwald, Aviel and Richard Stites (eds.), *European Culture in the Great War. The Arts, Entertainment and Propaganda, 1914-1918* (Cambridge, 1999), pp. 215-42.
Key, Kerim K., *An Outline of Modern Turkish Historiography* (İstanbul, 1954).
Keyder, Çağlar, *Türkiye'de Devlet ve Sınıflar* (İstanbul, 1993).
Koloğlu, Orhan, 'II. Abdülhamid'in Basın Karşısındaki Açmazı' in *Tanzimat'tan Cumhuriyet'e Türkiye Ansiklopedisi* (İstanbul, 1985), I, pp. 82-4.
Koloğlu, Orhan, '"Muzır" Ararken Alay Konusu Olan Rejim: II. Abdülhamit Sansürü,' *Tarih ve Toplum*, 38 (January 1987), pp. 14-18.
Köroğlu, Erol, *Türk Edebiyatı ve Birinci Dünya Savaşı (1914-1918). Propagandadan Milli Kimlik İnşâsına* (İstanbul, 2004).

Kumar, Krishan, *The Making of English National Identity* (Cambridge, 2003).

Kuran, Ercümend, *The Impact of Nationalism on the Turkish Elite in the Nineteenth Century* (Ankara, 1966).

Kuran, Ercüment, *Türkiye'nin Batılılaşması ve Millî Meseleler* (Ankara, 1994).

Kuran, Ercüment, 'Ottoman historiography of the Tanzimat period' in Lewis, Bernard and P. M. Holt (eds.), *Historians of the Middle East* (London, 1962), pp. 422-9.

Kushner, David, *The Rise of Turkish Nationalism 1876-1908* (London, 1977).

Küçük, Cevdet, 'Bulgar İhtilali'nin (1876) İngiliz Kamuoyunda Uyandırdığı Tepki ve Bunun Osmanlı-İngiliz İlişkilerine Tesiri,' *Güney-Doğu Avrupa Araştırmaları Dergisi*, 8-9 (1979-1980), pp. 117-66.

Kütükoğlu, Bekir, *Vekayi'nüvis Makaleler* (İstanbul, 1994).

Lewis, Bernard, *The Emergence of Modern Turkey*, second edition (London, Oxford, and New York, 1968).

Lewis, Bernard, 'Watan' in Reinharz, Jehuda and George L. Mosse (eds.), *The Impact of the Western Nationalisms. Essays Dedicated to Walter Z. Laquer on the Occasion of his 70th Birthday* (London, Newbury Park and New Delhi, 1992), pp. 169-79.

Lustick, Ian S., 'History, historiography, and political science: multiple records and the problem of selection bias,' *The American Political Science Review*, III/90 (1996), pp. 605-18.

Jelavich, Barbara, *History of the Balkans. Eighteenth and Nineteenth Centuries* (Cambridge, 1997).

Jelavich, Charles and Barbara, *The Establishment of the Balkan National States, 1804-1920* (Seattle and London, 2000).

Judah, Tim, *The Serbs, History, Myth and the Destruction of Yugoslavia* (New Haven and London, 1997).

Macar, Elçin, *Cumhuriyet Döneminde İstanbul Rum Patrikhanesi* (İstanbul, 2003).

Mackridge, Peter, 'The Greek intelligentsia 1780-1830' in Clogg, Richard (ed.), *Balkan Society in the Age of Greek Independence* (London, 1981), pp. 63-84.

Makdisi, Ussama, 'After 1860: debating religion, reform and nationalism in the Ottoman empire,' *International Journal of Middle East Studies*, XXXIV/4 (2002), pp. 601-17.

Mardin, Şerif, *Jön Türklerin Siyasi Fikirleri 1895-1908* (İstanbul, 1983).

Mardin, Şerif, *Makaleler 1, Türkiye'de Toplum ve Siyaset*, edited by Mümtaz'er Türköne and Tuncay Önder (İstanbul, 1994).

Mardin, Şerif, *The Genesis of Young Ottoman Thought. A Study in the Modernization of Turkish Political Ideas* (Syracuse, N. Y., 2000).

Masur, Gerhard, 'Distinctive traits of western civilization: through the eyes of western historians,' *The American Historical Review*, LXVII/3 (1962), pp. 591-608.

Mazower, Mark, *The Balkans* (London, 2001).

Millas, Herkül, 'Türk Edebiyatında Yunan İmajı: Yakup Kadri Karaosmanoğlu,' *Toplum ve Bilim*, 51/52 (Autumn 1990-Winter 1991), pp. 129-52.

Millas, Hercules, 'Non-Muslim minorities in the historiography of Republican Turkey: the Greek case' in Adanır, Fikret and Suraiya Faroqhi (eds.), *The Ottomans and the Balkans. A Discussion of Historiography* (Leiden, 2002), pp. 155-91.

Millas, Iraklis, '*Tourkokratia*: History and the image of the Turks in the Greek literature,' *South European Society and Politics*, XI/1 (2006), pp. 47-60.

Neumann, Christoph K., *Araç Tarih Amaç Tanzimat. Tarih-i Cevdet'in Siyasi Anlamı* (İstanbul, 1999).

Neumann, Christoph K., 'Bad times and better self: definitions of identity and strategies for development in late Ottoman historiography, 1850-1900' in Adanır, Fikret and Suraiya Faroqhi (eds.), *The Ottomans and the Balkans. A Discussion of Historiography* (Leiden, 2002), pp. 57-78.

Ortaylı, İlber, *İmparatorluğun En Uzun Yüzyılı* (İstanbul, 1999).

Ortaylı, İlber, *Osmanlı İmparatorluğunda İktisadi ve Sosyal Değişim - Makaleler 1* (Ankara, 2000).

Özbaran, Salih, *Tarih, Tarihçi ve Toplum* (İstanbul, 1997).

Özbaran, Salih (ed.), *Tarih Öğretimi ve Ders Kitapları* (İzmir, 1998).

Özbaran, Salih, 'The image of the «Other» in history textbooks: Turkish case' in Xochellis, Panos D. and Fotini I. Toloudi (eds.), *The Image of the «Other»/ Neighbour in the School Textbooks of the Balkan Countries (Proceedings of the International Conference. Thessaloniki, 16-18 October 1998)* (Athens, 2001), pp. 289-97.

Özerdim, S. N., 'F. Köprülü'nün Yazıları. 1908- 1950' in Eren, H. and T. Halası Kun (eds.), *Türk Dili ve Tarihi Hakkında Araştırmalar I* (Ankara, 1950), pp. 159-248.

Özyürek, Esra (ed.), *Hatırladıklarıyla ve Unuttuklarıyla Türkiye'nin Toplumsal Hafızası* (İstanbul, 2001).

Pawlowitch, Stevan K., *The History of the Balkans 1804-1945* (Longman, 1999).

Pawlovitch, Steven, 'Society in Serbia, 1791-1830' in Clogg, Richard (ed.), *Balkan Society in the Age of Greek Independence* (London, 1981), pp. 137-56.

Paxton, Roger V., 'Identity and consciousness: culture and politics among the Habsburg Serbs in the eighteenth century' in Banac, Ivo, John C. Acherman and Roman Szporluk (eds.), *Nation and Ideology: Essays in Honour of Wayne S. Vucinich* (Boulder, N. Y., 1981), pp. 101-19. .

Peckham, Robert Shannan, 'Map mania: nationalism and the politics of place in Greece, 1870-1922,' *Political Geography*, 19 (2000), pp. 77-95.

Petrovich, Michael Boro, *A History of Modern Serbia, 1804-1918*. Vol. I (New York, 1976).

Popovic, Alexandre, 'La presse de langue Turque dans les Balkans: vue d'ensemble' in *Cultures musulmanes balkaniques* (İstanbul, 1994), pp. 209-13.

Quataert, Donald, *The Ottoman Empire, 1700-1922* (Cambridge, 2000).

Robinson, Chase F., *Islamic Historiography* (Cambridge, 2003).

Rodinson, Maxime, *Europe and the Mystique of Islam*, translated by Roger Veinus (London, 2002).

Selim Nüzhet, *Türk Gazeteciliği 1831-1931* (İstanbul, 1931).

Seth, Sanjah, 'Rewriting histories of nationalism: The politics of "moderate nationalism" in India, 1870-1905,' *American Historical Review* (February 1999), pp. 95-116.

Smith, Anthony D., *National Identity* (London, 1991).

Smith, Anthony D., *Nationalism and Modernism* (London and New York, 2003).

Somel, Selçuk Akşin, *The Modernization of Public Education in the Ottoman Empire 1839-1908 - Islamization, Autocracy and Discipline* (Leiden, 2001).

Spender, Harold, *Byron and Greece* (London, 1924).

Spengler, Oswald, *The Decline of the West*. An abridged edition with a new introduction by H. Stuart Hughes (New York and Oxford, 1991).

Spiegel, Gabrielle M., 'Memory and history: liturgical time and historical time,' *History and Theory*, 41 (May 2002), pp. 149-62.

Stavrianos, L. S., *The Balkans Since 1453* (London, 2000).

Stokes, Gale, 'Dependency and the rise of nationalism in Southeast Europe,' *International Journal of Turkish Studies*, I/1 (1979-80), pp. 54-67.

Strauss, Johann, 'İstanbul'da Kitap Yayını ve Basımevleri,' *Müteferrika*, no. 1 (1993), pp. 5-17.

Şimşek, Sefa, *Bir İdeolojik Seferberlik Deneyimi Halkevleri, 1932-1951* (İstanbul, 2002).

Tanpınar, Ahmed Hamdi, *XIX. Asır Türk Edebiyatı*. Vol. I (İstanbul, 1956).

Tekeli, İlhan and Selim İlkin, *Osmanlı İmparatorluğu'nda Eğitim ve Bilgi Üretim Sisteminin Oluşumu ve Dönüşümü* (Ankara, 1999).

Timur, Taner, *Osmanlı Kimliği* (Ankara, 2000).

Todorova, Maria, *Imagining the Balkans* (New York and Oxford, 1997).

Todorova, Maria, 'Afterthoughts on *Imagining the Balkans*,' *Harvard Middle Eastern and Islamic Review*, 5 (1999-2000), pp. 125-48.

Toumarkine, Alexandre, *Les migrations des populations musulmanes balkaniques en Anatolie (1876-1913)* (İstanbul, 1995).

Trix, Frances, 'The Stamboul alphabet of Shemseddin Sami Bey: precursor to Turkish script reform,' *International Journal of Middle East Studies*, XXXI/2 (1999), pp. 255-72.

Tunaya, Tarık Z., 'Osmanlı İmparatorluğu'ndan Türkiye Büyük Millet Meclisi Hükümeti Rejimine Geçiş,' *İstanbul Üniversitesi Hukuk Fakültesi Devletler Hususî Hukuku Ord. Profesörü Muammer Raşit Seviğ'e Armağan* (İstanbul, 1956), pp. 1-22.

Türkeş, Mustafa, *Ulusçu Bir Sol Akım: Kadro Hareketi (1932-1934)* (Ankara, 1999).

Türkeş, Mustafa, 'The Balkan Pact and its immediate implications for the Balkan states, 1930-34,' *Middle Eastern Studies*, XXX/1 (1994), pp. 123-44.

Vryonis, Speros, *The Turkish State and History. Clio Meets the Grey Wolf* (Thesaloniki, 1991).

Wei-ming, Tu, 'Cultural China: the periphery as the centre,' *Daedalus*, 120 (1991), pp. 1-32.

Winter, Jay, *Sites of Memory, Sites of Mourning. The Great War in European Cultural History* (Cambridge, 2003).

Wolff, Larry, *Inventing Eastern Europe. The Map of Civilization on the Mind of Enlightenment* (Stanford, 1994).

Yasamee, F. A. K., *Ottoman Diplomacy. Abdülhamid II and the Great Powers 1878-1888* (İstanbul, 1996).

Yazıcı, Nesimi, 'Sadrâzam Kâmil Paşa'nın Yabancı Basınla İlgili Bazı Görüşleri' in *Prof. Dr. Bekir Kütükoğlu'na Armağan* (İstanbul, 1991), pp. 413-7.

Yerasimos, Stephane, 'L'eglise orthodoxe pépinière des états balkaniques' in Panzac, Daniel (ed.), *Les Balkans a l'epoque ottomane* (Aix-en Provence, 1992), pp. 145-58.

Yıldız, Ahmet, *"Ne Mutlu Türküm Diyebilene." Türk Ulusal Kimliğinin Etno-Seküler Sınırları (1919-1938)* (İstanbul, 2001).

Zachariadou, Elizabeth A., 'Co-existence and religion,' *Archivum Ottomanicum*, 15 (1997), pp. 119-29.

Zengin, Zeki Salih, *II. Abdülhamit Dönemi Örgün Eğitim Kurumlarında Din Eğitimi ve Öğretimi 1876-1908* (Adana, 2003).

Zürcher, Eric Jan, 'Young Turks, Ottoman Muslims and Turkish nationalist: Identity politics 1908-1938' in Karpat, Kemal H. (ed.), *Ottoman Past and Today's Turkey* (Leiden, 2000), pp. 150-79.

Dictionaries and Reference Sources

Akbayar, Nuri, *Osmanlı Yer Adları Sözlüğü* (İstanbul, 2001).

Bursalı Mehmet Tahir Efendi, *Osmanlı Müellifleri 1299-1915*. Vol. III (İstanbul, 1975).

Andreev, Stephan, *Glossary of Settlement Names and Denominations of Administrative Territorial Units in Bulgarian Lands in 15th-19th Centuries* (Sofia, 2002).

Ceyhan, Abdullah, *Sırat-ı Müstakîm ve Sebîlürreşad Mecmuaları Fihristi* (Ankara, 1991).

De Lolme, et al., *A French and English Dictionary* (London, Paris, New York and Melbourne, 1901).

De Schlechta-Wssehrd, Le B^N O., *Manuel Terminologique Français-Ottoman* (Vienne, 1870).

Devellioğlu, Ferit, *Osmanlıca-Türkçe Ansiklopedik Lûgat* (Ankara, 2000).

The Encyclopaedia of Islam, second edition. Vol. VIII (Leiden, 1995).

The Encyclopaedia of Islam, New Edition- Glossary and Index of Technical Terms; to Volumes I-VII and to the Supplement, Fascicules 1-6, compiled by J. van Lent and H. U. Qureshi (Leiden, 1995).

Gövsa, İbrahim Alâettin, *Türk Meşhurları Ansiklopedisi* (n.p.p., n.d.).

İslam Ansiklopedisi (İstanbul, 1945-1988).

Koray, Enver, *Türkiye Tarih Yayınları Bibliyoğrafyası 1729-1955* (İstanbul, 1959).

Mehmed Cemaleddin, *Osmanlı Tarih ve Müverrihleri. Âyîne-i Zurefâ*, edited by Mehmet Arslan (İstanbul, 2003).

Mehmed Süreyya, *Sicil-i Osmani yahud Tezkire-i Meşahir-i Osmaniye* (İstanbul, 1308-1315 reprinted in Westead, 1971), four vols.

Mercanlıgil, Muharrem D., *Eski Harflerle Basılmış Türkçe Tarih Kitapları (Türkiye Tarih Yayınları Bibliyografyasına Ek)* (Ankara, 1959).

Pitcher, Donald Edgar, *An Historical Geography of the Ottoman Empire* (Leiden, 1972).

Redhouse, James W., *A Turkish and English Lexicon* (Constantinople, 1890).

Redhouse Yeni Türkçe-İngilizce Sözlük. New Redhouse Turkish-English Dictionary (İstanbul, 1968).

Simpson, J. A. and E. S. C. Weiner, *The Oxford English Dictionary*, second edition, Vol. X (Oxford, 1989).

INDEX

Abdullah Cevdet 92, 123
Abdullah Zühtü 23
Abdurrahman Şeref 15, 21, 34
Abdülaziz, sultan 4, 68
Abdülhak Hamit (Tarhan) 22
Abdülhamid II, sultan 5, 6, 10, 11, 13,
  14, 15, 21, 22, 25, 35, 36, 53, 61,
  62, 63, 64, 68, 87, 88, 90, 93, 98,
  106, 118, 119, 122, 150, 151, 177
Abdülmecid, sultan, 4
Adıvar, Adnan 13
Afet (İnan) 18, 27, 96, 126, 136, 137,
  157
Ağaoğlu Ahmed 44, 45, 91
Ahmed Celaleddin Paşa 22
Ahmed Cevdet Paşa 2, 11, 15, 21, 42,
  43, 45, 46, 47, 50, 51, 52, 62, 66,
  67, 74, 85, 86, 102, 105, 106, 111,
  125, 164, 190
Ahmed Hasır 70, 75, 142
Ahmed İhsan (Tokgöz) 128
Ahmed Lütfi Efendi 21, 30, 47, 50, 52,
  62
Ahmed Mithad Efendi 149
Ahmed Müfid 68, 174

Ahmed Nazmi 33
Ahmed Rasim 3, 39, 47, 52, 74, 78,
  82, 102, 106, 109, 111, 112, 115
Ahmed Refik (Altınay) 2, 17, 18, 23,
  25, 26, 39, 54, 67, 70, 88, 89, 184
Ahmed Salah Aldin 40
Ahmed Şerif 96, 122
Ahmed Vefik Paşa 10, 12, 21, 30, 36,
  42, 46, 65, 66, 67, 88, 105, 124
Akçuraoğlu Yusuf (Yusuf Akçura) 9,
  12, 19, 52, 55, 74, 75, 78, 86, 91,
  189
Akşam, 35, 111
Akyiğitzade Musa 86, 111
Alexander, Bulgarian Prince 76
Ali Cevad 13, 21, 30, 34, 36, 46, 66,
  67, 106, 124
Ali Efendi, Basiretçi 131
Ali Haydar Midhat 38, 101
Ali Paşa 52
Ali Reşad 2, 19, 26, 39, 41, 67, 70, 80,
  88, 89, 98, 107
Ali Seydi 40, 67, 70, 88, 89
Andrić, Ivo 60
Ankara 4, 6, 21, 41, 45, 64, 80, 81,

110, 117, 119, 122, 135, 136
Arda, Gültekin 180
Argyro-Kastro (Ergiri) 50
Arif Hikmet 121
Arif Oruç 121
Aristotle 97
Athens 3, 76, 79, 132, 135, 177, 179
Aydemir, Şevket Süreyya 3, 24, 131
Aydın 113, 118, 119, 132, 195
Ayni, Mehmet Ali 96, 134

Baku University 18
Balkan, 119, 121
The Balkan Pact 41, 79, 80, 83
Barkan, Ömer Lütfi 144
Basiret, 131
Baymur, A. Fuad 9
Bayur, Yusuf Hikmet 79, 80, 142
Beaufort, Francis 94
Bekir Fikri 100, 110, 113
Belene 61
Belgrade 77, 116, 177
Berane 122
Berlin 76, 138
Beyoğlu 86
Birgen, Muhittin 18, 23, 24
Bismarck, Otto von 34
Bitolj (Manastır) 62
Bolayır, Ali Ekrem 14
Borba, 179
Braudel, Fernand 84, 127
Bucharest 56, 107, 120, 195
La Bulgarie, 95, 180
Bulgaristan Türk Muallimleri Mecmuası, 188
Burhan Asaf 24
Burnaby, Capt. Frederick 180
Bursa 111, 113

Byron, Lord 97, 98, 100

Cairo 5, 14, 22, 38, 174
Cami (Başkurt) 202
Canning, Stratford 57
Carr, E.H. 9
Cavid, Minister of Finance 23
Celal Nuri (İleri) 92, 99
Cemal Paşa 3-4, 6, 30, 48, 78, 98, 132, 146
censorship 13, 14, 15, 23, 35, 36, 38, 58, 150, 160
Cetinje 76
cinsiyet 49, 50, 51
civilization 16, 17, 54, 70, 83, 84, 85, 86, 87, 88, 89, 90, 91, 92, 93, 94, 96, 97, 98, 99, 100, 101, 103, 104, 105, 114, 125, 143, 184
Constantin, Greek King 110
Cowen, Joseph 100
Creasy, Sir Edward S. 157
Cromer, Lord 84
Cumhuriyet Halk Fırkası/Partisi (Republican's People's Party) 7, 25, 26, 107, 137, 200

Çağlar, Behçet Kemal 129

Dagistan 22, 125
The Danube (Tuna) 30, 82, 103, 124, 127, 128, 129, 132, 142, 144
Darülfünun 16, 24, 40, 134
Deliorman 117, 118
Deliorman 120
Deliorman, M. Necmettin 83, 120
Delvinon (Delvina) 33
Demosthenes 97
Dimetoka 90

INDEX

Disraeli, Benjamin 101
Donanma Mecmuası, 113
Dukagin 33
Dulcigno (Ülgün) 61, 62
Duru, Kazım Nami 117

Ebüzziya Tevfik 22
Ecevit, Bülent 129
Economist, 119
Edirne 32, 38, 64, 103, 104, 126, 131
Elbasan 33
Emin Ali 16, 17
Engelhardt, Ed. 39
Enver Paşa 6, 126
Ergin, Osman Nuri 35, 105
Erzincan 126
Erzurum 198
Esad, Minister of Education 93, 184
Esmer, A. Şükrü 157
Etem Ruhi (Balkan) 196

Fahrettin 99
Faik Sabri (Duran) 41
Falih Rıfkı (Atay) 19, 111, 130, 142, 144, 146, 192
Fazıl Ahmet (Aykaç) 27
Fener 56, 134
Fesch, Paul 35
Freeman, Edward 93, 94
The French Revolution 13, 43, 44, 46, 47, 55, 56, 151, 171
Fuad Paşa 52, 57

Gagauz 138
Galata 56, 83
Gaspıralı İsmail (İsmail Gaspıranski) 86, 87, 90, 105
Gelenbevizade Ahmed Tevfik Bey 11

Genç Kalemler, 59, 109, 166
Gendov, Vassil 144, 145, 207
Gendova, Zhana 145
Geneva 22
George, Greek King 76, 135
Gladstone, William 100, 101, 102, 103, 188
Gramsci, Antonio 21
The Greek Patriarchate 55, 133, 134, 136
Grey, Sir Edward 84
Gülhane Hatt-ı Hümayunu 4
Günaltay, Şemdeddin 26, 156, 157

Hafız Latif 120
Hagia Sophia 83, 117
Hakikat 120
Hakimiyet-i Milliye 45
Halet Efendi 68, 175
Halide Edib (Adıvar) 3, 111, 113, 145
Halil Yaver 3, 83, 103, 129, 138, 194
Halka Doğru, 109
Halkevleri (People's Houses) 18, 26, 137, 153, 156
Halk Sesi 120
Hamdullah Suphi (Tanrıöver) 107, 108, 137, 138
Hancızade Mehmed Remzi 44
hars 54, 139
Hatay 127
Hegel, Georg Wilhelm Friedrich 86
Homer 97
Hugo, Victor 97, 98, 186
Hüseyin Hüsnü 120, 121
Hüseyin Kazım 40
Hüseyin Raci Efendi 101, 130, 200

Ibn Khaldun 11, 51, 168

Ioannina (Yanya) 33, 62, 68, 96, 174
Işın, Mithat 3
Ignatiev, Nicholas Pavlovich 102, 106, 190
Islahat Fermanı 52

İbrahim Paşa 69
İbrahim Rafet 102
İbrahim Temo 195
İctihad, 92
ihtilal 43, 44, 45, 46, 65, 73, 165
İhsan, Şeref 27, 116, 118
İmdad, 120
İnalcık, Halil 32, 59, 78
İnönü, İsmet 83, 120, 127, 194, 199, 205
İrtem, Süleyman Kani 23, 35, 61
İskan Kanunu 137
İstanbul 4, 5, 6, 7, 22, 30, 31, 32, 38, 43, 45, 55, 58, 64, 66, 70, 75, 76, 77, 82, 83, 86, 87, 101, 106, 119, 123, 124, 125, 130, 131, 132, 141, 143, 133, 146, 181
ittihad (union) 15, 52
İttihad ve Terakki (The Committee of Union and Progress) 6, 10, 15, 18, 23, 30, 58, 88, 90, 93, 96, 117, 119, 122, 126, 131, 132, 138
İzmir 110, 111, 113, 116, 126, 132, 135

Janevo (Yanova) 33

Kadare, Ismail 72, 73
Kadro, 24
Kamil Kapudan 3, 30, 58, 73, 74
Kamil Paşa 53, 55, 116, 118, 119, 195
Kaplan, Mehmet 11

Karal, Enver Ziya 23, 80
Kara Yorgi (Karajordge Petrović) 75, 116
Karaman 136
Kaskatı, Arif Necip 180
Kavala 114
kavm/kavim 49, 50, 51, 53, 141
kavmiyyet meselesi (nationalité) 50, 51
Kazanov, the leader of the Zveno group 108
Kazım Karabekir 30, 63
Kelekyan, Diran 40, 163
Kemalettin Şükrü 43-44
Kıbrıslı Mehmed Paşa 38
Kırkkilise (Kırklareli) 126
Koca Balkan 120
Komotene (Gümülcine) 120, 121, 197
Kosovo 139
Koyuncu, Akil 78
Köprülüzade Mehmed Fuad (Köprülü) 2, 16, 17, 18, 46, 55, 70, 106, 143
Kruševac (Alacahisar) 33
Kurtuluş Savaşı (Turkish National Liberation War) 6, 27, 30, 44, 45, 63, 82, 92, 110, 116, 127, 142

Levski, Vasil 144
London 101
Lütfiye Hanım 21, 36, 66, 67, 69, 105

Machiavelli, Niccolo 84
Mahmud II, sultan 68
Mahmud Celaleddin Paşa 40, 53, 82, 106, 108
Mahmud Nedim Paşa 102, 106, 190
Mahmud Şevket Paşa 126
Manisa 111
Marriot, J.A.R. 33

Mazower, Mark 29
Mecidiye 120
Mehmed V, sultan 5
Mehmed Akif (Ersoy) 25, 92, 109
Mehmed Ali, Minister of Interior 23
Mehmed Arif (Professor in Darülfünun) 16
Mehmed Arif 38
Mehmed Asım (Us) 111
Mehmed Emin (Yurdakul) 25, 112, 113
Mehmed Eşref 40
Mehmed Salahi 50, 59, 73
Mehmed Memduh Paşa 14, 118, 119, 195
Mehmet Şeref 104, 115
Mekteb-i Sultani, later Galatasaray Lisesi 21
Midhat Paşa 38, 101
Milan (Obrenović), Serbian King 76, 77
millet 13, 27, 36, 49, 50, 53, 54, 57, 61, 125, 126, 136, 150, 161, 167, 169
Miloš (Obrenović) 75
Misak-ı Milli (the National Pact) 54
Mizan, 22
Mizancı Murad 5, 22, 23, 36, 125, 150, 182
Mosul 127
muhacir 137, 140
Murad I, sultan 30
Mustafa Kemal (Atatürk) 6, 7, 18, 20, 27, 28, 80, 81, 98, 126, 127, 129, 136, 142, 152
Mustafa Muhsin 70, 75, 142
Mustafa Nuri Paşa 2, 12, 21, 42, 48, 66, 67

Mülkiye Mektebi 21, 22, 26
Müşir Süleyman Paşa 10, 13

Nahid Sırrı 32
Namık Kemal 5, 11, 12, 13, 14, 15, 22, 25, 30, 50, 51, 52, 85, 87, 88, 92, 125, 127, 169
Napoleon Bonaparte 60
Napoleon III 51, 52
nationalism 1, 15, 27, 49, 50, 51, 52, 53, 55, 56, 65, 66, 70, 141, 144, 195
national movements 43, 45, 46, 49, 54, 55, 56, 65, 67, 70
Navarino (Navarin) 65, 69, 70, 186
Necib Asım (Yazıksız) 16
Necip Ali 18
Nevesije (Nevesin) 43, 47

Okhrida (Ohri) 33
Ormanjiyev 79, 180
Ottoman History Thesis (Osmanlı Tarih Tezi) 18, 24
Ottomanism 6, 27, 122

Ömer Seyfeddin 3, 25, 113, 114, 115, 117, 122, 123, 131

Pakalın, Mehmet Zeki 33
Panslavism 53, 105, 106, 107, 108, 190
Paris 22, 61, 145
Peremeci, Osman Nuri 26, 103, 129, 188
Peyami Safa 20
Piccolomini, later Pope Pius II 84, 117
Picot, M. Georges 95
Phanariots 68, 133
Philiki Etairia 55, 65, 173
Plato 97

Pleven (Plevne) 30, 205
Plovdiv (Filibe) 119, 120, 179, 196
Politiki Erena 119
Pomaks 102, 138
Posta, 120
Prens Sabahaddin 90
Prizren 33, 138
Public Debt Administration 5, 22

Ragıb Rıfkı 39, 63, 64
Ramsay, William 77, 88, 178
Ranke, Leopold von 94, 143, 184
Recaizade Mahmud Ekrem 22
Recep (Peker) 107
Renan, Ernest 85, 181
Reşit Galip 24, 155-6
Rizospastis, 119
Rodop, 120, 121
Rome 76
Ruse (Rusçuk) 60, 119

Sada-i Millet, 119
Safveti Ziya 87
Said Paşa 126
Samsun 127
Schopenhauer, Arthur 10
Sedes, Halil 3, 74, 75
Siroz (Serez) 114
Servet-i Fünun, 87
Sevük, İsmail Habib 129
Seyfi 99
Shipka (Şıpka) 129
Sırat-ı Müstakim, later Sebilürreşad, 90, 92
Silistria (Silistre) 128
Skolpje (Üsküp) 33, 128, 145
The Slaves' Revolt 144, 145
Smederovo (Semendre) 33

Sofia 59, 64, 81, 103, 119, 121, 138, 196, 205
Sophia, Greek Queen 135
Söylemezoğlu, Galip Kemali 3
Stavropol (İstavropol) 22
Strangford, Lady 101
The Sunday Strand, newspaper 94
Sungu, İhsan 49, 97
Süleyman the Magnificient 25

Škodra (İşkodra) 51, 59, 73, 176
Šumen (Şumnu) 103, 188

Şemseddin Sami 30, 31, 32, 33, 40, 48, 50, 53, 86, 99, 163
Şinasi 5

Tahsin Paşa 35
Takanoğlu, Mehmet Lütfi 120
Talat Paşa 6
Tanin, newspaper 18, 96, 122, 163
Tanpınar, Ahmet Hamdi 9, 199
Tansu, Samih Nafiz 46, 95
The Tanzimat 4, 5, 12, 13, 15, 57
The Tanzimat Fermanı 52
Tarih-i Osmani Encümeni (Ottoman Historical Commission) 15, 16, 21, 151
Tarih-i Osmani Encümeni Mecmuası, later Türk Tarih Encümeni Mecmuası 15
Tekin Alp (Moise Cohen) 124
Tepedelenli Ali Paşa 65, 66, 67, 68, 69
Tergovişte 122
Tevfik Kamil 121, 205
Tevfik Rüştü 179
Thessaloniki (Selanik) 5, 33, 120, 133
Thessaly 62, 63

INDEX

The Times, 33, 34, 37, 88, 91, 188
Tirana 139
Todorova, Maria 29, 30
Togan, A. Zeki Velidi 19
Trakia, 103, 189
Travnik 60
Trikala (Tırhala) 62
Tsaldaris, Panagis 135
Turan, 121
Turgut, A. Hilmi 120
The Turkish History Congress 17, 18, 19, 24, 81, 92, 96
The Turkish History Thesis (Türk Tarih Tezi) 18, 19, 25, 80, 93
The Turkish National Liberation War see Kurtuluş Savaşı
Turkish Orthodox Church 133
Tüccarzade İbrahim Hilmi 35, 36
Türk Ocakları 10
Türk Tarihi Tetkik Cemiyeti, later Türk Tarih Kurumu (The Turkish Historical Society) 3, 9, 26, 134, 151
Türk Yurdu, 78, 109

Uhuvvet, 119

Ülkü Halkevleri Mecmuası 18

Vahideddin, sultan 6
Vahyi Efendi 78
Valona (Avlonya) 33
Varna 145
vatan (fatherland) 36, 49, 51, 82, 123, 124, 125, 126, 127, 128, 129, 142, 145, 161

Velbužd (Köstendil) 33
Vilčetrin (Vilçetrin) 33
Vienna 76

Washburn, George 101, 187
Wilhelm I, the German emperor 61
Williams, W. Llew. 94

Xanthi (İskeçe) 120

Yahya Kemal (Beyatlı) 25, 128, 130, 145
Yakup Kadri (Karaosmanoğlu) 3, 20, 111
Yaşar Nabi (Nayır) 26, 121, 122, 124, 139
Yemen 126, 143, 198-9
Yinanç, Mükrimin Halil 11
The Young Ottomans (Genç Osmanlılar) 4, 6, 11, 49
The Young Turks 5, 22, 38, 101, 195
Ypsilantis, Alexander 69
Yücel, Hasan Ali 127

Zagora (Zağra) 101, 130
Zaria, 81
Ziya Gökalp 25, 53, 54, 74, 87, 92, 125, 163, 201
Ziya Paşa 5, 13

Bayur, Yusuf Hikmet, *Türk İnkılâbı Tarihi, Cilt: II, Kısım: I* (İstanbul, 1943).

Beaufort, Francis, *Karamania, or a Brief Description of the South Coast of Asia Minor and of the Remains of Antiquity. With Plans, Views and & c. Collected during a Survey of that Coast, under the Orders of the Lords Commissioners of the Admirality, in the Years 1811 & 1812* (London, 1817).

Behçet Kami, *Tarihimizde Rumlar, Patrikhane ve Yunancılık* (İstanbul, 1339).

Bekir Fikri, *Balkanlarda Tedhiş ve Gerilla. Grebene* (İstanbul, 1976).

Belgelerle Mustafa Kemal Atatürk ve Türk-Bulgar İlişkileri (1913-1938) (Ankara, 2002).

Berkes, Niyazi (ed.), *Turkish Nationalism and Western Civilization. Selected Essays of Ziya Gökalp* (New York, 1959).

Bertelli, Sergio (ed.), *Niccolò Machiavelli, Il Principe e Discorsi sopra la prima deca di Tito Livio*, with an introduction by Giuliano Procacci (Milan, 1960).

[Beyatlı], Yahya Kemal, *Kendi Gök Kubbemiz* (İstanbul, 1961).

[Beyatlı], Yahya Kemal, *Siyâsî ve Edebî Portreler* (İstanbul, 1968).

[Beyatlı], Yahya Kemal, *Çocukluğum, Gençliğim, Siyâsî ve Edebî Hâtıralarım* (İstanbul, 1973).

Bilsel, Cemil, *İstanbul Üniversitesi Tarihi* (İstanbul, 1943).

Binbaşı Mehmed Nasrullah, Kol Ağası Mehmed Rüşdi, and Mülazım Mehmed Eşref, *Memalik-i Mahrusa-i Şahaneye Mahsus Mükemmel Mufassal Atlas* (İstanbul, 1325).

Birinci Türk Tarih Kongresi, Konferanslar, Münakaşalar (n.p.p., n.d.).

Brown, Robert F. (ed.), *Hegel Lectures on the History of Philosophy. The Lectures of 1825-1826.* Volume III. *Medieval and Modern Philosophy* (Berkeley, Los Angeles and Oxford, 1996).

Burnaby, Capt. Frederick, *On Horseback through Asia Minor*, with a new introduction by Peter Hopkirk (Oxford, 1996).

Cami, *Osmanlı Ülkesinde Hıristiyan Türkler. Hicret Yolları*, second edition (İstanbul, 1932).

Cebesoy, Ali Fuat, *Büyük Harpte Osmanlı İmparatorluğunun 1916-1917 Yılındaki Vaziyeti. Brüssebi-Gazze Meydan Muharebesi ve Yirminci Kolordu* (İstanbul, 1938).

Creasy, Edward S., *History of the Ottoman Turks: From the Beginning of Their Empire to the Present Time* (London, 1878).

Çambel, Hasan Cemil, *Makaleler Hâtıralar* (Ankara, 1964).

Doktor İbrahim Rafet, *Bulgaristan Ahvali* (İstanbul, 1329).

Durham, Edith, *High Albania. A Victorian Traveller's Balkan Odyssey* (London, 2000).

Atabinen, Reşid Safvet, *Les apports Turcs dans le peuplement et la civilisation de l'Europe orientale* (İstanbul, 1952).

Atasoy, Ahmet Emin (ed.), *XV. Yüzyıldan Bugüne Rumeli Motifli Türk Şiiri Antolojisi* (Bursa, 2001).

Atatürk'ün Özdeyişleri (Ankara, 1975).

Atatürk'ün Söylev ve Demeçleri II (1906-1938) (Ankara, 1959).

Atatürk'ün Söylev ve Demeçleri I. T.B.M.M. ve C.H.P. Kurultaylarında (1919-1938) (Ankara, 1961).

Atay, Falih Rıfkı, 'Tarih Kongresi,' *Ülkü Halkevleri Mecmuası*, X/55 (September 1937), pp. 1-2.

Atay, Falih Rıfkı, *Tuna Kıyıları* (İstanbul, 1938).

Atay, Falih Rıfkı, *Batış Yılları* (İstanbul, 1963).

Atay, Falih Rıfkı, *Zeytindağı* (İstanbul, 1964).

Atay, Falih Rıfkı, *Çankaya* (İstanbul, 1969).

Aybar, Celal, *Bulgaristan Nüfusu* (Ankara, 1935).

[Aydemir], Şevket Süreyya, 'Millî Kurtuluş Hareketleri Hakkında Bizim Tezimiz,' *Kadro Aylık Fikir Mecmuası*, I/12 (December 1932) [reprinted in Ankara, 1978], I, pp. 38-44.

Aydemir, Şevket Süreyya, *Suyu Arayan Adam* (Ankara, 1959).

[Aykaç], Fâzıl Ahmet, *Gelecek Asırlarda Tarih Dersi* (n.p.p., 1928).

Aykaç, Fazıl Ahmet, *Kırpıntı* (İstanbul, 1991).

Aynî, Mehmed Ali, *Milliyetçilik* (İstanbul, 1943).

B. A. [Burhan Asaf], 'Kronikler: Arkada Kalan Darülfünun,' *Kadro Aylık Fikir Mecmuası*, I/8 (August 1932) [reprinted in Ankara, 1978], I, pp. 47-8.

Baltacıoğlu, İsmail Hakkı, 'Biz Türkler Nereden Geliyoruz, Nereye Gidiyoruz ve Biz Neyiz' in *Konuşmalar* [CHP Halkevi Neşriyatı] (Ankara, October 1940), pp. 25-9.

Barkan, Ömer, 'Osmanlı İmparatorluğunda Çiftçi Sınıflarının Hukukî Statüsü,' *Ülkü Halkevleri Mecmuası*, 56/X (October 1937), pp. 147-58.

Barkan, Ömer Lûtfi, 'Osmanlı Tarihinde Rumelinin İskânı İçin Yapılan Sürgünler Meselesi' in *CHP Konferanslar Serisi. Kitap: 16* (1940), pp. 55-72.

Basiretçi Ali Efendi, *İstanbul Mektupları*, edited by Nuri Sağlam (İstanbul, 2001).

Baymur, A. Fuat, *Tarih Öğretimi* (Ankara, 1945).

Baysun, M. Cavid, 'Cevdet Paşa'nın İşkodra'ya Memûriyetine Âid Vesîkalar,' *Tarih Dergisi*, XVI/21 (1966), pp. 39-52.

Bayur, Yusuf Hikmet, *Yeni Türkiye Devletinin Haricî Siyaseti* (İstanbul, 1935).

Bayur, Yusuf Hikmet, *Türk İnkılâbı Tarihi, Cilt: I* (İstanbul, 1940).

Ali Haydar Midhat, *The Life of Midhat Pasha. A Record of His Services, Political Reforms, Banishment, and Judicial Murder* (London, 1903).

Ali Haydar Midhat Bey, *Midhat Pacha. Sa vie - son ouvre* (Paris, 1908).

Ali Haydar Midhat, *Midhat Paşa'nın Hayat-ı Siyasiyesi, Hizmatı ve Şahadeti* (Kahire, 1322).

Ali Haydar Midhat, *Midhat Paşa. Hayat-ı Siyasiyesi, Hidematı, Mena-i Hayatı* (İstanbul, 1325), 2 vols.

Ali Necip, 'Halkevleri Yıldönümü Nutku,' *Ülkü Halkevleri Mecmuası*, III/13 (March 1934), pp. 5-15.

Ali Reşad, *Avrupa ile Münasebet-i Hariciyemiz Nokta-ı Nazarından Tarih-i Osmani* (Dersaadet, 1329).

Ali Reşad, *Asr-ı Hazır Tarihi. Liselerin İkinci Devre Son Sınıflarına Mahsustur* (İstanbul, 1926).

Ali Reşat, *Umumi Tarih* (İstanbul, 1929).

Ali Reşad and Ali Seydi, *Tarih-i Osmani. Resimli ve Haritalı. Mekteb-i Rüştiyenin İkinci Senesi İçin Kabul Edilen Son Proğrama Tevfikan Tertib Edilmiştir* (İstanbul, 1327).

Ali Rıza, *Atlaslı Memalik-i Osmaniye Coğrafyası, Kısm-ı Evvel* (İstanbul, 1318).

Ali Seydi, *Resimli Kamus-i Osmani* (Darülhilafe-i Aliye, 1330).

Ali Seydi, *Resimli Yeni Türkçe Lûgat* (İstanbul, 1929).

[Altınay], Ahmed Refik, *Hilminin Mektep Kitapları: Küçük Tarih-i Osmani. Mekateb-i Rüşdiye İkinci Senelerine Mahsus Proğrama Tevfikan Tertib Edilmiştir. 32 Resim ile 8 Haritaya Camidir* (İstanbul, 1327).

[Altınay], Ahmed Refik, *Kadınlar Saltanatı* (İstanbul, 1332 [Vols I and II]; 1923-1924 [Vols III and IV]).

[Altınay], Ahmed Refik, *Kızlar Ağası* (İstanbul, 1926).

[Altınay], Ahmed Refik, 'Alman Müverrihleri: Ranke,' *Yeni Mecmua*, I/20 (22 November 1917), pp. 392-5 and I/21 (29 November 1917), pp. 403-6.

[Altınay], Ahmed Refik, 'Tarih ve Müverrihler: 4 - Tarih Bir İlimdir,' *Hayat*, III/63 (9 February 1928), pp. 6-7.

[Altınay], Ahmed Refik, *Türk İdaresinde Bulgaristan (973-1255)* (İstanbul, 1933).

Arıkan, Zeki (ed.), *Tarihimiz ve Cumhuriyet, Muhittin Birgen (1885-1951)* (İstanbul, 1997).

Arşiv Belgelerine Göre Balkanlar'da ve Anadolu'da Yunan Mezâlimi - I Balkanlar'da Yunan Mezâlimi (Ankara, 1995).

Arşiv Belgelerine Göre Balkanlar'da ve Anadolu'da Yunan Mezâlimi - II Anadolu'da Yunan Mezâlimi (Ankara, 1996).

Ahmed İhsan, *Tuna'da Bir Hafta* (İstanbul, 1327).
[Ahmed Lütfi Efendi], *Vak'a-Nüvis Ahmed Lûtfî Efendi Tarihi*. Vols. X-XV, edited by M. Münir Aktepe (Ankara, 1988-1993).
Ahmed Lûtfî Efendi, *Vak'anüvîs Ahmed Lûtfî Efendi Tarihi*. Vols. I-VIII (İstanbul, 1999).
Ahmed Müfid, *Tepedelenli Ali Paşa. 1744-1822* (Kahire, 1903).
Ahmed Müfid, *Tepedelenli Ali Paşa. 1744-1822* (İstanbul, 1324).
Ahmed Nazmi, *Rumeli Haritası* (İstanbul, 1329).
Ahmed Rasim, *Resimli ve Haritalı Osmanlı Tarihi*, Vol. IV (Konstantiniye, 1330-1328).
Ahmed Rasim, *Matbuat Hatıralarından. Muharrir, Şair, Edib* (İstanbul, 1342-1924).
Ahmed Râsim, *Osmanlı Tarihi (Seçmeler)*, edited by İsmet Parmaksızoğlu (İstanbul, 1968).
Ahmed Râsim, *Eşkâl-i Zamân*, edited by Orhan Şaik Gökyay (İstanbul, 1969).
Ahmed Salah Aldin, *Makedonya Meselesi ve Balkan Harbi Ahiri* (Dersaadet, 1331).
Ahmet Şerif, *Arnavudluk'da, Sûriye'de, Trablusgarb'de Tanîn*, Vol. II, edited by Mehmed Çetin Börekçi (Ankara, 1999).
Ahmed Vefik Paşa, *Fezleke-i Tarih-i Osmani* ([İstanbul], 1286).
Ahmed Vefik Paşa, *Lehçe-i Osmani* (Dersaadet, 1306).
Akçuraoğlu, Y., *Ulum ve Tarih* (Kazan, 1906).
Akçuraoğlu Yusuf, *Tarih-i Siyasi* (n.p.p., 1927).
Akçuraoğlu Yusuf (ed.), *Türk Yılı* (İstanbul, 1928).
Akçuraoğlu Yusuf, *Zamanımız Avrupa Siyasi Tarihi* (Ankara, 1933).
Akçura, Yusuf, *Osmanlı İmparatorluğunun Dağılma Devri, "Türk Tarihinin Ana Hatları" Eserinin Müsveddeleri* (İstanbul, n.d.).
Akkaya, Şükrü, *Ankara Tarih-Dil-Coğrafya Fakültesi Tarih Metodu ve Felsefesi Notları. II. Kısım. Tarih İlminin Tarihi* (Ankara, 1938).
Akkaya, Şükrü, *Tarihin Tarihine Kuşbakışı* ([Ankara], 1938).
Akyiğitzade Musa, *Avrupa Medeniyetinin Esasına Bir Nazar* (İstanbul, 1315).
Ali Cevad, *Memalik-i Osmaniyenin Tarih ve Coğrafya Lugatı* (Dersaadet, 1313).
Ali Cevad, *Mükemmel Osmanlı Tarihi* (İstanbul, 1316).
Ali Fıtri, *(91-92) Hersek Seferi, 292-293 Osmanlı-Karadağ Seferi* (Dersaadet, 1337).
Ali Fuad, 'Rumeli-i Şarki Meselesi,' *Darülfünun Edebiyat Fakültesi Mecmuası*, VI/1 (January 1928), pp. 1-51.